TEA PARTY WOMEN

Tea Party Women

Mama Grizzlies, Grassroots Leaders, and the Changing Face of the American Right

Melissa Deckman

NEW YORK UNIVERSITY PRESS

New York

NEW YORK UNIVERSITY PRESS
New York
www.nyupress.org

References to Internet websites (URLs) were accurate at the time of writing. Neither the author nor New York University Press is responsible for URLs that may have expired or changed since the manuscript was prepared.

ISBN: 978-1-4798-3713-7 (hardback)
ISBN: 978-1-4798-6642-7 (paperback)

For Library of Congress Cataloging-in-Publication data, please contact the Library of Congress.

New York University Press books are printed on acid-free paper, and their binding materials are chosen for strength and durability. We strive to use environmentally responsible suppliers and materials to the greatest extent possible in publishing our books.

Manufactured in the United States of America

10 9 8 7 6 5 4 3 2 1

Also available as an ebook

For Sean, Mason, and Gavin

CONTENTS

ACKNOWLEDGMENTS

My first debt of gratitude goes to the nearly thirty Tea Party and conservative women activists who took the time to meet with me and share their thoughts about women's role in the Tea Party. Many of them were also gracious enough to connect me with other women activists involved in conservative politics as well as providing me countless information about books, blogs, and research that they thought would help the project. While the interpretation of their words is my own, I hope that I have captured their thoughts clearly.

I am extremely lucky to be surrounded by such smart, supporting colleagues at Washington College, including Dean Emily Chamlee-Wright, who has always been a champion of the project. I conducted most of the interviews during a yearlong sabbatical from Washington College, which was critical to getting the project off the ground, so I am grateful to the college for providing me this invaluable opportunity. Funding from several Faculty Enhancement Grants from Washington College also paid for student assistance with the book and allowed me to attend Tea Party events. My Political Science Department colleagues have also been wonderful cheerleaders as I finished the project, particularly Andrew Oros, Jennifer Hopper, and Christine Wade. Jennifer and Christine were gracious enough to read my book prospectus and early writing, and their comments were invaluable. My colleagues also provided several initial forums to present my research, too, which allowed me to hone my arguments. I would also like to thank former Washington College president Mitchell Reiss for his help in securing several important interviews for the book and for his constant encouragement with the project. Caitlin Steele and Victoria Venable, two of my students from Washington College, provided valuable assistance in gathering materials for the book as well. My former student Lindsay Dodd, who is active in GOP politics in Maryland, also provided me some initial contact information of local women active in the Tea Party, which was critical to getting the ball rolling in terms of interviews.

I also wish to thank several frequent co-authors who also offered great insight and encouragement for the project. While I completed the final edits on this book, I was also completing the third edition of my textbook on women and politics. While I wouldn't recommend finishing two books in one summer—not to mention moving(!)—I couldn't have asked for two better collaborators to help me along: Julie Dolan and Michele Swers. Undertaking their own massive book projects at the same time, Julie and Michele always offered wonderful suggestions and raised great questions about my Tea Party project. These two women continually inspire and amaze and I am very lucky to count them as friends and colleagues. I have enjoyed working with the smart and savvy John McTague during the past two years on the "War on Women" issue. And I am very indebted to him for loaning me half of his "brain trust," Shanna Pearson-Merkowitz, who provided me with wonderful statistical help, patiently walking me through my questions about STATA as they related to my Mama Grizzlies book. Thanks, Shanna!

I had the pleasure of presenting parts of my research about women and guns on a panel about gun politics at Washington College, on which Josh Horwitz, executive director of the Coalition to Stop Gun Violence, also appeared. He read a draft of chapter 6 and provided me with helpful advice on gun terminology and history, for which I am grateful. Devin Burghart, vice president with the Institute for Research and Education on Human Rights, provided me with up to date data on Tea Party membership numbers from his organization before it was made available to the public.

While writing this book, I have had the pleasure of serving as both an affiliated scholar and board member with Public Religion Research Institute (PRRI), becoming board chair of this fine organization in 2015. PRRI's Dr. Robert Jones, CEO, and Dr. Dan Cox, research director, have graciously given me free rein with their data, which I use throughout the book. Dan, in particular, has been helpful with tracking down specific information about Tea Party members from their data sets from time to time. More important, both Robby and Dan have encouraged the project and provided a forum for some of my early thinking about conservative women on PRRI's *Faith in the Numbers* blog. Amelia

Thomson-Deveaux, formerly of PRRI, offered some wonderful feedback on my first chapter as well.

I would also like to thank several anonymous reviewers who read both the book prospectus and later the entire manuscript, providing invaluable advice that helped give the book more focus. Moreover, I have presented most of the chapters in some form as conference papers over the past several years, and I appreciate the comments from reviewers and fellow panelists about the work, especially Ronnee Schreiber, Laurel Elder, Brian Frederick, Holloway Sparks, Shauna Shames, and Sarah Fulton. It has been a delight to work with Caelyn Cobb, my editor at NYU Press. In addition to her enthusiasm for the project, her editorial suggestions have been spot-on and have made the book much stronger.

Lastly, I'd like to thank my family for its continued support. The old adage "it takes a village" applies for me, and I have a wonderful village in my corner. I have two beautiful boys, Mason and Gavin Fallon, who bring me joy on a daily basis. My parents, Lloyd and Diann Deckman, and my in-laws, Andrew and Lesley Fallon, continually offer their love and support, and have always been there to help with the kids so that I can write, think, and present my research in various venues. Andy Fallon, aka Grandpa Bear, in particular, delights in taking the boys on various Bear Adventures to museums, plays, and other activities, and both the boys and I are very grateful. For much of the research and writing of this book I have relied on a wonderful nanny to help with my boys, Fatma Jenkins, who has been a big help in so many ways. Last, but not least, I thank my husband, Sean Fallon, for his encouragement. An amazing father and partner, he has always had my back, and I appreciate his love and support more than he knows.

1

Introduction

Mama Grizzlies Rising Up

Former Alaska governor Sarah Palin, addressing the pro-life Susan B. Anthony List as its annual "Celebration of Life" Breakfast in 2010, famously warned political leaders in Washington to be wary of "moms who are rising up" in the Tea Party movement to fight against big government:

> And Washington, let me tell you, you no doubt don't want to mess with moms who are rising up. There in Alaska I always think of the mama grizzly bears that rise up on their hind legs when somebody's coming to attack their cubs, to do something adverse toward their cubs. No, the mama grizzlies, they rear up and, you know if you thought pit bulls were tough well you don't want to mess with mama grizzlies . . . And that's what we're seeing with all these women who are banding together, rising up, saying no. This isn't right for our kids and for our grandkids. And women leading the grassroots people's movements—many of the Tea Party leaders, most of them are women.[1]

Taking Washington to task for bailing out the financial institutions and the automakers during the Great Recession and increasing the national debt to unsustainable levels, Palin argued that women were playing a pivotal role in the Tea Party in order to protect their families and to stop what she called "this fundamental transformation of America, this road to national insolvency."[2]

Sarah Palin has become synonymous with the Tea Party in the United States, which burst on the political scene a few months after Barack Obama's election in 2008. Although the Tea Party is not a monolithic entity, what binds its many grassroots and national organizations together is its advocacy for limited government, rooted in a conservative interpretation of the Constitution. Reducing the federal debt, lowering taxes, and promoting American exceptionalism are key issues dominating the movement. While these issues have always found a home among conservative political movements in America's history, what is unusual about the Tea Party is how much of its leadership comes from women, a demographic usually not publicly aligned with conservative causes. In addition to Sarah Palin, arguably one of the most famous national politicians associated with the Tea Party from its inception is former Minnesota congresswoman Michele Bachmann, who started the Tea Party Caucus while serving in Congress. Studies of grassroots Tea Party organizations suggest that women dominate as leaders at the local level, while women are also making their mark in the Tea Party as organizational leaders nationally.[3] Amy Kremer, who gained prominence as the chair of the Tea Party Express, routinely appears on news outlets to promote the views of the Tea Party. Women dominate the board of the Tea Party Patriots, another leading Tea Party organization, whose co-founder, Jenny Beth Martin, was named by *Time* as one of the hundred most influential people in 2010.[4] There is no doubt that women are among the Tea Party's most active movers and shakers at all levels.

To be sure, women have always played important roles as volunteers in many earlier conservative causes, such as the anticommunist movement, the pro-life movement, and the Christian Right.[5] Women have also been active in Republican Party politics for much of the twentieth century, although their work was generally isolated to the "housekeeping" functions that take place behind the scenes at the grassroots and precinct levels of politics well into the 1970s, often channeled through ladies' auxiliary organizations such as the National Federation of Women's Republican Clubs.[6] There have been some notable exceptions to the historical rule that women in conservative political circles rarely emerged as leaders in their own right—Phyllis Schlafly, who was largely responsible for stopping the movement to ratify the Equal Rights Amendment and later founded Eagle Forum, and Beverly LaHaye, the evangelist who started the influential Christian Right organization Concerned Women for America in 1979 as a counterpart to the liberal National Organization for Women, both come to mind. More typically, women's role in conservative politics through most of the twentieth century was largely supportive, behind the scenes rather than front and center. Yet these twenty-first-century conservative women activists, blogging for change and rallying their fellow "Mama Grizzlies" from a nationally watched podium, are different, a visible force with which to be reckoned.

This book addresses why Tea Party women have emerged as leaders of this newest incarnation of conservative activism in ways that are unprecedented in American history, and what their emergence may mean for American politics. I spent 2012 and 2013 attending Tea Party rallies, following Tea Party blogs and Twitter feeds, and meeting with women Tea Party leaders at the national, state, and grassroots levels. I conducted extensive interviews with a variety of Tea Party women, ranging from those women leading national Tea Party organizations and longer-standing conservative women's groups to women who have formed or are very active in their own state and local Tea Party organizations. My research reveals several important findings about this influential group of activists.

First, the fluid nature of the Tea Party, with its decentralized structure, allows women unprecedented opportunity to engage in conservative activism on their own terms, in large measure because opportunities to get involved in mainstream Republican Party politics are limited or unappealing. Many of the Tea Party women I spoke with recount negative experiences with local and state Republican parties and instead believe that Tea Party activism is a better fit for their brand of activism. That said, there still remains a relationship, however tenuous and born of necessity, between Tea Party women and the Republican Party. Women in the Tea Party also point to a newer generation of very conservative Republican women who have served as role models to emulate and who have not only inspired them to become politically engaged but have given them hope that the Republican Party may become more conservative in its principles and policy positions. Moreover, I demonstrate that Republican women leaders in Congress have appropriated much of the rhetoric first developed by Tea Party women to defend or explain their conservative policy positions to other women.

This leads me to my second finding: Tea Party women have adopted a unique, gendered rhetoric to promote conservative policies. Using what I call the "motherhood frame," many Tea Party women argue that reducing both the size and scope of government is good for American families. Other Tea Party women move beyond motherhood rhetoric to make other gendered claims against "big government," arguing that federal government policies, including the Affordable Care Act, promote women's dependence on government rather than empowering them. Still other Tea Party women extend their gendered rhetoric to defend gun rights, viewing efforts by the federal government to regulate firearms as yet another attempt to restrict women's liberties, curtailing their ability to defend themselves and their families. Indeed, certain Tea Party women are even making the case that their endorsement of laissez-faire government policies in all of these arenas embodies a sort of "freedom feminism," to use a term coined by conservative political theorist Christina Hoff Sommers.[7]

Finally, while the rise of the Tea Party's women leaders is an important story in American politics, I find that such women are still likely to face an uphill battle when it comes to influencing the public opinion of American women on all these issues—in some cases, even women in the mass public who consider themselves part of the Tea Party movement. Using national survey data, I examine American women's attitudes about a host of measures about which Tea Party women leaders take pronounced stands, including the role of government in the economy, taxes, pay equity regulation, the Affordable Care Act, and gun rights. Not surprisingly, Tea Party women in the mass public espouse far more conservative positions than women who are either Democrats or Political Independents and are often slightly more conservative than Republican women nationally who do not identify with the movement—but not always. Yet, in some cases, Tea Party women in the mass public do not necessarily march in lockstep with Tea Party women leaders with respect to their policy positions. Moreover, Tea Party women in the mass public represent a small minority of American women, and it is clear from my public opinion analysis that the vast majority of American women are more supportive of a larger role for government to play in terms of the social safety net and the regulation of the American economy—attitudes that have long driven the gender gap in American elections, in which women have been traditionally seen as more likely than men to vote for Democrats.

Studying Tea Party Women

In this book I rely on qualitative methods, including interviews, participant observation, and textual analysis of Tea Party writings, to tell a more complete, nuanced story of Tea Party women and the role they are playing in American politics. I conducted twenty-nine semi-structured interviews with key Tea Party women leaders and local grassroots and state women activists, most in person, to determine why they became involved in the movement and to get their sense of the role that women are playing in it. (Appendix A contains a description of the women I interviewed and their organizational affiliations.) I tend to use the term "leaders" and "activists" interchangeably, although most of the women I interviewed either founded their own organizations or hold important leadership positions within the local or state groups; several have even established their own blogs and enjoy a dedicated following of readers. I met many of the activists while attending multiple Tea Party and national conservative events that drew many Tea Party activists, ranging from local and state meetings in Maryland to national conferences and rallies such as CPAC and Smart Girl Summit, sponsored by Smart Girls Politics Action. While I interviewed a few Tea Party leaders from Texas and Massachusetts, most of my interviews were done with the grassroots activists in Maryland. Given that I reside in the state of Maryland, interviewing Tea Party leaders in this state was certainly a matter of convenience, making it far easier for me to attend local and state events throughout 2012 and 2013, when I completed the primary qualitative research for the book. National studies of Tea Party membership show that most Tea Party members from the major national Tea Party organizations such as Tea Party Patriots and FreedomWorks reside in the South, although in sheer numbers California has slightly more Tea Party members than Texas and Florida, which rank second and third, respectively, according to research done by the Institute for Research and Education on Human Rights.[8] This same research organization estimates that Maryland has about 7,600 active Tea Party members in national groups. However, as a percentage of its state population, Maryland's Tea Party member levels rank similarly to California and are only slightly lower than Florida or Texas, so there is no reason to think that the Tea Party is more or less represented in my home state than in other states, despite its Democratic leanings.[9]

Given the fluid and dispersed nature of Tea Party activism, it is difficult to generate a random sample of women Tea Party members to interview. Instead, I relied on referrals from other activists for women to interview, compiling what social scientists refer to as a "snowball" sample. While I recognize that the comments and insights generated during these interviews, which lasted anywhere from one to two hours, are not fully generalizable to the population of female Tea Party grassroots activists nationally, they give valuable insight into the workings of smaller, local-level Tea Party groups.

I also interviewed women serving as leaders within national Tea Party organizations, including Tea Party Patriots, FreedomWorks, Smart Girl Politics, and As a Mom . . . a Sisterhood of Mommy Patriots, and other conservative leaders affiliated with national political organizations based in Washington, DC, which brings a national perspective on how and why women are heavily involved in the movement, especially compared with previous incarnations of conservative activism. Being a participant observer at numerous Tea Party events has also given me a clearer understanding of the political views of these activists and the strategies they are undertaking to effect political change.

Additionally, I rely on a textual analysis of primary source materials published by Tea Party activists and organizations, most of which I found online, published digitally via organizational websites, such as Smart Girl Politics Action's *Smart Girl Nation* and As a Mom . . . a Sisterhood of Mommy Patriot's *Minute Mom Magazine*. Throughout the course of this research, I regularly followed many Tea Party women's blogs and Twitter feeds. These writings helped me identify key issues for Tea Party women as well as the rhetorical frames they employ to build support for their cause. In particular, the interviews and textual analysis shed light on the motherhood frame, and other gendered, rhetorical appeals, employed by Tea Party women to encourage other women to become engaged in conservative political activism.

To gain a better sense of what Tea Party women in the mass public look like, and to determine what drives their support for the movement, I analyze survey data from the Public Religion Research Institute, a nonpartisan, nonprofit organization that polls regularly on numerous political issues, including those of special concern to the Tea Party. Through survey data analysis, I also take a closer look at the key demographic and political characteristics of Tea Party women in the mass public, such as religion, race, partisanship, and socioeconomic status, and compare them with American women nationally to determine how or if Tea Party women are noticeably different. I also consider what factors make women likely to identify themselves as part of the Tea Party, and I compare the roots of their support with those of men.

Through the national survey data analysis, I also examine Tea Party women's attitudes on economic policies, social issues, gender roles and feminism, and gun control, conducting multivariate analyses to determine how or if their support for the Tea Party may condition their attitudes on such issues compared with other women. In conducting multivariate, statistical analyses, I don't offer an exhaustive explanation for numerous public policy positions that animate many Tea Party women, but instead hope to determine if Tea Party membership among women independently drives such positions among American women, or if women's attitudes are better explained by partisanship, ideology, or other factors. I use similar controls for my statistical models in order to make comparable comparisons across a wide range of public policy positions. (Readers interested in seeing the full results of the statistical analyses can find them in appendix B.)

Tea Party women in the mass public are in many ways not the same as the activists I profile in the book. Emily Ekins, a pollster with the libertarian organization Reason, likes to call Tea Party sympathizers in the general public the "other Tea Party"—those Americans in national surveys who may consider themselves as part of the Tea Party but who do not necessarily engage actively in politics.[10] Examining these Tea Party women in the mass public not only gives me a chance to compare and contrast women Tea Party leaders on the front lines of the movement with women who may be sympathetic to many Tea Party policy goals nationally, it also allows me to determine just how amenable other American women more generally may be to the Tea Party women's gendered claims that smaller government is best for women's interests. As such, I compare Tea Party women's attitudes on such policies nationally with those of other American women—both Republican women who do not identify with the Tea Party, and American women who are Democrats or Political Independents—as a way to gauge how receptive other American women may be to the Tea Party's message that smaller government, reduced taxes, and fewer business regulations are in women's best interests. Enacting the type of conservative legislation touted by the Tea Party—including the women featured in this book—will come about only if the Tea Party can convince more Americans to vote for conservative candidates at all levels of government. My analysis of national survey data provides an indicator of the potential areas in which the Tea Party's gendered message may work with women nationally, and where it may not.

The Tea Party in American Politics and the Opportunities It Offers Women

When it comes to labeling which groups and activists are part of the Tea Party, there are those that embrace the Tea Party moniker, but there are also activists within the movement who are more likely to consider themselves part of a broader "Patriots" or "Liberty" movement. Some activists prefer to think of themselves not as Tea Partiers but instead as true "Constitutional Conservatives."[11] Regardless of the title such deeply conservative activists use, for the purposes of this book I consider them all part of the Tea Party movement given that such activists share largely similar goals with respect to shrinking the size and responsibilities of the federal government. The Tea Party movement is a broad coalition of national, state, and grassroots organizations that is often unwieldy and diffuse, described by some analysts as following a "starfish" as opposed to "spider" organizational structure.[12] The starfish analogy comes from an organizational theory book by Ori Brafman and Rod Beckstrom, *The Starfish and the Spider: The Unstoppable Power of Leaderless Organizations* (2006), which is popular with many Tea Party leaders. The basic idea is that the Tea Party (and similar diffuse organizations that lack a traditional leadership structure) derives its power from being modeled on a starfish, which can survive if one of its parts is severed, as opposed to a spider, which ceases to exist when its head is chopped off. The organizational structure that the Tea Party inhabits brings both strengths and weaknesses in terms of political activism. While the dispersed and somewhat sporadic nature of the Tea Party may make it difficult to achieve sustained impact in shaping public policy, it allows a broader range of highly motivated people to get involved in the political process. While political parties are often more hierarchical, with fewer leadership opportunities, the "open source" nature of the Tea Party—as described by Jenny Beth Martin and Mark Meckler, co-founders of Tea

Party Patriots—effectively allows any political entrepreneur to begin a political group or to become active with the Tea Party. The fluidity of the movement helps to explain why so many women who are passionate about conservative politics can be found on the Tea Party's front lines.

While much of the activism of the Tea Party is situated at the local and state level of politics, several groups have emerged nationally that work to coordinate Tea Party activities and facilitate training and cooperation among Tea Party groups at the grass roots. These groups, such as Tea Party Patriots and Tea Party Express, have also become the "public face" of the movement, and their leaders, such as Jenny Beth Martin, often appear as spokespeople for the Tea Party cause on national media outlets or are the ones who organize and appear at large rallies and major conservative events, such as CPAC or the Faith and Freedom Coalition's Annual "Road to Majority" Conference. Additionally, several long-standing libertarian organizations whose founding predate the Tea Party, such as FreedomWorks, have capitalized on the Tea Party movement by courting Tea Party activists—many new to politics—and training them to be effective political advocates in their home states and communities. Although Matt Kibbe currently leads FreedomWorks, many women hold important leadership roles within the organization as well.

Although it is difficult to know just how many Tea Party groups exist at the local and state level, the *Washington Post* in October 2010 attempted the first national "canvas" of Tea Party groups at what was arguably the height of the movement's influence, before the midterm elections in 2010 that gave Republicans control of the U.S. House of Representatives and many state legislatures. Their canvas identified almost 1,400 Tea Party groups with some sort of online presence but was only able to validate and verify 647 of them.[13] Of those groups, the vast majority of their members—86 percent—were first-time political activists, which lends credence to the notion that the Tea Party has a solid grassroots presence and is not primarily an "astroturf" movement, as alleged by Democratic leaders such as Nancy Pelosi. (In a radio interview in San Francisco, Pelosi said that the hundreds of Tax Day rallies held on April 15, 2009, by Tea Party activists were not an expression of authentic, grassroots concerns but instead orchestrated by FreedomWorks and Americans for Prosperity.)[14] Half of these groups in the *Post* study indicated some affiliation with a national Tea Party group such as Tea Party Patriots (the leading affiliation by far), while 272 indicated that they did not work with any national organizations; the remaining groups did not indicate whether they worked with national groups. Similarly, political scientists Theda Skocpol and Vanessa Williamson found in their national study of the Tea Party that approximately eight hundred Tea Parties maintained an active web presence in the spring of 2011.[15] Unfortunately no newer canvas of local groups currently exists, as it difficult and time-intensive to gather such data. However, the Institute for Research and Education on Human Rights (IREHR)—a progressive organization that monitors Tea Party and right-wing activity—has tracked membership numbers of the six largest Tea Party national organizations, several of which have local affiliates. In raw numbers, they estimate that in September 2015 such groups had a little more than 556,000 members, compared to membership levels near 186,000 in June 2010.[16] However, while IREHR notes that these Tea Party organizations witnessed dramatic increases in national membership numbers through 2012, their level of growth tapered to just 3 percent over the course of 2015 from the year before.

In examining this diverse array of Tea Party organizations, while all espouse liberty as their primary value and argue for a reduction in the size and scope of government, certain differences do emerge. Some organizations are primarily libertarian in orientation, avoiding social issues, such as FreedomWorks and Tea Party Patriots, which emphasize smaller government, lower taxes, and more freedom from government regulation. Others marry conservative economic positions with socially conservative positions. For example, Ralph Reed, the former executive director of the Christian Coalition in the 1990s, started the Faith and Freedom Coalition in 2009 to bring together social conservatives and the Tea Party movement. While the Faith and Freedom Coalition is adamantly pro-life and supports a traditional definition of marriage, which are standard positions long espoused by Christian Right organizations, it also promotes "limited government, lower taxes, and fiscal responsibility to unleash the creative energy of entrepreneurs."[17] Other groups, such as the 1776 Tea Party, are vehemently opposed to immigration reform and have links to the Minuteman Project, both having been founded by conservative activist Jim Gilchrest.[18] Still others, such as Tea Party

Nation, share all of these concerns and also routinely emphasize national security and the rise of Islam as potential threats to the United States.

Moreover, several Tea Party organizations specifically geared toward women have emerged that mirror similar splits above. In this book I profile Smart Girl Politics, founded in 2008, which prioritizes economic concerns more than social issues. By contrast, another women's Tea Party organization I profile, As a Mom . . . a Sisterhood of Mommy Patriots, founded in 2009, is adamantly opposed to gay marriage and abortion, and its website includes many articles and links designed to appeal to the stay-at-home mother. Yet both groups are united in their opposition to Barack Obama, other Democratic Party leaders, and their public policy positions. I also talk with leaders from several longer-standing women's organizations established well before the Tea Party that often work together with newer Tea Party organizations and whose members are often sympathetic to many Tea Party goals, to gauge their insight into the role that women are playing in the Tea Party. The Independent Women's Forum is primarily libertarian in its orientation, while Eagle Forum and Concerned Women for America draws on socially conservative women as the bases for their membership. These longer-standing groups may not be considered (or consider themselves) Tea Party organizations per se, but they share similar goals with other Tea Party groups, so I consider them part of this broader, more diffuse coalition of pro-liberty groups.

While the fluid organizational structure of the Tea Party has allowed women unparalleled opportunities to rise as leaders, many of these very conservative women have flocked to the Tea Party as an alternative to a more traditional avenue of political participation for conservatives: the Republican Party. My research reveals that many Tea Party women activists, particularly at the state and local level, have had difficulty breaking into what they often describe as the GOP's "old boys' network," and in a few cases they describe outright sexist treatment at the hands of party insiders when they have tried to become active within the party. They also point to the negative treatment that high-profile, "authentic" conservative women such as Sarah Palin and Michele Bachmann, early Republican politicians affiliated with the Tea Party, received at the hands of those they consider "establishment" leaders within the GOP as evidence that women face a more difficult road to becoming leaders within the party. Other women I spoke with complain that the Republican Party is too slow-moving and overly bureaucratic, which makes it difficult for women to advance as leaders within the party, a point acknowledged by Jenny Beth Martin, who says that an appealing aspect of the Tea Party is that you "don't have to cut through all of these different [party] layers to become a leader."[19] Other Tea Party women, like many of their male counterparts, find the Republican Party "establishment" weak-kneed and too willing to compromise instead of standing by firm conservative principles, and thus believe that the Tea Party allows a better forum for their brand of pro-liberty activism.

Not only does the diffuse organizational structure of the Tea Party allow women unprecedented opportunities to emerge as leaders within the movement, especially as an alternative to engagement with the Republican Party, the ubiquity of social media allows for easy organization and communication, further facilitating women's roles as activists and leaders. Popular social media sites such as Facebook, Twitter, and Pinterest have reduced the "barriers to entry" to political activism for many individuals—particularly for those who have little to no political experience. Kristen Soltis Anderson, a political consultant who has been described as the Republican Party's "leading millennial pollster," says that social media has provided women enhanced opportunities for leadership within the Tea Party, especially as the GOP and more established conservative organizations are slow to change.[20] Anderson says, "If [conservative] establishment structures tend to be led by men, what you can now do is start a blog or tweet or set up your own meetings, organize on your own and wield influence that way. That has been one of things that has been so unique about the Tea Party movement."[21] Carrie Lukas, managing director of the Independent Women's Forum, believes that social networking in particular may be key to explaining why *women*, especially, appear to be leading the Tea Party in their local communities, as women are very adept at using this new technology and have little problem with the "blurring of public and private life." According to Lukas, "The stay-at-home mom is on Facebook, sharing pictures of her kids. She can easily be informed online, and then start sharing things, and building a network, and finding like-minded people, then organize a rally once every two months. Our politics, because of new technology, has really paved the way so that it is much easier for people to have a voice, in particular, women."[22] Lukas also notes that unlike "traditional forms" of political participation, such as campaigning for candidates or working within established party structures, which are time-intensive, women, especially busy mothers, can effectively participate in Tea Party politics primarily through social media and retain some balance in their lives.

In fact, Smart Girl Politics, now one of the leading Tea Party organizations for women, began through social media, employing just the sort of the network building described by Carrie Lukas. During the 2008 elections, political novice Stacy Mott began her own political blog to voice her conservative views and, with three young children at home, "to stay sane!"[23] She notes that after the election, she invited the readers of her blog to "continue the conversation" and within a week had more than sixty e-mail messages from her readers, many of whom later became part of the leadership team of Smart Girl Politics. Tami Nantz, who now serves as Smart Girl Politics national director of new media, also got her start in politics after launching a political blog during the 2008 election. An ardent supporter of Sarah Palin, Nantz was outraged at the criticism the Alaska governor received shortly after her selection as John McCain's running mate. According to Nantz, "The attacks started, and something clicked in me and I immediately got on my computer, and created a website, and I thought, 'What can I call it, what can I call it? Hurry up, I have so much to say!' And I called it Moms4Sarah-Palin. And I started blogging. And I hit a nerve."[24] Her blog became so popular that CNN's *Anderson Cooper 360* show did a feature on her during the 2008 presidential election. She is adamant that social media has been vital for women in the Tea Party as an organizational and motivational tool. Nantz says, "It has given women like me, stay-at-home and work-from-home moms, a voice." Not incidentally, most of the women who run Smart Girl Politics do not work for the organization full-time.

Another reason women have emerged as leaders in the Tea Party to a degree not seen in earlier generations of conservative activism is that the social context in which these women operate has changed dramatically. In addition to the development of social media, Tea Party women themselves bring to the political arena resources such as higher education levels and modern-day work experience that were not as available to older generations of conservative women activists. In their book *The Private Roots of Public Action* (2001), political scientists Nancy Burns, Kay Lehman Schlozman, and Sidney Verba find that men have traditionally been more likely to participate in politics than women because their life experiences in the workplace and their higher levels of education have long provided them with the resources, such as access to social networks in which politics are a common feature, and the skills, such as a greater understanding of how politics works, that make active involvement in politics easier.[25] Moreover, Burns, Schlozman, and Verba find that these gender imbalances in political participation are reinforced by a political system in which most visible political actors are male: women are simply less likely to see themselves as political activists, and they often express less political ambition than men, a finding that is corroborated in studies that examine why it is that women are less likely to run for political office.[26] However, both adolescent girls and women more generally report higher levels of political engagement when they are exposed to female political role models, including both political candidates and officeholders.[27]

It is likely no coincidence, then, that the rise of many women leaders and activists in the Tea Party comes at a historical point when women are reaching parity in the workforce and surpassing men in higher education. Far more likely to have higher levels of education and work experience than their mothers and grandmothers, many Tea Party women are combining these personal resources with new technology to become more engaged in conservative political activism. Moreover, they now have a greater number of conservative female role models to emulate, whether they are media personalities such as Michelle Malkin or Dana Loesch, or elected officials such as Michele Bachmann, New Mexico Governor Susanna Martinez, South Carolina Governor Nikki Haley, Senator Joni Ernst (R-IA), and, of course, Sarah Palin. For conservative mothers, especially, Sarah Palin may hold the key to why we see more "Mama Grizzlies" taking the lead in the Tea Party. Palin's impact in inspiring a new generation of younger, conservative women activists should not be underestimated, according to Kristen Soltis Anderson:

> If you think about it, if you are a stay-at-home mom or a working mom who is conservative, who is trying to be there for your kids and [you are]

focused on a lot of these at-home, pocketbook issues; you are pro-gun, pro-life. Who in politics could you have pointed to before her and say, "Oh, they get what I'm going for"? . . . I think in this case she was just so unique, that for women who were just "I'm trying to live my life, be a good mom and live my values, live my faith," . . . All that you looked at in Washington and saw [were] men who may not have gotten what was going on in my life, or women who were on the left, who don't get what's going on in my life. So Sarah Palin was, finally, someone in politics who gets what I am going for and maybe it's worth getting engaged in this process.[28]

What Anderson calls the "Sarah Palin effect" may have galvanized a new generation of conservative women whose lives and political beliefs more closely mirror someone like Sarah Palin than female political icons on the left, such as Hillary Clinton or Nancy Pelosi. And, as indicated by several women activists I interviewed, having more prominent conservative women in the spotlight will likely inspire local activism on the part of conservative-leaning women who have until now been unengaged in the process. As one grassroots Tea Party activist in Maryland put it, "Conservative women need to see more [conservative] women in office for validation."[29]

In short, several factors help to explain why conservative women have emerged as such a powerful force within the Tea Party in ways that previous generations of right-wing women did not. The diffuse organizational structure of the Tea Party has allowed political entrepreneurs, including many women, to start their own organizations or to find a place within organizations that best meet their specific political goals, aided in large measure by social media. Likewise, these Tea Party women bring to the movement an unprecedented amount of personal resources in terms of their educational and professional backgrounds and have new political role models to emulate. The Republican Party's lukewarm relationship with such women has also propelled many of them into Tea Party activism, as the Tea Party provides a better fit ideologically and more opportunities to rise as organizational leaders in their own right. In the language of social movement scholars such as Sidney Tarrow, these external conditions have provided such right-wing women with the "opportunity structure" to become engaged in the

Tea Party. In his book *Power in Movement*, Tarrow writes that people join social movements "in response to political opportunities, then, through collective action, create new ones."[30] Social media, the rise of inspirational conservative women who have encouraged more involvement, and a less-than-welcoming GOP have effectively lowered the costs of collection action for these Tea Party women—many of whom are new to political activism. Put off by what they see as a "fundamental transformation" of the United States in a political direction that alarms them, these conservative women have found the Tea Party an appealing home to channel their anger and resolve. And, in what is a new development in American politics, these women are adopting specific, gendered rhetoric to defend their very conservative political positions as a way to galvanize other like-minded women to their cause and to challenge the political discourse about what constitutes "women's issues."

Conservative Issues Are Family Issues: Linking Motherhood and Politics in the Tea Party

Many Tea Party women view the growth of government spending and newly established government programs under the Obama administration—particularly the Affordable Care Act, dubbed Obama-Care by its critics—as dire, moral threats that threaten the sanctity of America's families. For example, Sarah Palin writes in her book *America by Heart*, "When we have government taking over our health care choices and seeking to influence our end-of-life decisions, we have a government that doesn't respect the sanctity and privacy of families . . . When we have a government that is spending away our children's and grandchildren's patrimony, we have a government that no longer regards us as citizens of a republic, but as subjects of an all powerful nanny state—which is to say, as children of an all-encompassing, all-wise, all-powerful mother. Our federal government was never intended to become this."[31] In directly appealing to "Mama Grizzlies" to become engaged in conservative political activism, Palin and other Tea Party women leaders call on women's role as mothers to protect and preserve their families. Dana Loesch, a conservative talk radio host, blogger, and frequent CNN commentator, makes the case that motherhood is a political act. She writes about her political involvement on the now-defunct website *ConservativeWatchNews*: "I speak out because I don't want my children saddled with debt. I don't want my children's generation to be the first generation that comes out of the gate with a lower standard of living because of our recklessness."[32]

This appeal by Palin and other Tea Party women activists to mothers as special protectors of the family—what I call the motherhood frame—is in keeping with conservative political activism historically.[33] Long before Sarah Palin, Dana Loesch, and other Tea Party women arrived on the political scene, conservative activists used similar motherhood rhetoric to appeal to women to become engaged in what was then largely viewed as the masculine world of politics, whether aimed at stopping the sale of alcohol, the growth of the New Deal and America's entry into World War II, and the spread of communism, especially in local arenas such as school districts.[34] In the 1970s Phyllis Schlafly directly appealed to mothers to fight ratification of the Equal Rights Amendment by warning that its passage would result in their children using "unisex" bathrooms and their daughters being eligible for the draft. Further, Schlafly maintained that the ERA directly threatened housewives' traditional way of life and their most valuable property right—the right to be provided for by their husbands, even in cases of divorce. Her message had resonance for many individuals whose conservative religious beliefs were grounded in the traditional, patriarchal view of society, which held that families worked best when mothers stayed home to raise their kids while fathers worked and engaged in public life.

In some respects, then, the appeal to mothers by Tea Party women is a time-honored tradition in conservative political circles. However, the motherhood frame employed by Tea Party women differs in two important respects from their conservative forebears. First, Tea Party women expand the motherhood frame beyond ideological or religious appeals to include fiscal issues as a moral threat to the well-being of the family. Rather than an overt, public focus on social issues as being of utmost concern to American families, free market economic policy has become for Tea Party activists a "pro-family" cause—one to be championed by mothers. There are three themes related to the "motherhood" frame that explains why, in the minds of Mama Grizzlies, moms should promote conservative economic policies. In the first theme, Tea Party women often call on mothers to become engaged in politics as "kitchen table" conservatives. In this take on the motherhood frame, moms have experience balancing the budget at home, so those skills are needed to help balance the federal budget. In the second theme, moms should become engaged in reducing the debt burden for future generations. In this theme, moms are compelled to become active in politics as a means to protect their kids from what Sarah Palin calls generational theft. Lastly, moms should become engaged in fighting for reduced government and lower taxes because large government programs usurp the role of the family and often encourage "family disintegration," in the words of one Tea Party leader.

Second, many Mama Grizzlies have taken up the mantle of gun rights as an extension of their role as protectors of the family, another unique dimension to their motherhood rhetoric compared with previous generations of conservative women activists. In wake of gun tragedies in 2012, such as the movie theater shooting in Aurora, Colorado, and the Newtown, Connecticut, school shooting, gun control advocates have lobbied for extended background checks and bans on semiautomatic weapons at the federal level and in some state legislatures. This lobbying by gun control advocates has provoked a strong response from gun advocates, including many from the Tea Party, who view gun ownership as an essential constitutional right. While men are still far more likely than women to use guns, hunt, and participate in shooting sports, rates of hunting and gun ownership among women have risen in the past decade.[35] Moreover, pro–Second Amendment organizations such as the National Rifle Association have actively promoted gun culture to women via social networking, online video profiles of women hunters and sports enthusiasts, and training seminars that teach women how to safely use guns or promote women's self-defense more broadly. Certainly, many women who promote gun rights avoid the use of motherhood appeals in their political rhetoric—if anything, references to their own physical safety are more common—but among some Tea Party women there is a deliberate connection made between the right to bear arms and the potential need to protect their children.

Conservative Issues Are Feminist Issues: Reading Big Government as Harmful to Women

The motherhood frame is not the only gendered frame employed by many women active in the Tea Party to defend a reduction in the size and scope of government. Tea Party women also believe that a large government state essentially usurps women's agency, paints women as "victims," and promotes dependence on government. Other right-wing women believe that government regulation of firearms also usurps women's ability to defend themselves, arguing that attempts to restrict certain types of firearms is patronizing to women. Some Tea Party women go so far as to insist that an expansion of government in terms of spending more on social programs, increasing workplace regulation against sex discrimination or requiring companies to provide family leave, and enacting more gun control—all policies heavily touted by liberal feminist organizations as vital to women's interests—actually betray the original vision of the women's movement, which promoted the idea that women are equally as capable as men. This line of thought has resulted in a number of prominent right-wing women reclaiming the feminist mantel. As Amy Jo Clark, who cohosts a popular conservative radio show and blog called *Chicks on the Right*, said to me, "We say that we are the real feminists and liberals have hijacked the term. I think feminism is when you are accountable to yourself. You are only empowered when you are actually responsible, accountable, and you are able to take care of yourself."[36]

Returning to the case of Sarah Palin highlights what may be a new dimension for conservative women's activism—one that possibly, albeit slightly, shifts conservative women's orientation more toward feminism. In 2006 Palin was elected as Alaska's youngest governor after having served as mayor of Wasilla, Alaska, for two terms while raising a family of four children. While she is an avowed social conservative and evangelical Christian with strong pro-life credentials—even carrying to term her fifth child, Trig, who was born with Down's syndrome in 2008 while she was serving as governor—Palin says that the women's movement was important in providing her with opportunities that led to her history-making turns as Alaska's first female governor and as the first woman to be named to the Republican presidential ticket. A former basketball player and cross-country star in high school, Palin singles out the importance of Title IX—the federal law first enacted in 1972 that mandated equal educational opportunities, including in sports, for boys and girls in public education—to her own experience.[37] Palin goes on to write that she is a feminist: "It surprises some people to hear that I consider myself a feminist. I believe that both women and men have God-given rights that haven't always been honored by our country's politicians. I believe women and men have important differences, but those differences don't include the ability of women to work just as hard as men (if not harder) and to be just as effective as men (if not more so)."[38] Palin makes clear, however, that her feminism is traced to the ideas promoted by the early women's movement, such as those embodied in the Seneca Falls Declaration of 1848, which she believes made the case for greater legal rights and opportunities for women steeped in Enlightenment principles of individual justice. She avowedly denounces the modern feminist movement and its argument that women's rights are necessarily linked to abortion rights, or its view that systematic institutional and societal barriers still hinder women's progress.

Moreover, like other female conservative critics of the current feminist movement, Palin argues that modern feminism is actually "antiwoman" as it portrays women as victims who need to rely on government to promote fairness in society.[39] She writes, "Instead of being seen as fully capable of taking care of ourselves, we [women] began to be portrayed as in constant need of protection . . . At some point the message of the women's movement came to be one that seemed designed to support not independence for women, but dependence on government. In short, the message of feminism became 'no we can't—at least not unless government helps.'"[40] In this respect, Palin's emphasis on the importance of self-reliance for women is part of a larger theme that dominates Tea Party discourse, that Americans have become too dependent on "big government" and that only dramatic cuts in the size and scope of government will fix the nation's ails and, in turn, allow individuals (including women) to prosper. Palin's brand of feminism fuels, and is fueled by, the Tea Party's celebration of self-reliance and personal responsibility.[41]

Virtually all of the Tea Party women I spoke with reject modern feminism for many of the same reasons as Palin. Some who are avowedly socially conservative believe that feminism is too conflated with abortion rights and would never entertain calling themselves feminists. Other Tea Party women take offense with the feminist movement not necessarily because they themselves are opposed to abortion, but because they believe liberal feminists groups wrongly prioritize reproductive rights over other issues, which means that women in American politics, in the words of one of the activists I interviewed, become politically "pigeon-holed by their body parts."[42] In the 2012 election cycle, debate about the role of such issues in defining women's interests became a national flashpoint in the form of the "War on Women." Tea Party women took to the airwaves and to their social media sites to lambast the Democrats' claim that Republican policies, particularly the party's opposition to the Affordable Care Act's birth control mandate and its attempt to defund Planned Parenthood, amounted to a War on Women, maintaining instead that the "real" War on Women came as a result of Democratic economic policies. The key to liberating women, according to these Tea Party women, is not having the federal government protect women's reproductive rights. Instead, it lies in the adoption of free market fiscal policies, which they believe will allow the economy to grow at a faster pace, allowing women more opportunities and choices in the job market (and, by extension, give women ample resources to pay for their own birth control).

While many Tea Party women I interviewed reject the feminist label, others I spoke with celebrate the capacity of women to live full lives, both professionally and in politics and are willing to define themselves as feminists if allowed to define the term, which for them is a rejection of government assistance or government overregulation as women should be expected to take care of themselves. This line of gendered rhetoric, in addition to the motherhood frame, represents a potentially important new development in American politics, as it offers a distinct contrast to the gendered rhetoric that dominates the liberal women's movement, which promotes a more heavy-handed regulatory state and more social welfare spending as being vital to women's political interests— particularly lower-income women. For some Tea Party women, then, embracing the free market is far more feminist than embracing "big government" and thus better for women.

Tea Party Women, the Republican Party, and the Representation of Women's Interest in American Politics

As baby boomers age and the sustainability of politically popular programs such as Medicare and Social Security becomes harder to maintain at their current funding levels, the nature and scope of the role of government in our lives will continue to dominate American political discourse, which is why the Tea Party—or some version of it—is likely to maintain its political relevance in the near future. Yet most American women continue to support the social safety net in greater numbers than men and have yet to buy into the argument put forth by the Tea Party that such government programs do more harm than good, ultimately usurping individual responsibility. Through motherhood rhetoric and other gendered appeals, Tea Party women and other prominent conservative women hope to rebrand conservatism and ultimately change women's attitudes about these public policies. For this reason, the rise of women in the Tea Party cannot be ignored.

Understanding the role of women as leaders in the Tea Party is also important because such women, with a few notable exceptions such as Phyllis Schlafly, challenge our perceptions of what "typical" female political leaders look like. Most prominent national women leaders until the arrival of Sarah Palin and the Tea Party have been Democratic, progressive, or, in the case of nationally known Republican figures such as former elected officials Nancy Kassebaum, Olympia Snowe, or Christine Todd Whitman, politically moderate. Whereas the Democratic Party and progressive groups have devoted resources to training women to run for office or established rules to ensure that women serve in party leadership roles (for example, the stipulation that half of its national convention delegates be female), the Republican Party has been reluctant to embrace identity politics and thus has been far less successful at recruiting women candidates or leaders.[43] Other research suggests that the gender of party leadership matters when it comes to candidate recruitment and that women's lack of representation among Republican Party leadership, especially compared with the Democrats, has likely hindered women's electoral opportunities at the state level.[44] My book shows similar dynamics at play at the local level of politics as well. Several of the local Tea Party activists I interview share that they were motivated to start their own organizations after being effectively "shut out" by their local Republican organizations, which were often headed by men. Partly in reaction to a party establishment they believe does not represent them well, conservative women have found a home in the Tea Party.

At the same time, however, most of the Tea Party women I profile in the book acknowledge that, like it or not, the Republican Party by far is the party most likely to promote their preferred policy choices, so while there are certain tensions between Republicans and Tea Party activists, there are also opportunities for shared activism. Given the Republican Party's difficulty with women voters in recent elections, particularly in wake of the Democratic Party's largely successful strategy to paint the Republicans as starting a "War on Women," I argue that the Republican Party has recently adopted much of the gendered, maternal rhetoric first employed by Tea Party women to make their party's pro-market policies more appealing to women voters. The GOP has also sought to feature women, particularly mothers, more prominently as spokespersons for the party. While the political careers of prominent Republican women such as Cathy McMorris Rodgers and Michele Bachmann predate the Tea Party, such women are often featured prominently at public events sponsored by Tea Party women's groups or on the websites of such organizations as a way to inspire their grassroots members—and the Republican Party is benefiting from this relationship as Tea Party supporters constitute a disproportionate part of its donor and voter bases. As the Republican Party deliberately tries to rebrand itself as a party for women, the prominent role of women within the Tea Party has the potential to play an important part in this effort. Whether the arrival of such conservative women on the national stage and in grassroots activism means that women's presence in the GOP will one day rival the presence of women in the Democratic Party, however, is yet to be seen.

Setting aside the political and partisan reasons for examining the role of women in the Tea Party, the emergence of Tea Party women is significant for theoretical reasons, too, as it calls into question the prevailing narrative of just what constitutes women's interests. Political theorists have long been concerned about the nature and importance of representation for democracy. Essentially, our political institutions are said to be legitimate only if they reflect the views of their citizens. But how do we ensure that multiple views are represented? In her classic work *The Concept of Representation* Hanna Pitkin (1967) distinguishes between two types of representation: descriptive representation, which is the idea that groups, such as women or racial minorities, will best be represented by political actors who share their same identity (i.e., women will be better represented by female elected officials, and so on), and substantive representation, which alternatively posits that the identity of a representative is less important than the action of elected officials taken on behalf of such groups.[45] While Pitkin maintained that descriptive representation was not a necessary condition for minority groups to receive substantive representation, other theorists such as Virginia Sapiro and Jane Mansbridge argue that while not wholly sufficient, the election of more women legislators, for instance, will improve the representation of women's interests.[46] Among other reasons, Sapiro posits that increasing women's presence in government is important because it will "undermine the perception that politics is a male domain."[47] Additionally, Mansbridge believes that having women serve as political leaders brings a different voice to the political table, one that grants a certain moral authority to issues before governments that disproportionately affect women.

Studies of female lawmakers in state legislatures and Congress, however, are mixed as to whether once in office, women legislators best serve the interests of other women or govern in ways that are markedly different than their male counterparts.[48] While women legislators from both parties at the national and state level routinely express an interest in or special responsibility to represent women and their interests through the policy process, empirical studies that examine the impact of gender on women lawmakers' legislative behavior offer a conflicting picture.[49] Earlier studies have found that women legislators vote more liberally on women's issues, such as abortion and family leave, than do their male counterparts.[50] Other studies find that women lawmakers are more likely to champion legislation that focuses on women's rights, health care, children and families, and social welfare issues, particularly legislation that has a progressive bent.[51] Yet other studies challenge these findings, arguing that the adoption of liberal, "women friendly" policies has little to do with women's presence as elected lawmakers in state legislatures, but instead is linked to the effects of parties and constituency on legislative behavior, especially in an era marked increasingly by party polarization.[52]

Republican women lawmakers, especially, are split on what denotes "women's interests" and on the centrality of the role of gender in their roles as elected representatives. Political scientists Michele Swers and Carin Larson identify different archetypes among Republican women in Congress, from socially conservative Republican lawmakers who promote conservative social and fiscal policies as being good for families and stay-at-home mothers, to more moderate Republican lawmakers who self-identify as feminists and champion women's interests, and who are more likely to hail from Democratic-leaning districts.[53] A final archetype of Republican legislative women can be described as "the libertarian," who "rejects the notion that there are women's issues" and "any notion that they are somehow different because they are women."[54] Yet, much like their Democratic counterparts, Republican women in Congress are routinely called on to serve as "spokeswomen" for their parties and to appeal to women voters, denoting how their proposed legislation is good for women's interests and the needs of families.[55]

The finding that conservative women lawmakers are split on the idea that they can or should speak on behalf of women's interests echoes earlier work on conservative women activists by sociologist Rebecca Klatch. Klatch first wrote about "women of the New Right" during the Reagan Era, placing female conservative activists into two distinct types: social conservatives, who champion traditional family roles and promote active government intervention such as passing laws that they believe reinforce mothers' traditional roles in society, whether restricting abortion, gay rights, or pornography; and laissez-faire conservatives, who view the world through the "lens of liberty" and who place far greater emphasis on free market economic policies and advocate for limited government as being good for both men and women.[56] While socially conservative women view feminism as a threat to their way of life, Klatch argues that laissez-faire women have been willing to acknowledge and decry discrimination against women in public life and the workplace, although they oppose using government action to stop such behavior, which results in a paradox among right-wing women: "The paradox is that those [socially conservative] women who are further from the feminists in their beliefs actually do act in their own interests as women, while laissez-faire women, who partly share a feminist vision, do not act collectively in the interest of their gender . . . social conservative women act as women *for* themselves, while laissez-faire conservative women remain women *in* themselves."[57]

These two distinct worldviews of conservative women continue to distinguish the two most prominent conservative women's political organizations in the United States from each other, the socially conservative Concerned Women for America (CWA) and economically conservative Independent Women's Forum (IWF).[58] Yet, while CWA and IWF differ in their constituency base, which precludes them from working together on issues such as abortion and gay rights—unlike CWA, IWF as a libertarian-leaning group avoids these issues—both organizations have shown a willingness to criticize modern feminism as being out of touch with the majority of American women. Both groups work together to oppose progressive policies often touted by feminists as being good for women and families such as stronger antidiscrimination laws, gun control, or welfare programs.[59] By defending conservative public policies on behalf of women's interests, political scientist Ronnee Schreiber argues that both groups, in essence, extend the idea of descriptive representation for women, providing "legitimacy to issue positions that would be dismissed if conservative men were the ones making the political claims."[60]

This book considers where Tea Party women fit into the larger debate about women's representation in American politics, and whether Tea Party women are noticeably distinct from the women who currently belong to CWA and IWF. My research demonstrates that self-identified Tea Party women in the mass public are more socially conservative and religiously devout than other American women and, as a result, are more likely to support restrictions on abortion, which means that a majority of Tea Party women—though not all—share similar values that have animated Christian Right women for decades. However, most of the Tea Party women I interviewed place economic concerns far ahead of social concerns in their advocacy, even when they hold traditionally conservative views on social issues. They do so because they recognize that social issues are a potential fault line for some Americans, and they believe it is prudent to focus on concerns that might find more support among the general public. Or as one pro-life Tea Party woman activist in Maryland told me, "I pick what I can win. I can sit here and beat the drum about abortion, but the debt is going to keep going up and the country is going further and further to the left. I think the issues of the debt and deficits and things of this nature are critical, we have to stick to those things."[61] In this respect, then, Tea Party women differ from Christian Right and pro-life women in that they prioritize economic issues over social issues.

Another way that Tea Party women are distinct from earlier waves of conservative women activists is the extent to which they link economic policy to their "pro-family" values. Tea Party women have made a deliberate connection between free market economic policies and their role as family caregivers. So, for Mama Grizzlies, lower taxes, reducing the debt, and limiting the scope of government have all become pro-family concerns for American women, which are not issues that have historically animated Christian Right activists. In this vein, Tea Party women's organizations and leaders continue in the tradition of the libertarian Independent Women's Forum in their advocacy of free market economic policies, but move beyond libertarian rationales that promote the freedom of individual actors to pursue policies in their own self-interest. For Tea Party women, laissez-faire economic policies—and not merely policies that promote cultural conservatism—enhance parents' ability to protect their kids and provide for their well-being. By employing motherhood and other gendered rhetoric to pursue conservative economic policies and, to a certain extent, pro-gun legislation as well, Tea Party women put a conservative, gendered spin on a variety of public policies and challenge current public discourse about what constitutes women's interests, extending the concept of descriptive representation and perhaps even redefining elements of feminism in the process.

Here to Stay? Women, the Tea Party, and the Future of American Politics

Despite the Tea Party's rapid growth and influence on American politics during the Obama years, its future remains uncertain. For the Tea Party to find lasting success in shaping public policy, it needs to broaden its support, especially among women voters, who tend to vote for Democratic candidates. However, its message that the well-being of American families depends on reducing both the size and the scope of government, and fiercely defending constitutional rights such as gun ownership, may have difficulty appealing to American women more generally for two major reasons. First, previous social science data shows that women in general are less inclined than men to support the policies espoused by the Tea Party, such as curtailing the social safety net, reducing taxes, and limiting gun control.[62] Indeed, women's greater support of social welfare programs has largely driven the gender gap in American politics, which finds that women are more likely to identify as and vote for Democrats.[63]

Second, public opinion about the Tea Party has soured after its initial burst of success resulted, in part, in Republicans making big electoral gains in Congress and in state legislatures in 2010. While support for the Tea Party has remained relatively stable since its inception, the percentage of Americans who view the movement unfavorably has grown steadily,[64] likely because some Tea Party–backed candidates and elected officials have been extreme and attack-oriented in their rhetoric and have shown an unwillingness to compromise on issues such as the federal debt limit.[65] Some research suggests that women are less likely than men to respond positively to attack-oriented rhetoric in politics, so the perception of the Tea Party as strident and uncompromising may hurt its cause among American women more generally.[66] In addition, support for the movement more generally among the American public has never peaked above 25 percent, demonstrating that a relatively small portion of the electorate shares the views of the Tea Party. Americans who consider themselves actual *members* of the Tea Party represent an even smaller slice of the population.

Whether Tea Party women's organizations and women Tea Party leaders can overcome such perceptions is still to be determined; however, it is their *potential* for recruiting more women that is examined in this book. As I demonstrate, women are a driving force in the Tea Party, which challenges old assumptions about women's political behavior and the role of gender in political rhetoric. Mama Grizzlies and other Tea Party women are making the case that reducing the size and scope of government can be good for women and their families, which runs counter to the progressive narrative shaped by liberal women activists, who argue that American families and American women will only be better off if government offers more help in the form of expanded social safety net programs, additional regulations on the economy and workplace, and more restrictions on access to firearms. To a more limited extent, some Tea Party women are reclaiming the feminist mantle, arguing that their brand of laissez-faire politics celebrates women's independence and capabilities, decrying the need for "big government" to make victims out of women. In so doing, these Tea Party women confront the charge that the policies espoused by their movement, and the Republican Party more generally, entail a "War on Women."

In the end, the extent to which the Tea Party succeeds in making a lasting impact on American politics, and shapes our perception of what constitutes women's politics, will be determined by whether it holds appeal for a relatively small number of conservative women; or whether, by framing its message around the role of women as caregivers and mothers called to put the state's fiscal house in order and to protect their rights to bear arms, or insisting that government programs actually keep women beholden to an activist state, it is able to appeal to and mobilize a broader segment of American women. But do the Tea Party and the right in general have what it takes to make this happen? In this book I will explore their efforts to do just that—and the long way they may have to go to earn the trust of more women supporters on the national level.

2

Top Conservatives and Grassroots Leaders

The Women behind the Tea Party

Shortly after President Barack Obama's inauguration, millennial and libertarian Keli Carender started a blog under the pen name "Liberty Belle" called *Redistributing Knowledge*, with the tagline "Because knowledge is the only commodity that needs redistributing." Calling for fellow conservatives in her native Seattle to organize politically, she wrote in her initial blog post:

> My first thought is that we are not organized enough to complete the "revolution" our country so desperately needs again. I think the reason why we are not is due to the fact that many Republicans and Conservatives live in the shadows, especially those of us that live in very liberal cities. I myself am in a mecca of radical liberalism. It wasn't until I saw the threat to our liberty embodied in one man, yes, Barack Obama, that I decided that I could no longer stay quiet. The funny part is that as I slowly "came out" to my theater friends and old school friends, a few other people started to "come out" with me. That's when I realized that we have bought into the Democrats [*sic*] and mainstream media's lies that we are somehow alone in our opinions, or strange, or dinosaurs who need to progress, etc. BUT WE ARE NOT!!! There are tens of millions of us, if not more. I think if we chose a day to show the world, scary coworkers be damned, that we exist and we are just as passionate about the direction of our country, that we could maybe finally find each other. We need to find our voices, and we need to use them!![1]

The day that Keli Carender decided to "show the world" that conservatives in Seattle were a force to be reckoned with was February 15, 2009, when she organized the Porkulus Protest to demonstrate against passage of the American Recovery and Reinvestment Act, known more broadly as the "stimulus package." The first major piece of legislation passed by the 111th Congress to address the massive economic recession, the stimulus package came with a price tag of close to $800 billion, infuriating many fiscal conservatives such as Carender. Drawing national media attention for the Porkulus Protest, Carender is credited with holding the first Tea Party rally in the United States, several weeks before the movement began to take shape nationally.[2] Carender's role in spearheading the Porkulus Protest ultimately led her to become the national grassroots coordinator for the Tea Party Patriots, one of the largest national Tea Party organizations founded as part of the larger Tea Party movement in America.

Armed with an unprecedented degree of resources, including high education levels, work experience, and access to social media, and inspired by a new generation of conservative women political leaders such as Sarah Palin, women such as Keli Carender are making their mark in the Tea Party. In this chapter I profile women who make up the leadership of the most influential Tea Party organizations in the country, examining why they became involved with the Tea Party and their thoughts on why women are heavily engaged in the Tea Party as leaders and activists. Some of these organizations, such as Tea Party Patriots, are dominated by women: in 2014, for instance, five out of six of its national coordinators were women, and the group was co-founded, and continues to be led, by Jenny Beth Martin. While most of my focus is on national leaders, I also include the perspectives of several women who have formed their own Tea Party organizations at the grassroots and state level of politics for their thoughts as to why women are so active in the movement.

I also analyze the role that conservative women's organizations—both well-established groups such as Concerned Women for America (CWA), Eagle Forum, and the Independent Women's Forum (IWF) and newer groups such as Smart Girl Politics and As a Mom . . . a Sisterhood of Mommy Patriots—are playing in the Tea Party by examining the political strategies such groups use to build support among women for their cause. For more established conservative women's groups, the Tea Party has given them a chance to reach out to a new set of female activists, as representatives from these preexisting organizations facilitate networking opportunities and provide grassroots political training.

Both the older and the newer groups often work together, promoting similar causes by speaking at one another's events, writing articles or features on their websites, and by re-tweeting comments and news alerts in the blogosphere. I take a closer look at the women who run these organizations, their rationale for getting involved in politics, and their thoughts as to why women find the Tea Party appealing, particularly as an alternative to the Republican Party. I also examine to what extent their role as mothers inspires their activism in the Tea Party.

There is debate among the leadership of the two newer organizations, Smart Girl Politics and As a Mom . . . a Sisterhood of Mommy Patriots, whether their groups can be classified as part of the Tea Party. Unlike groups such as Tea Party Patriots or Tea Party Express, whose monikers clearly indicate alliance with the Tea Party movement, Smart Girl Politics and As a Mom avoid calling themselves Tea Party organizations per se, but they do acknowledge that many of their members are part of the movement. While their leadership may consider their groups as distinct from the Tea Party, for the purposes of this book I consider them part of the Tea Party given that their policy goals and perspectives on politics are generally the same as self-identified Tea Party groups and that their origins came amid the development of the Tea Party in early 2009.

Whether helping to organize new national organizations within the Tea Party, forming local and state organizations, or building coalitions with longer-running conservative women's organizations, the conservative women activists profiled here share similar views on why the Tea Party holds appeal for women and why women are rising as leaders within the movement. First, all believe that the "open source" nature of the Tea Party affords women multiple opportunities to become leaders on their own terms. Social media has given these women unprecedented networking opportunities and has allowed them to bypass more bureaucratic conservative organizations, particularly the Republican Party, to lead their own groups. Many of the women activists I interviewed also believe that women are more adept than men at using social media, which gives them an advantage in the Tea Party given the vital role that social media plays in this movement. Moreover, compared with earlier generations of conservative women, many women come to the Tea Party with high levels of work experience and education, giving them the skills and confidence they need to be effective at political activism.

While many of these women activists still work with the GOP to direct the party in a more conservative direction, campaigning on behalf of "authentic" conservative candidates—and in some cases challenging establishment Republicans in party primaries themselves—they also acknowledge that the party has not always been welcoming of women to its ranks. Instead, the Tea Party offers these women an opportunity to organize politically and to make their own conservative voices heard. That said, they point to a newer generation of very conservative Republican women, such as Sarah Palin and Michele Bachmann, who have served as role models to emulate, which has not only inspired them to become politically engaged but has given them hope that the Republican Party may become more conservative in its principles and policy positions at the national, state, and local levels of government.

For many women active in Tea Party groups, their status as mothers or "Mama Grizzlies" and their concern for the fiscal health of the nation have prompted them to become involved in conservative grassroots activism for the first time. For others, particularly those who profess libertarian leanings, their status as mothers is not as relevant—instead, their commitment to reducing the size and scope of government, combined with their opposition to Barack Obama and his party's passage of the stimulus package in 2009 and ObamaCare in 2010, have fueled their involvement. Regardless of their primary motivations, many of these women Tea Party leaders felt compelled to lead their own organizations because they believed men were simply not stepping up to do so or, in the case of groups like Smart Girl Politics and As a Mom, they wanted to create groups that would appeal directly to women.

The conservative women leaders and activists I profile here—both those whose first sustained political engagement came with the advent of the Tea Party and those who have been involved in right-wing politics for a much longer period of time—represent only a relatively small slice of the American population. While most Americans vote on a regular basis—at least in presidential election years—the vast majority of Americans cannot be described as political activists. For example, a 2009 study by the Pew Center found that while two-thirds of Americans indicate that they took part in one form of political participation an-nually, such as signing a petition, contacting a government official, or working to solve a community problem, less than one in six Americans engage in more than five or more such activities annually.[3] Moreover, just 15 percent of Americans indicate that they are an "active member of a group that tries to influence public policy of government," and 12 percent indicate that they attended a political protest or speech in the last year.[4] In this respect, the women leaders and activists engaged in Tea Party politics represent a true political elite. Shaping public policy, however, doesn't typically come about merely by holding a few protests, joining political organizations, writing letters, or posting political blogs online. Enacting the type of conservative legislation touted by the Tea Party—including the women featured in this book—will only come about if the Tea Party can convince more Americans to vote for conser-vative candidates at all levels of government.

To that end, the Tea Party faces particular challenges with American women, who have been far more likely to vote for Democratic candi-dates in recent elections and are likelier than not to hold more pro-gressive policy positions, especially compared with American men, resulting in the much-touted gender gap in American politics. As I demonstrate in my analysis of national survey data in the last part of the chapter, which gives us a much more complete picture of what Ameri-can women who support the Tea Party look like, Tea Party women are true outliers when it comes to public opinion compared with most American women. In this and in subsequent chapters, I argue that while the emergence of women as leaders and activists within the Tea Party is an important development in conservative political activism, the national data show that such outspoken, right-wing women may still face an uphill battle in shifting most American women's attitudes on issues that matter to the movement. The gendered arguments that Tea Party women make in support of conservative policies, however, may find some support among Republican women who do *not* identify with the Tea Party, although even here there are some important differences between non–Tea Party GOP women and Tea Party women. Lastly, and perhaps most surprisingly, I reveal some differences in opinions, par-ticularly with respect to economic policies such as paid family leave and the minimum wage, between the elite Tea Party women activists I interviewed and self-identified Tea Party women in the mass public—known as the "other Tea Party," which represents Americans in national surveys who identify with the Tea Party but who do not necessarily engage actively in politics.

The Tea Party Pathbreakers: The Women Who Started the Movement

Women Leaders in the Tea Party Patriots

Arguably the most well-known national Tea Party organization in the United States is Tea Party Patriots, which claims to represent more than three thousand grassroots affiliates in the United States with membership in the "tens of millions."[5] Although Jenny Beth Martin, Mark Meckler, and Amy Kremer originally founded the group, Martin is now the public face of the organization.[6] In their book *Tea Party Patriots: The Second American Revolution* (2012), Meckler and Martin attribute the founding of their organization to social media. Both adept at Twitter, Meckler and Martin routinely followed and participated in the Top Conservatives on Twitter (#TCOT) hashtag, established in November 2008 as a way for like-minded conservatives to follow one another's tweets. The founder of the #TCOT group, Michael Patrick Leahy—who started the Nationwide Tea Party Coalition—sponsored a conference call in February 2009 after an on-air rant by CNBC reporter Rick Santelli from the floor of the Chicago Mercantile Exchange, in which Santelli famously called for a Chicago Tea Party to protest the passage of the stimulus bill and Obama's subsequent announcement that stimulus funds would be used to help homeowners who were delinquent in their mortgage payments. Santelli argued (quite passionately) that the decision to help delinquent homeowners "promoted bad behavior" among consumers, arguing that government policy instead should "reward people who could carry the water, instead of drink(ing) the water."[7] The famous rant was later rebroadcast by popular conservative commentator Rush Limbaugh and made headline news nationally as a sign of increasing unhappiness with Washington's reaction to the economic downtown. Many Tea Party activists, including Jenny Beth Martin, credit the rant with helping to inspire their engagement with the Tea

Party. The 2009 #TCOT conference call, in which Jenny Beth Martin participated, set the groundwork for the Tea Party movement (notably, Stacy Mott and Teri Christoph, the founders of Smart Girl Politics, also participated in the call).

Jenny Beth Martin was inspired to organize the first Tea Party rally in Atlanta later that month. She writes in *Tea Party Patriots* that despite having never attended or organized a protest before, "as I looked at my young children, I could not shake the thought that this was my personal responsibility as a citizen and as a mother."[8] Although public protesting may have been new to Martin, she was no stranger to politics. Involved in state-level Republican Party politics in her home state of Georgia, in the 1990s she was part of the Newt Gingrich Farm Team and attended the Coverdell Leadership Institute, a training program sponsored by the late Georgia senator Paul Coverdell to train young conservatives to become engaged in political activism. Martin believes that her prior political training gave her an edge when it came to the Tea Party. She said of her time at the institute, "It trained me and prepared me so when the opportunity presented itself in the Tea Party movement, I was already prepared and was able to be involved at a very active level faster than most people around the country who are involved in the movement. Most of the people who have been involved in this movement . . . a lot of them, I would say the vast majority of them who are active, had not been active in politics before."[9] After the success of the Atlanta rally, Martin continued networking with like-minded conservative activists nationally, quickly forming a connection with Mark Meckler, who had organized a similar Tea Party protest on February 27, 2009, in Sacramento, California, on the same day that Martin organized the Atlanta Tea Party. Along with several others, the two decided to launch the Tea Party Patriots as the "go-forward organization" for the movement, to serve as an organizing platform for other grassroots activists with the goal of sponsoring Tea Party rallies nationally on Tax Day, April 15, 2009. By their account, more than 1.2 million people attended more than 850 Tea Party events that day across the country.[10]

While the level of their public protesting has diminished since the early, heady days of the Tea Party's emergence, Tea Party Patriots has grown in terms of its organizational structure since 2009. As of 2014, Tea Party Patriots had six national coordinators who work to train activists and create networking opportunities for right-wing conservatives at the grassroots level. Of the six coordinators in 2014, five were women, including Keli Carender and Diana Reimer, who represent different generational facets of the Tea Party movement.[11] A millennial and a math teacher by training, Keli Carender, thirty-one at the time of our interview, became politically active in her native Seattle just prior to the Tea Party's emergence, blogging as Liberty Belle. Her first foray into conservative politics came when she spoke out at a City Council meeting to protest a proposed law that would have banned firearms in public places prior to the 2008 presidential elections. But it was the financial crisis, the 2008 campaign, and Barack Obama's proposals for a large stimulus bill if elected president that Carender credits with inspiring her activism: "I personally saw what candidate Obama was saying and thought he was a total radical and I couldn't understand why everyone thought he was a moderate. Not that I liked McCain, but this guy [Obama] is totally far out in left field. What are you guys thinking? So, it spurred me to action and to do something."[12] Like Keli Carender, Diana Reimer of Pennsylvania was also fairly new to politics before the Tea Party began to brew. In 2008 Reimer was frustrated with the economy, noting how her husband had been forced into early retirement because of the recession and that she was only able to find work in retail that paid very little. As she recounted:

> We were really annoyed with Bush and the bailouts. And then Mr. Obama comes out with more bailouts and we're struggling like many other Americans. I saw on the news about the first Tea Party, on February 27, 2009, and that happened right after Rick Santelli's rant. And I said that is it; that is what I want to do. I just went online and signed up to be the coordinator of the Tax Day Tea Party in Philadelphia. And when my husband came out, he said he happened to have the same idea. That's what we did and that is what we have been doing ever since.[13]

The subsequent activism of both Reimer and Carender at the grass roots caught the attention of Tea Party Patriots, and both women began to work full-time for the organization along with Jenny Beth Martin.[14]

All three of these national Tea Party leaders acknowledge that women are playing a large role in the Tea Party. When asked about women's participation in the movement, Keli Carender laughed before saying, "I think it is funny whenever someone tries to characterize the Tea Party as this group of white males who are angry. Have you ever been to a Tea Party meeting or rally? There are so many women involved. . . . In terms of numbers, I have never noticed a problem with not having women involved. Every meeting that I go to, there are tons of women involved; in the leadership positions of groups. I mean, it is not even a THING." Diana Reimer also has had similar experiences, noting that women are very present at the events she attends and have been from the start of the movement. She attributes women's involvement, in part, to their instincts as mothers: "We had an opportunity to save our children from what is going to happen in this country and what is happening today in this country." Jenny Beth Martin believes that women may be heavily involved in the movement because the Tea Party message "naturally resonates" with women: "We are the ones, oftentimes, in the houses and families, who are balancing the checkbooks and buying the groceries and looking for whether we need to use coupons or not or seeing what sales make sense. When it comes to their own personal family checkbook, women are the ones who pay such close attention to it. And we are saying we want the government to do the same thing. And I think that message does appeal to women because women are doing this anyway in their own houses." Moreover, Martin also told me that conservative women may have an easier time finding leadership opportunities within the Tea Party compared to more formally structured organizations such as the GOP: "I would say more than anything, men and women and others who are active in the Tea Party, we don't have the same sort of bureaucracy that the Republican Party has. You don't have to cut through all of these different layers to become a leader in the Tea Party. We want as many leaders as we can possibly have. And we make it easy for people who have leadership goals to step up and become leaders." But, as Martin makes clear, this same "open source" structure that allows easier access to leadership opportunities for women is also good for men who are new to the movement and want to organize their own political organizations.

Indeed, while all three of the Tea Party Patriots national coordinators agree that women play a pivotal role in the Tea Party and may enjoy more leadership opportunities as a result of the diffuse nature of the movement, particularly compared with the GOP, they have largely avoided engaging in what Republican pollster Kellyanne Conway has called "identity politics."[15] According to Keli Carender and Diana Reimer, making overt appeals to women runs counter to their libertarian principles and runs the risk of political pandering. As Carender explained, "We want freedom for everybody. It doesn't matter who you are. We don't want to be a part of the balkanization of our society, and to some extent if you really, really change your messaging for different groups of people you are contributing to that. We'd rather teach people why our message is a unifying message and why everyone should support it and it doesn't matter who you are. It is a good way to live life and have society follow that model." As a fan of libertarian author Ayn Rand's school of individualism, Carender believes that every individual is unique, with his or her own talents and challenges, so she questions whether it is wise or even possible to develop a strategy geared solely at women to build support for the movement.

Jenny Beth Martin also agrees that Tea Party Patriots, up until now, has not developed a strategy for "differentiating" its messaging along gender lines in order to appeal to more women. But she says that their organization may be more open in the future to finding a way to connect with different groups of people, particularly in wake of the reelection of President Obama in 2012, who extended his party's advantage with women voters from the 2008 elections. In fact, she believes the Obama campaign did a "very good job" of figuring out which messages work best with different groups of voters, recognizing that "there is value in making sure that [although] your end goal is the same, that you [can] enhance your message depending on whatever group you are talking to." At the same time, of course, Tea Party Patriots is not a women's Tea Party organization in the mold of Smart Girl Politics or As a Mom . . . a Sisterhood of Mommy Patriots—it just happens to be led primarily by women. Developing a strategy that speaks to potential women supporters, then, has to be balanced with its larger mission, which, according to its website, is to "restore America's founding principles of fiscal responsibility, constitutionally limited government, and free markets."

Tea Party Express

Similar to Tea Party Patriots, Tea Party Express is not a women's organization, but it was led by a woman, Amy Kremer, for five years, until she stepped down as its national director in April 2014. Tea Party Express is the largest Tea Party political action committee and endorses candidates for federal office. However, it is probably best known for sponsoring national bus tours in conjunction with local Tea Party rallies, often bringing along well-known Tea Party leaders, including women such as Sarah Palin and Michele Bachmann, as featured speakers. Bachmann, in fact, was tapped to give the Tea Party Express's first annual response to the presidential State of the Union address in 2011 as a more conservative alternative to the Republican Party's official minority party response. Tea Party Express, whose tagline boasts of the group's aims to "restore liberty" and "honor the Constitution," began during the 2008 presidential campaign as a political action committee called Our Country Deserves Better, which sponsored Sarah Palin's bid to become vice president, and later morphed into its current incarnation as Tea Party Express.

Kremer got her start in politics as a co-founder, along with Jenny Beth Martin and Mark Meckler, of Tea Party Patriots.[16] Prior to her activism in the Tea Party she was a political novice—a stay-at-home mother with previous experience in the real estate business and as a flight attendant.[17] In a profile in *The Guardian* newspaper, she relates how she became involved in the nascent Tea Party movement almost by happenstance.[18] A news junkie who was adept as using social media, she began to tweet her conservative viewpoints using the #TCOT hashtag that other early Tea Party activists adopted in February 2009. Kremer suddenly found herself organizing the Atlanta Tea Party in April 2009—one of the largest of the initial Tea Party rallies held that spring across the country. However, Kremer had a falling out with Martin and Meckler when she decided to begin traveling with Tea Party Express on its campaign tours, so she left Tea Party Patriots to work full-time with Tea Party Express in summer 2009.[19] Her work with Tea Party Express and her success as a speaker at subsequent rallies and on national television—including on the *Colbert Report* and *The View*—launched Kremer's career as a visible national spokeswoman for the Tea Party cause.

Kremer believes strongly that women are playing a pivotal role in the Tea Party. In an op-ed for *Investor's Business Daily* in 2012, she wrote that financial issues and debt have driven many women into the movement: "The left and its Big Government, big-spending, big-debt policies are destroying the American dream that should be afforded to every citizen. It's strapping trillions of dollars of debt on the backs of our children, and is failing to leave our nation a better and more prosperous place for future generations."[20] Her op-ed was a strong rebuttal to the narrative pushed by Democrats in that election season that Republicans and conservatives were launching a "War on Women." She maintains that the Tea Party movement has given her a voice to express frustration at mounting debt and stagnating job growth, but that she is just one of many "women who are fighting to take our country back."[21] Although no longer affiliated with Tea Party Express, Kremer continues to work with Tea Party–backed candidates in elections.

FreedomWorks

Tea Party Patriots and Tea Party Express are the two most prominent Tea Party groups formed in wake of the Tea Party's rise in 2009. However, they are not the first organizations geared at grassroots political organizing to promote free market policies. One national organization, in particular, has a longer history fighting for libertarian causes and has gained momentum, visibility, and a greater number of members as a result of the Tea Party's insurgency: FreedomWorks.[22] The organization, whose founding predates the Tea Party by five years, claims to have more than six million members, from all fifty states.[23] In terms of a gender breakdown, approximately one-third of FreedomWorks members are women, which is slightly less than the gender breakdown of self-identified supporters of the Tea Party commonly reported in other national surveys, which typically find that anywhere from 37 to 40 percent of Tea Party supporters are women.[24] That men outnumber women as members of FreedomWorks should not be surprising given that men outnumber women among libertarians more than two to one.[25] However, women make up more than 40 percent of the national staff of FreedomWorks and hold some important, high-profile positions within the organization.[26]

One such leader at FreedomWorks until the summer of 2014 was Whitney Neal, who served as the organization's national grassroots organizer. Neal now works as director of marketing for the Bill of Rights Institute, which is a 501(c)(3) nonprofit organization that promotes educational programming about the Bill of Rights, running constitutional seminars nationally for teachers and parents. Both FreedomWorks and the Bill of Rights Institute have ties to organizations founded by the Koch brothers, well-known billionaire investors who hold libertarian values and who have for years funded a variety of conservative causes.[27] Prior to her work with the Bill of Rights Institute, Neal came to FreedomWorks after her involvement with Senator Ted Cruz's 2010 campaign in Texas. A teacher by training and a young single mother, she became active in conservative politics because she was frustrated with education policy. A proponent of school choice, part of her job at FreedomWorks was to work with their grassroots members in opposing the state standards education movement known as the Common Core.[28] Neal agrees that FreedomWorks could be described as a Tea Party organization, but she notes that groups representing "other pieces of the conservative, limited government spectrum," such as organizations that have spun off from Glenn Beck's 9/12 Project[29] (including As a Mom) and local Republican clubs, are also part of the FreedomWorks family, which she characterizes as an umbrella organization that connects conservative activists around the country.[30]

Neal believes that the Tea Party appeals to women, especially mothers. She said that her decision to become involved in grassroots, conservative activism stems from her own role as a mother, given her belief that the size and scope of government directly relates to an individual's chance at prosperity and freedom later in life:

> For me personally, I think about my son. And I want him to be personally responsible. I want him to be independent. I want him to challenge himself. I don't want him to live in a world where the government has told him what he can be or how to be it. Or the government says, I can solve your problems. Because as a mom, I would think any mom, they want their children to go out and make something of themselves, whatever it is that they want that to be, and not have to fall back and say the government has to help me, unless it is absolutely necessary. So, I think that is appealing.

It is not just the philosophical commitment to a limited government, however, that is driving women's activism in the Tea Party, according to Neal; their motivation is also issue-based. For instance, she describes how she has met many women across the country whose first political involvement in conservative grassroots activism came about because of the Common Core standards being implemented in their school districts. Education has always been an issue of special interest to women, certainly, but FreedomWorks has worked hard to connect opposition to the Common Core with other themes regarding limited government among its local members. Neal also believes that women's changing economic circumstances, particularly as they have become more likely than ever to be their family's sole or primary breadwinners, has prompted many to rethink their stance on taxes: "Moms . . . are looking at their family finances in a way that maybe women weren't [before.]. . . . You do see a lot more single moms out there right now. With the economy the way it has been, the dad has lost his job and the mom is out there. I see our role in the family as changing because we have women saying, 'Whoa, wait a minute. Why does this much of my check go in taxes? What is this going toward?'" In this respect, Neal and other Tea Party activists suggest that women's growing economic clout, as documented by journalists such as Liza Mundy in *The Richer Sex* (2012) and Hanna Rosin in *The End of Men* (2012), could have the potential to shift women's thinking about taxes and the size and scope of government—issues about which men and women have traditionally held very distinct views, with men being far more conservative than women.

While at FreedomWorks, Whitney Neal noted that the organization reaches out to women's organizations such as local Republican women's clubs and women's liberty groups. However, Neal stops short of saying that FreedomWorks pursues a gendered strategy. True to her libertarian roots, Neal rejects what she calls a political approach that focuses on women's issues more broadly, or mother's issues more narrowly, as such issues may "alienate the people for whom home is not an issue." She deals with a diverse array of women and men in the course of her work, believing that "everyone brings unique qualities to their activism." Herself a twentysomething, she often worked with young people in her role as grassroots coordinator, noting that there is no one-size-fits-all approach to dealing with activists. For example, she says that it is impossible to categorize all twenty-five-year-old women similarly among the FreedomWorks membership base. "There is the woman who is twenty-five who just got out of college; the twenty-five-year-old who is living with her parents, the twenty-five-year-old who is already a mom and who has a career already," she explains. "That is the most wonderful thing about our movement. There are so many unique individuals, including women, involved. Of course, as one, I think women bring great ideas to the table, we bring different perspectives, but so do men."

Women in State and Local Tea Parties

On a national level the Tea Party has developed organizations, often led by women, that seek to coordinate activism at the grassroots level and to speak for the movement. Many local and state organizations have also emerged that claim the Tea Party mantle, although it is difficult to know the exact number of organizations that exist given the fluid nature of the Tea Party movement, let alone the percentage of women who are serving as leaders of such groups or as active members within them. Some case studies, however, suggest that women may play a dominant role at the grassroots level. For example, in one of the first studies of the Tea Party at the grass roots in 2012, sociologist Clarence Lo profiled four local Tea Party groups formed in Boston, Punta Gorda (Florida), Houston, and Atlanta—three were founded or co-founded by women. Anecdotally, Emily Ekins of the libertarian Reason Foundation think tank, who has conducted extensive quantitative and qualitative research about the Tea Party, believes that women are more active on the ground than men in Tea Party activists, telling me, "When it comes to the activists, which are a distinct group, that's where you honestly encounter more women than men."[31] Skocpol and Williamson, who attended Tea Party meetings in Massachusetts, Virginia, Maine, and Arizona as part of their research, validate Ekins's observations, writing in their book *The Tea Party and the Remaking of Republican Conservatism* that "women provided active leadership" at the grass roots, and some such women "have used grassroots Tea Party activism as a stepping-stone to state and national influence."[32]

Several women who have started Tea Party organizations at either the state or local level serve to illustrate how and why the Tea Party may appeal to women, including two local groups based in Texas and Maryland, respectively, and one statewide umbrella organization from Maryland.[33] Katrina Pierson[34] of Dallas helped to found the Garland Tea Party in 2009 and currently serves as a member of the steering committee of the Dallas Tea Party, one of the most active local Tea Party organizations in the country. Pierson describes the Dallas Tea Party as an umbrella organization for some "three hundred local and county Tea Party groups in Texas, with a membership of more than one hundred thousand."[35] The Dallas Tea Party helps build connections between its members and finds guest speakers to attend regular meetings of its local Tea Party affiliates. A single mother in her mid-thirties, Pierson worked her way out of poverty to become a successful health care administrator in Dallas. As a Tea Party organizer, she has found success as a media spokesperson for the movement, having established a career as a political consultant and paid speaker since 2009, often appearing on Fox News and other conservative media outlets. Pierson has also made a name for herself as one of the few women of color to be associated with the Tea Party movement, profiles of which show that membership in the Tea Party is predominately white.[36] (Of course, in 2014 Mia Love, the first African American woman elected as a Republican to the House of Representatives, also generated headlines; Tea Party Express endorsed her bid for Congress.)[37]

In 2014 Pierson made the decision to move from activist to political candidate, attempting unsuccessfully to unseat longtime U.S. Representative Pete Sessions, who chairs the powerful House Rules Committee. Her campaign initially gained national attention as she racked up endorsements from FreedomWorks president Matt Kibbe, conservative pundit Michelle Malkin, and Tea Party Express. Moreover, Pierson was the first candidate of the 2014 election cycle to have received the endorsement of Sarah Palin, who described Pierson as a "feisty fighter" who is "an emerging leader and important voice for the future of the grassroots conservative movement."[38] But Pierson lost the March 2014 primary, in part because she was unable to generate much enthusiasm outside the most conservative base of Tea Party activists, raising just $144,000 compared with Sessions's $1.5 million.[39] She told the *Dallas Daily News* that her campaign, which garnered about 30 percent of the vote, "exceeded expectations" and that her main goal was keeping the

Republican establishment honest on conservative principles. She added, "This is a beginning of a big shift in the [Republican] party. There are several like myself who are young conservatives who aren't going away, and we're going to keep doing what we've been doing, which is working to keep these [party establishment] folks accountable."[40] After her loss to Sessions, Pierson became the national spokesperson for the Tea Party Leadership Fund in August 2014, a Tea Party political action committee dedicating to supporting conservative candidates for political office.[41]

Katrina Pierson argues that part of the impetus for many women to be involved in the Tea Party is that they are mothers: "Motherhood is important to the movement. The problems we face are so much greater than twenty or thirty years ago . . . There is a whole slew of debt that our children and grandchildren will face and no parent wants their children to have less opportunities than they did." Pierson believes that women have been able to rise up as leaders within the movement because many of them bring to the table professional work experience. Also, she notes the importance of social media networks in giving women an opportunity to take a leadership role within the Tea Party, which has allowed women to speak on their own terms about politics. She told me, "Women can't be overlooked with this platform. It used to be that men in the GOP or male leaders could take a woman's idea as their own—I have had this experience—but with social media women can be attributed, they can define their own brand, and define yourself and have your ideas heard. You don't have to go through the good old boys' club any longer and that has been huge for women." Pierson's complaints about the tension between the "establishment" Republican Party and more conservative grassroots activists, or "authentic Republicans," is a frequent complaint heard from many Tea Party activists who are attempting to reshape the GOP into a more conservative party.[42] But many of the women activists I spoke with point out that the GOP has been particularly bad for women. As Pierson noted, "They don't call is a good old boys' club for nothing," pointing to the "lashing" that national women figures such as Sarah Palin or Michele Bachman faced for "not agreeing with the party leadership."

Similar to Katrina Pierson, *Jennifer Jacobs*[43] has also faced hostility from "establishment" Republicans in her years of local political activism. Jacobs started her Tea Party organization, We the People, several weeks after the Tea Party phenomenon emerged in February 2009, when she realized that "no one else was doing it."[44] Her group, We the People, serves as a conduit for conservative activists in western Maryland, one of the more conservative, though sparsely populated, regions of the state. The group holds bimonthly meetings, organizes the occasional protest, recruits volunteers to help with the political campaigns of conservatives running for office, and operates a website to promote its views and publish the blog posts of its more active members. While their members work from time to time with other state and national Tea Party activists, We the People is a truly unaffiliated, grassroots organization. The group is not incorporated, and its small budget, coming from member donations, is typically donated to charity or used to rent buses for events.

A small-business owner and grandmother, Jacobs did have prior political experience before founding We the People, serving for one term on her county's Republican Central Committee in the 1990s. However, she soon figured out, in her words, that "being a woman was a detriment" to party involvement. She told me, "The party tries to put you in a box, and if you think outside of the box or try and do things outside of the box, you are punished." For example, she recounted the time when she waged a challenge to an established Republican officeholder in a local primary, whom she described to me as a "skirt-chaser" and "misogynist," only to find her tires slashed. By contrast, she found what Jenny Beth Martin calls the "open source" nature of the Tea Party appealing: "It's all about the individual. This is what the Founders knew, it is what we women already know—our country is broken and it needs to be fixed. We have allowed the men to 'muff' it up. I don't take no for an answer." She believes that women have played such a large role in leading the Tea Party because men have not stepped up—a theme that was echoed by several of the local activists I spoke with, including Katrina Pierson of Dallas. "We want men to help protect us, to do the manly thing, so when they don't, we look to women who do it for us," Jacobs stated.

While Jacob's group, We the People, is a local organization, the Maryland Citizen Action Network (MD-CAN) is a statewide group that "exists to form a network of communication among liberty-minded individuals and groups throughout the State of Maryland."[45] Among other activities, MD-CAN sponsors a yearly weekend conference, "Turning the Tides," that brings together conservative activists from across the state, often headlined by high-profile Tea Party leaders and other prominent conservatives. In recent years, Smart Girl Politics co-founder Teri Christoph, American Majority's Anita MonCrief, and Stop Islamization of America co-founder Pamela Geller, who is known for leading efforts to prevent the construction of a mosque near the World Trade Center bombing site, have spoken at the conference. The conference also provides an opportunity for local candidates or elected officials who are conservative to speak and recruit volunteers for their campaign efforts. Three out of the four founders of MD-CAN are women, and what ultimately convinced them to join forces was their volunteer experience for the 2010 gubernatorial campaign of Brian Murphy, a young entrepreneur and small-business owner from Chevy Chase, Maryland. Although Murphy's bid to win the Republican Party's gubernatorial nomination was unsuccessful against former Republican governor Robert Ehrlich, he was beloved by Tea Party activists for his willingness to challenge the much better-known Ehrlich, who the Tea Party believed was too politically moderate and lacked fiscal discipline.

The three female co-founders brought different levels of political experience to MD-CAN. *Ellen Sullivan* was one of the founders of the Hagerstown Tea Party in 2009 but had cut her teeth in grassroots activism in the 1980s as part of the property rights movement. Although she had not been very political during her upbringing, she said she became conservative after purchasing a horse farm near Antietam National Park, routinely battling what she refers to as the "ruling class" over land management issues. She successfully fought developers and local government officials, who she claims wanted to take away private property from landowners in order to extend the national park and to establish a convention center that would become a tourist destination. Her success in stopping the developers led her to organize her own property rights newsletter, which gained a national following. In those days before the Internet, it took her thirty hours a week to research and put together the newsletter, for which she charged subscribers to cover the cost of postage and materials. But after five years, with two children she was schooling at home, the volunteer activism became too much. However, her organizing, research, and writing background came in handy as the

Tea Party hit its stride two decades later. Sullivan now publishes her own blog, the *Potomac Tea Party Report*, which has many readers, and she continues to help organize MD-CAN.

Another founder of MD-CAN, *Elizabeth Reynolds*, had previously worked on Capitol Hill in the 1980s as a congressional staffer but left discouraged about politics. She became a stay-at-home mother, but her interest in politics was rekindled by the advent of the Tea Party movement after she attended an organizing "boot camp" sponsored by Freedom-Works that she read about online.[46] After attending the workshop, she read Sullivan's Tea Party blog and contacted her; the two became friends and decided to start MD-CAN with two other Maryland activists, one of whom was *Renee Wilson*. A young stay-at-home mother and former personal trainer, Wilson was just cutting her teeth in politics with the advent of the Tea Party movement. A devoted follower of Glenn Beck at the time, she became interested in his 9/12 Project and decided to join As a Mom . . . a Sisterhood of Mommy Patriots, the online networking organization that was partly inspired by Beck. Wilson claims that she was politically awakened after the Obama administration pushed the stimulus bill through Congress, after which she decided to become more politically active in Maryland, volunteering for the Murphy campaign in 2010 and later helping to launch MD-CAN.

When asked why women appeared to be taking a strong leadership role in Tea Party politics, Ellen Sullivan said she believes there is often "more of a fighting spirit" in women. In her earlier work as a property rights activist, she noted that women were the most "ferocious fighters" because they were "saving the nest, literally fighting to save their homes"; she believes that many women active in the Tea Party today bring that same mind-set to their political organizing. Renee Wilson, the stay-at-home mother, believes that many women are drawn to the Tea Party because the movement is about "protecting our families."[47] She added, "I think there has been a shift in the way women view themselves. There has been this realization among women that women need to take an active part in what is going on." She attributes some of this to the homeschooling movement, as she finds that many of the women who work with MD-CAN are homeschooling parents who are concerned about overregulation from the government, so they stay informed about events in local government. Prior to the Tea Party, she believes that many women were reluctant to take an open, visible role in conservative politics. She said, "For a long time, women faced a stigma in American politics, especially among conservatives, who are old school when it comes to women's involvement in American politics." But she believes that now, women's "consciousnesses have been raised, and because many women have work experience they are more capable of being effective in politics."

Moreover, Wilson noted that conservative women activists now have relatable role models to emulate, such as Sarah Palin and Michele Bachmann. She believes that Sarah Palin, in particular, was an important source of inspiration for young women activists in the Tea Party because she brought an authenticity and a "much-needed emotional voice" to conservative politics. By contrast, Wilson believes that many men who lead the Republican Party are "too damn brainy." She added that "these old white men like to talk over people." She particularly lauded Sarah Palin's ability to speak plainly, praising her ability to "condense complicated things down to sound bites that people could understand."

Similar to Katrina Pierson's experience in Texas, all of the women leaders of MD-CAN cite social media as critical to women's ability to serve as leaders of the Tea Party. Studies routinely show that women are more likely to use social media than men.[48] Joanne Bamberger, founder and editor-in-chief of *The Broad Side*, a popular news site dedicated to commentary from women, argues in her book *Mothers of Intention* that mothers from both sides of the political aisle have used the Internet to bypass traditional media structures to get their voices heard in ways that are unprecedented, echoing the experiences of the women interviewed in these case studies. Sullivan, the co-founder of MD-CAN who writes her own successful local blog, believes that social media is especially well suited to women's multitasking and communication skills in comparison to men, telling me that "women are willing to share details" about political organizing that are often neglected by men. Tea Party women use social media to build their own grassroots networks but also to bypass a Republican Party culture that they view as hostile—both to women and to "true conservatives." As Renee Wilson told me, she believes she has gotten little respect from the state GOP, but she is unsure if it is because of her gender or her avowedly conservative principles. This sentiment was also shared by Ellen Sullivan, who believes that while the GOP establishment, led by longtime Republican consultants such as Karl Rove, does not seem keen on recruiting women, it also seems hesitant to engage with the self-described "authentic" conservatives active at the grass roots, among whom she includes herself and her fellow Tea Party patriots.

While some Tea Party women leaders with more experience in political activism have had a more positive experience with the GOP, such as Jenny Beth Martin, who attributed early party training she received in her home state of Georgia more than a decade ago as vital to her ability to take up the Tea Party mantle and run with it, other Tea Party women have often received a cool reception from Republican Party insiders. The negative interactions that many of the Tea Party women featured here have had with the Republican Party echo difficulties other women have found advancing within the GOP, albeit those who come from a more moderate bent. While the past several election cycles starting in 2010 have witnessed the election of more conservative Republican women to Congress, such as Representatives Martha Roby (AL) and Renee Ellmers (NC) in 2010, Senator Deb Fischer (NE) in 2012, and Senator Joni Ernst (IA) and Representative Mia Love (UT) in 2014, studies based on data drawn from the previous two decades show that GOP women legislators are less conservative than their Republican male counterparts, particularly on social issues and welfare policies, both in Congress[49] and state legislatures.[50] More recent research also shows that female Republican state legislators are nearly three times as likely as male Republican state legislators to identify as ideologically moderate.[51] Thus, as both parties have become more polarized over time,[52] moderates within both parties have been largely squeezed out, which has been particularly bad for women seeking positions as Republican candidates for office.[53] Studies that examine recruitment and gatekeeping behavior among party elites also find that the Republican Party is less adept at recruiting women to run for office than the Democratic Party, which prioritizes diversity and promotes the representation of Democratic women.[54] Experimental studies find that Republican voters may punish female candidates within the GOP as well, believing that such women are less conservative than their male counterparts,[55] so the perception of women being less ideologically conservative may hurt women's chances to emerge both as candidates and as party leaders within the Republican Party. These perceptions about Republican women, then, may have spillover effects for women in the Tea Party, despite their very conservative orientation: if Republican party leaders, most of whom are men,[56] believe that women within the party are less conservative than men, Tea Party women may be hindered in their ability to wield influence within the GOP, making involvement in the Tea Party a more appealing alternative.

Of course, engaging in the Tea Party, as compared to more traditional party activism, offers other benefits to the right-wing women profiled here (and, no doubt, right-wing men as well), such as eschewing the need to compromise that often comes with governing or appealing to a broader general electorate as opposed to conservative purists. More-over, for some women, their activism within the Tea Party allows them to focus on a more narrow set of conservative issues from a particu-larly gendered perspective. As I detail below, forming new groups such as Smart Girl Politics or working with more established conservative women's organizations allow these right-wing women to develop a par-ticular niche within Tea Party activism that traditional involvement within the political parties may not as readily allow.

A Network of Women: Conservative Women's Organizations and the Tea Party

Another notable development within the Tea Party is the establishment of new *women's* organizations that are devoted to Tea Party causes such as limited government, free market policy, and constitutional conserva-tism. Their willingness to identify as organizations with the clear goal of building support among women for conservative causes sets them apart from national organizations such as Tea Party Patriots, Tea Party Express, and FreedomWorks. As their target audience is women, their messages and marketing are designed to appeal to them, which is not to say that their approach is monolithic. The two largest women's organiza-tions to emerge in wake of the Tea Party movement, Smart Girl Politics and As a Mom . . . a Sisterhood of Mommy Patriots, in fact, utilize dif-ferent rhetorical strategies in their appeals to conservative women.

As its name implies, As a Mom . . . a Sisterhood of Mommy Patriots, is very comfortable discussing how motherhood should be married with conservative principles, and while the group maintains that its message applies to both moms and "moms at heart," it is clear through the topics it discusses on its website and on its now-defunct quarterly newsletter, *MinuteMom Magazine*, that this organization is designed to appeal to socially conservative women and traditional homemakers, with particular attention paid to the history of the Founding Era. Many Tea Party organizations, in fact, emphasize American colonial history, often claiming that the federal government today usurps the original goals and meaning of the U.S. Constitution. As historian Jill Lepore documents in her book *The Whites of Their Eyes: The Tea Party's Revolution and the Battle over American History* (2010), relying on Revolutionary analogies is nothing new in American politics—but the extent to which many Tea Party activists conflate the causes and motivations of our nation's Founders with the "true patriots" of the Tea Party, she argues, is unprecedented.[57] By contrast, Smart Girl Politics has more of a libertarian feel, focusing primarily on economic issues and the size and scope of government while largely avoiding social issues. The organization, for example, quotes Margaret Thatcher on its homepage: "There is no liberty unless there is economic liberty." However, as the organization has grown, it has begun to address some cultural issues, with a special focus given to criticism of modern feminism among many of its bloggers.

In many respects, As a Mom and Smart Girl Politics are newer incarnations of the more established conservative women's organizations that have been active in national politics as a reaction to the women's liberation movement of the 1970s. Similar to Phyllis Schlafly's Eagle Forum (founded in 1972) and Beverly LaHaye's Concerned Women for America (founded in 1979), As a Mom embraces motherhood and a religious, socially conservative view of the world, adopting positions and advocating for public policies that celebrate the traditional, nuclear family. Smart Girl Politics, by contrast, has largely avoided "motherhood" appeals in its political rhetoric, as its stated goal is to appeal to conservative women of all stripes—mothers and non-mothers alike—although, somewhat ironically, two stay-at-home moms, Stacy Mott and Teri Christoph, started the organization. Much like the Independent Women's Forum (founded in 1991), Smart Girl Politics largely focuses on economic freedom, avoiding controversial social issues such as gay rights. Both organizations share common political goals, however, including the promotion of free market economic policies and education reform, and both exist primarily as social media groups that hope to educate their members about conservative politics and to serve as a networking resource. Smart Girl Politics, however, does hold an annual summit for its members and has several active state chapters that meet in person on occasion as well.

This distinction between the social conservatives who lead As a Mom and the more libertarian-minded leaders of Smart Girl Politics is indicative of a larger, sometimes tense divide that exists between socially and economically conservative activists within the Tea Party. While some national Tea Party groups such as Tea Party Express, Tea Party Patriots, and FreedomWorks purposively avoid promoting social and cultural issues as part of their political agendas and insist that the Tea Party is primarily an economic movement devoted to reducing the size and scope of government, groups such as Ralph Reed's Faith and Freedom Coalition and the American Enterprise Institute, through its Values and Capitalism Initiative,[58] seek to build connections between the Tea Party and the Christian Right. Studies show that self-identified Tea Party activists are significantly more likely to identify as social conservatives than the general public. For instance, the Public Religion Research Institute (PRRI) finds that 52 percent of Tea Party identifiers also self-identify as part of the Religious Right or Christian conservative movement, and that Tea Party identifiers are far more likely to be conservative, not libertarian, on social issues.[59] Yet PRRI finds that about one-quarter of Americans who identify themselves as part of the Tea Party also identify themselves as libertarians, and that well-known libertarians, such as the Koch brothers, heavily fund many Tea Party causes.[60]

Different factions have always inhabited the right-wing spectrum of American politics—whether rooted in economic conservative principles, religious conservative values, and, in some cases, nationalistic and/or racist tendencies—sometimes in isolation or sometimes in combination. Those dividing lines have also extended to conservative women engaged in American politics historically, as sociologist Rebecca Klatch's classic work *Women of the New Right* (1987) illustrates. Klatch profiled conservative women activists who became engaged in politics as a result of the feminist movement and other liberal political trends of the 1970s, most notably Phyllis Schlafly, who would lead a successful decadelong battle to defeat ratification of the Equal Rights Amendment by 1982. Klatch found a divide in her interviews of conservative women activists between those who were primarily motivated by a religiously conservative vision to defend the traditional nuclear family and women's roles as homemakers, and those women who held a more laissez-faire worldview, promoting economic liberty and conservative foreign policy as primarily important in politics. Unlike the socially conservative women she interviewed, who espoused traditional gender roles, the laissez-faire women were more open to feminism, even recognizing that women sometimes faced discrimination in society. However, similar to their socially conservative counterparts, these laissez-faire women opposed the Equal Rights Amendment and any attempt by government to address such gender discrimination, believing instead that the free market would provide the best solutions to such problems. The Independent Women's Forum, founded in 1991, was the first woman's economic organization devoted to laissez-faire economic policy and continues today to make the case that free market policies, not government regulation, hold the key to women's greater economic success.

The two newer Tea Party groups discussed here, Smart Girl Politics and As a Mom, sometimes work in conjunction with Eagle Forum, CWA, and IWF when their political goals align. For instance, at the annual Smart Girl Summit, an annual weekend conference sponsored by Smart Girl Politics, speakers from these more established groups often appear on numerous panels. The Independent Women's Forum, in particular, routinely reposts links to the Smart Girl Politics website. For instance, in January 2013, as part of its monthly web column, "Portrait of a Modern Feminist," IWF.org featured Stacy Mott, co-founder of Smart Girl Politics, on its homepage.[61] In the section below, after profiling Smart Girl Politics and As a Mom, I consider how the more established women's organizations—IWF, CWA, and Eagle Forum—have approached these groups, in particular, and the Tea Party, more generally, considering what their leaders think about the role women are playing within the Tea Party and the larger conservative movement.

*Smart Girl Politics and As a Mom . . . a Sisterhood
of Mommy Patriots*

Smart Girl Politics—a social media organization whose primary goal
is to educate and empower conservative women about politics—got its
start shortly after the 2008 elections. According to its co-founder and
president, Stacy Mott, the organization has approximately sixty-five
thousand members.[62] Mott, a stay-at-home mom from New Jersey who
has a background in marketing, became interested in politics during the
2008 presidential election; in order to "stay sane" with three children
under the age of five at home at that time, she started her own political
blog featuring commentary about the campaign. Once the election was
over, however, she had caught the political bug; as a way to continue
having a voice in conservative activism, she turned her blog into Smart
Girl Politics:

> My husband and I came up with the name Smart Girl Politics. My back-
> ground is in marketing so obviously I wanted something catchy and re-
> latable. And I knew that the blog had gotten something of a following by
> the end of the political season but I had no idea just how big a following
> it had. Right after the election, I reached out to my readers and said, hey, if
> you are interested in continuing the conversation now that the election
> is over, shoot me an e-mail. And I'm thinking three or four women in a
> chat room, but I received more than sixty e-mails by the end of the week.
> So, most of those who responded are now part of our national leader-
> ship team. Smart Girl Politics then just kind of came into fruition. We
> grabbed the name everywhere on the Internet and really became a force
> on Twitter. So, that's my first venture into politics.

Mott joined forces with Teri Christoph, who was one of her readers,
to launch Smart Girl Politics officially in early 2009. Christoph, unlike
Mott, had more experience in politics, having volunteered for local
and state Republican campaigns in her native Virginia. Both Mott and
Christoph also participated in the famous teleconference that took place
among about two dozen leading conservatives tagged with the #TCOT
(Top Conservatives on Twitter) hashtag. Jenny Beth Martin, who served
on the board of directors of Smart Girl Politics during the organization's

early days, told me that Mott and Christoph were essential players in the formation of the Tea Party movement: "Had they not done what they did right after the elections in November of 2008, I don't know that the movement really would have happened. Because what they did, and what Michael Patrick Leahy and Rob Neppell with Top Conservatives on Twitter, who founded #TCOT, [did], both of those groups knew how to use Twitter and figured out what the left was doing with technology and how to learn from the left and be better. They positioned themselves without even knowing what they were positioning themselves for."[63] Indeed, it is their presence on Twitter and other social media outlets, Mott believes, that has set Smart Girl Politics apart from older, more established conservative women's organizations such as Eagle Forum, CWA, and IWF—organizations with which they share many conservative policy priorities. Another distinguishing characteristic of Smart Girl Politics is that its members are largely political novices. As Mott said, "Other organizations have more history, more political background, and I think there are many pros and cons to being outsiders and grassroots, but I think it has helped us to reach out to other women who are similar to us."

In its early days, Smart Girl Politics focused a lot of attention on building inroads with other Tea Party organizations, which Mott believes helped to grow their organization pretty quickly. Smart Girl Politics co-founder Teri Christoph echoed this thought, telling conservative political blogger Glen Asbury, "I call the beginnings of SGP 'the perfect storm' of Sarah Palin arriving on the scene, conservatives flocking to social media, and Obama becoming president. We had enough of a presence in early 2009 that we were able to jump right into the early tea parties and raise our visibility. Our organization grew by leaps and bounds during that period and we were off to the races."[64] However, while Smart Girl Politics continues to work with Tea Party leaders on occasion and often invites Tea Party leaders to speak at their summit (for instance, Amy Kremer, formerly of Tea Party Express, was a featured speaker at Smart Girl Summit in 2013), the organization decided that the primary mission of the group was to "educate women" and "not so much [to advance] the Tea Party." Mott and Christoph started Smart Girl Politics because they believed that what was missing in American politics was a network to encourage conservative women who "put themselves out there as candidates, activists and role models" in addition to educating them.[65] According to Teri Christoph, Smart Girl Politics is "not looking to portray conservative women as victims, but rather get more women involved in their communities and looking to grow the conservative movement as a whole."[66]

Given its primary focus on educating women about conservative principles and building a support network for like-minded women, Smart Girl Politics spends more time reaching out to more established conservative women's groups, such as the Independent Women's Forum and Independent Women's Voice, recognizing that those organizations have their own specialties that benefit Smart Girl Politics members. Said Stacy Mott:

> Independent Women's Forum and Independent Women's Voice—we highly respect them. They are policy wonks. They know the policy. We never pretended to be policy wonks, so it is natural for us to reach out to them on policy issues and take their knowledge and pass it along to our membership. It's a win-win for both. We are educating our members and we are helping them push their policies. There are groups like Eagle Forum who are more on the ground and they have a different demographic than we have. Each of us has a niche. We have tried and strategized and reached out to these groups to partner with them and to work with them. A lot of these groups have either sponsored or been speakers at Smart Girl Summit. We are more than happy to promote other women's organizations. We have found that many of them have reciprocated.

Another distinguishing mark about Smart Girl Politics has been its primary focus on economic concerns rather than social issues. While Mott believes that many of the members of her group may in fact be socially conservative, she says her members want to keep the focus on economics. As a member-based organization, Mott says that Smart Girl Politics allows its members "to dictate what issues we address and what direction we are going in," and that annual surveys of its members always show that the top four or five things that concern them the most are economic issues. Moreover, Mott believes that such issues hold more universal appeal for all types of women: "This economy, the spending that Congress continues to increase—look at sequestration. All of these things will directly impact women, such as college women graduating and not finding jobs. So our goal and the goal should be to turn the conversation around and to start discussing the financial aspects and how the economy is negatively affecting women and to help them to see these fiscal issues impact women more than the social issues. The financial issues impact everyone." Mott also believes that a focus on social issues by Smart Girl Politics is unnecessary because "there are other women's organizations that deal with or do a great job with the abortion issue, like CWA, which tackles the religious liberty issue, and we just needed our niche. And our niche is the financial aspect."

By contrast, As a Mom . . . a Sisterhood of Mommy Patriots is more at home with emphasizing *both* social and economic issues on its website and through its now-defunct newsletter, *MinuteMom Magazine*.[67] Moreover, although As a Mom is not formally a faith-based organization, religious values are evident in many of its writings, as blog pieces and magazine articles often quote scripture or offer religious encouragement to readers. Primarily a social media organization, with a membership of more than eighty thousand, As a Mom was founded in 2009 by graphic designer and stay-at-home mother Lori Parker, who was inspired by Glenn Beck's 9/12 Project.[68] The 9/12 Project has spawned several spin-off groups, including As a Mom, which lists on its homepage the twelve values identified by Beck as vital to Americans. Parker served as the first president for As a Mom and chair of the board through 2013.

Lori Parker says she was inspired to choose the name "As a Mom" by a comment from Frank Lutz, a Republican pollster who made a guest visit on Glenn Beck's Fox television special, *The Mother's Challenge: A 9/12 Project*. On Beck's show, Lutz said that women can have a strong impact on politics by embracing their status as mothers. He said, "If you begin everything with 'As a mom,' you win." That comment, according to Parker, helped set in motion the founding of As a Mom, which she did out a sense of duty to her children. Of her involvement with As a Mom, she told me, "I can look my children in the eye one day and say I have done everything I can to fight for your liberties."[69] As a result, most of the writers who contribute to As a Mom speak from their perspective as mothers, imploring their fellow "mommy patriots" to become engaged in politics on behalf of their children.

As a Mom's website and the now-defunct *MinuteMom Magazine* include both political and nonpolitical features: many of its members are homeschooling moms, so there are articles detailing resources and information for families who educate their kids at home. General civic information and citizenship guides can also be found in their publications, giving basic information to women new to political involvement about how the legislative process works in Congress or how state laws differ with respect to voter registration. Some education pieces are written by long-standing conservative activists, such as Phyllis Schlafly, founder of Eagle Forum, who encourages the women of As a Mom to become members of their local Republican Party's precinct committee as a way to influence candidates who run in political primaries.[70] The political news stories featured in these publications, however, are typical of the types of information one often finds on other Tea Party websites: stories about the national debt, immigration reform, and gun rights; and denunciations of multicultural education, gay marriage, feminism, and various initiatives sponsored by the United Nations—particularly the sustainable development action plan aimed at reducing climate change, Agenda 21—among other liberal political causes.[71]

As a Mom also heavily focuses on the nation's Founding period and colonial history in its publications, with a strong emphasis on educating its readers about the Constitution. However, what distinguishes As a Mom from other Tea Party groups, many of which also consider educating their members about the origins of the Constitution an important priority, is its profile of important Colonial Era women, many of whom were spouses of the Founding Fathers such as Abigail Adams (wife of John Adams) and Elizabeth Adams (wife of Sam Adams). In a regular "Founding Mothers" feature, As a Mom describes the contribution of these lesser-known women, arguing that they were just as important to the establishment of the new nation. For instance, Krisanne Hall writes in *MinuteMom Magazine*, "The founding women of our nation carried themselves with dignity and strength; believing with their hearts and souls the value of Liberty was worthy of their families' sacrifice. These were women of principle, courage, and of great resolve, willing to sacrifice all so that their children could be free."[72] Notably, the "Founding Mothers" feature links the involvement of such women, some of whom organized boycotts of British goods or took over the management of their families' farms to allow their husbands to devote their time fully to the cause of the Revolutionary War, directly to their motherhood status, to ensure that their children, as Hall puts it, "would live free." And in so doing, Hall and other "mommy patriots" who make up the membership of As a Mom hope to put to rest what they believe are misconceptions about these Founding Era women.[73] In reclaiming the role of women in America's Founding Era, As a Mom members hope to inspire conservative women today to "stay informed of the challenges and threats we face, to learn more about American history, and to look for opportunities to exercise patriotism."[74]

The link between the nation's Founding Era and today's politics informs much of what As a Mom does, as its leaders routinely draw parallels between today's "patriots" in the Tea Party and the Founding Fathers and Mothers. When asked why she co-founded As a Mom, Lori Parker told me:

> I am going to step back to the 1770s. I started looking at our Founding Mothers. They set up in Boston Common and spun linen, and they have basically a "spin-in" because they realized by making their own flax, they would be hurting the British economy by stopping their reliance on Great Britain. Almost four years before the Boston Tea Party, you had seven hundred women sign a petition saying they wouldn't have tea in their homes. We have lost a lot of what they were doing. And I think what they were doing is the same thing that we are doing. We are looking at what is going on and we are looking at our children. I think men look at what is going on and they look at their bank accounts. But I think the same thing that drove those early patriot women is what is driving us today. We look around and we want to see a future for our children. We look at this legislation [today] that goes through and this isn't helping.

As one example, she points to the Healthy, Hunger-Free Kids Act that was passed by Congress and signed by Barack Obama in 2010, which sets federal child nutrition standards and helps fund school breakfasts and lunches. The new guidelines were enacted, in part, to help combat childhood obesity. However, after some criticism of the legislation over calorie restrictions and limits on the amount of meat and grains children could eat—brought by members of Congress whose constituents complained that their children who participated in the program left lunch hungry—the Department of Agriculture tweaked the act to allow more flexibility within individual school districts.[75] Lori Parker believes the act is indicative of a federal government that usurps the roles of parents, particularly mothers, and helps to explain why women have become more active in the fight to promote conservative political causes since the Tea Party movement began. She complained to me: "Why on Earth is the federal government determining what our kids are eating in our schools? We look at our kids more, and a lot of men don't. Men may not register this, whereas women will be like, 'Little Sally isn't eating because the food is so bad.' This may be politically incorrect to say, but we do have maternal instincts and we look at our kids, that whole thing, since day one when we are in the delivery room, it is all about protecting them." In Parker's estimation, conservative women have a unique vantage point about how the federal government's policies may have a negative impact on children. Her organization routinely educates its members on what it believes are the deleterious effects of federal policies on families, using language that directly appeals to mothers.

Parker believes that As a Mom has been successful in appealing to busy mothers—both those who stay at home and those who work outside the home—because its social media format best fits into their busy schedules. While there was some debate among its membership about promoting regular face-to-face meetings shortly after the organization began, As a Mom concluded that such an approach would not work. She told me:

> Moms are so busy and their lives are so packed, to say let's meet Tuesdays at seven o'clock doesn't work. Where, if we say, we have a meeting 24/7 going on online, pop in whenever you can, read the latest on the farm bill, it works. It conforms better to everyone's life because it is much easier to pop into your iPhone while you are waiting for Junior to get done with piano lessons than it is to find a babysitter and show up to a meeting. We are social media. We wouldn't exist without social media, because that is how we completely run.

In that respect, As a Mom is similar to Smart Girl Politics, which also is primarily run as a social media organization for conservative women.

Another similarity between As a Mom and Smart Girl Politics is that their members largely determine which issues the organizations will promote through social media platforms, chat rooms, and blog posts. And it is in that similarity—member-driven activism—that we see a major difference between the two organizations. Unlike Smart Girl Politics, As a Mom places a strong emphasis on traditional homemaking skills. For instance, Lori Parker notes that many As a Mom members, as a "reaction to rising food prices and an uncertain economy," were submitting articles or questions to its website about "prepping," which is a movement geared at helping individuals have adequate food, water, and shelter in case of a national emergency. As a result, sandwiched between articles about the Common Core and economic policy in *MinuteMom Magazine* and on the As a Mom website is information devoted to prepping: gardening, canning, and food and water storage. The prepping movement ties into the traditional conservative philosophy of self-reliance: many prepping websites promote the idea that families should be prepared to take increased personal responsibility in providing for themselves, particularly in case of a natural or political disaster. Many of As a Mom's members grew up hunting or growing their own food. Parker, for instance, notes that, as a Mormon, "gardening and canning is a big part of my heritage." The other co-founder of As a Mom, Anita L. Reeves, notes in her written contributions to *MinuteMom Magazine* that she is a master gardener and licensed ham radio operator. Moreover, As a Mom often partners with Homemakers of America, whose tagline is "Liberty begins at home." The top officeholders of Homemakers of America were regular contributors to *MinuteMom Magazine* before it stopped circulation in late 2013. These contributions celebrate women's traditional homemaking role yet also politicize the homemaker by linking homemaking and safeguarding the nation's liberties. As Tammy Hulse, vice president of Homemakers for America, writes, "Now, more than ever, we need mothers and homemakers to stand up and exercise the tremendous influence they can have on their family and society."[76]

In addition to emphasizing traditional homemaking tasks, and linking this motherhood role to larger political goals, As a Mom differs from Smart Girl Politics in other ways. First, As a Mom avoids endorsing candidates running for political office or profiling individual legislators in its writings. According to Parker, As a Mom decided "not to focus on

people but instead issues because there may be a candidate who is really great and wonderful and a year later, they are not."[77] Instead, As a
Mom places its emphasis "on the legislation and how it is written, and
say, look, this is really bad wording." By contrast, Smart Girl Politics endorses conservative women running for office, such as Karen Handler,[78]
who ran for U.S Senate in the Georgia Republican primaries in May
2014. The Smart Girl Politics website published the following endorsement: "Karen has a strong conservative record and is a proven leader,
which is why we fully support her candidacy."[79] She did not win. Prior
to endorsing candidates more formally, Smart Girl Politics routinely
profiled conservative, Republican women in its writings and on its website, and invited them as speakers to its annual summit.

Another difference between As a Mom and Smart Girl Politics is that
As a Mom is more comfortable discussing socially conservative issues and
embracing religious themes. The group routinely promotes a pro-life perspective on abortion, defends marriage as a relationship between a man
and a woman, and decries the wall of separation between church and state
in the United States. Many of their writers also promote the religious origins of the nation, drawing connections between religion, motherhood,
and patriotism in an effort to inspire its base of women activists. Typical
of such inspirational writing is the following from Kami Watkins, who
wrote in a 2012 article titled "We Need Not Fear . . . God Is on Our Side":

> We've had enough! We are done with the pro-liberal mentality that seeks
> a communist approach to the leading of this nation. We are women of
> strength . . . We can help change this path our country is on by trusting
> ourselves and in our God-given gifts to make a difference. We will change
> the future because our children, our nation, our God is depending on us.
> We must see truth, liberty, and freedom prevail . . . everywhere. We are
> mothers answering the clarion call of God for freedom and we need not
> fear, "For God hath given us the spirit of fear; but of power, and of love,
> and of a sound mind" (2 Timothy 1:7).[80]

Lori Parker notes that the biggest challenge groups like As a Mom face
in recruiting religiously conservative women is convincing them that
politics is not solely a man's prerogative nor is it inherently corrupt. She
told me:

There is this attitude, among religious women, where we just let things go, and if you show up to vote in November, you have done your part. When, of course, the real candidates are chosen much earlier in the year. There is this perception that politics is dirty; you cannot be a clean person. How can you say you are a Christian and be involved in politics? But I say, how can you say you are one and NOT be involved and try to influence things? That's where I see it. The problem is to try and reach out to people of faith. There are things and ways you can be involved and not feel like you have been rolling around in the pigpen.

The emphasis on scripture and the role that faith played in the founding of the new nation are often invoked by As a Mom to lend credence to the larger political themes and policy priorities of the Tea Party movement, which routinely calls on its heritage as patriots to inspire many of its activists today. As a result, As a Mom fills a unique niche among Tea Party groups: promoting Tea Party activism among religious women.

The Mainstays: Eagle Forum, Concerned Women for America, and Independent Women's Forum

As a Mom . . . a Sisterhood of Mommy Patriots and Smart Girl Politics, while relative newcomers to the world of conservative activism, are not the first such groups to represent women on the right side of the political spectrum. Eagle Forum and Concerned Women for America have represented the viewpoints of socially conservative women for more than thirty years. The Independent Women's Forum has more of a libertarian bent, defining its mission as "improv[ing] the lives of Americans by increasing the number of women who value free markets and personal liberty."[81] While IWF touches on some cultural issues, it does so from a more libertarian perspective. For instance, many of its publications and articles denounce feminism from an economic standpoint, decrying efforts by feminists to call for more government regulation to enact economic equality between men and women. By contrast, while Eagle Forum and CWA may also criticize feminism for economic reasons, they primarily decry feminism's denunciation of the patriarchy as offensive to their religious beliefs. These groups also oppose abortion and gay marriage, whereas IWF does not publicly take a stand on these socially conservative issues.

I interviewed the leadership of all three organizations for their perspectives on why conservative women have become more outspoken as political activists with the rise of the Tea Party and to see what sorts of outreach these existing groups have made to Tea Party women. Colleen Holcomb, who at the time of our interview was the executive director of Eagle Forum's Capitol Hill office, indicated that her organization was among several more long-standing groups that were already active in grassroots conservative politics when the Tea Party first emerged. Of Phyllis Schlafly, Eagle Forum's founder, Holcomb remarked, "She was Tea Party before there was the Tea Party!"[82] The advent of the Tea Party has provided Eagle Forum the opportunity to train women who are new to politics. Holcomb noted that Eagle Forum still has many members who cut their teeth in political organizing during the battle to stop the Equal Rights Amendment in the 1970s, and they are happy to pass along knowledge to political newbies about how politics works at the state legislative level. Although they have worked with activists from groups such as Tea Party Express and Americans for Prosperity, Holcomb says Eagle Forum has had less success with Smart Girl Politics. This is not because the organizations don't share some similar views on policy, but instead because their membership bases are very different. As Holcomb notes, Eagle Forum's population of activists are older and less familiar with social media, which is the main forum for the members of Smart Girl Politics to stay informed and politically engaged. By contrast, Eagle Forum shares a similar base of religiously minded members with As a Mom, and Phyllis Schlafly's writings are often featured on the group's website.

Janice Shaw Crouse, senior fellow of the Beverly LaHaye Institute, which is the think tank of Concerned Women for America, said that many of its members are involved in the Tea Party and that CWA is very supportive of the movement. She notes that her organization's membership has grown since the arrival of the Tea Party, but she stops short of saying that reaching out to Tea Party groups is an important part of CWA's strategy per se. Instead, CWA has always been an organization devoted to socially conservative issues, and some members believe that focusing on economic concerns may detract from its larger goals. As

Crouse told me, her group has "gotten some criticism" for emphasizing the economy and fiscal issues. However, Crouse believes that the fiscal concerns have moral dimensions, too, noting that CWA's president, Penny Young Nance, often compares reckless government spending with the constraints faced by U.S. families:

> Penny [often] talks about how as a housewife, she does the budgeting, handles the health care decisions, and goes to the doctor and plans the doctor's appointments . . . how the country would not be required to stay on a budget when they know that families have to do that as well at home. We feel very strongly about how women make the financial decisions. This is very offensive to women that the country would not be required to stay on a budget. They know that they have to do that in their own homes and there are some who say we can't afford to do it. And yet as a country we are flying in the face of that. And our kids are the ones who will have to pay that debt. That's a theme you will see on our website.[83]

Concerned Women for America, according to Crouse, tries hard to marry their conservative social stances with conservative economic policy, but the group's core concerns remain "solidly social conservative issues."

Of the three conservative women's groups, the Independent Women's Forum has engaged in the most direct outreach to other Tea Party groups. Carrie Lukas, the managing director of IWF, says they are "thrilled" to see such an outgrowth of support for conservative causes among women with the Tea Party's advent. IWF often works with Smart Girl Politics, providing the group with information and supplying them with articles for the Smart Girl Politics website and its magazine, *Smart Girl Nation*, which ceased publication in 2013. The IWF also profiles events sponsored by Smart Girl Politics on its own website and often provides speakers for the Smart Girl Politics annual Smart Girl Summit.

While the level of direct involvement with women Tea Party organizations may differ, the leadership of Eagle Forum, CWA, and IWF all acknowledge that women have played a critical part of the Tea Party more generally and that motherhood may be a compelling motivator for such women. Carrie Lukas said that President Obama's economic and health care policies have driven more women into the Tea Party: "You could say this is a threat to my kids' economic future. And I don't want my kids to be in a country with a permanent 10 percent unemployment rate or leaving the labor force or a socialized medical system. People are worried about the budget and most parents are motivated by what's best for their kids. So I am sure that is behind a lot of the Tea Party moms."[84] Eagle Forum's Colleen Holcomb has seen an uptick in the number of women active in conservative causes in wake of the Tea Party. She told me that women are drawn to the Tea Party because of their maternal instincts:

> I remember growing up with the sense that we have the ability to exceed our parents' accomplishments and to leave a better country. We realized we are not doing that now. There was even a time I was questioning whether I want to have children in this kind of world. And that is not something I have ever questioned in my life. It's a strong threat. The Mama Grizzlies is a great analogy. It is very primal. It is a very strong sense of threat. You just feel like to be a good mother, you have to do something; to be a loving, protective mother, you have to speak out.

All three women believe that another compelling feature of the Tea Party is that it allows women to bypass the Republican Party, which has not always been welcoming to women and has not done a good job of considering women's perspectives on political issues. Carrie Lukas of IWF believes that "there is a truth to the idea that the Republican establishment is run by men and continues to see policy through a male lens. And to see women's issues as one of those things you have to check on a list and target similar to targeting a group like farmers, for example, as a small interest group. Sometimes the GOP tends to put women in a small box. Absolutely."

Janice Crouse of CWA bemoans the lack of inclusion of women among Republican leadership and conservative groups more generally. She recounted complaining to the Mitt Romney presidential campaign after his organization called an election strategy meeting of social conservatives but invited only men. She told me, "After all of the War on Women rhetoric [of the previous election], what message does that send that you have all men advisers?" Colleen Holcomb of Eagle Forum believes that the problem the Republican Party has with women is not that its current leadership is filled primarily with "sexist, old white males," but instead that Republicans tend to be "primogenitor Republicans, they just go with the next in line," which means conservative women, who may be newer to political activism, are typically excluded. "As moms, you just want to cut through some of the crap!" said Holcomb. "You don't want to go to meeting after meeting, doing the same old thing." Conservative women, she believes, "want some action," which is what the Tea Party allows women to do.

The ability to bypass traditional Republican structures, all three women believe, has been key to women's success in the Tea Party, particularly through the use of social media—a theme echoed by many of the Tea Party activists I interviewed. Said Carrie Lukas of IWF, "The main reason there has been a huge shift in political involvement and, in particular, women with children being more politically involved in the Tea Party, is that they can be. Most of our political dialogue now takes place on the Internet, through social media. So, if you are a stay-at-home mother of four or a working mom of four, you don't have time to go down to campaign headquarters, hand out leaflets and volunteer, or do x, y, and z." The "barriers to political entry" with the Tea Party, as compared with the GOP, are far lower, which has allowed conservative women a new way to express their political views and to become engaged in politics. And the reliance on social media as a major mechanism for political organization may also better suit women than men. As Lukas concluded, "Girlfriends are used to sharing with each other and tagging each other [on Facebook] . . . 'I thought this article was an interesting story that we should all pass around.' Women do this quite naturally, and I think men in general are more reticent to do stuff like that. And I think that that is the political basis for the organizational success of the Tea Party."

Women in the "Other" Tea Party: Support for the Tea Party among America's Women

Women have emerged as strong leaders within the Tea Party, whether forming self-described women's organizations, such as Smart Girl Politics, or leading national, state, and grassroots organizations that are not gender-specific. Yet the women profiled thus far in this chapter are true political elites—a rarity among America's citizenry. Next, I shift my focus to what Emily Ekins, director of research for the libertarian think tank Reason Foundation, describes as the "other Tea Party."[85] The "other Tea Party" comprises Americans who in national surveys may consider themselves part of the Tea Party but who do not necessarily engage actively in politics. As political scientists Christopher Parker and Matt Barreto report, relatively few Americans engage in Tea Party politics.[86] In their study, just 7 percent of Americans indicated participating in some Tea Party–related activity such as donating money to a Tea Party cause or attending a Tea Party meeting.[87] Moreover, they found that a mere 2 percent of Americans actually *joined* a Tea Party organization.

By contrast, more Americans express support for the Tea Party and its goals. Examining mass support among Americans for the Tea Party is important, given that while most Americans aren't engaged in political activities routinely, a majority of them do vote (at least in presidential election years). Political leaders and party candidates, looking at the issues that are most salient to the American public, frame their messages to appeal to voters. In primary elections, voters tend to be more ideological and committed. Evidence suggests that the GOP, in particular, has become a more conservative party because of Tea Party pressure at the grassroots. Understanding who supports the Tea Party nationally, then, becomes vital to understanding the current dynamics and future direction of American politics. Understanding *women's* propensity to the support the Tea Party in the mass public is also important, as it helps us to understand whether the gendered messaging Tea Party women have developed to promote conservative policies will have much success in reaching the general public and convince more women to vote for Republicans rather than Democrats in future election cycles.

Studies consistently find that only a minority of Americans expresses support for the Tea Party. Figure 2.1 documents support among Americans for the Tea Party dating from 2010 to 2015, derived from national surveys conducted by three leading polling firms, all of which use very similar question wording regarding movement support. The CBS News / *New York Times* Survey asks "Do you consider yourself to be a supporter of the Tea Party, or not?"; the AP/GFK Poll asks "Do you consider yourself a supporter of the Tea Party, or are you not a supporter of the Tea Party?"; and Gallup asks "Do you consider yourself a supporter of the Tea Party, an opponent of the Tea Party, or neither?" The range of responses indicating support for the movement span a low of 20 percent

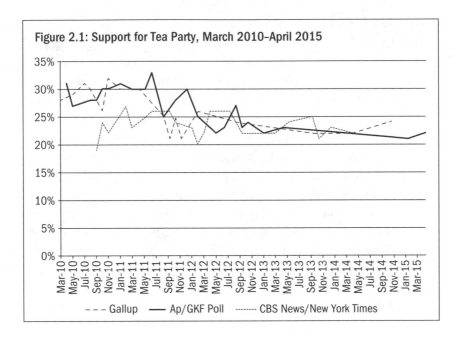

Figure 2.1: Support for Tea Party, March 2010–April 2015

(February 2012, CBS News) to a high of 33 percent (AP, June 2011), with a four-year average of 26 percent.[88] The most recent public opinion polls available in 2015 indicated just slightly lower support than the four-year average above: an AP/GFK poll showed that 22 percent of Americans identified themselves as supporters of the movement in April 2015.[89]

Expressed support for the Tea Party among the general public differs, however, depending on the language that surveys employ.[90] Some surveys elicit slightly higher approval ratings. For instance, the ABC News / *Washington Post* poll routinely asks respondents if they have a favorable impression of the Tea Party, and the responses from 2010 to 2014 ranged from a low of 26 percent (October 2013) to a high of 41 percent (February 2010). The Public Religion Research Institute (PRRI), which has tracked Tea Party support since 2010, uses a narrower indicator, asking respondents "Do you consider yourself a part of the Tea Party, or not?" This indicator finds fewer Americans describing themselves as part of the Tea Party. In 2010, PRRI's American Values Survey found that 11 percent of Americans identified as a member of the Tea Party—a percentage that held steadily through 2013. Its 2014 American

Values Survey, however, found that just 7 percent of Americans self-identified as part of the movement.[91]

Turning to *which* Americans are most likely to support the Tea Party, numerous studies all point to similar trends: Tea Party supporters are disproportionately white, older, well-educated, and, as Skocpol and Williamson (2012) phrase it, "comfortably" middle-class compared to other Americans.[92] Tea Party supporters are more likely to be married, attend religious services regularly, and identify as evangelical Protestants than Americans more generally.[93] Lastly, Tea Party supporters are more likely to be male, with most studies showing anywhere from a 15 to 20 percent gender gap in support for the movement, with roughly 60 percent of Tea Party supporters being male compared with 40 percent of supporters being female.[94] While national surveys consistently show this gender gap, few studies have systematically considered gender as an analytical category in their assessment of the Tea Party. For instance, we know little about what kinds of American women are likely to support the Tea Party, if Tea Party women differ from Tea Party men, or how their support for the movement may be predicated on different factors than men.

Using national survey data from PRRI, I profile Tea Party women nationally, examining their socioeconomic background and their religious and political beliefs. In subsequent chapters, I take a more thorough look at Tea Party women's attitudes regarding social welfare issues, income inequality and the role of government (chapter 4); feminism, gender roles, and gender-related policy issues such as abortion and sex discrimination (chapter 5); and gun rights (chapter 6). In this chapter I initially consider some basic policy differences that are not touched on in subsequent chapters between Tea Party women and two other groups of women—Republican women who do not identify with the Tea Party and other American women (Democrats and Political Independents). In particular, I consider attitudes about racial discrimination and immigration policy, given that some scholars argue that Tea Party mobilization can best be understood, in part, as a reactionary movement to Barack Obama's historic election as president and to larger demographic changes in American society.[95] Unfortunately, a more thorough examination of how gender interacts with Tea Party status to inform opinion about immigration and racial discrimination is beyond the scope of this study. Next, I compare and contrast Tea Party women with Tea Party men to examine how Tea Party women and men may differ from each other. Finally, using multivariate analysis, I showcase what characteristics lead American women to be likely to support the Tea Party and to determine whether women support the Tea Party for different reasons than do men. I then consider what my findings about these "other Tea Party women" nationally say about the ability for the Tea Party women leaders I profile here to convince more American women to support their conservative cause.

American Women and the Tea Party

To examine which American women are most likely to support the Tea Party and how they differ from other American women in terms of their socio-demographic, religious, political, and policy beliefs, I combine two surveys conducted by the Public Religion Research Institute in 2012: the American Values Survey (N = 3,003) and the White Working Class Survey (N = 2,501), which allows for a larger sample size and makes statistical inferences more meaningful between Tea Party women, non–Tea Party Republican women, and those American women who do not identify with either group (see appendix A for more details about the surveys).[96] Figure 2.2a shows the breakdown by gender of Americans who identify as part of the Tea Party, as Republicans who are not part of the Tea Party, and others (Democrats and Political Independents).[97] Roughly one in ten American women describe themselves as a Tea Party member, although they are significantly less likely to do so than men, which mirrors trends in other national data that has examined support for the movement by gender.[98] Among self-identified Tea Partiers, 58 percent are men and 42 percent are women, which demonstrates a significant gender gap in support among Americans who identify with the movement.[99] Most Tea Party women and men identify themselves as Republicans, although a sizeable portion identify themselves as Independents. However, while relatively few Tea Partiers of either sex identify as Democrats, women are significantly more likely than are Tea Party men to do so (see figure 2.2b). Turning back to figure 2.2a, American women are almost twice as likely (18 percent) to identify as "non–Tea Party" Republicans than they are to identify as part of the Tea Party (10 percent). Moreover, as figure 2.2c shows, among American

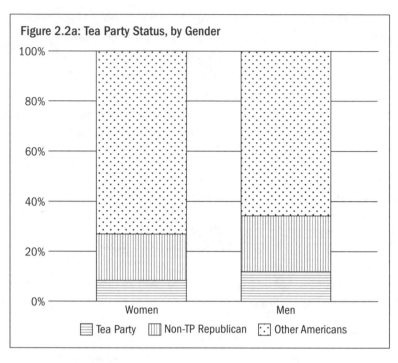

Figure 2.2a: Tea Party Status, by Gender

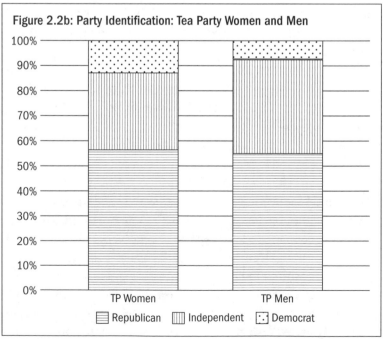

Figure 2.2b: Party Identification: Tea Party Women and Men

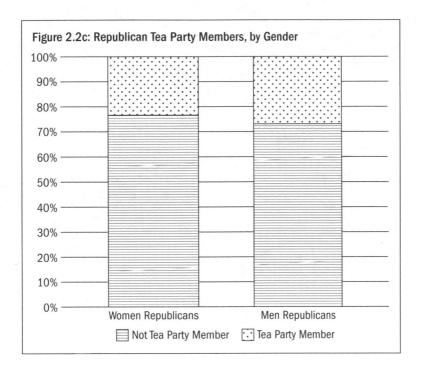

Figure 2.2c: Republican Tea Party Members, by Gender

women who identify as Republicans, just 22 percent consider themselves part of the Tea Party. Similarly, just 27 percent of Republican men in the United States also identify themselves as a member of the Tea Party. I'll return to further analysis of how gender affects Tea Party identification later this chapter. In the meantime, I compare Tea Party women with women who identify as Republicans but who do not consider themselves part of the Tea Party and women who identify as Democrats or Political Independents, whom I call "other American women."[100]

Tea Party women share many similarities with non–Tea Party Republican women but are measurably different from other American women in terms of key socioeconomic demographics. For instance, Tea Party women (50.3 years, average) and non–Tea Party Republican women (52.3 years, average) are older than other American women (47.6 years, average).[101] Tea Party women and non–Tea Party Republican women also report higher rates of marriage, 65 percent and 71 percent, respectively, than do other American women (53 percent).[102] Compared with other American women, both Tea Party and non–Tea Party Republican women are less

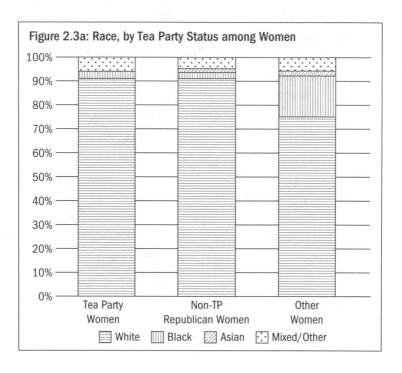

Figure 2.3a: Race, by Tea Party Status among Women

racially diverse (see figure 2.3a) and report higher incomes (see figure 2.3b).[103] While the modal response on employment status is full-time employment among all three women, other American women are less likely to list being full-time homemakers than are Tea Party or non–Tea Party Republican women (see figure 2.3c). One distinction between Tea Party women from both categories of the other women concerns education: Tea Party women are more likely than other women to report having a high school education or less (see figure 2.3d). However, all three categories of women report similar levels of parenthood: roughly 30 percent of all report having children under the age of eighteen.[104]

When it comes to religion, Tea Party women not only report higher levels of religious salience than do other women (see figure 2.4a), they are also more theologically conservative. More than half of Tea Party women, for example, believe that the Bible is the Word of God and literally true (see figure 2.4b). Moreover, more than two-thirds of Tea Party women describe themselves as born-again Christians, more than both non–Tea Party Republican women and other American women

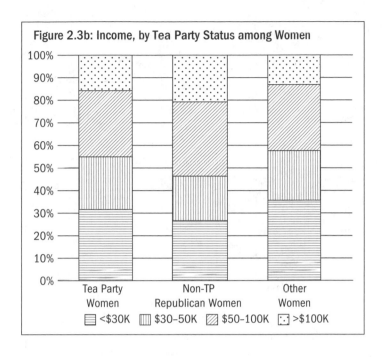

Figure 2.3b: Income, by Tea Party Status among Women

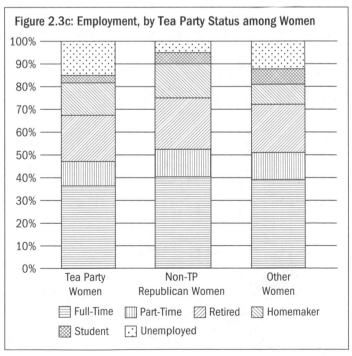

Figure 2.3c: Employment, by Tea Party Status among Women

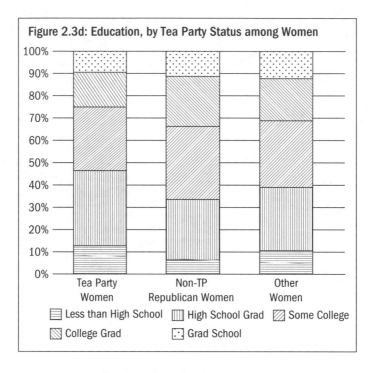

Figure 2.3d: Education, by Tea Party Status among Women

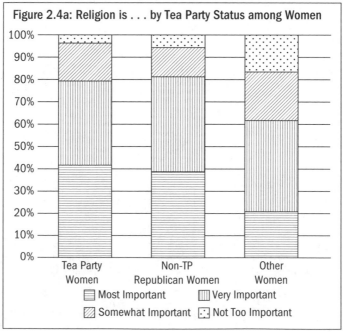

Figure 2.4a: Religion is . . . by Tea Party Status among Women

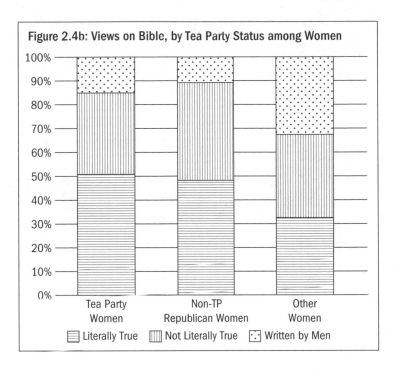

Figure 2.4b: Views on Bible, by Tea Party Status among Women

(see figure 2.4c). Tea Party women also report high levels of church attendance at rates comparable to non–Tea Party Republican women but higher than other American women (see figure 2.4d). Concerning support for gay marriage among American women, more differences emerge. While gay marriage is a social policy, most of the opposition to it is rooted in religious objection, and as revealed here, Tea Party women hold the most conservative position on gay marriage, although their views are fairly close to non–Tea Party Republican women (see figure 2.4e). By contrast, other American women express far greater support for gay marriage.

Turning to politics, Tea Party women are distinct from other American women in terms of their self-described ideological outlook, with 29 percent describing themselves as "very conservative," at almost twice the rate of non–Tea Party Republican women (see figure 2.5a). They also held the most unfavorable views of Barack Obama (see figure 2.5b). Similar to non–Tea Party Republican women, Tea Party women held far more positive views about Mitt Romney and the Republican Party (see figures 2.5c and 2.5d, respectively) than other American women, but

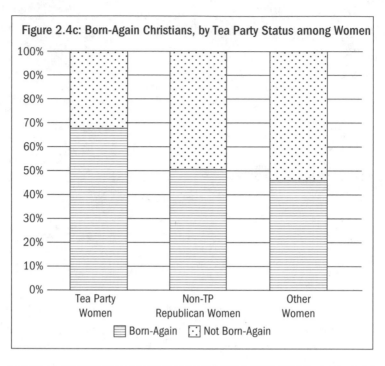

Figure 2.4c: Born-Again Christians, by Tea Party Status among Women

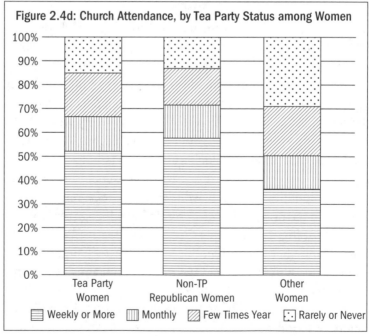

Figure 2.4d: Church Attendance, by Tea Party Status among Women

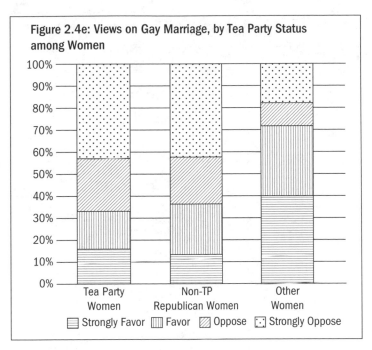

Figure 2.4e: Views on Gay Marriage, by Tea Party Status among Women

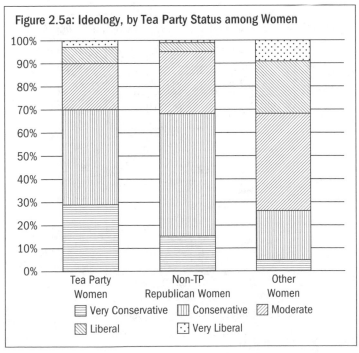

Figure 2.5a: Ideology, by Tea Party Status among Women

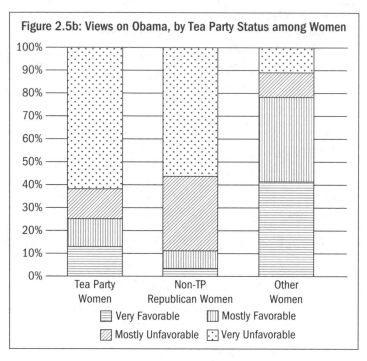

Figure 2.5b: Views on Obama, by Tea Party Status among Women

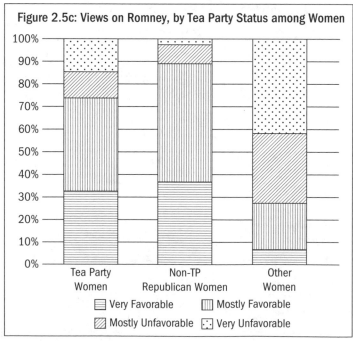

Figure 2.5c: Views on Romney, by Tea Party Status among Women

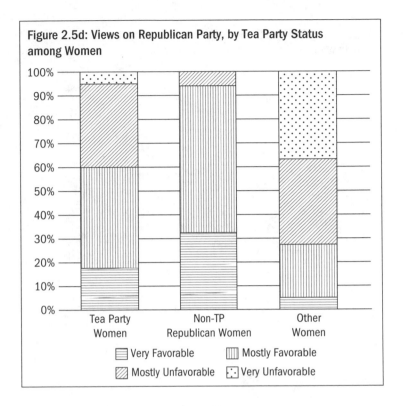

Figure 2.5d: Views on Republican Party, by Tea Party Status among Women

were more likely to be critical of both Romney and the GOP, and especially the Democratic Party (see figure 2.5e), than their non–Tea Party Republican women counterparts, reflecting the more general dissatisfaction that the Tea Party has with the political status quo, including "establishment" Republicans.

Subsequent chapters will demonstrate that Tea Party women hold far more conservative positions than do other American women on a variety of social and economic issues. I will explore these issue positions in much greater detail later in the book, but here I will briefly turn to Tea Party women's attitudes about immigration and race relations. Although the Tea Party positions itself as primarily an economic movement, some leaders within the movement have taken vocal stands against illegal immigration. In fact, illegal immigration reemerged as a big issue for some Tea Party activists in the summer of 2015, after derogatory comments about illegal Mexican immigrants made by Donald

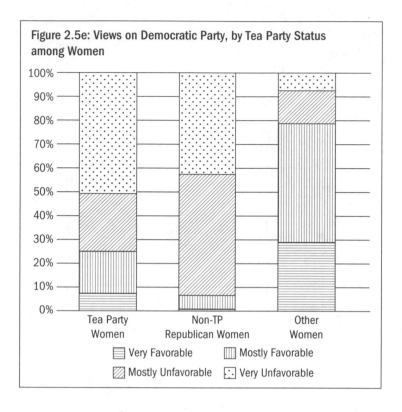

Figure 2.5e: Views on Democratic Party, by Tea Party Status among Women

Trump, who was seeking the GOP nomination for president, dominated national headlines for weeks and prompted many businesses to cut ties with the controversial business tycoon.[105] While Trump has not marketed himself as a Tea Party leader per se, many activists with ties to the movement have risen to his defense, including some of the women activists featured in this book. For example, the radio hosts and bloggers Miriam Weaver and Amy Jo Clark, known as the Chicks on the Right, defended Donald Trump on their blog: "The fact remains that when we continue to let people into our country illegally and not enforce immigration laws, criminals absolutely D O come into our country. And that includes rapists and drug dealers and lots of really bad people."[106] Yet, while Tea Party women in the mass public are more likely to hold conservative positions on the DREAM Act, a policy advocated by the Obama administration that under certain conditions defers deportment of the children of illegal immigrants who had been brought to the coun-

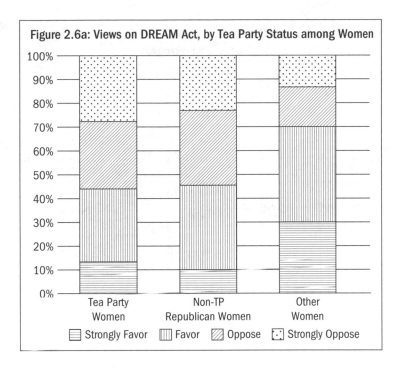

Figure 2.6a: Views on DREAM Act, by Tea Party Status among Women

Strongly Favor   Favor   Oppose   Strongly Oppose

try by their parents (see figure 2.6a), and are significantly more likely to so do than other American women, a surprisingly large chunk of such women—44 percent—express support for it. Similarly, 46 percent of non–Tea Party Republican women also support the DREAM Act.

Moreover, on matters of racial discrimination, there are relatively few differences among Tea Party women, non–Tea Party Republican women, and other American women in the PRRI data. Although Tea Party women are the most likely to completely agree that "discrimination against whites" has become a big problem, most Tea Party women, non–Tea Party women, and other American women are far more likely to disagree with that statement (see figure 2.6b). Just 20 percent of Tea Party women, 18 percent of non–Tea Party Republican women, and 17 percent of other women completely agree that discrimination against whites is a problem in the United States. Moreover, solid majorities of all three types of women disagree with the idea that government has "paid too much attention to the problems of blacks and other minorities" (see figure 2.6c). On both measures there were no statistically

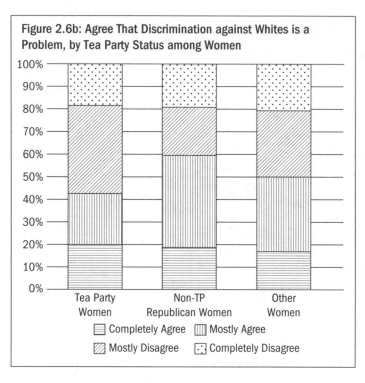

Figure 2.6b: Agree That Discrimination against Whites is a Problem, by Tea Party Status among Women

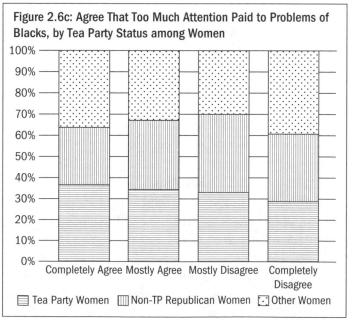

Figure 2.6c: Agree That Too Much Attention Paid to Problems of Blacks, by Tea Party Status among Women

significant differences among the three types of women. My data analysis data suggest that Tea Party women do not appear to hold attitudes
uniformly that demonstrate racial resentment—at least not at levels that
differ dramatically from other American women.

These findings with respect to racial resentment and Tea Party
women in the PRRI data are somewhat surprising given previous research that demonstrates a link between racial resentment and support
for the Tea Party.[107] However, these previous studies develop more so-
phisticated indices to tap into such resentment using a wider variety
of questions aside from the racial discrimination questions employed
by PRRI in its surveys. For instance, Parker and Barreto's racism index
considers the extent to which respondents agreed: (1) whether blacks
should overcome prejudice without "special favors" compared with
previous minority groups such as "Irish, Italians, Jews, and many other
minorities" who worked their way up; (2) that slavery and discrimination "make it more difficult for blacks to work their way out of the
lower class"; (3) that "blacks have gotten less than they deserve"; and
(4) that "if blacks would try harder than they could be just as well off
as whites."[108] By contrast, the racial resentment indicators in the PRRI
survey only tap into whether respondents believe that *government* pays
enough attention to discrimination. There could be social desirability
bias issues at play here as well. Social desirability bias is a tendency for
people to deny holding attitudes that may not conform to acceptable
societal norms or values. Given the controversy surrounding racism, respondents in the PRRI survey may not feel comfortable expressing what
some may view as overtly racist attitudes. Of course, we could be finding with respect to the DREAM Act and racial resentment that women
in the "other Tea Party"—women who identify with the movement but
who are not necessarily activists per se—may hold less conservative attitudes about such issues than many of the Tea Party movement leaders
featured in this book.

In sum, these descriptive data about Tea Party women show that
in many ways they are similar to other American women in terms of
their socioeconomic backgrounds, with some notable exceptions. For
instance, although Tea Party women are slightly more likely than other
American women to be full-time homemakers, they are still much more
likely to work outside the home than to stay at home full-time. Tea Party

women, comparable to other Republican women, are less racially diverse than other American women. Similar to non–Tea Party Republican women, Tea Party women attend church frequently, are more likely to hold conservative views on the Bible, and are more likely to describe religion as important than are other American women. Yet Tea Party women are slightly more theologically conservative and devout than even other Republican women.

While Tea Party women in the mass public and Republican women who do not identify with the Tea Party are often closer in their policy positions and political orientations than Democratic women and other American women, Tea Party women do express the most conservative options on most of the questions displayed here. On the political measures, which considered both ideology more generally and attitudes toward Barack Obama, Mitt Romney, and both parties, Tea Party women were especially distinct in their negativity. Their dislike of Obama and the Democratic Party was readily apparent, setting them very far apart from other American women. While Tea Party women generally held more favorable views of Romney and the GOP than of Obama or the Democrats, they were also more critical of them than non–Tea Party Republican women, indicative of the deep dissatisfaction that Tea Party activists have with the Republican establishment. Yet in some surprising areas, such as racial resentment as measured by the indicators here, Tea Party women look similar to women who do not identify as part of the movement.

Gender Differences among Tea Party Members Nationally

Women who identify as part of the Tea Party are more conservative and more religious than other American women, including Republican women who do not self-identify as part of the Tea Party. They also hold much more negative attitudes about Barack Obama and the Democratic Party. By and large, however, Tea Party women share remarkable similarities to their male counterparts when it comes to their demographic makeup. They share similar ages (50.3 years for women; 50.5 for men), similar rates of marriage, and similar income levels. Both disproportionately white, Tea Party women and men are just as likely to be parents of kids under the age of eighteen. Only on one demographic measure are Tea Party women and men distinct: Tea Party men are significantly

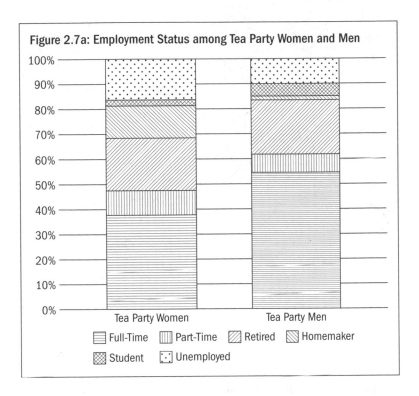

Figure 2.7a: Employment Status among Tea Party Women and Men

Legend: Full-Time, Part-Time, Retired, Homemaker, Student, Unemployed

more likely to work full-time (54 percent) than Tea Party women are (38 percent) (see figure 2.7a).[109]

When it comes to politics, Tea Party women and men again share strong similarities: 70 percent of Tea Party women and 76 percent of Tea Party men describe themselves as conservative or very conservative. They share similar views on both the Republican Party and the Democratic Party in the expected directions, and largely viewed Mitt Romney favorably. They both strongly disliked Barack Obama: 62 percent of Tea Party women and 63 percent of Tea Party men held "very unfavorable" views of Obama in 2012. However, Tea Party women were a little more tempered in their views on Obama, as they were significantly more likely to view him as either very or mostly favorably (25 percent) compared with Tea Party men (16 percent).

Where some statistically significant differences *do* emerge between Tea Party women and men concerns religion and social policy attitudes. As figure 2.7b shows, Tea Party women attend church more frequently,

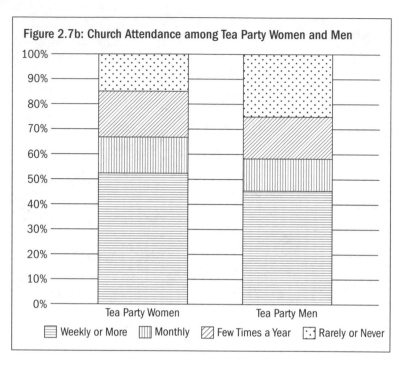

Figure 2.7b: Church Attendance among Tea Party Women and Men

Legend: Weekly or More | Monthly | Few Times a Year | Rarely or Never

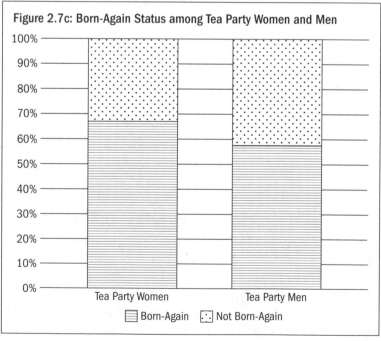

Figure 2.7c: Born-Again Status among Tea Party Women and Men

Legend: Born-Again | Not Born-Again

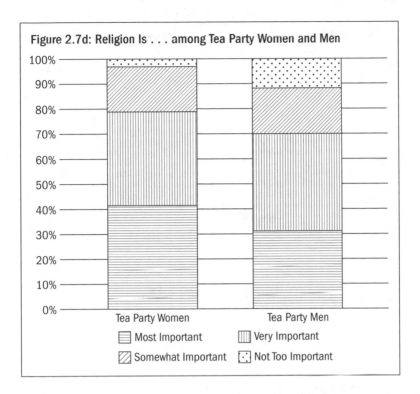

Figure 2.7d: Religion Is . . . among Tea Party Women and Men

Legend:
- ▤ Most Important
- ▥ Very Important
- ▨ Somewhat Important
- ⠙ Not Too Important

are more likely to identify as born-again Christians (see figure 2.7c), and view religion as more important than do their male counterparts. While Tea Party men are more religious and conservative theologically than other American men more generally,[110] they still are less religious than Tea Party women (see figure 2.7d). Whether these trends demonstrate that the Tea Party holds special appeal to conservative women of faith compared with Tea Party men, or simply reflect larger trends among Americans that routinely show that women are more religious than men, is unclear.

When it comes to social policy, while strong majorities of both Tea Party women and men are pro-life on abortion and oppose gay marriage, Tea Party women are significantly more likely than their male counterparts to say that abortion should be legal in all cases (15 percent to 10 percent, respectively) and to favor or strongly favor gay marriage (33 percent to 22 percent, respectively) (see figures 2.7e and 2.7f). National studies routinely show that women are more supportive of LGBT rights than are men, including the right to marry, so perhaps this gender

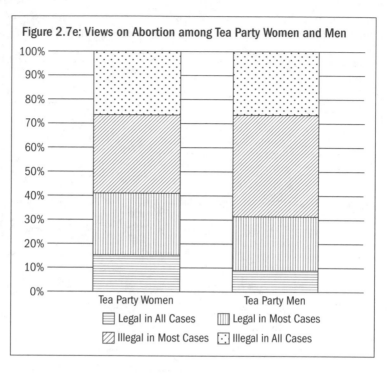

Figure 2.7e: Views on Abortion among Tea Party Women and Men

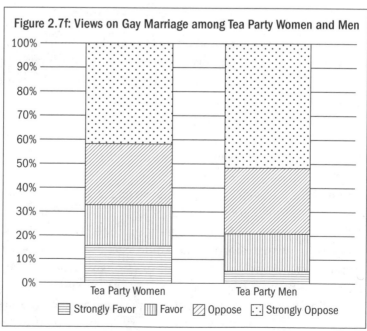

Figure 2.7f: Views on Gay Marriage among Tea Party Women and Men

division concerning gay marriage is following larger trends.[111] On abortion, while most studies show that majorities of American men and women believe that it should remain legal under most circumstances, there is also a persistent finding that women are significantly more likely than men to hold the most "absolutist" position: that abortion should be banned in all circumstances or that abortion should be legal in all circumstances.[112] This gender difference with respect to support for abortion's legality in all circumstances, then, is not wholly without precedent. Turning to other policy attitudes, Tea Party women and men hold largely similar views on immigration policy and racial discrimination.[113] And though not reported here, Tea Party men and women hold similar attitudes on a range of issues concerning economic policies.

In sum, Tea Party women share far more in common with Tea Party men than they do with other American women. The Tea Party movement is uniting men and women who are very conservative and who hold very negative views about Barack Obama and the Democratic Party. However, there are some differences between Tea Party women and men. Tea Party women are more religious than their male counterparts. Moreover, while Tea Party women are still overwhelmingly conservative on matters such as abortion and gay rights, there is a tendency for them to express less conservative positions than Tea Party men do on these issues. By and large, however, Tea Party women and men are awfully similar.

Factors That Drive Support for the Tea Party among Women and Men

Now that I have a picture of what Tea Party women and men in the United States look like and their general attitudes about a wide range of political and policy issues, I analyze which of these characteristics actually *drive* identification with the Tea Party among them while accounting for alternative explanations. I identify which factors are statistically linked to identification with the Tea Party and then calculate the predicted probability that an individual would be likely to identify him- or herself with the Tea Party, while holding a variety of factors constant.[114] Recall that in the 2012 PRRI data, 58 percent of self-identified Tea Partiers are men, compared with 42 percent of women, a statistically significant difference that is comparable to the gender gap in support for the Tea Party found in previous studies. When subjected to multivariate analysis, using logistic regression, I find that this gender gap remains statistically significant: men are more likely than women to identify themselves as part of the Tea Party (see appendix B for the coding of the variables used for the models and for the full model results). Holding all other variables at their mean values, the predicted probability of men identifying as part of the Tea Party is 10 percent while for women it is 6 percent. In other words, men are 4 percent more likely than women are to identify as belonging to the Tea Party. While this is not a large increase, it is important to stress that the model includes controls for a host of other factors.[115] The model shows that propensity to identify with the Tea Party among Americans more generally is also driven by ideology, attitudes about Barack Obama, and religion. Figure 2.8 presents each significant variable's change in predicted probability of supporting the Tea Party, moving from the minimum to the maximum value of each variable. Individuals who identify themselves as politically conservative are 7 percent more likely to identify as part of the Tea Party than are moderates (the reference category), born-again Christians are 4 percent more likely to identify as part of the Tea Party than are other Americans, and those who hold very unfavorable views of Barack Obama are 16 percent more likely to identify as part of the Tea Party than are those who hold very favorable views of Obama.

Next, I ran two separate statistical models—one for women and one for men—with identification with the Tea Party as the dependent variable, with the goal of determining whether identification with the Tea Party is driven by different factors for women and for men. (See appendix B for the full results of both models.) In looking at the data, I find that women and men are largely indistinguishable in terms of why they identify as part of the movement. Attitudes about Barack Obama are the largest factors driving identification with the Tea Party for women and men, followed by ideology and, to a lesser, though still statistically significant extent, born-again status.[116] Turning to men, and setting all over variables at their mean values, conservative men are 7 percent more likely to identify themselves as part of the Tea Party than are moderates, while men who hold very unfavorable views on Obama are 26 percent more likely to identify as part of the Tea Party than are men who hold

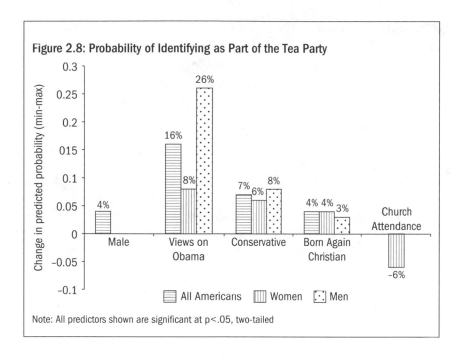

Figure 2.8: Probability of Identifying as Part of the Tea Party

Note: All predictors shown are significant at p<.05, two-tailed

very favorable views (see figure 2.8). These two factors are also the most important predictors for women: being a conservative makes women 6 percent more likely to identify with the Tea Party than other women, while holding very unfavorable views about Obama increases the probability that women will identify with the Tea Party by 8 percent. Being a born-again or evangelical Christian also matters in this analysis for both men and women. For women, being a born-again Christian makes them twice as likely to identify with the Tea Party: the predicted probability of identifying as part of the Tea Party is 8 percent, compared with 4 percent for those who are not born-again Christians; for men the difference is 3 percent. One difference that does arise between men and women, however, concerns church attendance, although in a somewhat surprising way. Women who report attending church weekly or more than weekly are 6 percent *less* likely than are women who never attend church to identify with the Tea Party. This finding might be driven by race—for instance, my analysis shows that nonwhite women are significantly more likely to attend church than are white women[117]—or could indicate that women from faith traditions aside from evangelical denominations, perhaps Catholics, for example, may find the Tea Party off-putting. Nonetheless, the analysis here shows that conservative, evangelical men and women who strongly dislike Barack Obama and the Democrats are far more likely to identify as members of the Tea Party.

The Tea Party's Appeal for Women in the United States

The Tea Party's core message of defending constitutional conservatism, scaling back social welfare programs, and promoting tax cuts while cutting federal spending is more likely to appeal to American men than American women, given that men are far more likely to identify as politically conservative. Indeed, my study, and other research, finds a persistent gender gap among Tea Party members. The Tea Party's message, however, does appeal to some American women in the mass public: those who identify as politically conservative, those who are better off financially, and those who are born-again Christians, but such women represent a small minority of Americans numerically. The challenge for the Tea Party has been to build support among a broader base of American women. However, given that women are more economically vulnerable and more likely to support a strong social safety net than are men—and my study finds that women with lower levels of income are less likely to identify with the Tea Party—it is difficult to imagine how its core message, which includes cutting government services, will resonate with larger numbers of American women. Moreover, as we will see in the chapters ahead, the vast majority of American women hold very different views on the economic policies often touted by the movement, which further complicates the task of the Tea Party to grow support for its cause.

My finding that religion motivates women to identify as part of the Tea Party, however, presents some opportunities and challenges to the movement in terms of building broader support. On the one hand, religion has been a powerful source of inspiration for political activism among many Americans, particularly evangelical Christians in recent decades. Moreover, as I detail in chapter 3, women have long used religion to justify their political engagement, especially before it was socially acceptable for women to take an active part in public life. If the Tea Party begins to merge its fiscally conservative message with socially conservative viewpoints that touch on religion, such a strategy could appeal to more conservative women of faith. Some argue that this merging of the Tea Party and the Christian Right is already happening.[118]

At the same time, while a greater emphasis on religious values by Tea Party leaders may add some women to the ranks of the Tea Party, such a strategy has serious limitations for growing the movement among Americans more broadly, especially given the fact that Americans—particularly the millennial generation—are becoming increasingly secular and more accepting of gay marriage. Furthermore, as the 2012 elections demonstrated, campaigns becoming mired in debate about social issues such as abortion and the birth control mandate can be detrimental to the fortunes of conservative Republican candidates—those who are most likely to be sympathetic to the Tea Party cause.[119] Lastly, given that there is a strong libertarian thrust within the Tea Party movement, any effort toward promoting socially conservative policies alongside economically conservative issues—the bread and butter of the Tea Party—would also potentially weaken the movement.

Facing these limitations, members of the Tea Party have nonetheless worked to convince more American women to support their cause. One way they have achieved this is to convince American women that smaller government, tax cuts, and reducing the federal debt is good for them and their families. In the next chapter, I consider how Tea Party women leaders are trying to accomplish this very task: by incorporating motherhood rhetoric in defense of conservative economic policies in their appeals. Such motherhood appeals have a long history in American politics, used by social movements on the left and right to build support for political causes—but they have potentially negative implications as well.

3

A New Civic Motherhood?

The Evolution of Conservative Women's Political Rhetoric

I've had a passion and a determination to change Washington DC but never as much as when I had three children. You look at your kids and then you look at what is going on in Washington and you want so much for them to have the same America that you've had. And I think that is why you see so many moms and so many wives standing up and saying I have to do this for my children.
—Jamie Radtke, former Virginia Republican U.S. Senate candidate and former head of the Virginia Tea Party Patriots Federation

While the technological format may be new, the message contained in Jamie Radtke's June 2012 web advertisement for her unsuccessful Senate bid is not: when their children's future is as stake, it is only natural that mothers are compelled to fight on their behalf, even if it means entering the unseemly world of politics.[1] Long before Radtke's web ad or Sarah Palin's call to "Mama Grizzlies," when a woman's role in the workforce or in politics was far less acceptable, conservative women often invoked their status as mothers and defenders of the family to justify their political activism in a variety of conservative causes throughout American history. Reliance on motherhood rhetoric, often steeped in religious fervor, provided these traditional women a legitimate rationale to engage in the male-dominated world of politics. As social movement scholars have long recognized, social movement leaders often frame their issues and grievances in such a way as to not only build support for their movement, but to give movement activists a sense of shared, common identity,[2] so an examination of their rhetoric is important to understand what motivates movement actors.[3]

In contrast to earlier female conservative activists, Tea Party women are involved in political advocacy at a time when women are more fully engaged in public life and in the workforce, maximizing new technology such as social media, which facilitates their involvement in politics to an extent that was not possible in earlier eras. Yet much of their political rhetoric remains steeped in motherhood appeals—but with a twist. Whereas earlier, twentieth-century conservative women activists used maternal rhetoric to fight against what they perceived to be the evils of communism and the women's movement, many Tea Party "Mama Grizzlies" aim to build support among American women by appropriating conservative economic policy and debates about the size and scope of government, and to a lesser extent gun rights, as being pro-family.

In this chapter I identify three "motherhood" frames that Tea Party women commonly use in their writing, speeches, or social media communications to explain why they have become politically active and to inspire other like-minded women to get involved. I also rely on interviews with activists and leaders in the Tea Party for further insight into Tea Party women's use of such frames. First, Tea Party women often call on mothers to become engaged in politics as "kitchen table" conservatives. In this take on the motherhood frame, moms have experience "balancing the budget" at home, so those skills are needed to help balance the federal budget nationally. Second, moms should become engaged in reducing the debt burden for future generations. In this theme, women are compelled to become active in politics as a means to protect their kids from what Sarah Palin calls "generational theft." Lastly, mom should become engaged in fighting for reduced government and lower taxes because large government programs usurp the role of the family.

In my discussion of each of these three frames, I consider how such rhetorical strategies either extend or delineate from maternal appeals made in earlier eras. While invoking their status as mothers is a time-honored political strategy for many conservative women up to the present day, some Tea Party women have deliberately avoided using this type of rhetoric as a way to build broader support for the Tea Party movement. This examination of the use of motherhood rhetoric—and when and how it is employed—is important to understanding the political motivation of many Tea Party women.

However, to understand more fully the appeal of motherhood as a rallying cry for many Tea Party women today, I first consider how previous generations of conservative women political activists relied on their status as mothers as both a justification for their own political engagement and a call to other women to become involved in the male-dominated world of politics. Although brief, this background is essential in not just understanding today's Mama Grizzlies when it comes to their political motivations, but also explains the internal division among conservative women with respect to feminism, a topic I explore in greater detail in chapter 5, and which has spawned a larger public debate as some Tea Party women seek to reclaim the feminist label. By placing Tea Party women in larger historical context, it is possible to compare and contrast Tea Party women's political participation in the twenty-first century, highlighting both the opportunities and challenges that face activists who use maternal themes as political strategy.

"Old" Maternalism: Motherhood as a Political Strategy before the Women's Movement

Women's political participation in the nineteenth century was often circumscribed by societal norms, which long mandated "separate spheres" for men and women in American society, rooted in strongly held patriarchal religious beliefs.[4] Home was the woman's domain, whereas politics and public life was best suited for men, in a society that was steeped in what historian Barbara Welter called the "Cult of True Womanhood."[5] In surveying most women's magazines and religious literature published between 1820 and 1860, Welter identified four "cardinal" virtues that the ideal woman was thought to embody at the time—piety, purity, submissiveness, and domesticity. That women should submit to men, according to this line of thinking, was based on the notion that man, as one magazine at the time put it, was "woman's superior by God's appointment, if not in intellectual dowry, at least by official degree."[6] As Theda Skocpol argues, the social thought behind True Womanhood was to pit women in stark opposition to the "selfishness of masculine identity in the world of commerce and politics."[7] Hence, women could only participate in advocacy for causes if the pursuit of such public virtue centered on the home as the "touchstone of feminine identity."[8]

While political and commercial activity was beyond the scope of what people thought women *ought* to be doing in American society, women could fulfill their womanly duties by volunteering in houses of worship, as church work would not "make her less dominant or submissive, less a True Woman."[9]

When women did become engaged in a variety of reform causes throughout the nineteenth century and well into the next, they had to justify their involvement in ways that did not challenge these prescribed gender roles or society's prevailing religious beliefs. To alleviate concerns that women's public advocacy violated the assumed, rightful place of women at home, for example, early woman abolitionists justified their public opposition to slavery in patriarchal terms, often invoking biblical heroines to bolster their claims that women were just as compelled religiously to speak out against injustice as were men.[10] Many women in the late nineteenth and early twentieth century who were engaged in a variety of social causes—such as the progressive movement, which sought to improve schools and other public services while reforming corrupt government practices, and the temperance movement, whose largely female leadership urged legislators to ban the sale of alcohol— did so by invoking their roles as mothers or as homemakers to justify their political engagement.[11] Scholars who have traced the evolution of such progressive reforms as the establishment of mothers' pensions, tenement houses, and juvenile and women's prisons, for instance, note that the women who helped to lead these efforts, largely through their work in voluntary social service organizations such as the National Congress of Mothers, often described their involvement as "municipal housekeeping."[12] The popular muckraking journalist Rheta Childe Dorr, who served as an editor of the women's section of the *New York Evening Post*, argued in her best-selling 1910 work *What Eight Million Women Want* that women's involvement in municipal reform would not violate women's natural role as mothers, but instead merely extend it to the public sphere. Dorr famously wrote, "Woman's place is in the home. This is a platitude which no woman will ever dissent from . . . But Home is not contained within the four walls of an individual home. Home is the community. The city full of people is the Family. The public school is the real Nursery. And badly do the Home and the Family and the Nursery need their mother."[13] Suffragists also began to invoke motherhood as the paramount reason that women should get the vote, successfully recruiting both progressive and conservative women to their cause by invoking maternal and religious themes in their rhetoric, what historian Ellen DuBois calls "women's special, maternal-based vision."[14] For instance, suffragists successfully persuaded many social reformers to fight for the right to vote for women, which they argued would allow for widespread, progressive reforms to take shape faster if elected officials faced pressure from newly franchised women, who, it was thought at the time, would support such policies.[15] Women involved in the temperance movement also came to believe that their goal of abolishing the sale of alcohol would only be achieved through women obtaining the right to vote.

Not all women—or men—were on board with securing the vote for women, however. Many "anti-suffragists" pointed to numerous arguments to deny women the right to vote, fearful that moving too hastily to grant women more rights could have profound implications for women's place at home and in society, thereby challenging the True Womanhood ideology and the "separate spheres" it entailed for men and women.[16] Aileen Kraditor argues in her history of the suffrage campaign that anti-suffragists based their opposition on a "sentimental vision of Home and Mother": "It was the link of woman to the home that underlay the entire ideology [of the anti-suffragists]. The antis regarded each woman's vocation as determined not by her individual capacities but by her sex. Men were expected to have a variety of ambitions and capabilities, but all women were destined from birth to be full-time wives and mothers. To dispute this eternal truth was to challenge theology, biology, or sociology."[17] Somewhat ironically, conservative women who opposed the franchise were compelled to take public action to justify their position, although this activity was often done through writing, as such women found it undignified to speak in public.[18] For example, an early history of the women's suffrage movement in Massachusetts recounts the activity of about two hundred women, calling themselves "remonstrants," who wrote to their state legislators to oppose extending the elective franchise to women in their state. In their written appeals to state legislators, these women argued that granting women the right to vote would "diminish the purity, the dignity, and the moral influence of woman, and bring into the family circle a dangerous element of discourse."[19] These conservative women founded the Women's Anti-suffrage Association of Massachusetts and published, until 1920, their own quarterly magazine, *The Remonstrance.*[20]

Long before the debate about women's ability to vote was settled, however, religious women who opposed the use of alcohol staged public marches and held prayer vigils outside saloons to place pressure on localities to stop the sale of alcohol.[21] Temperance activists argued that men's alcoholism bankrupted families and led otherwise responsible men to violence, leaving women and children in a vulnerable position within the family. By 1875 what had been disparate efforts of religious women to protest local saloons, known collectively as the Woman's Crusade, became more formally organized under the auspices of the Women's Christian Temperance Union, which would become the largest American women's organization by the end of the nineteenth century.[22] Francis Willard, who would serve as president of the WCTU from 1879 until her death in 1898, in 1875 became the first temperance leader to make the case for the elective franchise, in her home state of Illinois, although she initially argued that this right should apply to women only in local elections, as localities and towns determined whether the sale of alcohol would remain legal. As historian Barbara Epstein notes, Willard convinced the Illinois Union to pass a resolution calling for local franchise rights for women under the "Home Protection" ballot, which stated that since "woman is the greatest sufferer of the rum curse," a woman should be allowed the "power to close the dramshop" so near to her home.[23] By the time Willard ascended to the presidency of the WCTU, she had convinced its members to fight for women's wider suffrage rights. Willard argued women should have the ballot for "no selfish ends," but rather asked for it "only in the interest of the home, which has been and is women's divinely appointed province . . . there is no clamor for 'rights,' only a prayerful, persistent plea for the opportunities of Duty."[24]

Moreover, Willard and her followers promoted not just the cause of women's voting rights but other social reforms under the auspices of the WCTU, arguing that alcoholism was a "symptom of poverty, crime, and injustices done to women."[25] The decentralized organizational structure of the WCTU allowed local branches to determine which additional projects to take on, dubbed by Francis Willard as the "Do Everything" policy, as such projects were designed to "serve better the causes of temperance, the home, and the public good," running the gamut from suffrage to municipal and prostitution reform to labor organization.[26] Willard was successful in linking these causes to the central problem of the father being absent from the home. Whether it meant closing saloons or fighting for an eight-hour day for male workers, Willard's plea was based in a worldview that sought to secure family life, shoring up both the roles of mothers and fathers in the home. Willard's attempt to broaden the political aims of the WCTU to incorporate larger social reform was not without controversy; indeed, many activists broke from the WCTU to work more closely with the National Prohibition Party, whose major aim was solely to stop the sale of alcohol. Those contro-versies aside, Willard was successful in leveraging aspects of the "True Woman" ideology to convince traditionally conservative women to become engaged in the public sphere by claiming that their political actions were an extension of their role as mothers.

From Progressivism to Anticommunism: Motherhood, Feminism, and the Red Scare

Progressive reformers worked to enact women's universal voting rights because they believed that women, as mothers and caregivers, would be willing to embrace a larger role for government to provide social services for poor families. In her history of the development of early social welfare programs in the United States, Theda Skocpol argues that Congress passed the Sheppard-Towner Act in 1921, which established maternal health centers around the country as a way to lower infant-morality rates, because lawmakers worried that newly enfranchised women would hold them accountable in future elections.[27] Yet within eight years, the Sheppard-Towner Act was dismantled, ironically, due to the same "maternal-based" concerns that had been used success-fully by progressive reformers in securing women's voting rights and in promoting social service programs and municipal "housekeeping" efforts. Only this time, conservative activists, including many women, were successful in linking government social policy to the burgeoning anticommunist movement in the United States by arguing that such programs directly challenged the sanctity of families.

One organization active in early anticommunist movements was the Woman's Patriot Corporation, which was started by several women who had been active in the National Association Opposed to Women's Suffrage. When anti-suffragists lost the battle to deny women suffrage, some of the more radical women within the "anti" movement turned their attention to the triple threat of communism, bolshevism, and feminism.[28] Although the United States had won the First World War, anticommunist activists feared communist infiltration at home and identified women's political activism in the progressive movement, the expansion of the social welfare state, and feminism more broadly as the primary avenues by which communism could expect to take root in America.[29] For these "Women Patriots," suffrage rights represented just the beginning of a radical effort by feminists to alter gender roles in the home. In the organization's bimonthly publication, *The Woman Patriot*, female columnists wrote that making the home a "sweeter, happier, and better place for her family" was the highest patriotic service a woman could undertake, which would reinforce men's leadership in society, an arrangement that was in "the best interests of the family and state" because male leadership was "divine and democratic."[30] The Women Patriots were especially concerned that a burgeoning feminist movement, whose ideas they feared were taking root in women's colleges and through Progressive Era political reform efforts, sought to grant women economic independence, allowing men to their shirk their responsibilities as their families' providers.

For these conservative women activists, feminism was bad not merely because it would prompt women to step outside their proscribed gender roles by pursuing their own economic interests apart from the family. Feminism was also dangerous because it sought—through the progressive reform movement, legislation such as the Sheppard-Towner Act, the Child Labor Amendment (aimed at amending the U.S. Constitution to allow Congress to regulate or limit child labor), and the establishment of a national department of education—changes that would aid and abet feminists and socialists alike in their efforts to nationalize the family by having government usurp parental roles.[31] For example, historian Kim E. Nielson recounts efforts by one women's group, the Massachusetts-based Citizens' Committee to Protect Our Homes and Children, to oppose the Child Labor Amendment, described by its membership as a plot "hatched in Moscow."[32] Typical of the arguments waged against the measure, Nielson cites the following passage from the Citizens' Committee's formal statement in opposition to the amendment:

> The amendment aims, not at the exploitation of child labor, but at the right of the individual under eighteen to work for a living, for his own advancement, or for service to others; at the right of parents to direct their children and receive from them such assistance as may be essential to the maintenance of the family. It seeks to substitute national control, directed from Washington, for local and parent control, to bring about the nationalization of children, and to make the child the ward of the Nation.[33]

Such scare tactics by Women Patriots and other antifeminist women's organizations were successful in linking feminism and radicalism with Progressive Era reforms, creating a "political culture that was hostile to the largest female remnants of the Progressive Era" and helping to lay the groundwork for the twentieth-century conservative movement.[34] Indeed, many of these same arguments, namely, that communism posed a dire threat to the nuclear family, were only amplified when the Red Scare began in earnest in the 1950s.

By the end of World War II, women had possessed the right to vote for more than twenty years. Moreover, American women in large numbers had left lives of domesticity during the war effort, including many "Rosie the Riveters," who were encouraged by the U.S. government to work manufacturing jobs that had long been the purview of men in order to keep the country running and to provide equipment and essential services for the war effort. Despite women's initial foray into previously male-dominated working environments, as American GIs returned home social pressure and government-funded media campaigns compelled women to return to family life.[35] As the image of "female domesticity" once again became the social norm of the day, most women's career and political aspirations were effectively stymied. However, some conservative women found a political outlet in the movement against communism during the 1950s by employing the same motherhood rhetoric used by their female predecessors in the first Red Scare.[36] Working as self-appointed "housewife activists," many of these women formed study groups and watchdog organizations to monitor the work of locally elected officials, library boards, and boards of education to be on the lookout for subversive activity, which for such activists included school desegregation efforts, promotion of federal aid to education, and curricular changes in local schools that broadened discussions of world politics and the United Nations.

As their female forebears had done in earlier conservative political causes, Red Scare activists called on women's moral sense of duty to become engaged in the broader fight against communism. Take, for instance, the right-wing American Woman's Party (AWP), which argued in its writings that without immediate intervention by right-minded women, Americans risked "blundering into socialism."[37] Refusing to "give up what we prize most," members of AWP invited all women to join them in the quest to protect the "freedom, liberty, and independence of these United States."[38] The U.S. government also undertook efforts to compel housewives to become part of nuclear-preparedness planning through the Federal Civil Defense Administration (FCDA), established by Harry Truman after World War II.[39] Through government-printed brochures, pamphlets, and education campaigns, the FCDA implored women to train their children to cope with the aftermath of a nuclear attack and to prepare well-stocked bomb shelters, similar to their "grandma's pantry," in the event of an atomic war. In so doing, such propaganda served to reinforce women's appropriate gender roles within their families, as the family became the central means of both protecting Americans in the wake of potential nuclear holocaust and in stopping communist infiltration domestically.[40] Under this school of thought, feminism was to be avoided. Working mothers, and by extension their children, it was argued, would be vulnerable to Red influence. The nation depended on women to stay at home and educate their kids against the evils of communism. Hence, political activism undertaken by women during the Red Scare was viewed as patriotic as long as such activities did not subsume their domestic responsibilities or, even better, went hand in hand with those responsibilities.

As the Red Scare abated by the end of the 1950s, conservatism became, in the words of historian Michelle Nickerson (2012), a "self-conscious" movement at the dawn of the 1960s, one in which conservative women played an important part in two ways.[41] First, some conservative women found a political outlet for their beliefs through the Republican Party, largely through the work of the National Federation of Republican Women, which was established in the late 1930s and sought to bring together disparate groups of local Republican club women nationwide to work on behalf of electing Republican candidates to office.[42] While the founding of the National Federation of Republican Women predates the Cold War, anticommunism and morality-based politics led to a surge of membership in the 1950s and 1960s, its leaders, such as federation president Elizabeth Farrington, who served from 1949 to 1953, "presented politics in catastrophic, gendered terms believed to resonate broadly with the women it targeted—white, middle class, civil minded, patriotic, Protestant women . . . focusing on simple (yet vague) moral themes that gave a wide spectrum of women a means of identifying with the party."[43] For instance, Farrington routinely called on women to support "the moral issue of a free America," promoting policies that would "safeguard our Christian civilization," all the while emphasizing in her rhetoric women's differences from men, appealing to women in their roles as "religious crusaders and moral purifiers."[44]

Second, while some conservative women were drawn to political activism through the National Federation of Republican Women in the 1950s and 1960s, where they generally performed the organizational "housework" of government but lacked real power, other conservative women found a political outlet by forming their own local study groups, opening conservative book stores, and organizing in the local political campaigns of conservatives who were fighting not just communism but other disconcerting social trends wrought by the civil rights movement, liberal campus politics, and a burgeoning sexual revolution.[45] Through participation in local affiliates of the John Birch Society, the Christian Anticommunist Crusade, and similar groups, these women activists, by creating "homey settings" for politics, in feminine, modest dress and motherly demeanor, "contributed to the middle-class maternal ideal central to the conservative movement's social reform goals."[46]

Far-right conservative Barry Goldwater's presidential campaign in 1964 brought together conservative women from the GOP with those women active in local, grassroots organizations. Indeed, Goldwater's campaign made targeted outreach to these conservative women a priority through the establishment in 1964 of "Mothers for Moral America";

Nancy Reagan, among other spouses of prominent Republicans, served on its executive board.[47] The aim with Mothers for Moral America was to put a more "feminine" face on Goldwater's tough "law and order" platform that emphasized America's moral decline.[48] While Mothers for Moral America's morality campaign ultimately did little to help Goldwater's electoral chances, historian Michelle Nickerson argues that "its mix of spiritual, emotional and patriotic overtones would soon guide conservatism into a more triumphalist phase" as the feminist movement galvanized a fierce counter-reaction among conservative women, led by one of Goldwater's most fervent supporters, Phyllis Schlafly.[49]

Phyllis Schlafly, the ERA, and Feminism

More than fifty years after she became a well-known national political figure, Schlafly continues to inspire legions of conservatives, especially women who continue to see value in maintaining traditional gender roles. Although Schlafly became best known as the grassroots activist who dealt the Equal Rights Amendment its stinging defeat, she has long been active in Republican Party politics, critical of efforts by some within the GOP to moderate many of its positions beginning in the 1950s. It was the fight against the ERA, however, that would make Schlafly into a household name. In so doing, Schlafly relied on appeals to mothers in the United States, arguing that without their political participation, the American way of life stood threatened—gender-based, maternal arguments that some women in the Tea Party continue to make today for conservative economic policies, a reduced regulatory state, and, in certain cases, even gun rights.

In 1972 the U.S. Congress passed the Equal Rights Amendment, which sought to amend the U.S. Constitution to guarantee equal rights for women, with overwhelmingly bipartisan support. Pressure mounted across the nation for the ratification of the Equal Rights Amendment in state legislatures, as polling showed that a strong majority of Americans initially supported the measure.[50] But below the surface, at least among Republicans, there was brewing a conservative backlash to the more moderate factions within the GOP that was linked, in part, to the fight over the Equal Rights Amendment and to other cultural changes confronting Americans, such as the legalization of abortion after the

Supreme Court's decision in *Roe v. Wade* in 1973. The pitched battle over the ERA, led by Schlafly and many of her conservative women followers, as well as the fight over the legality of abortion, which became politically linked to its ratification efforts, is yet another example in twentieth-century American politics wherein conservative women at the grass roots employed motherhood rhetoric to justify their political activism. Conservative women called on Americans to reject the feminist-backed ERA because it was, in their minds, an affront to the traditional, nuclear family and would threaten the well-being of America's homemakers. The success of Phyllis Schlafly and her followers in framing the political fight over the ERA, abortion rights, and feminism as hostile to the natural order of family life helped to shepherd in a more conservative tilt to the GOP by the late 1970s, leading to Ronald Reagan's election in 1980 and solidifying ties between social conservatives, defense hawks, and mainstream business interests under the Republican Party's "Big Tent" strategy.

Phyllis Schlafly was no stranger to political activism by the time she emerged as the nation's leading opponent against the ERA in the 1970s. A devout Catholic and mother of six, Schlafly began her political career after she worked her way through college (working at an ordnance factory testing ammunition), graduating Phi Beta Kappa from Washington University in St. Louis in 1944. Her strong performance in college earned her a fellowship the following year, to Radcliffe College, the sister institution of Harvard, where she earned a master's in government.[51] Upon her graduation from Harvard, she accepted a position with the American Enterprise Institute, which helped to shape her conservative views of the free market system and her fierce opposition to communism. After returning to her native Missouri, she worked as an assistant to Towner Phelan, the vice president for advertising of a prominent bank and trust company in St. Louis, who was a frequent political speaker and penned a regular newsletter defending capitalism and criticizing the growth of the welfare state. Her responsibilities under Phelan grew, and she soon began writing for the newsletter (a practice she continued when she later established her own *Phyllis Schlafly Report* in the early 1970s) and became a sought-after political speaker in the St. Louis area. While she became a full-time homemaker upon her marriage to local attorney Fred Schlafly and moved to Illinois, she remained active in Republican Party politics, campaigning for congressional candidates and ultimately unsuccessfully mounting a campaign for Congress in 1952; indeed, historian Donald Critchlow notes in his biography of Schlafly that, similar to women who were venturing into uncharted political territory in earlier eras, Schlafly said that part of her motivation for running was her desire as a woman to shed virtuous light on the corrupt world of politics. He quotes Schlafly on the campaign stump urging voters to "turn out of office men who openly boast that governments are not bound by moral law . . . Since women have always been the guardians of morality in the home, our country would benefit if women exercised their voting rights to restore morality to our federal government."[52]

Although her bid for Congress was unsuccessful, she remained involved in GOP politics, largely at the grassroots and state level, where she and other activists opposed the more moderate wing of the party, believing it was too weak on the communism issue. A huge proponent of Barry Goldwater, in 1964 she self-published what many conservative Republicans now consider a classic work, *A Choice Not An Echo*, in which Schlafly attacked the moderate, GOP elite "kingmakers" who selected the Republican Party presidential nominees without regard to the wishes of the more conservative Republican voters at the grass roots.[53] Now a recognized national figure within the party, Schlafly sought to enhance her leadership role by seeking out the presidency of the National Federation of Republican Women during its national convention in 1967. However, she narrowly lost to Gladys O'Donnell, who was viewed as a more centrist, accommodating candidate, willing to back the male party leadership's more moderate agenda, whereas Schlafly had argued that the federation needed to offer a different perspective within the party, incorporating the more conservative political positions held by the female activists she worked with at the grassroots level. As historian Catherine Rymph writes, "Schlafly did not see the point of a large women's political organization whose actions were circumscribed and manipulated by the imperatives of male politicians—especially when male politicians endorsed political positions she believed many women opposed."[54] This chain of events prompted Schlafly's departure from the federation, and she instead formed her own political organization, Eagle Forum, in 1972.

Initially, Phyllis Schlafly did not hold a position on the ERA, as her political passions had always been linked to the anticommunist cause and to the promotion of a smaller, more limited federal government, as befit her strong belief in free market capitalism. However, by 1972 Schlafly had come to believe that the ERA was harmful to American families, linking her antistatist views to her opposition to the amendment, fearing that its passage would embolden the government to enact policies that would "threaten traditional gender roles in families and make women sexually and economically vulnerable."[55] Moreover, her opposition was also rooted in her long-held belief that the ERA stemmed from a movement of political elites who continually disregarded the more conservative views of average citizens; indeed, Gladys O'Donnell as president of the National Federal of Republican Women was a supporter of the ERA.

In her November 1972 *Phyllis Schlafly Report* she wrote exclusively about her opposition to the amendment for the first time, in which she challenged the claims made by ERA supporters that its passage would result in more job employment opportunities for women, equal pay for equal work, or other "desirable objectives which all women favor."[56] Instead, she argued that the ERA would result in making women subject to the draft and would undermine the legal authority that required husbands to financially support their wives and children, and in cases of divorce would deny women guaranteed custody and alimony rights. Moreover, she painted a picture of women's liberation activists as radicals who sought to change fundamentally the U.S. social order:

> In the last couple of years, a noisy movement has sprung up agitating for "women's rights." Suddenly, everywhere we are afflicted with aggressive females on television talk shows yapping about how mistreated American women are, suggesting that marriage has put us in some kind of "slavery," that housework is menial and degrading, and—perish the thought—that women are discriminated against. New "women's liberation" organizations are popping up, agitating and demonstrating, serving demands on public officials, getting wide press coverage always, and purporting to speak for some 100,000,000 American women.
>
> It's time to set the record straight. The claim that American women are downtrodden and unfairly treated is the fraud of the century. The

truth is that American women never had it so good. Why should we lower ourselves to "equal rights" when we already have the status of special privilege?[57]

Schlafly carefully cultivated this theme regarding the special, privileged status of American women, particularly mothers, in many of her writings and speeches. At the height of her efforts to prevent ratification of the ERA in 1977, Schlafly wrote *The Power of the Positive Woman*, defending the two-parent family as designed by God and biology, and arguing that the ERA specifically, and the larger feminist movement more generally, sought to undermine this uniquely American way of life:

Americans have the immense good fortune to live in a civilization that respects the family as the basic unit of society. This respect is not merely a matter of social custom. We have a great deal of federal and state laws designed to protect the institution of the family . . . The results of these laws are highly beneficial to the wife. Based on the fundamental fact of life that women have babies and men don't—which no legislation or agitation can erase—these laws make it the obligation of the husband to support his wife financially and provide her with a home. Since God ordained that women must have babies, our laws properly and realistically establish that men must provide financial support for their wives and children. The women's liberation movement has positioned itself in total opposition to the entire concept of "roles," but in so doing, they are opposing Mother Nature herself.[58]

Hence, working under the auspices of Eagle Forum, Schlafly named her grassroots campaign, STOP ERA, an acronym for "Stop Taking Our Privileges."

Under the STOP ERA banner, Schlafly's followers—mostly comprised of stay-at-home mothers who organized politically through their local churches—lobbied state legislators in key states to oppose ratification by writing them daily letters, handing out baked goods at their offices, and bringing their children with them to state capitals to protest the ERA.[59] Moreover, in a testament to Schlafly's influence on conservative state political elites, political scientist Jane Mansbridge notes how some state legislators, often from rural areas, echoed Schlafly's exact language in voicing their disapproval of the ERA. Take, for instance, state legislator Henry J. Hyde from Illinois, who argued in one speech that the ERA was "really an attack on the home. It is an attack on motherhood. It says that for a woman to have to be a mother and have to be a homemaker is somehow degrading."[60]

Ultimately, the efforts by Phyllis Schlafly and her followers at the grass roots were successful in stopping the ERA. By shifting the debate from the broad principles of fairness emphasized by the ERA's supporters to the possible ramifications the amendment would have on women's daily lives, from the somewhat probable (changes in alimony and child custody laws, for example) to the outlandish (forcing citizens to use "unisex" bathrooms in public spaces), Schlafly and her supporters effectively put the ERA's supporters on the defensive. They cast enough doubt on the amendment's merits to stop the quick momentum its ratification once had, having passed in thirty state legislatures by 1973, but ultimately failing to be passed by the thirty-eight states necessary by the congressional deadline of 1982.[61]

In addition to stopping the ERA campaign, Schlafly helped to shape public opinion against feminism more broadly in American society. As communications scholar Martha Solomon points out in her study of Schlafly's anti-ERA rhetoric, Schlafly was adept at "paint[ing] an unappealing picture of the feminists' physical appearance and nature, emphasizing their disregard for traditional standards of feminine attractiveness and sexuality."[62] By casting pro-ERA supporters as unfeminine women's libbers who disdained motherhood, Schlafly was able, by contrast, to portray traditional homemakers as the wholesome, "positive" women who embraced their biological destiny, for the good of their families and the nation.[63]

Other conservative women activists quickly adopted Schlafly's arguments about the challenges that feminism posed to American society, arguing the feminism was both antifamily and narcissistic. The Heritage Foundation's Onalee McGraw, for example, renounced the feminist movement in her work *The Family, Feminism, and the Therapeutic State* for "urging women to liberate themselves from the chains of family life and affirm their own self-fulfillment as the primary good."[64] Socially conservative women were also worried that feminism would ultimately reshape the definition of families and further serve to belittle the status of mothers in society. For example, Rebecca Klatch's study *Women of the New Right* details how local women activists began to organize in response to the national conference for International Women's Year, sponsored by the United Nations. Social conservatives were alarmed that most of the female delegates who attended the meeting were in favor not just of passage of the ERA, but also called for federal funding of abortion, an expansion of government-sponsored child care, and gay rights. Their alarm only grew when the Carter administration in 1980 sponsored the White House Conference on Families, which brought together various interest groups to discuss the impact of government policies on the family. The very definition of family, whether it constituted blood relatives or a broader definition that also incorporated unmarried parents and gay couples, met with fierce debate.[65] Klatch cites Rosemary Thomson, who was tapped by Schlafly to be the national Eagle Forum coordinator for the White House Conference, on why the definition of family was so crucial to the involvement of social conservatives: "The pro-family movement was, indeed, engaged in a spiritual battle—a struggle between those who believe in Biblical principles and ungodly Humanism which reject's God's moral absolutes! . . . Somehow, it was to the organizers of the White House Conference on Families as if the Lord had never spoken in history. As if He had never declared that taking an innocent life was forbidden. That sexual activity outside of marriage was fornication, and that homosexuality was an abomination to Him—sin, not gay."[66] As Thomson's statement reveals, social conservatives believed that feminism was clearly tied to abortion and gay rights—all in ways that challenged their sacred, deeply held values derived from the Bible. Political appeals made by Schlafly and other leaders at Eagle Forum that expressed reverence for the stay-at-home mother and defended the traditional family as designed by God had resonance for conservative, religious American women. In the midst of larger societal changes that they believed threatened their way of life, such as increases in divorce, a rise in the number of women working outside the home, and the legalization of abortion, conservative women likely found in such calls for action "a stable and comforting rationale" to become engaged in politics.[67] Similar to the appeals to apolitical homemakers made by suffragists, temperance activists, and anticommunists long before them,

Schlafly and her followers persuaded traditional women who viewed politics with wariness instead to view their participation as a chance to have their distinct voices heard, voices that "honored, validated, and protected women's traditional roles and their position in the family and society."[68]

Phyllis Schlafly, at the age of ninety in 2015, is still active in the conservative cause, fighting against feminism, abortion, and the overreach of the federal government—themes that continue to resonate with many activists engaged in the Tea Party. Schlafly's stamina and commitment are certainly remarkable, as was her ability to galvanize many previously apolitical conservative women to become engaged in the battle against the ERA and other Christian Right causes in the 1970s and 1980s, especially given that most national leaders of the conservative Christian movement were men. But Schlafly's leadership likely resonated with so many conservative, traditional women precisely because she shared with them their identity as a devout mother. Many of the concerns first raised by Schlafly decades ago, particularly as they pertain to the size and scope of the federal government, have been revived under the auspices of the Tea Party as a new generation of conservative women carries on Schlafly's legacy.

Mama Grizzlies, Motherhood, and the Tea Party

Mama Grizzlies, many brought to political activism for the first time through the Tea Party movement, also continue the legacy of employing motherhood as a rationale for their involvement in right-wing politics. Unlike previous eras in which their female conservative forebears were engaged in politics, there is no Cold War to fight, the struggle to ratify the ERA is no longer an issue, and the notion that women's primary responsibility is to stay home and raise children is largely outdated. While it is true that some conservative women involved in the Tea Party, particularly those who are religiously devout, continue to celebrate the stay-at-home mom and invoke a passionate defense of traditional gender roles, the economic reality is that most mothers—even those who hold conservative political views—work outside the home, either part-time or full-time. Even those conservative Tea Party women who are currently full-time homemakers or work part-time are far more likely than women from their mother's generation to have either a college degree or professional work experience, as American women continue to delay marriage and childbirth. Yet motherhood remains a powerful rhetorical device, as many Tea Party women compel their conservative sisters to become politically active out of a sense of motherly duty.

What *has* changed from previous eras of conservative activism in the twentieth century, however, is how Tea Party women activists frame their motherhood appeals. Rather than an overt, public focus on social issues, such as feminism, or religious issues, such as "godless" communism, as being of utmost concern to American families, the Tea Party movement has made conservative economic policy a "pro-family" cause—one to be championed by mothers. Moreover, as I discuss in chapter 6, some Tea Party activists frame their defense of gun rights in motherhood terms as well, although to a more limited extent than in their defense of free market policies.

Turning to economic policy and the more general concern about the role of government in society, I identify three motherhood frames that many Tea Party women activists use that relate to the movement's commitment to reducing taxes and limiting the size and scope of government. First, Tea Party women often call on mothers to become engaged in politics as "kitchen table" conservatives, arguing that because mothers balance the budgets at home, they can be counted on to support policy that balances the federal budget nationally. In essence, Tea Party women argue that since American families have to be accountable in their budgeting, so should the American government. Second, in what I describe as the "generational theft" frame, Tea Party women call on mothers to pressure political leaders to reduce the federal debt. In this theme, moms are compelled to become active in politics in order to safeguard future generations from reckless spending and to make sure that our children and grandchildren maintain a high standard of living. In the final motherhood frame, Tea Party women compel mothers to fight for limited government, arguing that large government programs usurp the role of the family, thereby fostering family disintegration. As such, Tea Party women persuade mothers to become engaged in politics to protect their kids from an overreaching government that threatens liberty, the preeminent value at stake for Tea Party activists, and to allow their children to "keep the same America" as they have had.

While evidence of all three motherhood frames can be found in much of the rhetoric used by Tea Party women, there are some women active in the movement who do not employ such language. In fact, for these women, particularly those of a more libertarian bent, reliance on gendered appeals steeped in motherhood imagery, at best, potentially limits the ability of the Tea Party to build support among women who are not mothers while reinforcing in their minds outdated stereotypes of women's roles; at worst, it contradicts their vision of a society in which all people, regardless of gender, creed, or race, should be treated as individuals and not as members of specific groups who warrant special treatment. I examine the concerns of these Tea Party women activists toward the end of this chapter.

Kitchen Table Conservatives

One motherhood frame Tea Party activists employ to encourage greater activism by women concerns the practical experience that moms gain as managers of their household finances. In this take on the motherhood frame, Tea Party leaders argue that mothers, who often balance their family's budgets, are needed to relay that ability to elected officials in Washington who seem incapable of balancing the federal government's books. Take, for example, the following claim by Jenny Beth Martin, co-founder of the Tea Party Patriots. She maintains that the Tea Party message naturally resonates with women because "we are the ones, oftentimes, in the houses and families, who are balancing the checkbooks and buying the groceries and looking for whether we need to use coupons or not or seeing what sales make sense. When it comes to their own personal family checkbook, women are the ones who pay such close attention to it. And we are saying we want the government to do the same thing. And I think that message does appeal to women because women are doing this anyway in their own houses."[69] Janice Crouse, senior fellow with the Beverly LaHaye Institute—a think tank affiliated with Concerned Women for America—agrees, adding that it is "very offensive to women that the country would not be required to stay on a budget" given that their families are not afforded such a luxury.[70] The national director of new media for Smart Girl Politics, Tami Nantz, also believes that discussing the economic issues that confront families, such as grocery and utility costs, "is a huge way to reach women" to be supportive of the Tea Party cause.[71]

This "family budget" theme was on full display in the campaign appeals of women candidates who rode the Tea Party wave in 2010, such as Kelly Ayotte, a Republican elected to the U.S. Senate from New Hampshire. In her announcement speech in 2010, she remarked, "You can't spend money you don't have. Like most New Hampshire families, [my husband] Joe and I sit around our kitchen table, and we have to prioritize and live within our budget. Our government should be no different. Our elected officials must be willing to make the same hard decisions."[72] Another example of a campaign theme that used a family budget analogy came from former U.S. Senate candidate Jamie Radtke—a leading figure in the Tea Party in Virginia—who called for a "2 Percent Solution" to balance the federal budget by 2016. In an op-ed written for the *Richmond Times-Dispatch*, which calls for Congress to cut annual spending by 2 percent of current federal outlays to eliminate the federal budget deficit in five years, Radtke used a motherhood analogy:

> It is a plan so simple, even my children can comprehend and support it. My husband and I give our three children (ages 9, 8 and 5) a weekly allowance of a few dollars. Now, suppose I went to my kids and I told them the following: "Mommy and Daddy don't have a lot of money right now. Things are very tight for us as a family. We need to cut 2 cents out of every dollar we give you each week. If we only give you 98 cents instead of one dollar, our family can keep our house, car, buy groceries and provide for you. But if you insist that Mommy and Daddy give you the entire dollar and don't cut 2 cents, then there is a very decent chance we will lose all those things." What would be the response from my children? "Sure, Mom, you can keep the 2 cents!" My kids would have no problem cutting 2 cents out of their allowance so we could ensure that we can provide for their basic needs.[73]

While some observers questioned the "ease" of Radtke's solutions to the budget deficit crisis—critics claimed that she had glossed over some important political and budget details[74]—what is telling is that her approach is clearly aimed at families, explaining conservative fiscal policy in a way that is meant to resonate especially with mothers.

Many Tea Party women activists I spoke with also extended their budget analogy to incorporate their views on taxes. One activist in Maryland said women are drawn to the Tea Party because they are savvy about budgeting, very cognizant of "where their money goes and where their money comes from," and are thus "sick and tired" of taxes being raised to pay for programs they don't support.[75] Another activist from Maryland, *Joan Duncan*, said that government programs today, at all levels, are hitting American families harder, with taxes "coming in and reaching in further and further and now we are saying that you are taking it too far."[76] Duncan, a small-business owner, believes that her background and many of her female friends who own their own businesses has given them the confidence to "understand taxes and regulations that are being placed upon them in all different aspects of their life."[77] Combined with managing her family's finances, these business experiences have provided Duncan with a big source of inspiration for her involvement in Tea Party grassroots activism.

On a similar note, Sarah Palin often extols the virtues of mothers as "common-sense conservatives," noting in her online video advertisement for SarahPAC, her political action committee that endorses federal- and state-level candidates, that women "all across this country . . . are standing up and speaking out for common-sense solutions."[78] She goes on to write in her book, *America by Heart*, that conservative women's "common-sense" approach to politics and the expertise they gain as multitasking moms offers a new and important voice to the political debate: "We're busy enough to know that time must be spent efficiently; in fact, we're too busy to waste time with typical political games and power struggles."[79] Several of the local women Tea Party activists I interviewed also expressed a similar theme to Palin: that the skills they derived from juggling home, work, and community activism made them well suited to grassroots advocacy. For example, consider what I heard from this activist in Maryland: "We tend to be pretty organized. Certainly not that men aren't, but again, as a mother . . . There are so many qualities you use as a mom, [such as] taking care of your household, [that apply] to politics. You know, if you handle the budget, the planning, the organizing—all of that can carry over into working with a campaign, especially when it comes to event planning."[80] The practical skills that these conservative women bring to the table, combining their family budget skills with their abilities to organize their household's many events and responsibilities, has given many of these local women advocates the capacity to handle political organizing at the grassroots and state level, while making them responsive to Tea Party messages that advocate for a smaller, fiscally responsible American government.

Generational Theft

Another common appeal used in the "motherhood" frame is "generational theft," so dubbed by Sarah Palin, who writes in *America by Heart*, "Moms can be counted on to fight for their children's future. And when politicians start handing our kids the bill for their cronyism and irresponsibility—when they engage in generational theft—moms rise up."[81] Tea Party women routinely insist that part of their motivation for getting involved in politics is to save children from the large debt burden that they face. This line of rhetoric also appears to be influencing the argumentation of more "establishment" Republican women leaders. For example, Cathy McMorris Rodgers, a Republican member of Congress from Washington who now serves as the highest-ranking woman in House GOP leadership, described House Republican women on the conservative *RedState* blog—a website popular with Tea Party activists—as "mothers and grandmothers who want to eliminate the debt burden for the next generation" and as conservative reformers "committed to leaving America better for our children and grandchildren than it was for us."[82]

Similarly, Tami Nantz cites her "greater responsibility" to her sole child's future as a pivotal reason she became involved in the Tea Party. She told me, "I feel like what we are doing right now will directly impact her future and that will get a mama fired up!"[83] That sentiment was echoed by another Tea Party activist I interviewed from Indianapolis, Miriam Weaver, who cohosts a nationally syndicated radio show with Amy Jo Clark called *Chicks on the Right* and who writes a political blog of the same name that is popular with many Tea Party women. She said that concern about their children's future, tied to the large debt generated by the federal government, has special resonance with mothers in particular: "We tend to be the Mama Bears; we're Mama Grizzlies. We are the ones who are thinking—not that fathers don't, of course—but I think that it is more of a natural female instinct to be thinking about the protection of and the future of her cubs. I think that is why we see such a strong engagement with women now. Everyone is feeling very 'growly' about what is happening with our kids' future."[84] Colleen Holcomb, former executive director of Eagle Forum's DC office, the lobbying arm of Phyllis Schlafly's group, also agrees that the Mama Grizzly metaphor is an apt description that captures why many women are engaging in Tea Party activism. As she told me, their activism is "primal," as many conservative Moms believe "there is a real perceived threat to our way of life and our freedoms and to our children's future. . . . I remember growing up with the sense that we have the ability to exceed our parents' accomplishments and to leave a better country. We realized we are not doing that now."[85]

Jenny Beth Martin agrees that motherhood is a powerful source of inspiration for their activism because parents are concerned with the fiscal health of the nation. She believes that many women are getting involved in the Tea Party because "they are looking at their children and thinking we have got to leave a country that is fiscally sound for their children, they deserve that. It is motherhood and it is looking at our children and making sure that we have or are leaving the right country for them."[86] As Martin's quote above suggests, however, Tea Party activists believe that the debt issue also speaks to underlying moral concerns. Witness the words of this Tea Party activist in Maryland, who feels that the debt is a larger indicator of the moral breakdown of society:

> The very first thing that comes to mind is my kids. I am concerned about the state of our nation and the state of the state that I am in. Just really trying to secure a better future for my children. That is a huge issue . . . When I think about how the country has changed overall, just morally, and the overwhelming debt is huge, I feel like I need to do something to try and get involved and to try and make a difference. I want the U.S. to be a better place for them to grow up.[87]

Other Tea Party women link the federal debt directly to an overbearing government, pursuing policies that run counter to the free market, as does this activist and political blogger in Maryland, a grandmother who got involved in politics to make the "world different for my grandchildren and the direction that I see it going in."[88] As she explained, "I don't want this for them; I don't want this massive debt. I don't want them to just know a socialist kind of government. It is not the America I grew up with and it is a scarier place, a less free place, and I don't want that for my children or for my grandchildren."[89]

Limited Government as Family Protection

Another prominent Tea Party theme that employs motherhood rhetoric concerns the protection of the family from a federal government that is too large and that usurps family prerogatives—an idea that was commonly used by earlier incarnations of conservative women activists who opposed the growth of the welfare state during the Progressive Era and the Red Scare. Tea Party activists, including many women, repeatedly extol the virtues of limited government as good for families. Their arguments are based on a narrow, conservative reading of the Constitution—one that says the federal government's powers should be limited to what was prescribed in the Constitution at the time it was ratified. For example, Dana Loesch writes that her political activism is grounded in the fact that she doesn't want her children's future to be "squandered" on things "non-essential to the operation of our basic Article 1 Section 8 government," which for Loesch includes entitlement programs such as Social Security.[90] She goes on to write in the same essay that she doesn't want her "children robbed of their ability to have [an] effect in their communities because the power was sucked up and centralized at the federal level."[91]

Amy Kremer, former head of Tea Party Express, believes that women are at the forefront of the Tea Party movement because they oppose an expansive federal state, which has been made only bigger under the Obama administration. Kremer writes, "The truth is that Tea Party women are leading the charge to tackle the fundamental problems brought on by the ever-expanding Big Government agenda. Women are not only the most protective of loved ones. They are also the most familiar with how policies will affect their family on a micro level."[92] Or, as Colleen Holcomb told me, "I can see how government can be detrimental to families. In order for government to grow, families have to shrink." Holcomb directly ties her organization's socially conservative views, which seek to protect the family, to its promotion of conservative economic policy:

> If you protect the family, if you have mothers and fathers together supporting each other and raising their own children, not only does that limit welfare use—marriage is the solution to poverty and the greatest indicator of prosperity. It limits the need for things like special education, need for prisons, drug abuse, law enforcement. There are all kinds of benefits that the family provides. . . . And the capitalist system . . . provide[s] the most opportunity for economic equality, too. That is one of the issues that we fight. Liberals are always fighting for equality. We [already] believe everyone has equality and the greatest thing a government can do to provide equality is to keep everyone safe and to give us economic freedom.[93]

Holcomb's views are echoed in many of the interviews I conducted with local-level Tea Party activists, who argue that previously apolitical conservative women have become engaged in the Tea Party because far-reaching government policies, particularly at the federal level, are threatening the well-being of families. In the words of one Maryland activist, women are participating in the Tea Party because "this movement is truly about protecting our families."[94] Or as another Tea Party activist new to the political world put it, "Conservative women always hung out and did the right thing, and they realized now wait a minute, [the government is] stepping on my toes, on my property, on my rights, on my family, and we're not going to take it."[95]

Nothing raises the ire of Tea Party activists—including women—like the Affordable Care Act, dubbed "ObamaCare" by its critics. Tea Party activists decry it as federal overreach; many Tea Party women also believe that ObamaCare will restrict their ability to make health care decisions for their families. For example, Darla Dawald, national director for the Patriot Action Network, believes that women's activism in the Tea Party is based in part on the health care overhaul legislation. She was quoted in *Politico* as saying, "Statistically, healthcare is something that women drive . . . They usually decide where their families will be cared for and are the ones making the appointments and so forth, so [the Tea Party's opposition] became something that was being driven very strongly by women."[96] Tea Party women also believe that "big government," as embodied for them by new federal programs such as Obama-Care, essentially usurps the role of the family and even threatens the family unit. Thus Tea Party activists, including its women leaders, call for a more drastically limited federal government and a reduced tax burden for families. They also believe that government entitlement spending and social welfare has created a culture of dependency among the poor. Hence Jamie Radtke's Senate campaign website, quoted in the beginning of the chapter, which states that social welfare spending, including in politically popular programs such as Social Security and Medicaid, actually encourages "family disintegration." Or as Eagle Forum's Colleen Holcomb stated, in order for government to grow, "families have to shrink." In more pointed rhetoric, Tara Kozub, a member of As a Mom . . . a Sisterhood of Mommy Patriots, writes in *Smart Girl Nation*, "So as Moms who strive to be the modern-day patriots of our time, how can we respond to our country's current crisis? We can begin by teaching our children this simple equation: Dependence on government + a spirit of entitlement = slavery. Dependent on God + a spirit of self-reliance = Freedom."[97]

In the latter passage, Kozub clearly believes that reducing the size and scope of government has religious overtones. Kozub's language harks back to the rhetoric employed by right-wing women during the Red Scare, who called on mothers as religious crusaders to safeguard Christian civilization by promoting a "free America" and to teach their children about the importance of self-reliance and small government as a defense for America's liberties.[98] Additionally, the attempt by Kozub and many other Tea Party women to compel mothers to advance conservative economic policy mirrors earlier efforts by Christian Right organizations to "fuse" conservative economic policy goals with social policy during the Reagan Era—a tendency that has only become more pronounced with the rise of the Tea Party.[99] For instance, Ralph Reed, former executive director of the Christian Coalition—the leading Christian Right group in the 1990s—founded the Faith and Freedom Coalition in 2009 to marry conservative economic policy with socially conservative values.[100] Reed's organization states that the "greatness of America lies not in the federal government but in the character of our people—the simple virtues of faith, hard work, marriage, family, personal responsibility and helping the least among us."[101] So while its mission statement advocates for policy that strengthens traditional families and respects the sanctity of life, it also seeks to "lower the tax burden on small businesses and families" and to require the "government to tighten its belt and live within its means"—a clear echo of the "kitchen table" rhetoric and other maternal themes employed by many Mama Grizzlies.

The Downside of Motherhood Appeals

Calling on mothers' own expertise as 'budget managers" at home and stoking fears among mothers about how the federal debt and overreaching government programs will affect the nation's children and grandchildren provide powerful, compelling reasons for conservative mothers to become engaged in Tea Party activism. As demonstrated in much of the writing done by Tea Party women leaders and in the interviews I conducted with local, state, and national activists, many women involved in the Tea Party routinely explain that their participation is rooted in their experiences as mothers. However, while evidence of all three motherhood frames can be found in much of the rhetoric used by Tea Party women, there are some women active in the movement who pointedly avoid such "motherhood" rhetoric in their calls for political engagement. Some female Tea Party leaders avoid using such rhetoric for fear of alienating many potentially politically like-minded women, whether they are young and single and not yet thinking about having children, older yet choosing to remain childless, or not capable of having children. Moreover, there is concern among some Tea Party leaders that too much reliance on motherhood as a justification for involvement in conservative politics promotes older stereotypes of what conservative women activists "should" look like.

One of the newest Tea Party women's organizations to emerge since 2009 is Smart Girl Politics, co-founded by Stacy Mott, who continues to serve as the group's president. The group, which now claims a membership of about sixty-five thousand at the grassroots level and in various state chapters, sponsors an annual conference, Smart Girl Summit, which brings together its activists to meet with and hear from prominent conservative pundits and leaders. Her organization also runs a popular political blog, *Smart Girl Politics Action*, and until 2013 published a web magazine, *Smart Girl Nation*. Mott told me that while many of her members are mothers—both those who stay at home and those who work full-time—her organization has deliberately avoided using overt motherhood appeals in its marketing approach. Mott believes that the political left has been successful at painting all conservative women as "women of the 1950s, [where] we're in the kitchen barefoot and pregnant, that stereotypical woman." By avoiding motherhood appeals as their main rhetorical strategy, Mott and her organization hope to paint a modern portrait of conservative women who hail from diverse backgrounds and life experiences, mothers and non-mothers alike. Moreover, she fears that using motherhood rhetoric as a deliberate marketing strategy may be counterproductive; she believes that "the quickest way to offend or alienate different categories of women is by putting a generalized label on that," recognizing that many of her board members are single women.[102]

The Republican pollster Kristen Soltis Anderson also cautions against the Tea Party's overreliance on motherhood rhetoric because it may potentially feed into old stereotypes of what conservatives look like. She told me that while it may be good for individual Tea Party women to speak to their own personal experiences as mothers, "the caution is that you want to make sure that your message still has relevance to women who don't have children. If the right is really trying to . . . [change] this misperception that it is a movement of old institutions" they need to acknowledge "what family looks like these days in America is changing."[103] Whitney Neal, formerly director of grass roots at Freedom-Works, echoed these thoughts about motherhood appeals and the Tea Party. Although a single mother herself who was inspired by her son to become active in conservative politics, Neal told me, "When you start talking motherhood, you do alienate the people for whom it is not an issue."[104]

Moreover, for many libertarian-minded activists in the Tea Party, making large "group" appeals to women or mothers runs counter to their underlying philosophy, which embraces individualism. Keli Carender, a national grassroots coordinator for the Tea Party Patriots, acknowledges that while certain people may respond differently to different political messages, she believes that the Tea Party in general should avoid making targeted appeals to different demographic groups such as mothers or racial minorities. She says that the Tea Party wants "freedom for everybody. It doesn't matter who you are. We don't want to be a part of the balkanization of our society, and to some extent if you really, really change your messaging for different groups of people, you are contributing to that. We'd rather teach people why our message is a unifying message and why everyone should support it."[105]

Some Tea Party libertarian women also worry that reliance on motherhood rhetoric more specifically, or gender-based appeals more broadly, unnecessarily limits the political dialogue in which women can engage. Carrie Lukas, managing director of the Independent Women's Forum, finds such political messaging potentially problematic. She told me, "The IWF uses as a tagline [that] all issues are women's issues: tax policy, education, health care . . . we don't put people in a box, with girls out here."[106] She does acknowledge, however, that psychological research suggests that women are more risk-averse than men, so that political messaging on economic issues that may work for men—for example, promoting tax cuts as a way to yield more economic growth—may not be as relevant for some women, who may be more concerned with ensuring financial stability.

This "split" among Tea Party women activists into those who seek to employ motherhood rhetoric as a way to galvanize socially conservative women into political activism and those who are primarily committed to a libertarian view that prioritizes individual liberty is not new among women engaged in right-wing politics, at least since the ascendancy of the "New Right" in the late 1970s. Sociologist Rebecca Klatch found that both socially conservative women—the type engaged in antifeminist advocacy such as the campaigns to stop the Equal Rights Amendment or abortion—and laissez-faire conservative women—those who placed a far greater priority on economic issues as the basis for their political activism—were both active in grassroots right-wing politics at this time but were far apart in terms of their worldviews. Most of the libertarian women Klatch interviewed vehemently disagreed with the viewpoint that government policy should enhance and strengthen a patriarchal vision of society, rooted in traditional beliefs about women's inherent biological gender roles; instead, laissez-faire conservative women "see themselves as no different than men, self-interested actors working for a political cause."[107]

In a more recent work, *Righting Feminism*, which profiled the activism of the libertarian Independent Women's Forum along with the socially conservative organization Concerned Women for America, political scientist Ronnee Schreiber found that this divide among conservative women activists predated the Tea Party at the start of the new millennium.[108] Although their worldviews differed, Schreiber did find that when these two sets of activists shared common ground on policy issues, they could work together quite effectively, though clearly using differing narratives to speak to their primary constituencies. However, the tension was still there in some ways. For instance, IWF refuses to take a position on social issues such as abortion or gay rights, which are often more compelling for conservative women than are economic issues. In some respects, finding disagreement about Tea Party women in the 2010s as to the utility of motherhood appeals should not be surprising. By emphasizing how conservative economic policy can strengthen families, however, as many Tea Party women routinely make the case, perhaps the divide between these two groups of conservative women activists may prove less important if they can stay focused on economic issues primarily.

The Tea Party, Motherhood, and the Future

Tea Party activists routinely decry the size and scope of the federal government as a betrayal of the vision they believe motivated the Founding Fathers. They believe that taxes are too high, income distribution through "socialist" policies such as ObamaCare and (in some cases) Social Security is economically wasteful, and government programs that bailed out failed corporations and unlucky consumers who took out risky mortgages are unjust to those Americans who worked hard and played by the rules.[109] They fear that the massive debt incurred by the United States threatens their children's way of life. As the qualitative analysis shows here, many—but not all—Tea Party women activists also echo these themes, but with a twist, by employing "motherhood" rhetoric to justify their call for reduced government spending and lowering taxes. For many such activists, these policies represent a loss of liberty and a challenge to them keeping for their kids what activist Jamie Radtke refers to as the "same America" they have enjoyed.

While these Mama Grizzlies tout relatively mainstream conservative principles, including fiscal responsibility, reducing the size and scope of government, and freer markets, as a way to safeguard their families' liberties, critics argue that some of the rhetoric, such as Radtke's appeal to mothers to "keep the same America" as they have had, smacks of troubling racist and xenophobic undertones, whether such activists do so consciously or not.[110] When Tea Party activists—including many of the Tea Party women profiled here—call on their fellow conservatives to "take back America," it begs the question, From whom are they taking it back? Political scientists Christopher Parker and Matt Barreto argue in their book *Change They Can't Believe In* that Tea Party activism is a reactionary response to changes in American politics and society, such as the election of Barack Obama, the rise of Latinos and other ethnic minorities as part of the U.S. population, and the decline of traditional religiosity, which includes the broader acceptance of LGBT Americans. Such changes represent "a threat of the mostly male, middle-aged and older, middle-class, white segment of the population on par with the ethnocultural and political threats that motivated participation in right-wing movements"[111] historically such as the John Birch Society. Moreover, political theorist Holloway Sparks argues that the angry Mama Grizzly rhetoric employed by many women in the Tea Party, as depicted here, trades on white privilege: "The Tea Party women called to identify with the Sisterhood of Mommy Patriots and to channel their righteous Mom anger at the president, Congress, and so on, are most clearly white women."[112]

The adoption of motherhood rhetoric by Tea Party women in defense of their political activism, Sparks also points out, gives cover to women whose anger is often viewed by larger society as "irrational and shrill."[113] In other words, Tea Party women adopt the Mama Grizzly rhetoric as a way to rationalize not merely their involvement in right-wing politics per se, but as a way to legitimate tough, masculine behavior in the political sphere. Of course, progressive women often employ motherhood appeals as a way to encourage women to fight for more liberal policies. But unlike many of their conservative counterparts, liberal women political activists have also been more comfortable grounding their political appeals in the language of individual rights. Accordingly, women as *individuals* should be granted equal rights as a matter of justice, not because they are mothers first and foremost. Several of the women libertarian activists profiled here, in fact, reject motherhood appeals based, in part, on this logic. Yet, for most of the women I interviewed, motherhood remains a powerful reason to engage in Tea Party politics.

At the end of the day, perhaps the use of "Mama Grizzly" rhetoric may not prove to be a divisive issue among Tea Party women activists after all. One benefit of the diffuse nature of grassroots movements is that organizations can spontaneously form that, while working together for a common cause, can take different approaches with different messages that their members find most appealing. As Kristen Soltis Anderson points out about the Tea Party and its female groups, "You've got Smart Girl Politics, you've got As a Mom—there's no one right way to be. If that message resonates with you, you can go in that group or you can go somewhere else."[114] If the Tea Party can stay focused on its message of fiscal responsibility and smaller government, then motherhood appeals may work more seamlessly with other Tea Party appeals. If instead the Tea Party begins to focus most of its attention on social issues and the promotion of patriarchal gender roles, then perhaps the nature and tone of the rhetoric its leaders use, particularly if steeped in motherhood appeals, could prove more divisive.

4

The Sexist Safety Net

Free Enterprise as Feminist Principle

In May 2012, at the height of the election contest between Democrat Barack Obama and Republican Mitt Romney, the Obama campaign's website launched an infographic it dubbed "The Life of Julia."[1] In this animated slideshow, the Obama campaign illustrates how one fictional woman, "Julia," benefits over her lifetime from government programs that Obama supported, such as Head Start, Pell Grants, Medicare, and Social Security, and how these programs were threatened by spending cuts proposed by the Romney campaign. "The Life of Julia" placed special emphasis on two signature pieces of legislation signed by Obama: the Lilly Ledbetter Act and the Affordable Care Act. With respect to the former, the Obama campaign stated, "Because of steps like the Lilly Ledbetter Fair Pay Act, Julia is one of millions of women across the country who knows she'll always be able to stand up for her right to equal pay." Later, when the fictional Julia turned twenty-seven, the infographic said, "Thanks to ObamaCare, her health insurance is required to cover birth control and preventive care, letting Julia focus on her work rather than worry about her health." Four years later, when "Julia decides to have a child," the Obama campaign maintained that she benefits from "maternal checkups, prenatal care, and free screenings under health care reform."

The condemnation of "The Life of Julia" by Tea Party women, not to mention Republicans and conservative groups more generally, was swift.[2] Conservative blogger Michelle Malkin wrote that the infographic "inadvertently exposed the real Barack Obama: a chauvinistic control freak who would tether every last woman and child to his ever-expanding, budget-busting Nanny State."[3] Smart Girl Politics featured several posts critical of "The Life of Julia" and created a bumper sticker, "I'm Not Julia," available for purchase. As Kristen Hawley wrote on the site, "The problem with 'The Life of Julia' . . . lies in the Administration's assumption that the average American woman would want or need government assistance. Shouldn't it be the goal of our leaders to create a culture of self-reliance, which is the pinnacle of individual liberty and freedom?"[4] Tami Nantz, Smart Girl Politics director of social media, was even more pointed in her response: "It seems to me that President Barack Obama is trying to make women a slave to the almighty government plantation."[5]

In the last chapter I discussed three motherhood themes that Tea Party women employ in their promotion of conservative economic policies. Many Tea Party women argue that balancing the budget, eliminating the federal debt, and scaling back or overturning government programs such as ObamaCare would be good for American families, and that as "Mama Grizzlies" conservative women should fight against "big government" as a way to safeguard the American way of life for the next generation. Conservatives in the United States have long maintained that a growing federal social safety system is not only unsustainable from a budgetary perspective, but does little to stem poverty. Moreover, many social conservatives reject a growing welfare state because they believe that government programs designed to help the poor ultimately usurp family responsibility and discourage marriage. Recall the comment by Colleen Holcomb, former head of Eagle Forum, DC: "For government to grow, families have to shrink." These conservative activists feel that the growth of government is intrinsically linked to troubling societal changes, such as decreasing marriage rates and increased rates of single motherhood,[6] which they believe exacerbate income inequality and threaten the well-being of many children.

However, as their responses to Obama's "Life of Julia" campaign infographic illustrate, Tea Party women sometimes move beyond motherhood rhetoric to make other gendered claims against "big government." Many Tea Party women, as well as elected Republican women leaders, argue that federal government policies, including the Lilly Ledbetter Act, the Affordable Care Act, and long-standing social welfare programs, promote women's dependence on government rather than empower them. An overreaching government not only usurps the proper responsibility of mothers to best meet the needs of their children, it also circumscribes women as autonomous actors, in ways that some Tea

Party women argue is sexist. In this chapter I take a closer look at Tea Party women's attitudes about the size and scope of government and why they think government social programs and a large regulatory state are ultimately bad not just for mothers with children, but for women in general.

The fierce opposition that many Tea Party women feel toward the federal government stands in direct contrast to progressive women leaders, who argue that government should do *more* to help struggling families, whether that means expanding social welfare programs, increasing the minimum wage, or requiring businesses to provide mandatory paid sick and family leave to help Americans better balance their work and family lives.[7] Liberal women's organizations also tout the importance of passing new legislation, such as the Paycheck Fairness Act, that would make it easier for women to sue for pay discrimination, focusing their attention on the wage gap in the United States, which shows that women typically earn between 77 and 84 percent of what men do.[8] These debates about the size of government and the sorts of regulations it should put on businesses has never been more relevant: wages in the last decade have been largely stagnant, helping to contribute to the most pronounced income inequality in the United States since the Great Depression.[9] Yet, as this chapter illustrates, Tea Party women and conservative women's organizations resoundingly reject government solutions to these problems, arguing that although well intentioned, such policies actually harm women more than help them. Instead, Tea Party women point to economic data that show women's wages are rapidly coming into line with men's, which they believe demonstrate that the free market is the best way to close the wage gap, raise wages, and lessen income inequality for both men *and* women.

Next, I consider the extent to which self-identified Tea Party women in the mass public share such views with the Tea Party women who are helping to lead the movement and who are shaping public rhetoric about such policies. In addition, I compare Tea Party women's attitudes on such policies nationally with those of other American women—both Republican women who do not identify with the Tea Party and American women who are Democrats or Political Independents—as a way to gauge how receptive other American women may be to the Tea Party's message that smaller government, reduced taxes, and fewer business regulations are in women's best interests. Using data from the Public Religion Research Institute, I examine American women's more general orientation toward government's obligation to help the poor as well as their perceptions about welfare recipients. I also consider how American women feel about the economic system in this country more generally, including their perceptions about whether all Americans enjoy equal opportunities to succeed. I then examine American women's attitudes about numerous policies that tap into both the size and regulatory scope of government: the Affordable Care Act, the birth control mandate, tax cuts, the minimum wage, and paid family and sick leave. In between examining the attitudes of American women on these policies, I also consider through my interviews and through their writings what Tea Party women have to say about these policies and why they believe they are detrimental to women.

Tea Party Women and the State: Viewing Government Programs as Harmful to Women

Debates about the size and scope of government have dominated domestic politics in the United States for more than a century, with women activists on both the left and the right reaching very different conclusions about whether government policies to help the poor are beneficial or detrimental to women and their families. Among the American public, women have always been significantly more likely than men to believe that government should do more to help the poor—a difference that helps drive the gender gap in American politics, in which women have been significantly more likely to vote and identify as Democrats than have men.[10] Some scholars argue that women's more liberal orientation toward government spending may be grounded in inherent biological differences or socialization experiences, particularly given women's roles as caregivers.[11] Others point out that women are more economically vulnerable than men are, which may lead them to be more supportive of government providing a social safety net.[12] Still others maintain that women support a larger government because they are more likely than men are to work in occupations affected by redistributive government politics.[13] Lastly, work by social psychologists and economists finds that women are more empathetic than men and less

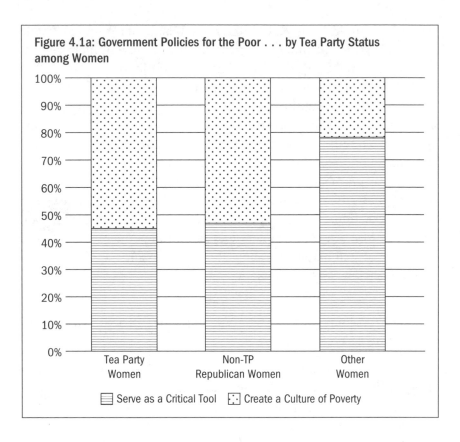

Figure 4.1a: Government Policies for the Poor . . . by Tea Party Status among Women

Serve as a Critical Tool   Create a Culture of Poverty

risk-averse, which may also help explain why women are more likely than men to support a strong social safety net.[14]

However, the rise of Tea Party women—not to mention the growing number of Republican women elected to Congress and to governors' mansions in the past few election cycles—reminds us that women's views on government social programs are far from monolithic. Data from two surveys conducted by the Public Religion Research Institute—the 2012 and 2014 American Values Survey—demonstrate that both Tea Party women in the mass public *and* Republican women who are not part of the Tea Party hold distinct attitudes from other American women when it comes to how large a role the government should play in helping the poor. (See appendix A for more information about the surveys.) Figure 4.1a shows that when respondents in the 2012 American Values Survey were asked whether government policies aimed at helping the poor either "serve as a critical safety net, which help people in hard times get back on their feet," or "create a culture of dependency where people are provided with too many handouts," more than half of Tea Party women (55 percent) and non–Tea Party Republican women (53 percent) chose the latter option, compared with just 22 percent of other American women. When Tea Party status is regressed onto the notion that poverty programs create a culture of poverty among women, it remains a statistically significant explanatory factor. In other words, being part of the Tea Party has a conservatizing influence on women's attitudes about antipoverty programs even while controlling for partisanship and other demographic and religious factors. (See table 4.1 in appendix B for full model results.) Not surprisingly, given the parties' well-documented stands on such issues, Republican women are significantly more likely, and Democratic women significantly less likely, than women who identify as Independents[15] to believe that government programs aimed at reducing poverty create a culture of dependency.

Moreover, from the 2014 American Values Survey, 56 percent of Tea Party women and 55 percent of non–Tea Party Republican women either mostly or completely disagree that the "government should do more to reduce the gap between the rich and the poor," which is in stark contrast to the 22 percent of other American women who disagree (see figure 4.1b). Again, controlling for other political and demographic factors in a statistical analysis, I find that Tea Party status among American women is a significant factor in explaining attitudes about whether government should do more to reduce the gap between the rich and the poor. (See table 4.1 in appendix B for full model results.) Party also matters, but only for Democrats: Democrats are significantly more likely than Independents to believe that government should address income inequality, while Republican status is not a statistically significant variable in this model. On the role of government in addressing income inequality, then, self-described Tea Party women nationally hold more conservative positions than do Republican women in the mass public.

In their own words, Tea Party women explain why they believe such social welfare programs ultimately do more harm than good to women as individuals. In some cases, they believe these programs promote the false premise that women are incapable of taking care of themselves. Amy Jo Clark, who along with Miriam Weaver runs the popular blog

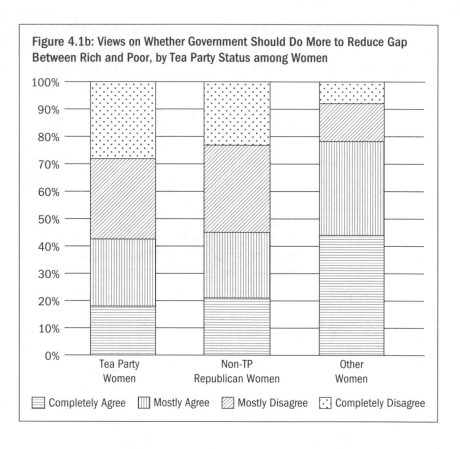

Figure 4.1b: Views on Whether Government Should Do More to Reduce Gap Between Rich and Poor, by Tea Party Status among Women

and radio show called *Chicks on the Right*, says that although many women support government social programs out a sense of empathy, "what they don't hear in the messaging is really how these programs keep women down. The cyclical things that keep these women down, it keeps them poor, it keeps them dependent on these programs. They don't see how absolutely non-empowering these programs are."[16] Jennifer Jacobs, who heads a local Tea Party organization in Maryland, believes that "women are socialized into thinking they need government support." She recounts the time she separated from her first husband and people told her she should apply for housing assistance, welfare, and food stamps, which she refused to do. She told me, "Once women are a part of the [government] system, they can't leave the system. These women think that standing on their own two feet is being on welfare when they are actually dependent."[17] Gabriella Hoffman, a 2012 graduate of UC San Diego, who runs the blog *All-American Girl for the Restoration of Values*, also believes that government today usurps individual responsibility and ultimately restricts the freedom of women. She says, "Big government policies want you to have government dependency from cradle to grave. And, when you are beholden to the government, you have no decisions over what you can do. You are going to be told to have as many abortions as you want, or as many sexual partners, and to not be accountable for your actions, leading you to beg the government for certain items or certain rights or privileges, that you don't necessarily need and which are contrary to being what an independently minded female is."[18] Instead, Tea Party women maintain that women should be expected to take care of themselves, and if they cannot, the onus should be on charity groups or families—not government—to help. Said Elizabeth Reynolds, co-founder of the statewide conservative organization Maryland Citizen Action Network (MD-CAN), "I think we have veered away from our community and religious groups to be the providers of the social safety net. I don't think government should provide social services unless for the very destitute. I guess my bottom line is, What promotes freedom? What promotes individual liberty? I think social programs are better being addressed in your community and by your family. You need to take responsibility for yourself."[19] The common theme connecting these responses is that government programs ultimately undermine women's ability and responsibility to be self-sufficient.

The argument that women themselves as individuals should be responsible for their own livelihood reflects classic conservative positions that promote self-reliance and industry. It also assumes that all women are equally capable of solving their own problems and enjoy the same opportunities to succeed as one another—a premise that is often challenged by progressive activists, who believe government must help those who come from less-privileged backgrounds and who face structural barriers to overcoming poverty. In the 2014 American Values Survey, the Public Religion Research Institute asked respondents the extent to which they thought "children from all income groups have adequate opportunities to be successful," which suggests that upward mobility is still a key characteristic of American society—74 percent of Tea Party women either completely or mostly agree with this statement

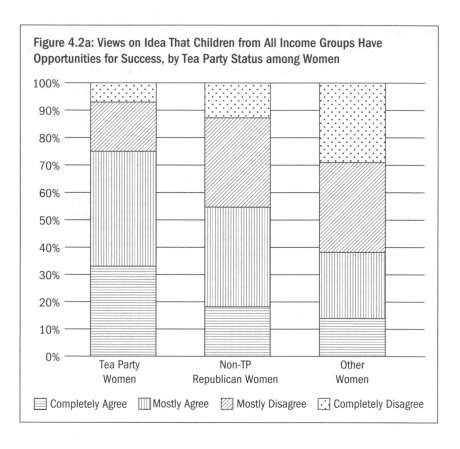

Figure 4.2a: Views on Idea That Children from All Income Groups Have Opportunities for Success, by Tea Party Status among Women

Completely Agree ▤ Mostly Agree ▥ Mostly Disagree ▨ Completely Disagree ⋮

(see figure 4.2a). By contrast, 55 percent of non–Tea Party Republican women agree with this sentiment, compared with only 36 percent of other American women. These findings suggest that Tea Party women in the mass public, and to a lesser extent Republican women, hold a very different orientation about individuals' abilities to shape their own destinies than do other American women. Given these results, it should come as little surprise that Tea Party women and non–Tea Party Republican women are far more likely, 77 percent and 70 percent, respectively, than other American women (41 percent) to believe that "most people on welfare are taking advantage of the system" rather than being "genuinely in need of help," as asked by the 2012 American Values Survey (see figure 4.2b). In the case of both dependent variables examined here, Tea Party status remains a statistically significant predictor of attitudes about upward mobility and welfare recipients once additional

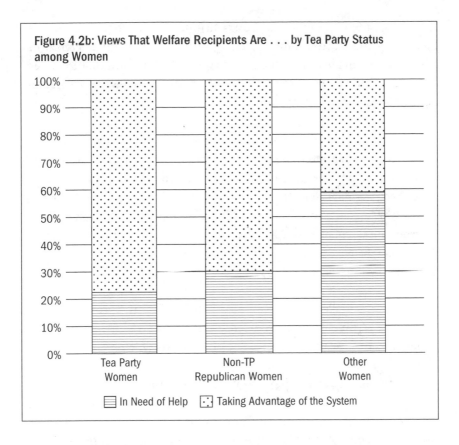

Figure 4.2b: Views That Welfare Recipients Are . . . by Tea Party Status among Women

controls are included in a regression analysis. (See table 4.2 in appendix B for full model results.) In other words, identifying as part of the Tea Party has a conservatizing impact on the attitudes of American women when it comes to these opinions. Notably, party also significantly shapes women's attitudes on these issues: Republicans are significantly more likely than are Independents to believe that all children enjoy equal opportunities of success and that most people on welfare take advantage of the system, while Democrats are significantly less likely than are Independents to hold conservative positions on these measures.

Tea Party women's opposition to these social safety net policies also evoke more traditional themes, which is not surprising given that many socially conservative women believe that government programs today have come to usurp family roles. Janice Shaw Crouse, senior fellow at the Beverly LaHaye Institute, worries that the growing acceptance of the social safety net maligns the traditional family structure and detaches any stigma from unwed parenthood. In referencing a claim that Mitt Romney made during the 2012 presidential election that President Obama had the votes of the 47 percent of Americans who "are dependent upon government,"[20] Crouse said:

> Now unmarried women don't have as much to fear. The government is the provider. The government is the husband. The government provides better than most men can provide. And that colors the whole culture. Romney was right about the 47 percent. The way he said it was offensive. The way he said it was distorted. But it is true that close to half of the people in the country are dependent on government and not all of them find that shameful. And so stigma has been removed. And that is producing a sea change of attitudes about the role of government.[21]

Eagle Forum's Colleen Holcomb also believes that the growing acceptance of government-sponsored programs to alleviate poverty by many Americans obfuscates the real solution to poverty, which in her mind is linked to the traditional family structure. She maintains that if "you protect the family, if you have mothers and fathers together supporting each other and raising their own children, not only does that limit welfare use. Marriage is the solution to poverty and the greatest indicator of prosperity."[22] Even conservative women whose activism is not rooted in their religious beliefs argue that single women and married women often view the role of government in their lives quite differently. Carrie Lukas of the secular Independent Women's Forum believes the divide between married women with children and unmarried women with children is incredibly important, because "a lot of single people are more concerned and more interested in the government safety net as they are on their own and don't have the family infrastructure."[23]

Criticism about the impact of the social safety net on American women derived from socially conservative and libertarian perspectives need not be mutually exclusive. When denouncing "The Life of Julia" meme, for example, many conservative women such as Meredith Jessup of *The Blaze* not only decried the portrayal of Julia as a "completely helpless and hopeless cretin who depends on government assistance to function," but also expressed dismay that the infographic did not once mention a father or family structure.[24] Conservative blogger Dana Loesch described the spot as the "Dads Are Unnecessary, Single Women Are Helpless Campaign," writing, "As a woman, the idea that I can't accomplish anything in life unless a male in government plans it out for me is offensive. It's amazing to me how progressives reject the oversight of the divine and the gift of free will but embrace the oppressive oversight of flawed men who reject free will. Men, too, should be offended at their lack of representation in the life of 'Julia'—the white, faceless female stereotype that the Obama administration sees as the average female voter."[25] Loesch's comments reveal that Tea Party women take issue with what they perceive as government's paternalistic assumption—that women need or want government assistance in their lives. They also worry that such programs belittle men and their role in helping women raise families. Instead, Tea Party women believe that scaling back the size and scope of government is ultimately good for American women and their families, making women more self-reliant. As the PRRI survey data show, Tea Party women are far more likely than other American women in the mass public to believe that if individuals work hard enough, they can still get ahead in American society, no matter what station in life they were born into, which helps to explain why they are more likely to believe government social safety programs are not only unnecessary, but downright damaging to women.

ObamaCare and the Birth Control Mandate

Tea Party women's opposition to an expansion of the social safety net also extends to two specific policies that dominated headlines during the 2012 presidential election: the Patient Protection and Affordable Care Act, which critics dubbed ObamaCare, and its corresponding birth control mandate. The Affordable Care Act was the widest expansion of federal government social welfare policy since the Great Society programs under LBJ.[26] President Obama, working with Democrats in Congress, passed the Affordable Care Act in 2010, with the aim of providing health care to the majority of the nation's uninsured. Based on a model first developed in Massachusetts (ironically, under Romney's leadership as governor of the state), the Affordable Care Act legislated that individuals would be required to purchase health care or face a tax penalty. It also mandated that states set up online health care exchanges to allow Americans to shop for private insurance policy, while expanding Medicaid to provide subsidies for lower-income Americans to purchase policies.[27] Requiring that businesses with more than fifty full-time employees provide health insurance coverage, the Affordable Care Act also made changes to the types of coverage that insurance companies had to provide. For example, it eliminated the ability of insurance policies to drop customers with preexisting conditions. Moreover, it mandated that health care policies provide prescribed birth control to women patients without a copayment as part of several gender-specific preventative health care services.[28]

Controversy erupted over the Obama administration's decision not to exempt certain religious nonprofit organizations, such as Catholic universities, hospitals, and charities, from the birth control mandate despite the Catholic Church's longtime opposition to the use of contraceptives. While the administration did exempt churches and houses of worship from having to comply with the mandate if they had religious objections, its initial refusal to extend this exemption to religiously affiliated organizations such as hospitals and universities deeply offended many religious leaders. Republican leaders denounced the Obama administration for not backing down on the rule, arguing that it amounted to a violation of religious liberty. Ultimately, the administration announced a series of compromise measures, first mandating that companies providing insurance for religious organizations foot the bill themselves for any contraceptive coverage for female employees, and then instituting a plan by which insurance companies would offer separate policies covering only birth control directly to employees of such organizations.

To say that the Affordable Care Act, and its corresponding birth control mandate, was opposed by Tea Party activists and Republicans is an understatement. Debate about the Affordable Care Act helped fuel the flames of the Tea Party movement in 2009: Tea Party activists jammed town hall meetings that summer to express their opposition to "ObamaCare,"[29] and prominent Republican leaders denounced the policy. While a detailed examination of the Tea Party's opposition to the Affordable Care Act and its birth control mandate is beyond the scope of this study, examination of Tea Party women activists' opposi-

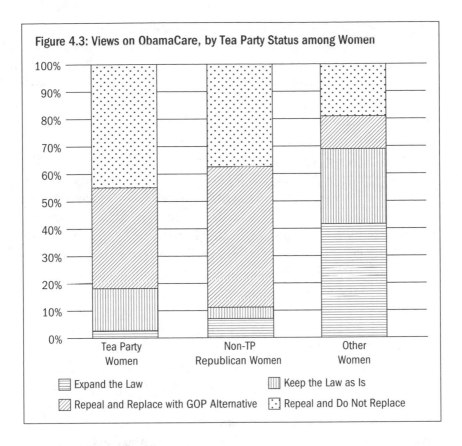

Figure 4.3: Views on ObamaCare, by Tea Party Status among Women

tion to these measures demonstrates that they think ObamaCare and its birth control mandate are bad for American women.

Nationally, American women's attitudes about ObamaCare strongly fall along party lines. In 2014 the Public Religion Research Institute queried Americans about the Affordable Care Act, asking them whether the health care law should be expanded, kept as is, repealed and replaced with a Republican alternative, or repealed and not replaced. As figure 4.3 illustrates, Tea Party women and non–Tea Party Republican women hold very different views compared to other American women: just 18 percent of Tea Party women and 11 percent of non–Tea Party Republican women believe the law should be expanded or kept as it, which contrasts sharply with a solid majority of other American women. Instead, both Tea Party women and non-TP Republican women express strong support for repealing the law, although Republican women do tend to support replacing ObamaCare with a Republican alternative (52 percent) at higher levels than do Tea Party women (37 percent). Nonetheless, when the data are grouped into two categories—support for repeal or support for expanding/keeping the law—and Tea Party status is considered alongside repealing ObamaCare while controlling for other factors, Tea Party status remains a significant predictor of opposition to the law (as does party). (See table 4.3 in appendix B for full model results.) In other words, being a member of the Tea Party makes women in the mass public significantly more likely to oppose the Affordable Care Act.

All of the Tea Party women activists I interviewed strongly opposed the Affordable Care Act. While many of them argued that ObamaCare was an unnecessary, "socialist" expansion of government that they feared would ultimately do little to control costs but instead restrict consumer choices, several used specifically gendered argumentation as to why they believed the Affordable Care Act was bad for women and families. Janice Shaw Crouse, of Concerned Women for America, believes that women will feel ObamaCare's impact disproportionately, given that the woman in the family is the one who "handles the health care decisions, and goes to the doctor and plans the doctor's appointments."[30] Her remarks echo similar concerns expressed by Republican Congresswoman Cathy McMorris Rodgers, who in an interview with Smart Girl Politics stated her belief that women's activism in the Tea Party was largely motivated by the health care reform debate: "Women make 85 percent of the healthcare decisions in their household . . . Women in America do not like the idea of the federal government getting in the way of them being able to make healthcare decisions for their families."[31]

In a study penned for CWA called "Obamanomics," Crouse elaborates on why ObamaCare is especially harmful for women and their families. She takes aim at the employer mandate, which requires employers of more than fifty employees to offer health care, arguing that the financial penalties that nonparticipating small businesses face will likely result in less hiring and that "women, employed disproportionately in small businesses, will be especially hit hard."[32] This theme was also taken up by the Republican Conference of the U.S. House of Representatives, which in a press release titled "3 Things House Republicans Are Doing for Women," argued that ObamaCare "introduced a slew of problems that hit women harder than men," including the employer mandate, which they claim is leading many companies to cut workers' hours to avoid falling under the mandate. The House GOP states that the mandate "affects women at a rate 64 percent more than male workers— meaning more women are being demoted to part-time positions instead of the full-time jobs they held before ObamaCare."[33]

Crouse also makes the case that ObamaCare effectively enforces a marriage penalty, noting that unmarried, cohabiting couples earning smaller salaries individually would be eligible for larger health care subsidies to offset the cost of insurance than they would if they combined their incomes as a married couple. She writes that the policy is a "boondoggle for older, unmarried mothers (in their 20s and 30s)" at the expense of married mothers.[34] The result for Crouse is that "instead of encouraging single mothers to marry the father of their children and to become financially independent by facilitating job growth, ObamaCare creates another avenue of dependency through health insurance subsidies."[35] CWA president Penny Young Nance, writing for Fox News, also argues that ObamaCare is bad for married women, expressing dismay that if government forces "women to pay for health care services they do not need or want . . . married women and their families will bear the brunt of ObamaCare's income redistribution." Young believes that the increased taxes embedded within the policy are especially harmful to women compared with men, "because women enter and exit the labor force more often and for longer periods of time. Furthermore, women typically have an additional 15 to 18 more years of life than our male counterparts. Citizens on Medicare and Medicaid, mostly women, will receive less, and possibly worse, care under ObamaCare than under privatized health services."[36] In this last point, Young references cuts to both programs that bill designers argue would be offset by stopping overpayments to hospitals and other wasteful spending.

The Independent Women's Forum also cites research showing that both younger and older women who need to purchase individual plans through health care exchanges will be hit especially hard by Obama-Care's individual mandate. For instance, Carrie Lukas cites a study by economists from the Wharton School that found that premiums and out-of-pocket expenses for women between the ages of fifty-five and sixty-four buying individual plans on the health care exchange, as compared to their expenses prior to passage of the Affordable Care Act, increased by 50 percent—more than any other demographic group.[37] Hadley Heath, also of IWF, cites other research that predicts women thirty years and younger who buy their own insurance will face higher premiums than those they faced prior to enactment of the law.[38] She also points to a decline in student plans offered by colleges and universities as a result of ObamaCare, leading her to quip, "Perhaps some of the 67 percent of single women who voted to reelect President Obama will feel some buyer's remorse."[39]

Writing in *Forbes* with April Ponnuru, policy director for the conservative think tank YG Network, Carrie Lukas makes the case that ObamaCare "lets women down" because many are forced to buy plans for their families that often result in changes in provider networks.[40] Noting that women, unlike men, require both a primary care physician as well as an obstetrician-gynecologist, Ponnuru and Lukas argue that ObamaCare stands to threaten long-standing relationships women have developed with their doctors: "Good doctor-patient relationships often take years to form and they are not easily remade. But many women will have a very difficult time finding an ObamaCare plan that covers the two or more doctors that they require, because physician networks are being narrowed dramatically by many ObamaCare plans in an effort to keep costs down. Hospitals are being cut out, too. The upshot: many women are losing their access to first-rate care they have come to expect."[41] Fear of unwanted changes to their health insurance was a major concern that drove many women to become active in the Tea Party, at least according to Eagle Forum's Colleen Holcomb: "Health care was huge. As a woman of childbearing age, I certainly don't want to go into labor under Obama-Care in this state-run hospital. Who wants to sit in waiting rooms for two hours more than you have to? So there was this general sense that our whole way of life was under attack and was only going to get worse."[42]

Conservative women activists were also put off by the Affordable Care Act's birth control mandate. For some Tea Party women, their opposition to the mandate stemmed from religious convictions. Describing the birth control mandate as an "outrageous interference of religious liberty," conservative icon Phyllis Schlafly argued that ObamaCare includes "birth control, the morning-after pill (an abortion drug), and sterilization, at zero cost to the individual without any additional premium, co-pay, or out-of-pocket expense. And yes, this mandate does apply to religious hospitals, schools, colleges, and charities, even though their religion teaches them that these acts are immoral and wrong."[43] Even conservative women from secular organizations, such as Hadley Heath from IWF, joined forces with more religiously minded conservative activists to oppose the mandate based on liberty concerns. At a Heritage Foundation panel discussion about the mandate, Heath remarked that despite working for a secular organization, IWF believes "that individual liberties—like religious liberty—are vital to a free and flourishing country, and therefore we strongly oppose the most recent HHS mandate under discussion today."[44] Another conservative blogger, Rachel Bjorklund, described the birth control mandate in much starker terms on her blog, *Thoughts from a Conservative Mom*: "This isn't about birth control or women's choices or religion. This is about an elite ruling class who believe they can abuse unconstitutional powers to tell private citizens and organizations what to buy and sell, and at what price, and how, and to whom. We can't allow our liberties to be stripped away without a fight."[45]

Still other Tea Party women took issue with what they perceived as a bait and switch from the Obama administration, claiming that Obama-Care's stipulations that provide free, preventative health services for women, such as no-cost prescription birth control and free annual wellness exams, were in actuality anything but "free." Take for instance, the following point from CWA's Brenda Zurita: "When ObamaCare supporters tout the preventive health care services now mandated, especially for women, they fail to mention that somewhere along the line you are, in fact, going to pay for those, whether you use them or not. The charge will not be the day you receive those services, but they will be paid for with a higher deductible, higher premiums, and higher co-pay amounts. They might be paid for by the exclusion of another health service you actually use."[46] This line of thinking was echoed by Phyllis Schafly, who claimed that the Obama administration's compromise offer to allow employees of religiously affiliated organizations to purchase insurance for birth control separately was simply a red herring: "It's obvious that insurance companies will distribute and conceal the costs so nobody appears to be paying for the controversial procedures."[47]

Similar to their opposition to an expanded social safety net, some Tea Party women viewed the birth control mandate as yet another overreaching, paternalistic government handout. Said Tami Nantz of Smart Girl Politics, "I can't buy a four-dollar pack of birth control myself? Big Daddy Government has to provide that for me? I resent that. I don't want anybody thinking that I expect taxpayers to take care of me."[48] Moreover, Smart Girl Politics president Stacy Mott said that the birth control mandate was essentially a distraction from the more pressing issues women faced, in part because she believed this social issue was not as critical to women's well-being as were economic issues. She argued that the job of Smart Girl Politics was to "turn the conversation" around from birth control and social issues, and instead discuss how fiscal issues were more important to women's well-being, claiming, "The financial issues impact *everyone*. And you may have your beliefs on the social issues [such as the birth control mandate], but the bottom line is, the odds are that they are not directly impacting you."[49]

As these comments make clear, Tea Party women activists were outspoken critics of the birth control mandate. Nationally, Tea Party women in the mass public were the least likely among other American women to support the birth control mandate according to the 2012 American Values Survey: 31 percent of Tea Party women, followed closely by 35 percent of non–Tea Party Republican women, expressed support for the policy, compared to more than two-thirds (69 percent) of other American women (see figure 4.4). When controlling for other factors, however, Tea Party status does not remain a statistically significant predictor of attitudes about the birth control mandate among women. (See table 4.3 in appendix B for full model results.) Instead, partisanship, ideology, and religious factors shape women's attitudes about the birth control mandate. In particular, Democratic women appear to care more about this issue than do either Republicans or Independents. Church attendance negatively affects women's attitudes about the birth control mandate, as does holding more conservative ideological viewpoints.

The finding that Tea Party status does not predict attitudes about the birth control mandate may be a bit of a surprise given that women activists within the movement uniformly denounced it. Perhaps part of this reason is that even Tea Party women express nearly universal support for the use of birth control: PRRI's 2012 American Values Survey found that 85 percent of Tea Party women find the use of birth control to be "morally acceptable," and this is a rate similar to that of non–Tea

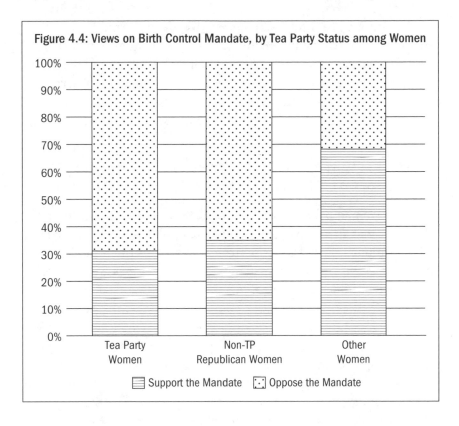

Figure 4.4: Views on Birth Control Mandate, by Tea Party Status among Women

Party Republicans and other American women.[50] Nonetheless, the lack of significance of Tea Party status in the full regression model indicates one instance in which self-identified Tea Party women nationally find this political issue to be less salient than do movement leaders. Instead, the more important drivers of attitudes on the birth control mandate among American women are religion and ideology—not identification with the Tea Party. Indeed, traditional Religious Right organizations, such as the Family Research Council, and longer-standing conservative religious women's organizations, including Eagle Forum and Conservative Women of America, emphasized the religious liberty angle of the birth control mandate debate more than the economics of the issue, which was a dominant frame employed by more secular conservative women's groups such as the Independent Women's Forum or newer Tea Party groups such as Smart Girl Politics. The statistical analysis shows that the religious liberty rhetoric may have been more effective at influencing the attitudes of conservative, devout American women regarding the birth control mandate than the economic rhetoric employed by Tea Party women's groups, given that ideology and religiosity are significant predictors of such attitudes. These findings also serve as a good reminder that Tea Party women in the mass public may not necessarily adopt all of the positions put forth by movement leaders.

The Scope of Government: Government Regulation of the Economy and Work/Family Balance Issues

Tea Party women believe that the social safety net has grown too large and worry that an expansion of government policies, although perhaps well intentioned, is bad for American women and their families. Not surprisingly, this opposition extends to ObamaCare as well, although attitudes about the birth control mandate are more mixed: my qualitative analysis shows that Tea Party women activists routinely denounced the mandate, while my analysis of national survey data finds that Tea Party status is not a significant predictor of birth control mandate opposition among women in the mass public. Instead, ideology and religion appear to be the driving factors in explaining attitudes about the birth control mandate. Next, I consider Tea Party women's attitudes about other aspects of the regulatory state. More specifically, I examine how Tea Party women feel about government regulation of the economy, and in particular, economic regulations that are often touted by *progressive* women leaders as being necessary for women to alleviate poverty, minimize their wage gap with men, and help them achieve a better balance between their work and family lives.

Turning first to attitudes about taxes and the role of tax cuts in stimulating economic growth, the 2014 American Values Survey shows that Tea Party women in the mass public (57 percent) and non–Tea Party Republican women (50 percent) are far more likely to oppose raising taxes on the most wealthy Americans—those earning more than $250,000 a year annually—than are other American women (31 percent) (see figure 4.5a). The relationship between Tea Party status and women's attitudes is statistically significant once additional controls are taken into consideration,[51] as is partisanship. White women and self-identified conservative women also are more likely to oppose raising taxes than are other

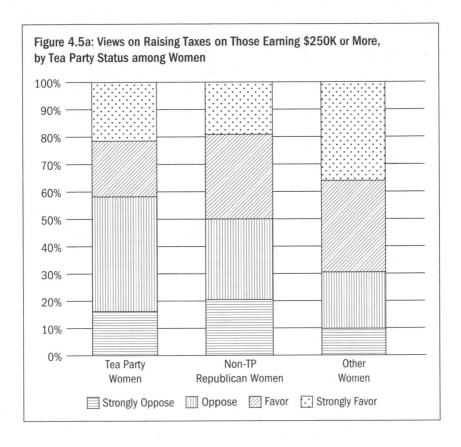

Figure 4.5a: Views on Raising Taxes on Those Earning $250K or More, by Tea Party Status among Women

women. (See table 4.4 in appendix B for full model results.) Moreover, when asked whether they believe economic growth would be best promoted by either "lower[ing] taxes on individuals and businesses and pay[ing] for those tax cuts by cutting spending on some government services and programs" or "spend[ing] more on education and the nation's infrastructure and rais[ing] taxes on wealthy individuals and businesses to pay for that spending," 64 percent of Tea Party women, along with 67 percent of non-TP Republican women, choose lowering taxes, compared to just one-third of other American women (see figure 4.5b). Again, once controlling for other factors, Tea Party status remains a statistically significant predictor of attitudes on economic growth: women who are part of the Tea Party (as well as Republican women) are more likely to believe that cutting both taxes and spending on government programs will spur economic growth. (See table 4.4 in appendix B for

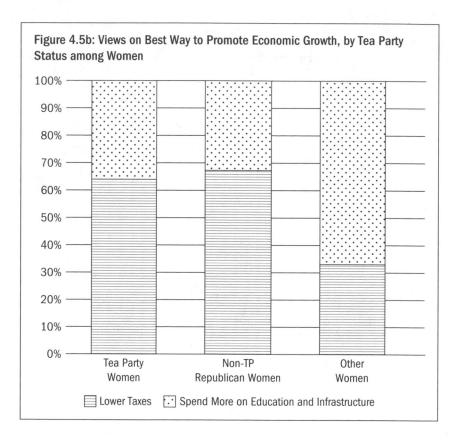

Figure 4.5b: Views on Best Way to Promote Economic Growth, by Tea Party Status among Women

full model results.) Additionally, ideology, income, age, southern residency, and religion also play a significant role in explaining women's attitudes about what best promotes economic growth.

That Tea Party women hold more conservative attitudes about taxes should come as little surprise given that Tea Party leaders such as Michele Bachmann (2014) often describe their movement as the "Taxed Enough Already" (TEA) Party. Adhering to free market philosophy, Tea Party activists are both quick to espouse that taxes are wasteful and economically inefficient, and often express profound distrust of the Internal Revenue Service.[52] While most of the Tea Party women I interviewed opposed taxes on economic principle, several did use gendered rhetoric to explain their hostility to taxes. As the last chapter demonstrated, Mama Grizzlies sometimes voice their opposition to taxes as part of a larger motherhood theme that promotes their political activism as "kitchen table" conservatives. Similar to moms whose families have to stay within their means, these Mama Grizzlies argue that the federal government should cut its spending and stop burdening families with onerous taxes to pay for programs they don't support.

Some Tea Party women, however, also believe that women's growing role in the economy, whether as small-business owners or as their families' breadwinners, may be leading more women to oppose taxes, especially single mothers. Whitney Neal, formerly of FreedomWorks and herself a single mother, notes that women may be looking at their family finances anew: "You do see a lot more single Moms out there right now. With the economy the way it has been, the Dad has lost his job and the Mom is out there. We see our role in the family as changing because we have women saying, 'Whoa, wait a minute. Why does this much of my check go in taxes? What is this going toward?'"[53] This theme is echoed by Republican strategist and pollster Kristen Soltis Anderson, who notes that there are lots of women who are becoming "financially self-sufficient and independent, who are starting their own businesses, even if it is something as simple as they are a stay-at-home mom who is making her own fun crafts on Etsy and she is selling them online." As a result, she believes many women are now discovering for the first time the heavy taxes and regulatory hoops placed on business owners, which provides for conservatives a "huge opportunity" with women "for a Republican message about how it is unconscionable, the [tax] burdens we place on people who just want to do something as simple as sell a few products online."[54]

Other conservative activists note, as they do about ObamaCare, that current tax policy enforces a marriage penalty, as married couples are often taxed at a higher rate when they file jointly. In their book *Liberty Is No War on Women*, the Independent Women Forum's Carrie Lukas and Sabrina Schaeffer make the case that such tax policies disproportionately hurt married women compared with single women: "Married women, for example, face some of the highest tax rates because they are often the second earner in the family, which means that the first dollar they earn is taxed at their husband's top rate. Those high marginal tax rates discourage some married women from going to work, leaving them with less work experience, which can be a real hardship in the event of divorce or widowhood."[55] Moreover, they add that such higher taxes may also push women who prefer to stay at home into the workplace, since "one after-tax salary isn't enough to make ends meet."[56] As a result, conservative women's organizations, such as the Independent Women's Forum, along with other conservative political groups, such as the Heritage Foundation, the Family Research Council, and the Cato Institute, call for tax cuts for families and the removal of "marriage penalties" in the tax code. Phyllis Schafly goes even further, writing on the Eagle Forum website that political leaders should eliminate "the sections of the tax code that reward non-marriage with lower taxes" and that "family allowances and child credits should be reserved for married parents who are raising their own children."[57]

While not as extreme as Schlafly's approach, the Republican Party has begun tapping its prominent female members in Congress to cosponsor and speak out on behalf of tax legislation specifically geared at married families with children. Writing in the *Washington Examiner*, Republican Representatives Lynn Jenkins (KS) and Diane Black (TN) discussed why they introduced legislation that would "help parents keep more of their hard-earned money to use for the mounting expenses of parents and help save for the costs of a college education."[58] In the Child Tax Credit Improvement Act, these congresswomen called for expanding the current $1,000 child tax credit by adjusting it for inflation, which has not been done since 2004, and by removing the marriage penalty embedded in the current tax credit, by increasing "the income level at which the child credit begins to phase out from $110,000 to $150,000 for married couples—which is twice the level for single filers."[59] Moreover, in July 2014 Representative Cathy McMorris Rodgers led a GOP press conference on the steps of the Capitol Building to tout the Child Tax Credit Improvement Act and other bills they argued would empower women, noting that women manage more than 80 percent of the household income and start two out of three new businesses.[60]

Support for conservative economic policies does not stop at tax cuts or tax credits, however, among Tea Party women. As figure 4.6 demonstrates, Tea Party women are the group of women (50 percent) most likely to oppose or strongly oppose raising the minimum wage to $10.00 per hour, which stands in stark contrast to the 18 percent of other American women who strongly oppose or oppose raising the minimum wage. Once again controlling for other factors in a multivariate model,[61] Tea

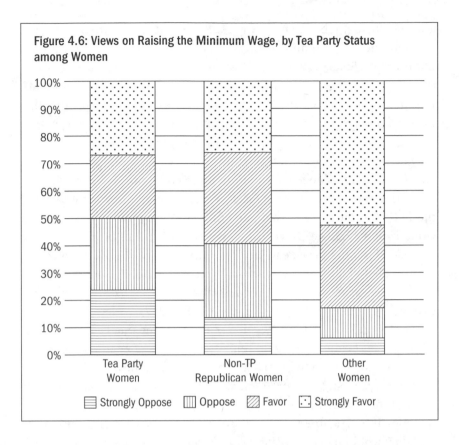

Figure 4.6: Views on Raising the Minimum Wage, by Tea Party Status among Women

Party status remains a significant predictor of attitudes among American women when it comes to the minimum wage. (See table 4.5 in appendix B for full model results.) Although it is notable that half of Tea Party women actually *favored* raising the minimum wage, their support still falls short of the nationwide average: PRRI data show that 69 percent of Americans favor increasing the minimum wage from $7.25 per hour to $10.10 per hour.[62] However, Tea Party women's mixed attitudes in the mass public about the minimum wage demonstrate that there are economic arenas in which self-identified Tea Party members nationally may not march in lockstep with national Tea Party leaders or libertarian policy experts.

Indeed, organizations such as the Cato Institute, the Heritage Foundation, and FreedomWorks strongly denounce the minimum wage as an unnecessary intrusion into the free market, which they believe does a more efficient job at setting wages. Such arguments often find their way into the language and writings of Tea Party women's organizations. For example, Smart Girl Politics features numerous blog writings about the minimum wage that draw heavily from such libertarian arguments. Brandi Frey, writing on the Smart Girl Politics blog, maintains that that minimum-wage jobs are meant to provide a stepping-stone to higher paying jobs and should not be made into a career. She argues that calls for raising the minimum wage, while compassionate on their face, hurt Americans in that "skilled citizens are priced out of the labor market because this rate is set by some faceless government bureaucrat and not the initial productivity of that person."[63] SGP's Elizabeth Vale cites the Congressional Budget Office's 2014 analysis of Obama's proposal to raise the federal minimum wage to $10.10, noting that the study estimates that such a policy change would result in the loss of about five hundred thousand low-wage jobs as business owners would be saddled with higher expenses.[64] Julie Borowski, policy analyst at FreedomWorks, also posted a blog entry on Smart Girl Politics Action maintaining that very few people with families below the poverty line earned wages at or below $10.00 an hour. Instead, most individuals earning the minimum wage do not work full-time, are young, and/or are unskilled workers.[65] She points out that some of these workers are, in fact, "mothers that are entering the workforce for the first time to provide second income to their household," and they would most likely be most susceptible to layoffs.

Further tying minimum-wage hikes to the detriment of women, Carrie Lukas of the Independent Women's Forum argues that efforts by congressional Democrats to raise the minimum wage as "part of their agenda for women" are disingenuous. She writes that politicians who promote increasing the minimum wage "make it sound as if those making minimum wage are heads of households working full-time throughout their working lives to support their families. However, that's not an accurate picture of minimum-wage workers or their typical work experience."[66] Instead, she notes that most minimum-wage workers either work part-time or work these jobs at entry-level, and that most are able to "climb the economic ladder" and receive pay raises so that they are earning more than the minimum wage within a year of work. Moreover, she contends that women will be especially hurt by a federal minimum-wage increase, citing studies estimating that such a hike will result in job losses, particularly in the part-time sector. In *Forbes* Lukas writes, "Women also account for nearly two-thirds (about 63 percent) of part-time workers, and part-time workers are more likely to earn the minimum wage. As the minimum wage goes up, these women may find that their part-time jobs are cut and consolidated. That's bad news for those who had sought out a part time schedule to balance their work and family responsibilities."[67]

Instead, free market conservatives maintain that there are better ways to address low wages and stem poverty among low-skilled women. Rachel DiCarlo Currie, a senior fellow at IWF, believes the government should expand the Earned Income Tax Credit, in which the government provides lower-income Americans with a refundable credit on their federal income taxes if their adjusted gross income falls below a certain amount, instead of raising the minimum wage. (In 2014, for example, a married couple with two children who earned less than $49,000 were eligible for a tax credit of approximately $5,460 according to the IRS.)[68] Although she believes the policy is far from perfect, Currie maintains that expanding the EITC is far preferable to increasing the minimum wage, given that "the credit lifts millions of Americans above the poverty line by incentivizing them to work and then augmenting their wages."[69] Moreover, Carrie Lukas argues that although they have their own drawbacks, direct aid to struggling families in the form of food stamps and Medicaid are preferable to increasing the minimum wage as they "have the virtue of doing less to distort the employment market." Ultimately, free market conservatives believe policies that raise the costs of hiring for employers are ultimately counterproductive and that creating more jobs is the ultimate solution to poverty.

Opposition to raising employers' costs also unites conservative women against government policy that would provide paid sick and parental leave for their employees. Many progressive women's organizations, such as the National Organization for Women (NOW), routinely note that the United States stands apart from other developed nations because it lacks such policies for workers. As a result, many American families, they contend, must "choose between their paycheck and caring for their families" in moments of health crises.[70] NOW argues that "improving current paid sick leave and paid family leave" would disproportionately help women, "especially those who are heads of households and primary caretakers." MomsRising, an online advocacy group that works to "achieve economic security for all families," lists paid family leave as among its top policy priorities.[71] MomsRising maintains that paid family leave not only combats poverty, but also lowers the wage gap between women and men by "providing structural support to balance work and family."[72] The group's promotion of family-friendly policies also extends to paid sick leave, arguing that "even Super Moms can't fight all germs!" Moms-Rising notes that lack of sick pay has the largest impact on low-wage workers, 80 percent of whom do not currently qualify for sick leave.[73]

Not surprisingly, conservative economic groups, including Smart Girl Politics and the Independent Women's Forum, do not look kindly on such policies, instead viewing them as yet more costs to be incurred by businesses and potentially hurting women more than helping them. For instance, Sabrina Schaeffer, IWF executive director, writes about her opposition to the proposed FAMILY Act (or Family and Medical Insurance Leave Act), introduced in Congress in 2014 by Democratic Senator Kirsten Gillibrand and Democratic Representative Rosa DeLauro. Modeled after paid leave programs run in New Jersey and California, the FAMILY Act would create an independent trust fund funded by employee and employer contributions of 0.2 percent of wages—similar to Social Security—that would provide up to three months of partial paid family leave to Americans who qualify based on employment history and contribution status.[74] Deriding it as the "enemy of flexibility and workplace opportunity," Schaeffer maintains that the FAMILY Act may, in fact, lead employers to be less likely to hire women:

> Not only would this program require its own dedicated payroll tax, and likely encourage many private companies to do away with existing leave policies, but it would also encourage businesses to avoid hiring women (particularly of childbearing age). Businesses would have good reasons to assume that such women are likely to take leave for several months' time, with no ability to negotiate partial-work arrangements that benefit both worker and employer. In the long run, women would become costlier and more difficult to employ. The result would be fewer opportunities— particularly leadership opportunities—as a result.[75]

Schaeffer argues that such policies are unnecessary, as many private companies are offering more generous leave packages and flexible schedules than ever before in response to the demands of working parents and to recruit and retain top professionals. Ultimately, Schaeffer maintains that the best solution for women to balance work and family life is a robust economy, so that "women can look for another employer and have a greater range of employment opportunities" if they are unsatisfied with their current job and the benefits it allows.[76]

Tea Party women in Congress have sought ways to legislate more workplace flexibility while remaining steadfastly opposed to paid leave policies. For instance, Representative Martha Roby, an Alabama Republican elected as part of the Tea Party wave in 2010, introduced the Working Families Flexibility Act in 2013, a bill that would allow private-sector workers to receive "comp" or paid time off instead of cash wages for overtime—a policy that is legal for public-sector employees but remains restricted by federal law for the private sector according to the Fair Labor Standards Act. As Roby stated in a press release, she believes her bill would strongly appeal to women: "As a working mom, this bill is personal to me. I understand the time demands on working families, including children's activities, caring for aging parents or even a spouse's military deployment. It only makes sense that our laws governing the workplace catch up to the realities of today's families. The Working Families Flexibility Act would finally offer Americans working in the private sector what their peers in the public sector already enjoy— more freedom and more control over their time."[77] As reported by USA Today, House Republicans purchased a $20,000 ad buy on more than one hundred websites frequented by women, such as MarthaStewart.com, to promote the bill, micro-targeting the ads so that they would be viewed by residents in various swing districts nationally. Viewers who saw the ad were encouraged to contact their Democratic representatives and tell them to support the bill, hyperlinking to a petition website that told lawmakers to "support more freedom for working moms."[78] Democrats opposed the measure, arguing that despite GOP assurances that such a policy would be purely voluntary on the part of employees, they feared that as written the bill would allow employers to withhold pay for overtime work or cut workers' hours.[79] Moreover, the progressive organization National Partnership for Women and Families (2013) argued

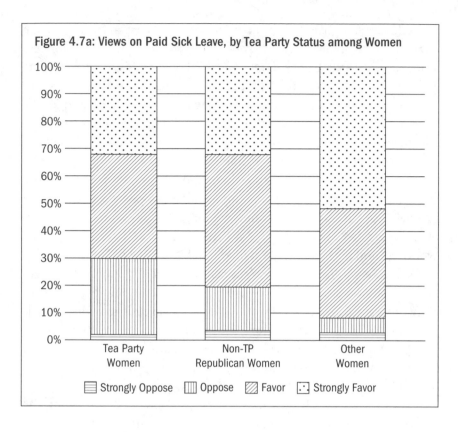

Figure 4.7a: Views on Paid Sick Leave, by Tea Party Status among Women

that the bill as written does not guarantee employees the opportunity to use comp time when they want to use it, and that it incentivizes employers to give overtime hours to employees as opposed to overtime pay as a cost-saving measure. Instead, the National Partnership advocates for increasing the minimum wage and legislation that would allow for paid sick days in addition to legislation comparable to Senator Kirsten Gillibrand's FAMILY Act.

When it comes to national public opinion on family leave and paid sick leave, however, far more American women support these initiatives than oppose them, *including* Tea Party women in the mass public and non–Tea Party Republican women. According to the 2014 PRRI American Values Survey, 69 percent of Tea Party women, 78 percent of non-TP Republican women, and a whopping 92 percent of other American women either favor or strongly favor paid sick leave (see figure 4.7a). Support for paid family leave is similarly high among all three categories

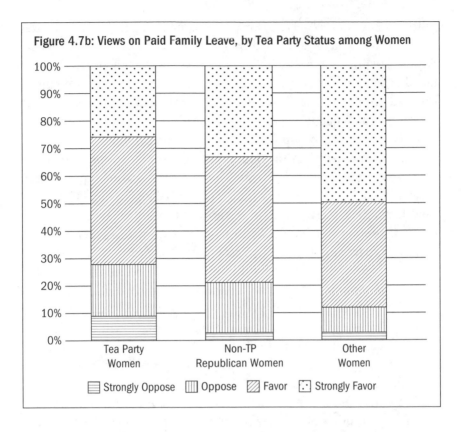

Figure 4.7b: Views on Paid Family Leave, by Tea Party Status among Women

of American women: 72 percent of Tea Party women, 81 percent of non-TP Republican women, and 88 percent of other American women favor or strongly favor paid family leave (see figure 4.7b). Regression analyses do demonstrate that Tea Party women hold distinct attitudes on paid sick leave, being significantly less likely to support the policy than other American women while controlling for other factors, but not when it comes to supporting paid family leave. (See table 4.6 in appendix B for full model results.) Yet strong majorities of Tea Party women nationally support both policies. Comparable to attitudes on the birth control mandate and the minimum wage, paid leave appears to be another area in which Tea Party women do not necessarily march in lockstep with Republican leaders or conservative women policy wonks.

Lastly, Smart Girl Politics and the Independent Women's Forum, as well as most prominent Republican women, also denounce efforts geared at pay equity concerns for women, including the Lilly Ledbetter Fair Pay Act, which was signed by President Obama in 2009, and the Paycheck Fairness Act, which was sponsored by Democratic leaders but failed to pass the Senate in 2012 and 2014. The Ledbetter Act, which was featured prominently in "The Life of Julia" infographic during Obama's reelection campaign, was passed by congressional Democrats in 2009 in response to a 2007 Supreme Court decision brought by Ledbetter, a manager at a tire plant in Alabama who sued her former employer, Goodyear Tires, when she learned she had been earning far less than male managers for the same work for decades. The Supreme Court denied Ledbetter's claim that she be allowed to sue for pay discrimination because she failed to file a formal complaint with a federal agency within 180 days after her pay was established, as mandated by the Civil Rights Act, despite the fact that Ledbetter did not learn of the pay disparity until years later.[80] Democrats in Congress worked to amend the law in 2009 to reset the 180 days to file a claim with each discriminatory paycheck, which was the first piece of legislation signed by President Barack Obama. Republicans in Congress largely voted against the measure, claiming that the bill does little to stem pay discrimination but instead is a boon to trial lawyers.[81]

Democrats did not stop with the Ledbetter Act, however. Barbara Mikulski and other Senate Democrats have sponsored the Paycheck Fairness Act for several years, which seeks to amend current federal law that bans gender-based wage discrimination. The legislation would close certain loopholes in the 1963 Equal Pay Act—which currently requires employers to pay women and men the same amount for the same job—by allowing workers to share information about salaries without threat of losing their jobs or other retaliation by their employers. As Mikulski (2014) stated on the Senate floor in defense of the bill before it failed to pass in 2014:

> The Lilly Ledbetter bill that we passed restored the law to where it was before the Supreme Court's decision. The *Paycheck Fairness Act* updates and strengthens it. It deals with the whole issue of retaliation. The Lilly Ledbetter bill did not address employers who are currently able to legally retaliate against workers who share salary information. The *Paycheck Fairness Act* would stop employers from being able to sue or punish

workers for comparing their wages. It also helps restore Congressional intent, which is to change how discrimination cases are litigated. And it makes sure that employers who claim that differences in pay are based on something other than sex are dealt with.[82]

Democratic leaders and progressive women's organizations, including MomsRising, the National Women's Law Center, and the National Organization for Women, support the Paycheck Fairness Act as a way to help eradicate sex discrimination and to close the wage gap between men and women, which, according to the White House, resulted in full-time working women earning just seventy-seven cents on average for every dollar that a full-time working man earned in 2014.[83] Again, Republican leaders and conservative organizations believe the Paycheck Fairness Act is misguided, raising the costs of doing business while doing little to eradicate the wage gap, which in their minds is greatly exaggerated.

Opposition to both the Lilly Ledbetter Act and the Paycheck Fairness Act by Republican women and conservative women activists does not mean that either constituency believes that sex discrimination has been wholly eradicated in the United States—as I demonstrate in the next chapter on Tea Party women's views about feminism, a majority of Tea Party women and non–Tea Party Republican women according to data from the Public Religion Research Institute agree that sex discrimination is still a problem in American society. Unfortunately, PRRI has not polled nationally on the questions of support for the Lilly Ledbetter Act and the Paycheck Fairness Act. However, many Tea Party groups and Republican women take issue with legislative solutions to eradicate sex discrimination proposed by Democrats and with the very idea that a pay gap between men and women necessarily represents such discrimination.

Prominent Republican women leaders who voted against the Lilly Ledbetter Act toed the party line as to why they voted against a bill that would remove the statute of limitations to sue for back pay—namely, that the law would result in unnecessary litigation. In an interview with *Glamour* magazine, for instance, Republican Representative Cathy McMorris Rodgers, while insisting that she and the GOP support equal pay for equal work, said she voted against the Ledbetter Act because it was "more of a treasure chest for trial lawyers."[84] Additionally, conservative women activists, including those from the Independent Women's Forum, also opposed the measure, including Charlotte Hays, director of cultural programs at the IWF. When discussing the role of women's issues in the 2012 presidential campaign, Hays told a conservative news website that "a better name for the Lilly Ledbetter Act would be the Tort Lawyers Full Employment Act."[85] Moreover, many conservative women argue that the Ledbetter Act does nothing to protect women against gender-based discrimination, nor does it, as IWF's Sabrina Schaeffer points out, "actually create equal pay . . . it simply extends the 180-day statute of limitations for filing an equal-pay discrimination suit established under Title VII of the 1964 Civil Rights Act."[86] In 2014, conservative women in Texas were quick to denounce a call by Democratic gubernatorial candidate Wendy Davis for a state version of the Lilly Ledbetter Fair Pay Act using similar logic. The executive director of the GOP in Texas, Beth Cubriel, criticized the proposal by Davis, asking in an interview with an Austin television news station, "Is it really fair to clog up the courts with litigation that you can take through another avenue and put that ahead of litigation that can only go through the state courts?" Instead, she encouraged women to become "better negotiators" in terms of salary grievances instead of "pursuing the courts for action."[87]

Tea Party women hold similar reservations about the Paycheck Fairness Act, which they believe would do little to stem pay disparities between men and women. Conservatives take issue with the proposed law's stipulation that employers must justify wage differentials between men and women with bona fide factors such as education, training, or experience. According Elizabeth Vale of Smart Girl Politics, "If a company can't prove that a female employee is earning less due to one of the above three factors, the company is '*liable in a civil action*' and the bill '*authorizes the Secretary of Labor to seek additional compensatory or punitive damages in a sex discrimination action*.'"[88] Vale argues that this stipulation would prove onerous to companies, which would be "at the mercy of the federal government" by having to document each reason given to workers for their salaries and wages. Rachel Greszler of the Heritage Foundation also argues that the bill would make it more difficult for employers to pay workers according to their merit.[89] Moreover, she contends that the law would have the perverse of effect of reducing employment opportunities for women. Facing the prospect of "frivolous class-action suits" that would effectively allow "lawyers to second-guess employers' business calculations," she contends that the Paycheck Fairness Act would "discourage business owners from selecting female job applicants, reducing women's opportunities and choices in the workplace."[90]

Prominent Republican women in Congress argue not only that the Paycheck Fairness Act would promote unnecessary litigation but also that it is simply redundant. Republican Senator Susan Collins (ME), who voted against the Paycheck Fairness Act in 2014, told the *Huffington Post* that current legislation, including the Equal Pay Act, the Civil Rights Act, and the Lilly Ledbetter Act, "provide adequate protections" for women who face sex discrimination in pay. She believes the Paycheck Fairness Act would "result in excessive litigation that would impose a real burden, particularly on small businesses."[91] Kelly Ayotte, Republican senator from New Hampshire, also voted against the bill, telling *Politico* that current legislation that bans sex discrimination should be better enforced. She also expressed concerns that the Paycheck Fairness Act could make it more difficult for employers to pay based on merit. She added, "And obviously I think it's self-evident that I'm for women receiving equal pay. In fact, I'd like them to be paid more."[92]

Collins, Ayotte, and Senator Lisa Murkowski (R-AK)—all of whom faced notable public scrutiny when they voted against the 2014 Pay Equity bill—joined with Republican Senator Deb Fischer of Nebraska to offer a conservative amendment to the Paycheck Fairness Act, which was ultimately unsuccessful. While dropping the controversial bona fide business rationale language, the amendment still would have would have prohibited retaliation against employees who request information about or discuss their salaries. Discussing the amendment in an op-ed for *Politico*, Fischer argued that their amendment would also "reinforce employers' obligations to fully apprise employees of their rights regarding pay discrimination."[93] By arming women with knowledge about their rights, according to Fischer, their proposal would equip "women who might otherwise be unaware of their ability to recover lost wages."[94] The amendment also pledged to commit existing federal grant funding to train women (and men) in underrepresented—and more lucrative— sectors of the economy that require more worker training, including manufacturing, energy, transportation and logistics, information technology, and health care.[95]

Fischer's *Politico* op-ed also calls into question the basic premise underlying pay equity proposals such as the Paycheck Fairness Act—that women's wage gap with men is based solely on discrimination. As Fischer states, "Much has been made recently of the difference in men and women's average salaries. I believe—and reports prepared for the U.S. Department of Labor confirm—that commonly used 'wage gap' statistics don't tell the full story. Factors including differences in occupation, education, fields of study, type of work, hours worked and other personal choices shape career paths and earning potential. Moreover, salaries alone don't account for total compensation." Fischer's arguments echo similar themes first raised by conservative women activists who routinely denounce federal government efforts to stem the pay gap between men and women. Prominent conservative women activists such as Christina Hoff Sommers, a resident scholar at the American Enterprise Institute, and Carrie Lukas and Sabrina Schaeffer of the Independent Women's Forum, have long maintained that the wage gap is a product of women's choices in terms of what they study in school, what career paths they find more appealing (and which happen to pay less), and their desire for more flexible work hours compared with men.[96] Writing in the *New York Times*, Sommers points to research showing that women are more likely to leave the workforce than men to take care of children or older parents, and thus place a higher preference on having flexible work hours, often in exchange for lower salaries.[97] Once these factors are controlled for, Sommers says economic studies show that the pay gap between men and women narrows dramatically.

Sabrina Schaeffer also rejects claims by liberal feminist groups that the current wage gap is largely a product of discrimination faced by women in the workforce. As Schaeffer puts it, "Choices—not widespread discrimination—explain the small pay disparity between men and women. But choices are a function of a woman's freedom, not an injustice imposed on her by society."[98] Krista Kafer, a senior fellow with the IWF, also opposes the Paycheck Fairness Act, writing that it is unnecessary because "women are not hapless victims but are intelligent decision-makers balancing work and life's demands."[99] Of course, liberal feminist groups take issue with this claim by conservative groups, arguing that women's choices are still "fraught with inequities" given the widespread sexist stereotypes that women face in society.[100] Moreover, liberal feminist critics say that the "choice rhetoric" often employed by conservative groups tends to divert attention from "oppressive social systems and focuses on the individual, avoiding the more difficult to tackle and achieve systemic change necessary in struggles for gender equality."[101] Nonetheless, Sabrina Schaeffer points to Pew Social Trends data from 2013 that show that women are for more likely than men to value workplace flexibility over higher pay—70 percent to 46 percent, respectively—and that relatively few married American working mothers—just 23 percent—would work full-time if they had the choice, all of which counters liberal feminists' claims that their solutions are what most women seek.[102] Schaeffer and other conservative women fear that legislation such as the Paycheck Fairness Act would actually limit workplace options that best meet the needs of women and their families. Rachel Greszler of the Heritage Foundation writes, "As a working mother, flexibility is a crucial component of my job. Sick days, doctor appointments, and snow days when school and daycare are closed all take time away from work. There are also accommodations and benefits such as teleworking, 'pregnancy parking,' and paid maternity leave. The value I place on these benefits and my use of them is reflected in the paycheck I negotiated to receive. The Paycheck Fairness Act would restrict the availability of such personalized, flexible work arrangements for women and men alike."[103] Instead, Tea Party women believe feminists should embrace free enterprise principles, as they believe the free market is the best way to expand the opportunities and job benefits for both women *and* men. In fact, they point to studies showing that "young, childless, single urban women" now earn more than their male colleagues do, mainly due to education differences, as evidence that the free market will ultimately provide salaries that are fair and nondiscriminatory. They also believe that a truly functioning free market, with expanded job growth, would allow women who are underpaid to seek new jobs that would "pay them according to their worth." Or, as GOP pollster Kristen Soltis Anderson told me, an unregulated free market would "be paying women the same as men and economic liberty would empower women more than a government program."[104] At the end of the day, Tea Party women worry that legislative efforts that seek to address pay equity perpetuate the notion that women, according to Sabrina Schaeffer, are a "victim class in need of special protections from government."[105]

Tea Party women also accuse congressional Democrats and President Obama of backing equal pay legislation, and of harping on the pay gap between men and women, purely for political ends. The Republican National Committee issued a press release from RNC Women in April 2014, shortly before the Senate voted on the Paycheck Fairness Act, in which they described the bill as a "desperate political ploy," claiming that the Democrats are resorting to this measure as they "don't have other issues to run on."[106] RNC Women criticized Democrats in the Senate for failing to consider "any of the 40 jobs bills the Republican House has sent them." Elizabeth Vale, writing on the Smart Girl Politics blog, also bemoaned the Paycheck Fairness Act and other wage gap actions by President Obama as pure political propaganda, claiming that Democrats are trying to extend the "War on Women" campaign theme they used to great effect in the 2012 elections. Vale points to an Executive Order issued by Obama on April 8, 2014, which extends the regulations proposed by the Paycheck Fairness Act to federal contractors, as advancing "the narrative that President Obama had to go around the Republican-run Congress to get something done about equal pay."[107] In Vale's opinion, such a move allows liberal Democrats and progressive women's organizations to continue the narrative that "Republicans hate women, Democrats love women—got that?"[108]

In short, Tea Party and Republican women promote a series of economic policies that stand in stark contrast to policies championed by progressive women's organizations and Democrats in Congress. While liberal women believe that raising the minimum wage, providing workers with paid and sick leave, and equipping women with more legal tools to fight sex discrimination in pay would help women, particularly on the lower end of the economic spectrum, conservative women counter that such policies—while seemingly well-intentioned—actually end up being more harmful to women and limit their choices. They believe that such policies are essentially political in nature, allowing Democrats to portray Republicans, and conservatives more broadly, as hostile to women's needs. Instead, they champion free market solutions as being best for women in the long run.

The Message Challenge for Tea Party Women

The qualitative and quantitative analysis shows that Tea Party women, along with their fellow Republican sisters, largely hold distinct attitudes about the scope and size of government compared with most American women. That such women hold conservative economic positions is not surprising given their affiliation with a movement and political party that promotes smaller government and free enterprise. But what is new in American politics are the gendered arguments that such women make to explain why they embrace a smaller social safety net and reduced workplace regulations. Tea Party and conservative women activists reject an expansion of the welfare state, to include ObamaCare, because they believe it encourages a sexist culture of dependence that assumes women are unable to take care of themselves. Moreover, they believe that workplace regulations such as increasing the minimum wage, providing for more generous leave policies, and making it easier for women to sue for pay discrimination will ultimately backfire, making women less desirable as potential hires for employers and threatening to jeopardize women's abilities to negotiate part-time work or other benefits with their employers. Instead, conservative women leaders and Republican women in Congress promote tax cuts, reduced business regulations, and smaller government, as they firmly believe that the United States is a land rich in opportunity, and that if left to her own devices any American women can succeed.

However, there are a few areas in which Tea Party women in the mass public do not sing the same tune as Tea Party movement leaders or prominent GOP congressional women. For instance, the national survey data from PRRI show that overwhelming majorities of Tea Party women, comparable to non–Tea Party Republican women and other American women, support businesses being required to provide paid family and sick leave. Moreover, Tea Party women are evenly split on minimum wage—while more conservative than most American women on this issue, about half of Tea Party women believe a raise in the minimum wage is overdue. While there are much fewer differences between self-identified Tea Party members nationally and Tea Party women leaders when it comes to their attitudes about the social safety net, taxes, Americans who are poor, or ObamaCare, the fact that movement leaders have yet to fully persuade even self-identified Tea Party

American women in the mass public on issues such as paid leave and the minimum wage show some of the challenges the Tea Party faces in convincing more American women that their economic positions are best for them.

How, then, will Tea Party women activists and Republican women leaders get more women to align with their views concerning the social safety net, ObamaCare, and a smaller regulatory state given that a majority of American women hold such opposing positions? Several of the activists I interviewed acknowledged that changing American women's minds about curtailing popular government programs will be difficult. Amy Jo Clark of *Chicks on the Right* said that it is understandable why most American women find appealing the message of Democratic leaders, as embodied by "The Life of Julia" infographic, saying, "What they see is the messaging that it's all puppies and skittles and rainbows. What they don't see is their kids being broke [in the future]."[109] She adds that conservatives are "sucking wind" at the messaging battle and that they need to do a better job of explaining why such programs lessen women's accountability. Robert Boland, chief of staff to former Minnesota representative Michele Bachmann, told me that "advertising the conservative message is hard" and that the left has been very successful in painting an appealing narrative for women voters: "Look at the War on Women [message] and ObamaCare. They boiled down a two-thousand-page piece of legislation into three things: no preexisting conditions, kids being covered until they are twenty-six, and free birth control."[110] By contrast, Boland acknowledged that the GOP does "not have a good story to sell," in part because most of their efforts have involved blocking President Obama's legislative agenda in Congress, so there are no concrete measures to point to as legislative successes.[111]

Carrie Lukas also acknowledges that changing women's minds about social welfare policies is a challenge, and that attempts by conservatives in the past to promote tax law and social security reform have largely fallen on deaf ears, in part because such policies are sold as a means to make individuals better off financially. She said, "There's reams of research that shows that women are more risk-averse than men . . . They don't worry about being rich. They just worry that they're safe and secure."[112] Similarly, Kristen Soltis Anderson also believes that the right will have to walk a fine line in promoting conservative economic poli-

THE SEXIST SAFETY NET | 173

cies, one that focuses on pocketbook issues that hit middle-class women directly rather than "the top marginal tax rate or corporate profits and the corporate tax rate."[113] She adds that in addressing women's concerns, Republicans need to clearly state how their policies will make it easier for Americans to "have the time that you can pay attention to your kids and your work at the same time" and that by reducing taxes you can work fewer hours and "your money will go further."[114] Anderson, Lukas, and other conservative women activists concede that current conservative, free market economic messages often touted by the GOP and Tea Party leaders don't tap into many women's economic insecurities.

Lastly, several Tea Party women also worry that the message of less government will be a hard sell to many younger women. Keli Carender of Tea Party Patriots says that millennials in particular will be hard to convince that reducing or eliminating certain government programs, such as welfare or student loan financing, will be in their best interests. Herself a millennial, Carender says:

> I think my generation and younger have had it handed to us. We are told that we are entitled to a college education, to this free thing and that . . . when you have schools telling us that and the culture telling us that and our parents telling us that, I don't think it is a surprise that a lot of young people vote for free stuff over freedom, so yeah, it is a huge undertaking to see how we are going to re-instill the desire and love of freedom even if it means it might make your life a little bit harder or you might have to have a little bit less of something because you are going to have to work for it instead of get it for free.[115]

Kristen Soltis Anderson agrees, adding that one challenge faced by conservative groups that often tout the linkage between economic prosperity and a strong, two-parent household is that the notion of family is rapidly changing. With people getting married later, having kids later, and living apart from their extended families, Anderson maintains that economic conservatives have to find a way to "talk about the importance of family [to economic well-being] while not sounding like they only want the nuclear family with a golden retriever and 2.7 kids."[116]

Faced with changing demographics, with an America that is increasingly populated by more diverse constituencies, including more single mothers, and with a majority of American women currently opposed to their policies, Tea Party women certainly face many challenges in promoting their message that smaller government is better for American women and their families. At the same time, however, Tea Party women may face new opportunities to advance their conservative economic beliefs given recent trends showing that women are beginning to outperform men in terms of educational and career achievement. Moreover, many economists and pundits argue that women appear poised to do better than men in many sectors of the twenty-first-century economy. If rising paychecks can convince women that tax cuts and conservative economic policy may better suit their needs, the Tea Party has a fighting chance of growing its movement among American women.

5

Freedom Feminism

Individualism, Conservatism, and Gender Roles

Since Republicans took control of the U.S. House of Representatives in 2010, the Democratic Party has garnered success electorally among voters with claims that the GOP is waging a "War on Women."[1] In the 2012 elections, for instance, President Obama and congressional Democrats repeatedly emphasized the Republican Party's opposition to policies important to liberal women's rights groups such as the Lilly Ledbetter Act, government funding of Planned Parenthood clinics, and the Obama administration's birth control mandate. The War on Women narrative also entailed debates about abortion, as several Republican U.S. Senate candidates made clear their position that access to abortion should be strictly limited. For instance, U.S. Representative Todd Akin, running for the Missouri Senate seat, claimed in a televised interview that a rape exception for abortion was unnecessary because victims of "legitimate rape" rarely get pregnant. In a debate against his Democratic opponent Joe Donnelly, Indiana Republican Senate candidate Richard Mourdock defended his stance that abortion should be outlawed in cases of rape because God intends pregnancies to happen "even when life begins in that horrible situation of rape."[2] Obama campaign spokeswoman Jen Psaki tied Akin and Mourdock to the Romney campaign, telling reporters that their positions were "a reminder that a Republican Congress working with a Republican President Mitt Romney would feel that women should not be able to make choices about their own health care."[3]

Republican and Tea Party leaders tried to counter claims that their policy stances were antiwoman. Prominent Republican women in Congress, such as Cathy McMorris Rodgers, took to the airwaves to discount the "War on Women," calling it a "Democratic myth" and insisting that Democratic economic policies entailed the real war on women.[4] Tea Party women leaders also took umbrage at the notion that their movement was to blame for the War on Women. For instance, Amy Kremer, former chair of Tea Party Express, lambasted the "left's War on Women," writing that "ironically, much of the Tea Party leadership is made up of a new generation of powerful conservative women."[5]

The War on Women also tapped into larger debates about gender roles. Returning to the 2012 presidential campaign, gender emerged as a significant political issue after an appearance by Democratic lobbyist Hilary Rosen on CNN's *Anderson Cooper 360* to discuss whether the War on Women narrative would help attract women voters for Obama. Several days before Rosen's appearance, Mitt Romney had told the nation's newspaper editors that his wife, Ann, in her capacity as his campaign surrogate, reported to him that "the issue women care about most is the economy."[6] Rosen challenged Ann Romney's authority to discuss economic matters because, as she put it, Ann Romney "never worked a day in her life."[7] Her insinuation that stay-at-home mothers like Romney, who raised five sons, didn't engage in real work set the blogosphere on fire, including this tweet from Ann Romney: "I made a choice to stay home and raise five boys. Believe me, it was hard work."[8] Even Michelle Obama tweeted in support of Ann Romney, claiming that "every mother works hard, and every woman deserves to be respected."[9]

Although Rosen was quick to apologize for offending stay-at-home mothers, her offhand comment did not prevent many conservative women leaders from speaking out. Said Republican Senator Kelly Ayotte (NH), herself a working mother with school-aged children, "It's insulting that the president's adviser would dismiss the value of the important and hard work women do in raising children."[10] On *Townhall*, a conservative website popular with Tea Party activists, columnist Rachel Alexander claimed that the real War on Women was coming from Democrats against conservative women: "Conservative women are under attack by the left for making lifestyle decisions the left does not approve of."[11] In a similar vein, Sabrina Schaeffer, executive director of the Independent Women's Forum, said on behalf of the Romney campaign that "many, many people in the Democratic Party view the choices that Ann Romney made as the greatest threat to feminism."[12]

The "Mommy Wars" rhetoric is certainly not new in American politics—recall the reaction to the comment Hillary Clinton made while campaigning for her husband's presidential race in 1992, defending her choice to work by stating, "I could have stayed home and baked cookies and had teas, but what I decided to do was fulfill my profession."[13] While the debate that ensued after Rosen's assertion that Ann Romney "did not work a day in her life" reminds us that Americans' views about gender roles remain politically salient, I argue that the growing prominence of conservative women in American politics as leaders of the Tea Party and within the GOP suggests that many conservatives have actually softened their position on what constitutes "appropriate" gender roles, which was a pivotal goal of the second-wave women's movement in the 1970s. Hence the Republican Party has been quick to showcase elected GOP women such as Cathy McMorris Rodgers, Martha Roby, and Joni Ernst as spokespersons for its brand to counter the perception that it is out of touch with women. Moreover, many Tea Party women, such as Amy Kremer and Sarah Palin, are quick to point out that women are playing a pivotal role as activists and leaders within the movement. Conservative pundit Ann Coulter in the film *Fire from the Heartland: The Rise of Conservative Women*, produced by the conservative nonprofit organization Citizens United, notes that it is "stunning how much of the passion [in the Tea Party] comes from conservative women." Conservative women, within both the Tea Party and the GOP, have taken a more public political profile than ever before, often making an overtly gendered case as to why conservative policies are good for women and their families. In the process, such women are challenging perceptions among many Americans that women who engage in politics largely hold progressive policy views or support Democratic candidates.

That the Tea Party and Republican Party have tapped mothers with small or school-aged children as visible spokespersons also illustrates a growing acceptance of changing gender norms even in the most conservative of political circles. At the same time, while there is a greater acceptance of women as conservative and Republican leaders, which represents an evolved view on gender roles considering that many conservative political activists little more than a generation before were fighting against the Equal Rights Amendment and defending the rights of the homemaker, this issue evolution does not extend to abortion. Many Tea Party women leaders and their Republican women counterparts remain steadfastly pro-life. If anything, the Republican Party has become more conservative with respect to abortion policy. As Republicans have taken control of many state legislatures in recent years, GOP lawmakers have introduced and successfully passed a record number of new regulations designed to place greater restrictions on a woman's ability to obtain a legal abortion.[14] Republicans in Congress have also been active on the reproductive rights front, passing legislation in the House banning taxpayer-funded abortions in 2011 and 2012 and attempting to strip federal funding from Planned Parenthood, the nation's leading provider of abortion and health services for poor women. (Both bills faced a Democratic majority in the Senate that refused to consider them; efforts to defund Planned Parenthood began anew in the summer of 2015, however, but will likely face a veto from President Obama if they pass Congress, despite the Senate now being controlled by Republicans.) Notably, such heightened legislative activity with respect to abortion restrictions came after the Tea Party wave in 2010 that brought more conservative Republicans to both Congress and many state legislatures.

In this chapter I consider what the emergence of debates about gender roles and reproductive health concerns as major campaign issues in recent elections, and the active part that many Tea Party and GOP women are playing in such debates, says about gender, politics, and the state of feminism in twenty-first-century America. Politically speaking, that the Republican Party has increasingly tapped its female members to "represent" the party on such concerns[15] makes sense as an electoral strategy given that the gender gap in the 2012 presidential election was at a historic high, with women far more likely to vote for Democrat Barack Obama than Republican Mitt Romney.[16] Moreover, from a theoretical perspective, when Tea Party and prominent Republican women make the claim that their policies, whether economic or social, are best for women and their families, they challenge current political discourse as to what constitutes the very definition of women's interests.

Both Tea Party women activists and prominent Republican women have begun to make an overt, gendered case as to why conservative economic policies are good for American women. Many Tea Party women describe why mothers should be up in arms about an expansive government state. Some Tea Party women and Republican women leaders move beyond the motherhood frame to argue that progressive economic policies, an expanded social welfare system, and regulations that seek to address work/family balance issues and sex discrimination in the workplace actually work *against* the interests of all American women, mothers or not. Instead, these Tea Party women believe that such policies do little to empower women, instead promoting women's dependence on government and, in the case of legislation aimed at addressing workplace issues, may make women less attractive as potential employees. What's more, some Tea Party women go so far as to insist that such progressive policies, heavily touted by liberal feminist organizations as vital to women's interests, actually betray the original vision of the women's movement, which argued, in part, that women are equally as capable as men to participate fully in public life. The result is that some conservative women, including Sarah Palin, have begun to reclaim the feminist mantle, declaring that they are, in the words of well-known conservative author Christina Hoff Sommers, "freedom feminists." Attempts by these conservative women to "take back" feminism in the twenty-first century potentially broadens the meaning of feminism by insisting that women with conservative views also fall under the feminist tent. In this chapter I examine Tea Party women's attitudes about feminism and show why some Tea Party women leaders are making the case for a conservative interpretation of feminism.

The case for a conservative feminism is rejected by liberal women's organizations (not surprisingly), but I find that it is largely met with ambivalence from many of the Tea Party activists and conservative women leaders I interviewed and from Tea Party women in the mass public. Some of the Tea Party activists I spoke with are open to identifying themselves as feminists, if allowed to define feminism on their own terms, particularly activists who are socially and religiously conservative, believe that the concept of feminism is too closely affiliated with reproductive rights and a denial of traditional family structures and would thus never consider themselves feminists. My data analysis of Tea Party women in the mass public shows that such women are far more conservative than women who are Democrats or Political Independents, and, in some cases, non–Tea Party Republican women, when it comes to several issues that are often linked to the liberal feminist cause, such as abortion rights and a rejection of more traditional gender roles. Yet, somewhat surprisingly, a solid majority of Tea Party women in the mass public also recognize that sex discrimination remains a problem in American society. Moreover, their attitudes about gender roles are also nuanced: only half of Tea Party women in the mass public agree that family life suffers when women work full-time. Such positions reveal that at least some Tea Party women nationally may view feminism, or more precisely, certain tenets of feminism, as comporting with their own views. Before turning to how Tea Party women view feminism, however, I provide a brief overview of the concept of feminism, both its history as well as the corresponding policy stands that liberal feminists today believe are essential to its cause.

Feminism and Feminist Principles

Although no clear definition of feminism exists, and indeed, its meaning over time has been changed and challenged by many, one place to start in establishing what constitutes feminism today comes from historian Nancy Cott, whose work *The Grounding of Modern Feminism* traces the term "feminism" to the early twentieth century.[17] While the early women's movement, led by abolitionists Elizabeth Cady Stanton and Lucretia Mott at Seneca Falls, New York, initiated the fight for greater political, legal, and social rights for women in the mid-nineteenth century, culminating in the national suffrage campaign for women's voting rights, the term "feminism" was not routinely used until the early twentieth century. During the last stages of the suffrage campaign, younger, more radical women's rights advocates rejected the maternal-based reasoning used by most suffragettes as the basis for granting women the right to vote. Instead, these radical women, such as Alice Paul, grounded their appeal for voting rights and later, the passage of the Equal Rights Amendment, in "women's common human identity with men"—a view rejected by most women social reformers of the day.[18] Calling themselves feminists, such radicals sought to articulate a broader ideology concerning women's rights, "proclaiming revolution in all the relations of the sexes."[19] The burgeoning feminist movement of the 1920s often had ties with other radical ideologies, such as communism and anarchism, and opponents of women's rights linked early feminists to the Red Scare, which further dampened the appeal of the "feminist" label.[20]

"Feminism" as a term would not be widely embraced until the second-wave women's rights movement, when a new generation of women began its struggle for greater rights under the banner of women's liberation beginning in the late 1960s. Second-wave feminists called not merely for legal and political action to challenge discriminatory laws and labor practices in the public arena, but also challenged interpersonal relations at home, by promoting the idea that "the personal is political." The most well-known feminist organization to emerge at the time was the National Organization for Women (NOW), which sought a legal strategy to ensure women's rights. Moreover, it championed reproductive rights, including legal abortion, as critical to women's liberation as well as the passage of an Equal Rights Amendment to the U.S. Constitution, which would effectively ban all discrimination based on sex. While abortion rights largely continue be to constitutionally protected, passage of the Equal Rights Amendment remains elusive.

Several key policy issues unite liberal feminists today. First, liberal women's groups continue to work to eliminate sex discrimination from the workplace, which they believe is still prevalent today, and were supportive of the Lilly Ledbetter Fair Pay Act of 2009. Currently, feminist organizations such as the National Woman's Law Center and the National Organization for Women support more government intervention to reduce the wage gap among men and women, including advocating for the Paycheck Fairness Act, which would "ensure full compensation for victims of gender-based discrimination."[21] Feminist groups also stand against laws or policies that discriminate against women of color and gay women or those individuals who identify as transgendered, so much of their legal advocacy also centers around LGBT rights and racial justice.

In addition to fighting sex discrimination in the workplace, or discrimination against marginalized groups in society, women's groups also fight sexual harassment in a variety of settings, including the military. They also seek to end violence against women through the enactment of federal legislation such as the Violence against Women Act, which was last reauthorized in 2013 and which, among other things, seeks to hold offenders accountable by strengthening federal penalties for repeat sex offenders, to train state and local law enforcement officers to better understand the realities of domestic violence, and to provide services for the victims of such violence.

Prominent women's rights groups also promote women's reproductive rights, calling for greater accessibility to birth control, emergency contraception, and abortion for women of all income levels. Abortion rights, in particular, are a prominent issue for liberal women's groups such as NARAL Pro-Choice America, the National Organization for Women, and the National Woman's Law Center. As NOW states on its website, it supports abortion rights and access to contraception because "all women have the right to have the children they want, raise the children they have, and plan their families through safe, legal abortion, and access to contraception, and pre- and post-natal care."[22]

Lastly, another common theme that unites a variety of progressive feminist groups is the fight for economic justice for women aside from pay equity concerns. Recognizing that women are more likely to be poor or near poverty compared with men, most feminist groups seek government solutions to help women overcome poverty, such as supporting increases in the minimum wage, maintaining more generous funding for social welfare programs such as Medicaid or welfare, and opposing cuts in food stamps or unemployment insurance. On matters of economic policy, as with sex discrimination, sexual harassment, violence against women, and reproductive rights, modern liberal feminists envision a large role for government, particularly the federal government, to intervene in these matters.

The Conservative Challenge to Broaden Feminism

At first glance, given the issues that most liberal feminists support and their belief that government must proactively address these issues, it seems unlikely that conservatives would seek to call themselves feminists. Indeed, many prominent conservative women continue to eschew the label in addition to the broad principles espoused by the modern feminist movement. Former House member Michele Bachmann, for example, when asked if she was a feminist while running for the GOP's presidential nomination in 2011 refused to characterize herself as such. Bachmann told the *Daily Beast*'s Kirsten Powers that she thought of herself as "an empowered American," stating, "I'm a woman comfortable in her own skin. I grew up with three brothers. My parents didn't see us [as] limited [by gender]. I would mow the lawn and take out the trash; I was making my own fishing lures. I went along with everything the boys did."[23] When asked in 2011 if she was a feminist, Penny Young Nance, the CEO and president of the largest group of socially conservative women, Concerned Women for America, instead called herself a traditionalist. For her, feminism today is too closely linked to what she refers to as "the ubiquitous female branch of the professional left." Claiming that modern feminism is steeped in Marxist thought, she says that the prevailing dictates of feminism are as follows: "The government must redistribute wealth, control businesses to make them hire us, and even take on the responsibility of raising our children via government daycare for us to be equal."[24]

Sarah Palin's candidacy for the vice presidency and the emergence of women leading the Tea Party, however, have led some prominent conservative women to "reclaim" the feminist label. In a highly touted speech given to the Susan B. Anthony List in 2010, a pro-life political action committee that raises funds for and endorses pro-life women political candidates, Palin declared that there is an "emerging conservative feminist identity" developing in American politics, one rooted in "Western" or "frontier" feminism. She expands on these views in her 2010 book *America by Heart: Reflections on Family, Faith, and Flag.* Palin comments on the ascension of conservative women in both the Tea Party and the GOP, likening them to Mama Grizzlies from Alaska, who "rise up" when their cubs are threatened. Palin compares the "Mama Grizzlies" of conservative politics today with the pioneers of the early women's movement. She writes, "Truth is, mama grizzlies have been with us for a long time. These are the same women who settled the frontier, drove the wagons, ploughed the fields, ran cattle, taught their kids, raised their families—and fought for women's rights."[25] Palin recounts her own childhood in Alaska, in which both boys and girls hunted, chopped wood, and grew their own vegetables, allowing them to develop the self-reliance that is a hallmark characteristic of Palin's version of the American frontier.[26]

Indeed, self-reliance, empowerment, and personal responsibility are keys to understanding the true nature of feminism, Palin argues, linking her views on feminism to the Enlightenment principles of individual equality that inspired early women's rights activists such as Elizabeth Cady Stanton and Susan B. Anthony. In doing so, Palin acknowledges that women have faced sex discrimination historically, as she writes "that both women and men have God-given rights that haven't always been honored by our country's politicians. I believe women and men have important differences, but those differences don't include the ability of women to work just as hard as men (if not harder) and to be just as effective as men (if not more so)."[27] In taking a page from the second-wave feminist movement, she claims that women are fully capable of participating as equals in public life, moving beyond the patriarchal view held by some social conservatives who continue to embrace women's primary role as mothers who stay at home. For example, one is struck in a September 2008 *New York Times* profile of the newly tapped GOP vice presidential nominee by her response to potential critics of her unintended fifth pregnancy while serving as governor of Alaska. She told her staff at the time that she intended to get right back to work after the birth of her fifth child and "to any critics who say a woman can't think and work and carry a baby at the same time, I'd just like to escort that Neanderthal back to the cave."[28]

In reclaiming feminism for conservatives, Palin sets "frontier" feminists apart from modern feminists in her book, describing the former as rejecting one of the basic goals she believes was a hallmark of the earlier women's rights advocates: women's empowerment. She writes, "I believe that women in the radical feminist movement of the 1960s and '70s became too heavily invested in the idea of women as powerless. They were preoccupied with themselves and their frustration to the degree that they made victims of themselves."[29] The downfall of this approach, according to Palin, is that by portraying women as not being fully capable of taking care of themselves, government is needed to provide social welfare programs for women. In short, Palin writes, the message of feminism became "no we can't—at least not unless government helps."[30] Palin also rejects modern feminism's position on the legality of abortion being a linchpin of women's equality. Instead, she maintains that liberal feminists who advocate for abortion rights do young women a disservice by underestimating their capabilities, writing, "Strangely, many feminists seem to want to tell these young women that they're not capable, that you *can't* give your child life and still pursue your dreams.

Their message is: 'Women, you are not strong enough or smart enough to do both.'"[31]

Reclaiming an "authentic feminism" is also the goal of Marjorie Dannenfelser, president of the Susan B. Anthony List. Writing an op-ed in *Politics Daly* during the 2010 midterm elections, Dannenfelser points to the record number of "highly credentialed" pro-life women candidates running that year who "both embody and embrace a vision of womanhood that bridges the modern feminist divide between motherhood and selfhood."[32] Like Sarah Palin, Dannenfelser links authentic feminism directly to suffragists such as Susan B. Anthony, who, she writes, viewed abortion as a tool "of male oppression." While Dannenfelser acknowledges that the modern feminist movement helped women by "advancing the economic rights of women, and in creating opportunities and legal protections in the workplace, athletic arenas, academia, and other areas of endeavor," she argues its linkage of abortion rights to the feminist cause divided women and diminished "their exceptional creative power as bearers and protectors of human life."

Palin's and Dannenfelser's claim that the true essence of feminism was stolen by modern feminists is not new—although the targeted audience of conservative women and men who may be likely to read Palin's book or Dannenfelser's writing might be new to this line of reasoning. Palin's arguments, in particular, share many similarities with the work of Christina Hoff Sommers, an affiliated scholar with the American Enterprise Institute, a conservative think tank based in Washington DC. One of Sommers's best-known works is *Who Stole Feminism? How Women Have Betrayed Women*, originally published in 1995, in which Sommers distinguishes between "equity feminists" and "gender feminists." Sommers believes that modern, gender feminists have betrayed the "traditional, classically liberal, humanistic" feminism that was initiated by first-wave women's rights advocates at Seneca Falls—a view of feminism that enjoys more widespread support among the American public. She writes that a first-wave or "equity" feminist "wants for women what she wants for everyone: fair treatment, without discrimination."[33] By contrast, Sommers argues that "gender" feminists offer a more radical take: "that women, even modern American women," are in thrall to a "system of male dominance" known as patriarchy. The goal of gender feminists, according to Sommers, is to raise women's consciousness so that they will view society through a sex/gender prism, seeking a more "radical transformation of our society than earlier feminists had envisioned," pitting women against men.[34] While Sommers does not go so far as Palin or Dannenfelser in advocating that a pro-life position on abortion is the true feminist position, she is highly critical of feminist scholarship that she believes inflates incidences of gender bias in U.S. schools and workplaces and violence against women as a means to further their own ideological goals.

The disagreement among prominent conservative women as to the merits and applicability of feminism to their own cause today reveals that conservative women are not monolithic on this issue. In earlier work, sociologist Rebecca Klatch uncovered two types of conservative women activists during the rise of the "New Right" in the 1980s: socially conservative and laissez-faire conservative women, a schism with historical antecedents found in the broader conservative movement of the twentieth century. Klatch found that while both sets of women shared important political goals, such as being unified against communism and the expansion of the federal government, their views on feminism differed. As might be expected, socially conservative women activists became politically active in part as a reaction against feminism, viewing the women's movement as antifamily, narcissistic, and a threat to the status of the homemaker. However, Klatch finds that laissez-faire conservative women supported part of the feminist agenda, rejecting the patriarchal view of gender roles espoused by social conservatives and believing that men and women are both rational, self-interested, and autonomous actors, and that both sexes "must be able to climb to the height of their talents in a marketplace free from outside interference."[35] Unlike their socially conservative counterparts, laissez-faire conservative women supported day care, abortion rights, and gay rights, arguing that individuals should be free to pursue these things as a matter of individual liberty. This is not to say that laissez-faire conservative women supported government efforts to fund or expand day care or abortion services for the needy—instead, they opposed any efforts to expand the role of government to provide such services or to enforce equality as an affront to their vision of a society with limited government interference.

Ronnee Schreiber's important work *Righting Feminism* further examines this divide among socially conservative and laissez-faire conservative political women in her analysis of the two leading women's interest groups that purport to speak for these constituencies, respectively, before the rise of the Tea Party: Concerned Women for America and the Independent Women's Forum.[36] As Schreiber documents, both groups oppose modern feminism and, by extension, the use of the government to expand opportunities for women. In challenging the ability of feminist groups to speak for all women, however, Schreiber finds that both CWA and IWF sometimes employ feminist rhetoric to claim that their groups do a better job of representing American women, what she calls "playing femball." In essence, while these groups "contest the validity of feminists to make identity-based political claims," they themselves "make gendered identity claims about *their* interests and goals."[37] Schreiber finds that the socially conservative women who populate CWA believe that their identity as a women's organization "hinges on women's differences from men."[38] By contrast, the more libertarian-leaning women from the IWF are typically only likely to "invoke gender identity to raise the question of *which* women's interests are getting represented."[39]

Schreiber's work, like Klatch's work before her, demonstrates that conservative women have had power and agency in American politics, even though most political scientists and scholars of women's history have more often emphasized the liberal women's movement in their studies of American politics. Arguably, Sarah Palin's historic nomination, women's growing prominence within the GOP, and the rise of women leaders in the Tea Party movement indicate that conservative women's political clout is growing. The question remains as to whether Tea Party women, more generally, have begun to embrace the term "feminism" or its historical precepts. Through interviews with Tea Party women leaders and activists and an examination of their writings in the form of blog posts, books, and articles, I find that Tea Party women are united in their opposition to what they view as the current excesses of modern feminism, arguing that liberal feminists portray women as incapable victims in need of government assistance. Socially conservative Tea Party women, like their Christian Right forebears who fought against the ERA in the 1970s and against abortion and gay rights in the 1980s and '90s, also take issue with liberal feminists' support for abortion rights and worry that feminism has led to the breakdown of the traditional family structure. Several of the Tea Party women who iden-tify as libertarians, moreover, generally reject the concept of feminism because their worldview promotes individualism, essentially consider-ing themselves "postfeminist."

At the same time, some—but not all—Tea Party women are open to reclaiming the feminist mantle *if* feminism is equated with the em-powerment of women and the equal treatment of women. While these women acknowledge that women have faced sex discrimination histori-cally, they believe that sex discrimination is not nearly as prevalent today as most liberal feminists maintain. Moreover, these "freedom feminists" largely reject the need for government to address any sex discrimination that may remain, arguing instead that a truly free market will eradicate sex discrimination (and in many cases has begun to do so). By compari-son, however, I find that Tea Party women in the mass public are actu-ally more likely than not to agree that women still face discrimination in American society. While Tea Party women nationally do hold more conservative views on the prevalence of sex discrimination and other women's issues compared with non–Tea Party women, my data analysis shows that even this most conservative category of American women has softened on some attitudes concerning traditional gender roles.

The Tea Party and Feminism: A View from the Activists

When asked if they consider themselves feminists, the reaction of the Tea Party women I interviewed was mixed. Several of the women, par-ticularly those who also identify as socially conservative, believe the chasm between conservatism and feminism was too great and refused to identify as a feminist. Most activists, however, were willing to iden-tify as a feminist if allowed to define the term as standing for broad principles of equality for women or "women's empowerment." Similar to Sarah Palin, a few Tea Party women even made the case that feminism has been "stolen" by liberal women's organizations and that conserva-tives should reclaim the term. However, several others, particularly libertarians, argued that they were, in a sense, postfeminist, rejecting the essentialist claims laid out by either feminists or antifeminists. Still others questioned whether feminism was even necessary any longer, given the many gains women had already made in society. One common thread uniting all the women I interviewed, however, was their outright rejection of the modern liberal feminist movement, to which I turn first.

Rejection of the Modern Feminist Movement

The modern feminist movement holds little appeal for Tea Party and conservative women. Most of the women I interviewed clearly believed that the liberal, "leftist," or "militant" branches of feminism (as described by many) did not represent their views or the views of most Americans. Several of the interviewees expressed outright hostility toward liberal feminists, such as one grassroots activist from Maryland who told me that she does "not feel that ugly feminists represent me, like the extreme Code Pink women who give all women a bad name."[40] Another Maryland Tea Party activist described modern feminists as "single women who hate men" or perhaps women who have children but "resent them." She adds that these women also "don't feel comfortable in their own skin, which is why they chastise someone like Sarah Palin."[41]

Most of the Tea Party women and conservative activists I interviewed believed liberal feminists promoted women as victims, in need of government assistance to alleviate their problems. Stacy Mott, president and co-founder of Smart Girl Politics, rejects liberal feminism, in part, because she does not necessarily believe that sex discrimination is rampant in society. She told me, "I don't like to be labeled as a victim and I think the word 'feminism' does [that]." In recounting the days when she worked full-time outside the house, before becoming a stay-at-home mother and now full-time activist, she said, "I worked for the same company as my husband doing the same work and we were equals. There was nothing that held me back differently from him, and I just believe in individualism. I think feminism puts you in a category in which you have to rely on your sex rather than who you are as a person."[42] Said another activist, a self-described libertarian living in Texas, the whole message of the mainstream feminist movement today is that "we should depend on government for everything, which to me is the antithesis of feminism." Instead, she counters that "women should be self-sufficient based on their own volition."[43]

Several Tea Party women argued that feminism is essentially outdated, including Ellen Sullivan, a co-founder of a state Tea Party organization in Maryland who came of age during the 1970s, at the height of the women's liberation movement. Today she maintains that the "women's liberation movement is a whole load of crap."[44] Elizabeth Reynolds, a Tea Party activist from suburban Washington DC who attended a woman's college in the 1970s, said, "I think harkening back to the old feminist days, that somehow we don't have the same opportunities—I don't think it's true anymore." Moreover, Reynolds added that when she attended a recent college reunion, she found that the women there who are "avowed feminists" were the "most miserable, divorced, bitter . . . and they [were] looking to blame someone for their unhappiness." She argues that women have plenty of opportunities today, and if they use their "talent, skill, and hard work" they will get ahead.[45]

Janice Shaw Crouse, senior fellow at the Beverly LaHaye Institute, rejects the idea that one can be a conservative and a feminist because the term "feminist" "is so muddled that no one wants to be called a feminist anymore."[46] Her opposition to the term stems in part from her belief that feminism has outlived its usefulness. She believes younger women, especially, reject feminism because they grew up in a world with enhanced opportunities and rights, so liberal feminists' claim that women face discrimination often rings hollow. However, she also believes that feminism is anathema to most of her socially conservative members because "radical feminists" promote both "man hatred" and "the abhorrence of maternity."[47]

Other Tea Party women who also identify as social conservatives reject modern feminism's notion that women perhaps *should* be treated equally in all things, and instead embrace gender differences as essential. Said Lori Parker, founder of the online Tea Party forum As a Mom . . . a Sisterhood of Mommy Patriots, "I'm not your ERA-type feminist. At the same time, I think women definitely have a role, a complementary role in what we do. I'm not the type of feminist that would say I have to be able to do everything a man does to feel worth. My husband can't do some of the things that I can do. We complement each other on what we can do."[48] Gabriella Hoffman, the conservative blogger who works as a field coordinator with the conservative Leadership Institute, also rejects feminism because feminists fail to recognize women and men's biological differences. She told me that feminists "have this view that women are equal to men in everything, but that's not true: we're biologically different, we're more prone to emotion, guys are naturally stronger than us." She believes that such a feminist worldview promotes women's careers over a traditional family life, saying, "It is sad to see a lot of career women who delay childbearing, marriage, even forgo marriage altogether, because of this notion that we have to prove ourselves because we have to defeat this patriarchy. . . . The so-called party of choice is not allowing women the choice to become a mother or to become a wife."[49]

The notion that modern feminists abhor the lifestyle choices of women to become mothers who stay at home to raise children was prevalent among other conservative activists I interviewed. Colleen Holcomb, formerly of Eagle Forum, argues against modern feminists' contention that "marriage and motherhood and anything masculine needs to be rejected or is a burden to women rather than a blessing that can enhance women."[50] Some of the conservative activists believed that feminists are to blame for any friction among women that exists in American society. Said *Brenda Jones*, who currently serves as a Republican state legislator in Maryland, "I wonder if [feminists] are the ones who are really offended by the way we want to live as women. I don't care if they want to work or not work or have one kid or ten kids or marry or don't marry. I think *they* are the ones who get worked up about women whose moral foundation is religious."[51]

For many of these women on the right, liberal feminists' view that abortion rights are paramount to women's liberation is highly problematic and leads them to reject the label of feminist. One Tea Party activist and blogger from Maryland, *Marilyn O'Leary*, told me that she initially joined the National Organization for Women in the 1970s in her early twenties. At that time, O'Leary personally faced sex discrimination working in a male-dominated industry and found appealing the efforts of the women's liberation movement to eradicate such discrimination. At the beginning, she found that NOW was a "big tent" that allowed women with a variety of views on abortion to fight together on issues such as sex discrimination. However, O'Leary gradually grew concerned that NOW "wanted me to march for abortion," which she could not do as a pro-life supporter. Ultimately, she dropped her membership and says that organizations such as NOW have only become more militant about the abortion issue over time, which she resents. She said, "Unless you stick with [feminists] on every issue, you are not a real woman. You are not free to have your own belief system. And if your belief system does not match up with theirs, you are stupid, judgmental, bigoted."[52]

Kristen Soltis Anderson, the Republican pollster, describes the current state of feminism as unappealing for most conservative women in large measure due to the issue of reproductive rights. She explained to me, "I think it is frustrating that the choices presented to conservative women are a feminism that doesn't feel like it is actually about insuring women have a voice and place in society. [Instead,] it is more about expanding government and fighting back any restriction on abortion. [There is this] sense that the feminist movement has gone astray."[53] In fact, Anderson believes that Sarah Palin was such an inspiration to Tea Party women not only because she projected a strong political leadership role as a principled conservative with young children, but also because she was the living embodiment of the pro-life cause, having chosen to give birth to her son with Down's syndrome.

Several socially conservative women I interviewed not only rejected the mainstream feminist movement's defense of abortion as morally problematic, as they believe life begins at conception, but they also took issue with feminists' efforts to promote government assistance in providing abortions to lower-income women. In several interviews Tea Party women activists brought up the debate about defunding the women's health organization Planned Parenthood.[54] Government funding of Planned Parenthood is anathema to Tea Party activists and a clear indication of what they believe is wrong with modern feminism (and, more generally, a government that is too big and overreaching). Consider the viewpoint of Gabriella Hoffman of the Leadership Institute: "Feminists want women to be genderless, beholden to big government, and not be accountable for their actions. They want moral relativism to take over women. When you see a lack of personal responsibility, that is what all of this lawlessness goes to. You see [feminist] women say, well I have every right to kill something in me because it is not human, and usually on taxpayer money, because Planned Parenthood gets about a half billion dollars [annually]."[55] As Hoffman argues, for social conservatives not only is the pro-choice position a moral outrage, but having government pay to provide such services also allows women to sidestep personal responsibility for their actions. Even among the relatively few self-identified pro-choice Tea Party women I interviewed, government spending on reproductive health is problematic because as a matter of principle fiscal conservatives and libertarians largely reject the welfare state, believing that entitlement programs foster dependence on government assistance and usurp individual responsibility. For many Tea Party women, modern feminists today embody the worse excesses of the liberal state, particularly in their advocacy of government spending on reproductive health policies as part and parcel of "big government."

Perhaps no other issue embodied this concern about government's "oversized" role in promoting reproductive rights for the Tea Party more than the Obama administration's birth control mandate, which became a majorly divisive point in the 2012 presidential election.[56] Many of the activists I interviewed mentioned the controversy surrounding the birth control mandate, and the role that feminist organizations and advocates, especially women's rights activist Sandra Fluke, played in fostering this debate, as emblematic of modern feminism's excesses.[57] As indicated in the previous chapter, many Tea Party women activists denounced the birth control mandate as part of their larger opposition to the Affordable Care Act, viewing both as unnecessary costs to business owners that, in their minds, would end up raising the price of medical care. But some also directly criticized the work of Fluke and liberal feminist organizations in promoting the birth control mandate as *good* for women, arguing instead that efforts to have government provide birth control (or mandate that businesses do so) usurped women's individual responsibility. For example, Tami Nantz of Smart Girl Politics argued that the work of liberal feminists activists such as Fluke is not in women's best interests: "I don't think that the feminist movement is helpful today. I think the feminist movement hurts today more than [it] helps women. For instance, I think of Sandra Fluke. In my opinion, she makes women look very meek and very needy. And that is not what I am. I am stronger than that. I resent a woman like that."[58] Amy Jo Clark and Miriam Weaver of *Chicks on the Right* also take issue with the birth control mandate because they believe it holds women unaccountable for their choices, leaving women "unempowered." Clark told me, "Feminism today has morphed into 'I am dependent, I am a victim, I need somebody else to pay for my birth control, to pay for my abortions. I need the government.'"[59]

Many Tea Party women activists also raised concerns about religious freedom with respect to the birth control mandate. Recall that the Romney campaign and conservative activists vehemently objected to the Obama administration's decision to require religiously affiliated organizations that formally oppose the use of contraception for religious purposes to provide birth control as part of their health care insurance plans. Dana Loesch, the conservative radio host and blogger, argued in one editorial that requiring *women* business owners who consciously object to the use of birth control to provide contraception as part of their benefits packages violates their personal freedom more profoundly than the needs of women whose birth control is not covered by their insurance policies. She wrote, "Many women see as a greater threat to their freedom the administration's insistence that employers—many of whom are also female—compromise their religious beliefs to provide for the contraceptive choices made freely by other women, women who can empower themselves by paying for their choices *themselves*. It's not 'feminist' to demand that another woman carry the yoke of your *free* choices."[60]

Tea Party women also strongly rejected the narrative put forth by liberal feminist organizations and the Democratic Party that the birth control mandate, access to abortion, and the defunding of Planned Parenthood entailed a "War on Women." Instead, many Tea Party women believed that the War on Women narrative essentially narrowed the scope of issues that could be defined as being of interest to women. Or, in the words of one Maryland Tea Party activist, Jennifer Jacobs, feminist leaders essentially "let us be pigeonholed by our body parts," which had the effect of discounting women's views on the more "important issues," namely, economic concerns.[61] Keli Carender, a national grassroots coordinator with Tea Party Patriots, echoed this point: "Personally, as a woman, I think it is incredibly insulting when politicians only talk about reproductive stuff to me. You know what? That is so low on my totem pole to me on what is important. I was a math and science major. I can handle tough talk on the budget. Could you just talk to me about what you are spending my money on?"[62] Tea Party women believe that liberal feminist groups, in portraying women as in need of government assistance to guarantee access to free birth control or to insure that abortion remains legal and funded, in fact "victimize women for the sake of using them as pawns in an election," in the words of Dana Loesch.[63]

Many Tea Party women also question the extent to which sex discrimination—another issue of particular concern to liberal feminists—actually exists. Recall the comment from Stacy Mott, who earlier said that when she worked full-time before becoming a stay-at-home mother she was paid the same as her husband for doing the same work, arguing that "there was nothing that held me back differently from him." Caroline Kitchens, a senior research associate at the American Enterprise Institute, told the Independent Women's Forum when she was featured as part of its online "Portrait of a Modern Feminist" series that "it's a shame that feminists who claim to be all about empowering women are teaching young girls that they will always be victims and that the cards are stacked against them. I just don't think that's true in our society anymore, and we're sending a horrible message to girls by teaching them to embrace victim status."[64] Instead, conservative women's groups such as IWF routinely paint a more positive picture of women's progress in society. In *Liberty Is No War on Women* (2012), IWF's Carrie Lukas and Sabrina Schaeffer question whether liberal feminists' aim of full equality for women and girls in society is "really such a distant goal." While acknowledging that some challenges for women remain, they argue, "Overall, American women and girls enjoy unprecedented opportunity to work and succeed in all aspects of life. Today, women are participating and excelling as never before in the workplace and academia. At the same time, new technologies and other advances are giving women more ways to pursue happiness than ever before in history."[65] Such activists believe that liberal feminist organizations who endorse policies such as the Pay Equity Act overstate the case for sex discrimination in pay, instead of acknowledging what in their mind is actually driving the statistic which shows that women make approximately eighty cents for every dollar a man does: women's choices for more flexible jobs that mean working fewer hours or for occupations that traditionally pay less. Or as conservative icon Phyllis Schlafly likes to say, feminists seek "equal pay for unequal work."[66] Moreover, as the analysis about conservative women's views on policies such as the Pay Equity Act in the last chapter demonstrates, conservative women activists such as Lukas and Schaeffer maintain that such policies may in fact harm women more than help if they lead employers to reduce their number of employees or makes them gun-shy about hiring more women.

As the above analysis indicates, Tea Party women and conservative women's organizations largely reject modern feminism and the public policies it promotes. For some socially conservative Tea Party activists, the promotion of abortion rights and the requirement under the Affordable Care Act that all insurance policies offered by employers offer women access to free birth control, even those who religiously object, violates their religious views. Regardless of their attitudes on reproductive rights, however, Tea Party women reject the idea that government should be providing such reproductive health services as a usurpation of women's responsibility. Tea Party women activists also take issue with the call by liberal feminist organizations to have government intervene on women's behalf, whether it means providing more social services to women or fighting sex discrimination. First, they think that such efforts "victimize" women, painting women as incapable of solving their own problems. This notion belies the capacity of individuals to be self-reliant, which is an important tenet of conservative ideology. Second, Tea Party women believe that many of the important issues that originally inspired the second-wave women's movement, such as a lack of opportunity for women or widespread sex discrimination, have largely dissipated. Instead, the "fixation" of modern feminists groups with these concerns, or moreover, their promotion of reproductive rights as essential to women's rights, unnecessarily narrows the scope of what defines women's issues in modern politics.

"Real" Feminists and Antifeminist Libertarians

While Tea Party women soundly reject modern feminism as incompatible with their personal beliefs, some Tea Party women do consider themselves feminists *if* feminism is equated with the empowerment of women and the equal treatment of women. Take Maryland grassroots activist *Angie Crawford*'s opinion of feminism: "I support equal pay for equal work. I support being taken seriously for doing our jobs. Women can be equal to men and should have that right."[67] Said another Maryland activist, *Linda Myers*, who owns her own small business, "I consider myself a conservative feminist. I can do anything a man can do, pretty much. I know that I am not as strong as some men, but I'm stronger than some. I think it is based on your individual capabilities, whether you are a male or female."[68] Carrie Lukas, managing director of the Independent Women's Forum, told me that while she understands for many conservatives the term "feminism" is problematic because "it has been so associated with radical big government leftism," she still thinks feminism can remain relevant. She said, "There is a need when I look around the world for a feminist movement now more than ever in terms of what is going on overseas. And who is willing to say that girls don't deserve the same opportunities as boys? So I think you *can* be a conservative and feminist and that feminism still has a role to play."[69]

Similar to Sarah Palin's arguments in *America by Heart*, several of the women I interviewed praised earlier incarnations of the women's movement for expanding legal and political opportunities for women while distancing themselves from modern feminists active in politics today. So, while Jennifer Jacobs from Maryland told me she considers herself "a feminist in the original sense of the word," she maintains that feminism today has become "perverse" so she rejects the term.[70] Another Maryland state activist, Renee Wilson, also acknowledged that the second-wave feminist movement opened doors for women. As she told me, "Our consciousness has been raised—many women have been working outside of the home and because of women's entry into the workforce, they are more capable of being effective in politics."[71] But she stopped short of identifying herself as a feminist. Jenny Beth Martin, the co-founder and spokesperson for Tea Party Patriots, told me that she does not really consider herself a feminist because "when I think about what I am capable of doing, my gender doesn't really affect me." She realizes, however, that the mere fact that she does *not* question her ability to lead this prominent national organization is a tangible result of the women's liberation movement, adding, "I guess in that respect, the feminist movement has been very successful in America, because . . . a lot of women in America think today, 'I can do anything, and I'm allowed to do anything. I am going to set out and do what I can to achieve my goals.'"[72]

Several of the Tea Party women I interviewed, similar to Sarah Palin, believe the true nature of feminism lies in women's empowerment—not in having government provide social welfare benefits or mandates that employees hire women or ensure that women are paid equally to men. While some activists are grateful to earlier feminists who paved the way for women to have more opportunities in life, they believe that feminism today has been "co-opted" by liberal feminist organizations. Said Amy Jo Clark, one of the *Chicks on the Right*, "We say that we are the real feminists and liberals have hijacked the term. I think feminism is when you are accountable to yourself. You are only empowered when you are actually responsible, accountable, and you are able to take care of yourself."[73] A libertarian activist from Texas I interviewed also supports feminism, which she believes "should be about individual female empowerment." Efforts by liberal feminist groups to have government intervene on behalf of women's economic rights, according to this activist, are wrongheaded and hypocritical. As she told me, "Looking for government consistently subsidizes the power structures that [feminists] oppose . . . It is illogical to me."[74]

Other self-identified libertarians I spoke with reject the "feminist" label, however, and instead argue for policies that empower women *and* men. Take for example Whitney Neal, who previously served as grassroots coordinator for FreedomWorks, the libertarian organization that works closely with Tea Party groups and activists. Neal told me, "I think because of being a libertarian, you believe in the power of the individual—man, woman, [it] doesn't matter. I don't define myself as a feminist or an antifeminist. I just define myself as an individual." While she does acknowledge that women today are playing a more prominent role in society because of the women's movement, she believes the women's movement today sends the wrong message. Instead, she feels that "the most important message we can give women is that *you* are in control of your path and destiny."[75] Keli Carender of Tea Party Patriots also believes that women don't face any particular challenges in politics or society more broadly and does not identify as a feminist. She said, "I think individuals have unique talents they can bring. I really abhor looking at people as groups and that women bring this or men bring that . . . I am very much an individualist and a fan of Ayn Rand's school of individualism. If you go down the road of grouping people together, even if it is for something good, I think that road always ends with collectivism."[76]

Aside from these libertarian women who eschew the term "feminist" and the socially conservative activists profiled earlier who claim that feminism is too closely linked with reproductive rights, some Tea Party women are open to being defined as feminists *on their own terms*. However, Tea Party women reject claims by liberal feminists groups that government needs to play a larger role in the economy, either in providing enhanced social services for lower-income women, which they believe reduces women's capabilities of taking care of themselves, or in passing new regulations to fight against sex discrimination, which they think is far less prevalent than feminist groups claim. If feminism were equated more with laissez-faire economic policies, Tea Party women may be receptive to efforts by Christina Hoff Sommers, Marjorie Dannenfelser, Sarah Palin, and other prominent conservative women in politics to establish what Sommers refers to as a "freedom feminism."

The Tea Party and Feminism: National Opinion Data

The qualitative analysis demonstrates that some Tea Party women may be open to embracing the term "feminist," if allowed to define the term devoid of activist government or abortion rights—a definition that directly counters major tenets of feminism as promoted by liberal women's groups today. However, these Tea Party and conservative activists and national leaders embody the rare "political elites" in American society who are actively engaged in the political process on either a part-time basis or as paid professionals. Turning attention to Tea Party women in the mass public, I consider the extent to which Tea Party women nationally are feminists.

Generally speaking, most Americans do not identify as feminists. Using data from the 1980s, Cook and Wilcox found that just roughly one-quarter of Americans possess what they term feminist consciousness, a measure that combines expressed support for the women's "liberation movement" and the extent to which individuals believe women should hold equal roles with men outside the home.[77] However, they did find that far more Americans could be classified as "potential feminists"—those individuals who are generally supportive of women's equal role with men in society but who hold negative feelings toward the feminist women's movement. In a separate study, Wilcox and Cook found that a solid minority of white evangelical women—40 percent—"believe that women should have an equal role with men,"[78] which is somewhat of a surprise given that evangelical denominations, and their pastors, have often interpreted in antifeminist ways scriptures that call on women to obey their husbands. Thus by the 1980s, a decade or so after the passionate battle that resulted in the failure of feminists to ratify the Equal Rights Amendment, many Americans, even those of a conservative bent, became more accepting of women's equal role in society.

As a political term, "feminism" remains largely out of favor with most Americans, due in no small measure to negative perceptions of the women's movement. Using 1996 General Social Survey data, for instance, Schnittker and colleagues found that only 27 percent of women and 12 percent of men self-identify with the term "feminist."[79] More recently, a 2013 poll by the *Huffington Post* shows that just 20 percent of Americans consider themselves feminists.[80] However, some goals of the women's movement, such as stopping sex discrimination and making the decision of women to work outside the home more socially acceptable, have been embraced by many Americans over time, showing huge shifts from several decades before. For example, the same 2013 *Huffington Post* poll found that a whopping 82 percent of respondents agreed that "men and women should be social, political, and economic equals."[81]

Turning to the attitudes of Tea Party women in the mass public about feminism, I analyze data from two separate surveys conducted by the Public Religion Research Institute: the 2012 American Values Survey and the 2011 Religion, Millennials, and Abortion Survey. (See appendix A for more detailed information about the surveys.) Unfortunately, neither the 2012 or 2011 PRRI surveys asked respondents specifically if they consider themselves feminists or how they view prominent feminists organizations vis-à-vis feeling thermometers. However, both surveys ask questions about issues on which liberal feminist groups take very public stands, in a sense providing us with proxy measures for certain aspects of feminism. The 2012 American Values Survey contains questions about abortion and gender roles, while the 2011 survey contains questions about sex discrimination and gender roles. I compare the views of self-identified Tea Party women with both Republican women who do not identify with the Tea Party and "other" American women (Democrats and Political Independents).

First, I consider attitudes about sex discrimination, based on a 2011 survey question that asked respondents if they agreed with the following statement: "Discrimination against women is no longer a problem in the United States." I also consider how Tea Party women feel about gender roles, tapping into two separate questions that consider child rearing and whether family life suffers when a woman works full-time. The 2012 survey asks respondents if they agreed with the following statement: "Women are naturally better suited to raise children than men." In the 2011 survey, PRRI asked respondents if they agreed that "all in all, family life suffers when a woman has a full-time job." Lastly, the 2012 American Values Survey asked respondents their views on abortion and whether they think it should be legal in all cases, legal in most cases, illegal in most cases, or illegal in all cases.[82]

Figures 5.1 through 5.4 graphically depict Tea Party women's attitudes about these issues compared with non–Tea Party Republican women and other American women. In all cases, Tea Party women in the mass public hold more conservative positions than women who identify as Democrats or Independents and, in some cases, hold more conservative positions than non–Tea Party Republican women. On the matter of sex discrimination, however, Tea Party women's responses are virtually indistinguishable from Republican women who do not support the Tea Party. The more interesting finding about both Tea Party and non–Tea Party Republican women's attitudes about this issue is that the vast majority—fully two-thirds—of these women still recognize that sex discrimination remains a problem in society. That an overwhelming majority of conservative women nationally largely agree that sex discrimination remains a problem contrasts strongly with the narrative pushed by prominent conservative women's groups and several of the Tea Party women activists I interviewed that instances of sex discrimination are largely overblown by liberal feminists (see figure 5.1).

That Tea Party identification may not drive women to have more conservative attitudes about sex discrimination is further supported by the multivariate statistical analysis. (See table 5.1 in appendix B for full model results.) My statistical analysis finds that membership in either the Tea Party or the GOP does not affect women's opinions about whether sex discrimination remains a significant predictor of such attitudes. Instead, education levels in particular, and ideology to a lesser

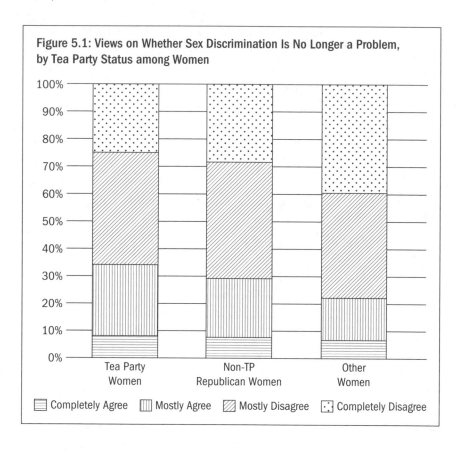

Figure 5.1: Views on Whether Sex Discrimination Is No Longer a Problem, by Tea Party Status among Women

extent, drive attitudes about this issue. Specifically, having higher levels of education makes women far more likely to indicate that sex discrimination remains a problem in American society.

On questions that tap into gender roles, Tea Party women initially express more conservative attitudes than do other women. About half—51 percent—of Tea Party women completely or mostly agree that family life suffers when a woman works full-time, compared with just 41 percent of non–Tea Party Republican women and 36 percent of other American women (see figure 5.2). Moreover, my multivariate statistical analysis shows that Tea Party women are more likely than are other women to agree that women working full-time causes family life to suffer. This attitude is more strongly affected, however, by additional factors among American women, including age, ideology, marital status, religion, and education. (See table 5.2 in appendix B for full model results.) American

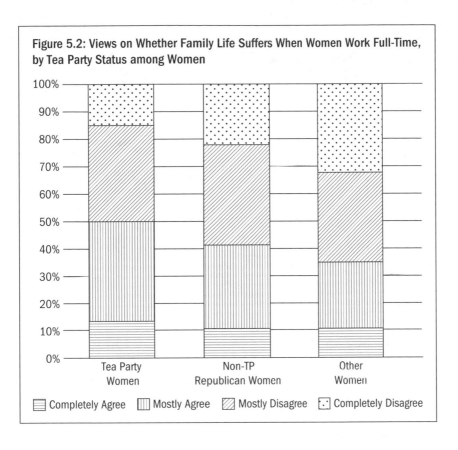

Figure 5.2: Views on Whether Family Life Suffers When Women Work Full-Time, by Tea Party Status among Women

women who are older, married, evangelical, and conservative hold more conservative attitudes about this issue; education, by contrast, drives women to hold more liberal attitudes on this measure. When asked if "women are better suited than men to raise children," 69 percent of Tea Party women either completely or mostly agree with that statement, compared with 61 percent of non–Tea Party Republican women and 51 percent of other women (figure 5.3). Indeed, that just 8 percent of Tea Party women, 9 percent of GOP women, and 16 percent of other American women completely disagree with this statement demonstrates that many American women, regardless of party status, continue to adhere to the very gendered notions of parenting that liberal feminists have often challenged since the second-wave women's movement. Nonetheless, the statistical analysis shows that belonging to the Tea Party acts, along with ideology, as a conservatizing influence on American women

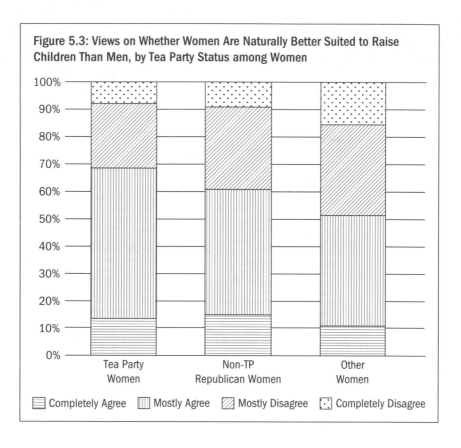

Figure 5.3: Views on Whether Women Are Naturally Better Suited to Raise Children Than Men, by Tea Party Status among Women

when it comes to their attitudes about whether women or men are better suited to raising kids. (See table 5.3 in appendix B for full model results.) Education acts in the opposite manner for American women: the more education women have, the more likely they are to disagree that women are better suited to raise kids than men. In both gender role statistical models, then, it is notable that Tea Party women hold statistically distinct, and more conservative positions, than do Republican women.

Turning to reproductive issues, Tea Party women hold more conservative views on abortion than both other groups of women (see figure 5.4). For instance, 29 percent of Tea Party women believe that abortion should be illegal in all cases, compared with 23 percent of non–Tea Party Republican women and 13 percent of other women. Non–Tea Party GOP women also trend pro-life, however, as 40 percent believe that abortion should remain illegal in most cases, compared with 37 percent of Tea

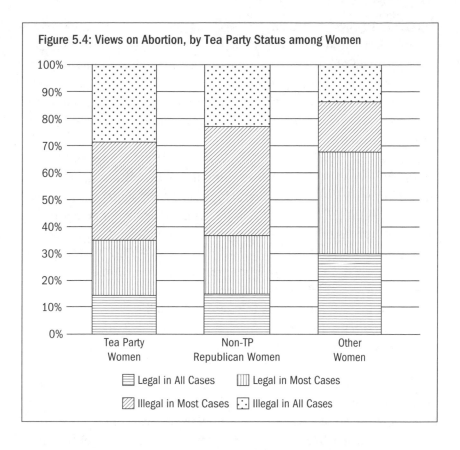

Figure 5.4: Views on Abortion, by Tea Party Status among Women

Legend:
- ☰ Legal in All Cases
- ⦀ Legal in Most Cases
- ▨ Illegal in Most Cases
- ⋮ Illegal in All Cases

Party women. These data stand in stark contrast to all other American women, as more than two-thirds of them believe abortion should be legal in all or most cases. However, when I control for partisanship, Tea Party status, and other factors in a statistical model, I find that Tea Party status is not a significant predictor of abortion attitudes. (See table 5.4 in appendix B for full model results.) Instead, partisanship is much more important to understanding women's attitudes about abortion. Republican women are far more likely to oppose abortion rights and Democratic women are far more likely to support abortion rights than are women who identify as Political Independents. Moreover, ideology, education, race, age, evangelical status, and church attendance also drive abortion attitudes among women. This finding does not mean that a majority of women in the Tea Party are not pro-life; rather, it suggests that there is nothing in particular about Tea Party membership that compels women to be pro-life. Given that Tea Party women are far more likely to be Republican than any other party affiliation—recall from chapter 2 that 57 percent of Tea Party women are also Republican—and that Tea Party women are avowedly conservative and more likely to be evangelical Christians than are American women more generally, it should not come as a surprise that so many Tea Party women in the mass public oppose abortion.

The national data from PRRI show that Tea Party women hold more conservative positions on sex discrimination, abortion, and gender roles than do other American women. However, when subjected to multivariate analysis, the data show that for women, being a member of the Tea Party only significantly shapes attitudes about gender roles. These findings might suggest that women who identify with the Tea Party may be more likely to be drawn from the ranks of stay-at-home mothers or women who work part-time—women who may believe that women are best suited to raise children and therefore seek a lifestyle that comports with that notion. However, 2012 data from Public Religion Research Institute, as revealed in chapter 2, find no significant differences between women who are Tea Party members in the mass public and other American women in terms of their employment status: both are equally likely to be homemakers (12 percent of Tea Party women; 11 percent of other women), employed part-time (12 percent each), or employed full-time (40 percent of Tea Party women compared with 38 percent of other women). It could instead be the case that Tea Party membership has a conservatizing influencing on women when it comes to gender roles because of religion. Recall also from chapter 2 that Tea Party women are significantly more likely to identify as Evangelical Christians than are other American women and that evangelical status is significantly linked to whether women are likely to join the Tea Party. Evangelical denominations, many of which continue to limit women's leadership roles in churches, are far more likely than are other faith traditions to espouse "complementarianism,"[83] which is the view that the Bible endorses separate, complementary positions for men and women, identifying men as spiritual leaders in church and at home while women are designed to be submissive.[84] Indeed, several of the Tea Party women I interviewed who identified themselves as social conservatives grounded their opposition to feminism in their belief that feminists are hostile to traditional gender norms. Recall the view from Eagle Forum's Colleen Holcomb, who believes that feminists, by definition, must reject marriage, motherhood, or anything masculine. Her views are rooted strongly in her conservative religious values and are likely shared by many women who have joined the Tea Party who also happen to be religiously conservative.

At the same time, while Tea Party women are significantly more likely to hold conservative positions on gender roles than are other women, it is worth noting that *most* American women, regardless of whether they belong to the Tea Party or their partisanship, hold conflicted views about such roles. As the PRRI data show, a majority of *all* American women continue to believe that women are naturally better suited to raise children than men are, although their feelings about the effects on children of women working full-time are more nuanced, which may reflect either a greater acceptance of women working or simply a resignation that mothers need to work due to economic conditions.

Given this ambivalence among American women about gender roles nationally, it is little wonder that no consensus has emerged as to the role government should play in addressing the work/family balances with which many American families struggle. In recent years, Democrats and progressive women's organizations have been promoting legislation aimed to help American families cope with work/family balance, such as paid family leave and paid sick leave. In 2015 President Obama introduced a proposal in his State of the Union address to help families deal with the high cost of paid child care that would give working families a $3,000 tax credit to defray day care costs, noting some families pay more in child care expenses than they do toward their mortgages.[85] However, those policies are strongly rejected by conservatives, likely due in some measure to their greater loyalty to traditional gender roles. For instance, Ramesh Ponnuru of the *National Journal* described Obama's proposed child care tax credit as a "War on Homemakers," arguing that it shows that the political left prefers mothers to be working outside the home rather than choosing to stay at home to raise their children full-time.[86] Although the Independent Women's Forum often champions women's growing role and success in the workforce, when it comes to tax credits to help American families pay for day care IWF's Carrie Lukas argues that the policy goes against public opinion data that shows many working families with child care needs often consider day care a last resort, noting that most working mothers wish to work less and "spend more time caring for children themselves."[87] Rather than pushing "parents toward their least preferred child-care arrangement," Lukas argues that a better approach would be to expand child tax credits for Americans with younger children across the board to give parents more flexibility in deciding who will take care of their kids.[88] Moreover, conservative leaders of both genders largely believe the free market should ultimately address these issues.

Tea Party Women, Feminism, and the Future of Public Policy

When it comes to feminism and attitudes about gender roles, Tea Party women hold a diversity of views. While rejecting the liberal feminist movement as extreme and too beholden to an activist state, some Tea Party women and conservative women leaders do show some willingness to self-identify as feminists. For Tea Party activists who hold conservative religious values, feminism is too conflated with abortion rights and a rejection of women's traditional gender roles, so they reject it. Other self-identified libertarian women active in the Tea Party also reject the feminist label, more as a commitment to their belief that society should place paramount importance on individuals as opposed to groups in society. Identifying as a feminist in their minds would mean embracing public policy that would give women preferential treatment, thereby violating their libertarian principles.

Liberal women's organizations, by contrast, believe that women remain unequal to men, due in part to structural barriers in society but also because of pervasive gender stereotyping that still colors many Americans' beliefs about men's and women's capabilities. While liberal women's groups do celebrate women's successes, they point to glaring inequality faced by women at the lower end of the economic spectrum, particularly by women of color, as indicative that women and men still face unequal treatment in the workforce and in society more generally. Such liberal groups also maintain that reproductive rights are essential for women's ability to lead empowered lives. As a result, these liberal feminists envision a large role for government to play in ensuring these rights and making sure that the marketplace truly levels the playing field for all women, regardless of their socioeconomic status, race, or sexual orientation. Thus liberal feminist groups support passing federal legislation aimed at stopping sex discrimination or requiring businesses to offer paid leave or higher minimum wages. Moreover, liberal women's organizations call for more government programs that help lower- and middle-income women pay for child care, preschool, and college as means to help women—this generation and the next—better prepare for the demands of the twenty-first-century economy.

While all the Tea Party women I spoke with reject the liberal feminist movement and its calls for more government programs to help women, many do embrace women's empowerment and some are open to reclaiming the term "feminist." Similar to prominent conservative women such as Sarah Palin, many Tea Party women celebrate the capacity of women to live full lives, both professionally and in politics—choosing to emphasize women's strides in these areas and rejecting claims by liberal women's organizations that structural barriers persist in keeping women down. The rise of women in the Tea Party, and the ascension of Sarah Palin, Michele Bachmann, Cathy McMorris Rodgers, and other women on the political right, does show in some ways that the women's movement has been successful in shaping women's attitudes about their own capabilities. Women such as Palin, Bachmann, Rodgers, and Stacy Mott of Smart Girl Politics and Jenny Beth Martin of Tea Party Patriots—all working mothers—in many ways embody what the women's liberation fought for: that women were capable of being more than mothers. In some respects, then, these Tea Party women are notably distinct from previous generations of right-wing political women, particularly those socially conservative women who fought in defense of the traditional homemaker at the height of the battle for ERA ratification.

Yet there remains a strong undercurrent of socially conservative women working within and alongside the Tea Party who continue to embrace traditional gender roles, rooting their opposition to abortion in their status as mothers and arguing that feminism has ultimately been damaging for women and their families. As the venerable Phyllis Schlafly writes with Suzanne Venker in *The Flipside of Feminism*:

> Men and women used to have respect for one another before feminism came along. They knew gender differences were real, so there was no need to fight over The Pedestal—each gender has its own pedestal. Wives

respected their husbands as breadwinners, and husbands were in awe of their wives' maternal capabilities. That didn't mean men didn't help with domestic duties or women never worked outside of the home (contrary to what feminists told us). But men tended to defer to women on matters related to the home, and women tended to defer to men when it came to making family income decisions.[89]

For women to be truly happy, argue Schlafly and Venker, women and men need to stop denying "each other's inherent nature" and climb back up on their own pedestals. Conservative women's groups such as Eagle Forum and Concerned Women for America, and some newer Tea Party groups like As a Mom . . . a Sisterhood of Mommy Patriots, carry on the antifeminist tradition of Schlafly. As a Mom's *MinuteMom Magazine* and its blog posts, for example, are just as likely to promote numerous conservative public policies as they are to feature articles celebrating the full-time homemaker or provide tips on "prepping," which includes gardening and canning.[90]

Given the decentralized nature of the Tea Party as a social movement, however, such traditionally minded women often find themselves working with more libertarian women, particularly as both are united in their opposition to liberal feminism and to progressive public policies more generally. Conservative women's organizations that are primarily motivated by their laissez-faire economic principles, such as the Independent Women's Forum and Smart Girl Politics, reject liberal feminists' policy solutions to economic policy as an abridgement of the free market. Unlike socially conservative women's organizations, though, their organizations do not argue that women (or men) will find happiness if they embrace traditional gender roles. Yet unlike conservative women activists who are largely driven into political activism because of their socially conservative religious values, laissez-faire women recognize and celebrate women who have been successful at balancing work and family, often profiling "modern feminist" women on their websites who are living the full lives that the second-wave women's rights movement championed. Instead, they seek public policy solutions that give families more flexibility in handling their work/family balance concerns, which in their minds means minimal government regulation. Liberal feminist groups, of course, would counter that such flexibility is an option largely available only to families on the upper end of the economic spectrum, and thus struggling families desperately need government to intervene on such matters.

Many free market feminists also recognize that a younger generation of women, who in the words of American Enterprise Institute's Karlyn Bowman "expect to work *and* have families, [and] . . . have more education than their male counterparts,"[91] are not likely to be open to overtures by the Republican Party and other conservative groups, mostly run by men, if they insist on treating women less seriously. As AEI's Christina Hoff Sommers argues, "Conservative leaders and funders don't take women's issues seriously. They tend to treat women's groups like the Ladies Auxiliary and women's issues as a distracting side show."[92] However, Tea Party women have their work cut out for them to convince other American women that conservative economic policy and their opposition to laws such as the Pay Equity Act to eradicate the lingering effects of sex discrimination are in women's best interests. As the national survey data demonstrate, most American women hold more liberal positions on all of these matters. This is why many conservative women activists such as AEI's Karlyn Bowman and the women who head the Independent Women's Forum implore the GOP to more vocally adopt their messages as to why conservative economic policy is good for women and their families.

There are some signs, perhaps, that the Republican Party has begun to get the message, due in no small part to the efforts of women involved in the Tea Party. In more recent years, as political scientist Michele Swers argues, the GOP has looked to Republican women in Congress as surrogates to "reach out to women voters who tend to favor Republicans, such as white suburban married women, and to defend the party against Democratic accusations that Republican policies are harmful to women."[93] The advent of the Tea Party, and Democratic claims that the Republican Party is engaged in a War on Women, have also spurred the GOP to embrace its female members in more visible ways. In 2015 the GOP tapped the newly elected senator from Iowa, Joni Ernst—a conservative favorite endorsed by both Tea Party Express and Sarah Palin's SarahPAC—to deliver its official response to Obama's State of the Union Address. The year prior, Cathy McMorris Rodgers gave the official response, carefully noting in her speech that all three of her children were born while she was serving in office. The selection of McMorris Rodgers to give the response to the State of the Union Address a mere eight weeks after delivering her third child prompted journalist Hanna Rosin to quip that Rodgers as Supermom is "the new model for a successful Republican woman . . . ambitious, urbane, pen in one hand, baby in the other, having it all, all by herself."[94] Moreover, the GOP has tapped its women members of Congress, such as Martha Roby, to cosponsor legislation such as the "Working Families Flexibility Act" to counter claims by Democrats that the Republican Party is not addressing women's concerns about balancing work and family.

Moreover, the GOP has led numerous initiatives to recruit more women to run for office and serve as party leaders at the state and local level.[95] In discussing such efforts, Cathy McMorris Rodgers told *The Hill*, "Messengers are important, and having a broad spectrum of members who represent that background—youth, women, Hispanics, every walk of life—is very important."[96] While the 2014 elections marked some significant milestones for Republican women—Mia Love of Utah and a Tea Party favorite, was the first African American Republican woman elected to the House; and Elise Stefanik of upstate New York, endorsed by Sarah Palin, at age thirty was the youngest Republican woman ever elected to Congress—the GOP still faces challenges in this area. Currently, women who choose to run for political office in the United States are still far more likely to be Democrats: Democratic women outnumber Republican women in state legislatures and in Congress by a margin of three to one.[97] And, as chapter 2 demonstrated, many of the local Tea Party women activists I interviewed also shared stories of their failed efforts to break into the good old boys' clubs that dominate their local Republican parties, finding that starting their own Tea Party groups served as a better outlet for their political activism.

One commonality shared by Tea Party women, conservative women leaders, and women on the left, however, is their belief that *more* women's voices are needed in politics, although there is no consensus among them as to what public policies are best for women and their families. Tea Party and conservative women *themselves* are still divided about public policy, with some promoting conservative social policy such as restricting abortion rights while others emphasize economic concerns. As Charlotte Hays of the Independent Women's Forum argues, women's issues should not "be limited to our anatomy," which is why the IWF does not take an official stand on abortion rights and instead "prefers to focus our discussion on issues of economic liberty and limited government," inviting both pro-life and pro-choice women to join them.[98] Regardless of how successful these women of the right are in changing American women's attitudes to better comport with their stances, women's emergence as leaders within the Tea Party, and their slow inroads into Republican leadership positions, at the very least signify that no women's group holds a monopoly on what constitutes women's issues. In the next chapter, I demonstrate how gun rights have also become a cause for conservative women to champion, with many conservative women using gendered rhetoric to make the case that relaxing gun restrictions are in women's best interests. Some women on the right even argue that gun ownership among women is an important feminist principle, further demonstrating that feminism may hold some appeal, at least, to conservative women.

6

Guns Are the Great Equalizer

Mama Grizzlies and the Right to Bear Arms

In December 2012 the nation mourned the loss of twenty schoolchildren and six staff in an unspeakable act of gun violence at Sandy Hook Elementary School in Newtown, Connecticut. The shooter, twenty-year-old Adam Lanza, used a semiautomatic rifle to kill the victims at Sandy Hook before killing himself. After the attack, many citizens called for a renewed effort for government to limit access to guns; one of those individuals was Shannon Watts, a stay-at-home mother who formed the group Moms Demand Action for Gun Sense in America, which later partnered with Mayors against Illegal Guns, creating a national, grassroots coalition of activists dedicated to ending gun violence. As stated on its website, the goal of Moms Demand Action is "educating, motivating, and mobilizing moms and families to take action that will result in stronger laws and policies to save lives."[1] The tendency for women, acting as mothers, to stand against gun violence politically is not new in American politics. For instance, Donna Dees-Thomases formed the grassroots movement Million Mom March in 1999—a year in which tragic gun shootings at Columbine High School in Colorado and the Granada Hills Jewish Community Center in Los Angeles gripped the nation's attention. The Million Mom March sponsored a rally at the National Mall and in communities nationwide on Mother's Day, 2000, to call for tighter gun control laws. Dees-Thomases told CNN she started the organization because "there is nothing more powerful than a mother's drive to protect her children. Mothers across the country are harnessing that energy, and it is their passion that will have the impact here."[2]

While the fiscal crisis of 2008, and efforts the following year by President Obama and congressional Democrats to expand the size and scope of government, initially sparked the emergence of the Tea Party, support for gun rights has become a dominant issue for the movement in wake of the Sandy Hook shootings and other national gun tragedies that have prompted efforts to regulate gun ownership. Part of the new effort to defend the right to bear arms has involved conservative women, who often invoke the desire to protect themselves and their families as the reason to defend gun ownership—a marked contrast from more progressive women activists who believe families will be safer when access to guns is more tightly restricted. Take, for instance, Sarah Palin's call at the NRA's 2014 Stand and Fight Rally for women to arm themselves as a way to protect their children: "Our Congressmen are [protected by guns], our president is, anti-gun mayors and celebrities are, our banks, our airports, our jewelry stores are. But our children? They are protected by a thin, tin sign that reads gun-free zone. Like that will stop the bad guy. That's stupid on steroids. . . . Maybe our kids could be defended against criminals on the spot if more Mama Grizzlies carried."[3] Palin's speech to the NRA is just one high-profile example of conservative women who are using gendered rhetoric, sometimes steeped in "Mama Grizzly" imagery, to promote gun ownership and Second Amendment rights.

While many women from the Tea Party and the ranks of elected Republican members of Congress use gendered appeals in their statements and messaging concerning economic goals or what they perceive as the excesses of the liberal feminist movement, in this chapter I examine the extent to which such women use gendered appeals to fight for gun rights. Not surprisingly, Republican women in Congress are strongly in favor of gun rights. Aside from Maine Republican Senator Susan Collins, who earned a C rating from the National Rifle Association in 2013, all GOP women serving in the Senate and House in recent years have earned an A rating or higher according to ProPublica, a nonpartisan, public interest news organization.[4] While the movement for gun rights has long predated the Tea Party, given the Tea Party's devotion to individual liberty, grounded in a conservative interpretation of the Constitution, it is little wonder that the Tea Party routinely champions gun rights along with groups such as the National Rifle Association. To consider how Tea Party women more specifically, and conservative women more broadly, make gendered appeals, I rely on several sources: interviews with Tea Party women, the blog posts and speeches by Tea Party women activists, and the writings promoted by conservative women's organizations, which include newer Tea Party groups such as Smart Girl Politics and As a Mom . . . a Sisterhood of Mommy Patriots, and longer-standing conservative organizations, particularly the Independent Women's Forum (IWF). Although perhaps best known as the leading conservative women's organization devoted to promoting libertarian economic policy as well as to debunking liberal feminist causes, IWF has also written extensively about gun rights as a gendered issue. Lastly, I examine the rhetoric employed by several pro-gun women activists and advocacy groups on their websites.[5]

I identify three common gendered arguments made by pro-gun women. First, pro-gun women often argue that guns are especially impor-tant for women's safety, as guns serve as an "equalizer" against men who may attack them or their families. Second, pro-gun women denounce efforts by gun control advocates to limit access to certain semiautomatic weapons because such weapons are not only more accurate, in some cases they are lighter and easier for women to use, than, say, shotguns. Third, some pro-gun women view attempts by gun control advocates to limit women's access to certain guns and ammunition as sexist and paternalis-tic, in addition to being unconstitutional. Pro-gun women maintain that women should have access to any gun they may need as a way to protect themselves, viewing self-defense as an important feminist principle.

To tackle the issue of whether gendered rhetoric concerning gun rights is likely to find greater appeal among American women at large, I analyze current public opinion about gun rights. Using data the Public Religion Research Institute collected with the Religious News Service in August 2012,[6] I examine how gender shapes attitudes about guns. While I find that a solid majority of American women agree that gun rights are an important constitutional right, most women still support passing stricter gun control legislation and are especially opposed to allowing Americans the ability to carry concealed weapons in churches, govern-ment buildings, and colleges, as is advocated by many pro-gun and Tea Party women activists. Tea Party women and Republican women, not surprisingly, share far more conservative positions on these issues com-pared with "other American women" (Democrats and Political Indepen-dents.). Yet my multivariate analysis shows that being a part of the Tea Party alone does not predict more conservative attitudes on gun con-trol legislation. Instead, what is more important in predicting attitudes about guns among American women is Republican status and ideology. In other words, while many Tea Party women themselves are pro-gun, and many activist women within the Tea Party proudly pronounce their support for gun rights, gun culture also extends to GOP women and self-identified conservative women more broadly in the United States. Gun attitudes are one area in which the Tea Party and Republican women may be more in sync than other policy areas.

Women and Guns in America

It is estimated that about one in four Americans personally own guns and that approximately 35 percent of Americans live in a house with a gun.[7] Gun ownership rates vary by region, type of residency, age, race, and partisanship. Gun owners are more likely to be older, white, Republican, and reside in rural communities and in the South, Midwest, and West. Moreover, there are large gender differences in gun ownership: men are much more likely to report owning guns compared with women. Philip J. Cook and Kristin A. Goss, in their book *The Gun Debate* (2014), find that 37 percent of American men compared with 12 percent of American women report owning a gun; other studies, including the 2012 General Social Surveys, show that about 10 percent of women report owning a gun.[8] Estimates vary, but Peggy Tartaro, who edits *Women and Guns* magazine, told the *New York Times* that between twelve and seventeen million American women likely own guns.[9]

According to the General Social Survey, self-reported gun ownership rates per household have decreased in the last four decades, from an average of about 50 percent of households having a gun in the 1970s to 35 percent in the 2000s.[10] Those who study household gun ownership rates believe that their decline stems from several national trends decades in the making: the United States has fewer hunters, fewer military veterans (many Americans first learn how to handle guns through military service), less violent crime, and more female-headed households. It is little wonder, then, that gun manufacturers and pro-gun organizations have stepped up efforts to market guns to women, who represent a largely untapped market. Such efforts to make gun ownership and shooting sports more appealing to women are certainly not new, however. In the mid-1990s the National Rifle Association famously launched its "Refuse to Be a Victim Program," which recommended that women purchase and carry handguns for self-defense.[11] The NRA maintains this program on-line today, featuring the stories of female survivors who used firearms to protect themselves or their families upon an attack. However, it has also expanded its programming for female gun enthusiasts to include its "Armed and Fabulous" video features, which profile women hunters and award-winning shooters. The "NRA Women" program also provides re-sources for women, including general overviews of gun basics, informa-tion about which sorts of guns are best suited for women, and links to local gun clubs, classes, and shooting ranges with programming geared for women. It also contains a portal for shopping, which includes links to well-known outdoor and sporting stores, such as Cabelas and Eddie Bauer, as well as more specialized gun shops for women, such as Armed in Heels, which sell guns and holsters specifically designed for women.[12]

The NRA is not alone in helping to build broader interest in gun ownership and shooting sports among women. In the past few years, several organizations devoted to such activities have appeared, such as Shoot Like a Girl and A Girl and a Gun, which promote both hunting and archery as sports that hold appeal to women.[13] Founded in 2009, Pistols and Pumps, whose tagline reads "Concealed and High Heeled," sells gun-related apparel and shooting accessories but also promotes knowledge about gun safety, recreation, and current legislation. The Well Armed Woman, founded in 2012 by gun instructor Carrie Light-foot, sponsors women's gun clubs throughout the country; its website claims that the group in 2015 has 222 chapters in 49 states.[14] In 2014 *Rolling Stone* featured a story about the rise of women's gun culture, in which the gun industry has shifted away from "token scantily clad females—the dreaded 'booth babes'—toward actual engagement with actual women."[15] Additionally, *Garden and Gun* magazine, though not necessarily marketed as a women's magazine, promotes hunting and gun ownership with a larger emphasis on southern culture, food, and heri-tage and has been growing in popularity since its founding in 2007.[16]

Regardless of whether the onset of such gendered appeals and pro-grams to promote gun ownership and shooting sports have increased women's interest in guns, or is merely a reflection of such an increase in women's gun interests, some data suggest that gun ownership and participation in hunting and shooting sports has increased among women. For example, Gallup shows an increase in gun ownership rates among women from 12 percent in 2007 to 15 percent in 2013.[17] The National Sporting Goods Association reports that women's participation in target shooting from 2001 to 2011 increased by 51.5 percent and by 41.8 percent for hunting.[18] Moreover, according to the National Shooting Sports Foundation, nearly 80 percent of gun retailers reported an increase in female customers in 2012.[19] Women's rates of concealed carry permits have also gone up significantly in the last decade, increasing sevenfold in Texas alone.[20] Paxton Quigley, who is a well-known self-defense and gun instructor, attributes women's greater interest in guns to several factors, including broader lifestyle changes, with more women choosing to live alone or to delay marriage. In books such as *Armed and Fabulous*, Quigley fiercely argues that women should carry handguns to prevent themselves from becoming rape victims (her activism in this area was prompted after a friend of hers was raped). Regarding women's rising interest in guns, she told the *Christian Science Monitor*, "There is a different attitude now, that women need to take responsibility for their own safety."[21]

Gender and the Right to Bear Arms

Gun ownership is significantly more likely among men than among women, although recent data suggest that women are more likely to own guns than in previous years. Not surprisingly, then, women have begun to take a more active role in promoting gun rights. This is not to say that a majority of women support relaxing gun control laws: as I demonstrate, a solid majority of women actually favor passing more gun control laws. Yet this has not stopped many women, including those with ties to conservative groups and Tea Party organizations, to make overt, gendered appeals to relax gun control measures as a means to protect women and their families.[22] Some suggest that women activists have been particularly successful in helping to relax gun controls legislatively, often by using gendered framing.[23] For instance, Julie Dolan's case study of the passage of a bill to relax the concealed carry provision in Minnesota's state legislature documents how the chief sponsors of the successful bill—both conservative, Republican women—framed increased access to handguns as a women's issue, affording women, in particular, greater potential protection against violent crime.[24]

In my review of interest group blog posts, writings, and interviews with Tea Party and conservative activists, I found that pro-gun women expressed several gendered themes about why gun ownership was important, although they also routinely relied on the more general rationales that have been employed by the gun rights movement for decades, including broad support for the Second Amendment as a matter of personal liberty, their right to self-defense, and the argument that gun control laws only harm law-abiding citizens, not criminals. For instance, Gabriella Hoffman, who writes the blog *All-American Girl for the Restoration of Values* and works at the Leadership Institute—a popular training program for conservative activists—told me that she plans to apply for her conceal license as she is a big proponent of gun rights. She said:

> For me, personally, the reason I want to keep and bear arms is not only [that] is it a constitutional right that we are afforded, but for me it is a statement hitting back at socialism and Marxism, because my parents never had the right to bear arms (they immigrated to the U.S. from communist Lithuania). Much like any society that has succumbed to socialism, Marxist–Leninism, the first thing they do is strip people of their guns and their protection. So, for me, I want to do my part to show that this is a birthright to everyone. . . . We have this great right in the event that someone breaks into your home or in the event that tyranny lurks somewhere. We have to be suspicious of our government. We can't trust it.[25]

That the right to bear arms is vitally linked to safeguarding democracy is a common refrain among many gun rights advocates, especially those in the Tea Party, who argue that government overreach in many areas of the lives of Americans—including the regulation of firearms—essentially amounts to a socialist form of government. This statement above is similar to those often expressed by Tea Party activists, men and women alike, in describing why they are so passionate about gun ownership. It is not, however, a particularly *gendered* rationale. Moreover, in examining the press releases of Republican women members of Congress who support gun rights, their rationales in defending the right to bear arms are largely gender-neutral. Many members relate that they themselves are gun owners, such as Representative Martha Roby (R-AL), who said the following in a press release in response to Obama's gun proposals after the Sandy Hook school shooting: "I'm a gun owner myself, and I strongly value the rights guaranteed in the Second Amendment."[26] Other GOP women, particularly those from more rural areas, also highlight the importance of gun rights to their families and culture. Take, for instance, the following statement from Representative Cynthia Lummis (R-WY), whose position statement on her congressional website reads, "As a fourth-generation Wyoming rancher, I know firsthand the importance of the Second Amendment to our way of life in Wyoming. Firearms are important tools for so many of Wyoming's citizens, whether for self-defense, recreation or even one's business occupation. Our Founding Fathers believed so strongly in our right to own and use firearms that they made it part of our Bill of Rights."[27]

While GOP women in Congress have yet to be tapped by party leaders to promote gun rights as a *women's* issue in the way that they sometimes are asked to defend their record on women's rights or economic and regulatory policy, many Tea Party women and conservative women activists do, in fact, use gendered language to defend their Second Amendment rights. There are three common arguments used by pro-gun Tea Party women to defend gun rights and oppose attempts to prohibit the sale of certain weapons. First, many pro-gun women paint the right to own guns as particularly important to women as a matter of personal safety. Viewing guns as a great "equalizer" for women, they believe women especially should be invested in the fight for gun rights because they often lack the physical strength to defend themselves in case of attack. In some cases, in true Mama Grizzly fashion, pro-gun women argue that gun rights enable women to protect their families and children. Second, and related to the first theme, pro-gun women reject attempts to limit the sale of certain firearms because such guns are lighter and easier to shoot, making them particularly well suited for women's physiques. Lastly, pro-gun women defend their right to bear arms as a matter of feminism, viewing attempts by the government to limit their access to guns as not just unconstitutional but paternalistic as well.

Guns as an Equalizer

The most common gendered frame used by pro-gun women activists is safety: many activists believe that guns rights are especially crucial for women as they lack the physical strength necessary to defend themselves if attacked.[28] As Carrie Lukas, managing director of the Independent Women's Forum, told me, "A lot of people are so passionate about this, and they talk about Second Amendment rights as an important constitutional right, and a lot of women see this as a great equalizer. A woman is going to lose a fight with a man due to his physical strength, but a woman can use a gun to protect herself and her family in a way that she can't unarmed."[29] While Lukas acknowledged that the gun issue is not a "major focus" for IWF, several of their senior fellows have written extensively about gun rights, particularly in wake of the Sandy Hook school shootings.

For example, IWF senior fellow Gayle Trotter regularly appears on conservative talk shows to promote this position. Trotter was the only woman to testify in January 2013 at Senate Judiciary Hearings convened to consider gun control reforms advocated by the Obama administration. In her statement, Trotter argued that guns make women safer, given that federal statistics show more than 90 percent of violent crimes occur without a firearm: "The vast majority of violent criminals use their size and their physical strength to prey on women who are at a severe disadvantage. In a violent confrontation guns reverse the balance of power. An armed woman does not need superior strength or the proximity of a hand-to-hand struggle."[30] She began her testimony by relaying the story of a young widow and mother, Sarah McKinley, who on New Year's Eve in 2011 called 911 as two intruders broke into her home to steal her late husband's prescription drugs. She killed one of the intruders with a shotgun, prompting the other man to flee. McKinley was not prosecuted given that she acted in self-defense. Her story has galvanized many women on the right to speak out on gun rights.[31] Trotter also argued that armed women can benefit those women who choose not to carry a gun, pointing to studies that show that in jurisdictions with concealed carry laws, women "are less likely to be raped, maimed or murdered than they are in states with stricter gun ownership laws."[32] She ended her testimony by saying that "for women, the ability to arm ourselves for protection is even more consequential than for men. Because guns are the great equalizer in a violent confrontation."[33]

Krista Kafer, another senior fellow with IWF, recounts her experience as a robbery victim as a reason to oppose Obama's gun control efforts. She writes on IWF's website, "If implemented, the Obama gun control plan will impact me, the victim who intends to arm herself, not the lawless man who can rely on his physical strength to assault a woman."[34] Anna Rittgers, also with IWF, directly invokes her role as a mother in response to the Newtown school shooting. In "A Mother's Case for Gun Rights," an online op-ed penned for Fox News, she argued that more law-abiding citizens, especially women, need to be armed:

> There was no good guy available to protect the children of Sandy Hook Elementary School in Newtown, Conn. from evil. Those poor, innocent, defenseless children had to wait 20 minutes for police to arrive, and the horror only ended when the gunman chose to take his own life. I am passionate about protecting the civil rights enshrined in the Second Amendment, particularly because I am a thirty-something year old woman with a three year old and a newborn. The only chance I have against one or more assailants seeking to harm me or my family is a firearm.

She closed by saying that "good guys—and gals—must be able to possess guns in order to fight evil."[35]

Other Tea Party women's organizations, like As a Mom . . . a Sisterhood of Mommy Patriots and Smart Girl Politics, also make gendered, pro-gun arguments from time to time. As a Mom's director of membership, Erin Williams, shares her decision to seek gun training, citing concerns about her family's safety as a motivation for learning to shoot. Williams wrote in As a Mom's online *Minute Mom Magazine*, "I began thinking about my kids and what I would do if anyone tried to break into our home with us in it, or attack us at the park, or while on my run. I started to see guns as a potential, self-protection device." Once she became comfortable with guns, she writes that she began to keep it loaded and by her side when her young kids were napping—"just in case someone tried to break into the home." Again, invoking her status as a mother, she believes being armed allows her to be "ready to get between a potential attacker and my children."[36]

Smart Girl Politics, similar to the Independent Women's Forum, does not promote gun rights as its major focus but has recently taken a more vocal pro-gun stance. As Stacy Mott, co-founder of the organization, told me, "We're not a gun organization, [but] we're about individual freedom, and women being secure and independent and being able to take care of ourselves away from the government."[37] In addition to promoting pro-gun pieces on its website, for the past several years at its annual Smart Girl Summit the group has sponsored a trip to the gun range for participants in a program it dubs "Armed and Fabulous," and several of its state chapters have sponsored gun clubs for women. Moreover, in February 2013 Smart Girl Politics sponsored a Google Hangout video chat on "Women and Guns" featuring Mott, Smart Girl Politics writer Maya Grim, and several other pro-gun women: Carrie Lightfoot of The Well Armed Woman, Natalie Foster of Girl's Guide to Guns, and Celia Bigelow, director of campus action for the conservative group American Majority Action.

Tara Kozub, a featured writer in the Smart Girl Politics e-magazine *Smart Girl Nation*, recounts her decision to buy a handgun as a measure of self-defense and family protection. Prompted by the appearance of a homeless person close to her neighborhood, Kozub wrote about being fearful that someone could break into her family's home: "This man and his message hammered home the reality that, within walking distance of my home, stood a potential threat to my family and me. My misplaced fear of guns began to wane, while the fear of an intruder breaking into my home to steal from me became a reality. For it is the lawless criminal who is to be feared, not the gun he may be wielding. For the first time in my life, I thought about purchasing a gun."[38] Kozub then tells readers about her day of gun training at Smith and Wesson Academy, followed by her decision to seek a license to carry from her local police station.

Since January 2013 gun activist Maya Grim has been writing regular features about gun rights on the Smart Girl Politics website. While many of her pieces provide basic information (for example, explaining gun terminology or describing the different types of firearms available) or use the more familiar Second Amendment rhetoric employed by gun rights groups to defend gun ownership, she also employs a lot of gendered appeals. In her blog post "Why I Carry," Grim said that she owns guns to protect herself and her kids: "Ladies, you have to be the

hero. You and your kids can fare much better, if and when you step between them and a monster you have a couple of magazines full or a
large caliber, and a high velocity lead delivery system known commonly
as a gun."[39] Grim implored women to carry a gun as they would other
items, including makeup and hand sanitizer, in their purses[40] as a matter of basic preparedness, noting that a gun is the only item women have
that can be used to "immediately stop a threatening person who has approached you in the grocery store parking lot and tries to force you into
his/her car." At the end, she argued that gun ownership is "the ultimate
woman's right and female empowerment issue rolled into one: defending our own lives."[41]

Last but not least, Tea Party activist and conservative columnist Dana
Loesch, who hosts a nationally syndicated radio show popular with
many Tea Partiers, has made gun rights a special concern of hers. She
argues that gun control is the "ultimate war on women" because women
would be left defenseless in cases of a violent crime:

> The average woman does not have the physical strength of a man. As
> much as I want to believe that I'm 6′6″ and 275 lbs, in reality I'm 5′6″ and
> a buck 20. If a dude wants to take me down, he will. The only method
> available of leveling the playing field is with my ultimate equalizer, my
> firearm. Women have had the right to bear arms since before we could
> vote. How amazing that the very men who sought to deny us the vote
> now seek to disenfranchise us of our Second Amendment liberties.[42]

As with other pro-gun women activists, Loesch describes guns as a great
equalizer for women. If women are now allowed to fight in combat for
their country, Loesch continues, they should have the right to "defend
themselves and their family at home. In their home, *they* are their own
first responders."[43] This latter point raised by Loesch is echoed by many
gun rights advocates, who believe that gun control experts urging
citizens to rely on 911 in case of emergencies instead of arming themselves is bad advice, particularly for women. For instance, in one blog
post, Loesch is critical of Milwaukee Mayor Tom Barrett, a member
of Mayors against Illegal Guns. In a tweet shared on Loesch's website,
Mayor Barrett was openly critical of efforts by Milwaukee County Sheriff
David Clark to encourage citizens to arm themselves for self-protection

"instead of calling 911." In her reply, Loesch wrote that Barrett and other progressive gun control politicians "would rather women gamble their lives, defenselessly, until police arrive."[44]

In examining these passages here, it is worth noting that while violent crime against women does occur in the United States, is it not nearly as common as these pro-gun women (or pro-gun advocates more generally) suggest. In fact, rates of violent crime, including rape, have dropped precipitously in the past two decades, according to data from the FBI.[45] Moreover, gun proponents rarely mention that guns in the home are more likely to be used in conjunction with a fatal or nonfatal unintentional shooting or suicide attempt rather than on an intruder in the home.[46] Of course, fear is a powerful rhetorical device often employed by Tea Party activists, whether it is fear of an invasion by an unnamed homeless man as described in Tara Kozub's piece for *MinuteMom Magazine*, fear of ObamaCare regulations taking away end-of-life decisions from Americans as we saw in chapter 4, or fear more generally that the United States is headed in a direction that does not respect the values and priorities of conservatives, hence the frequent call to "take back America" that is often invoked by Tea Party leaders, men and women alike. It is also worth noting that the gun proposals first introduced by President Obama with the support of most congressional Democrats—proposals that ended up going nowhere in the Senate—would not, in fact, have affected the ability of most women to carry or possess a gun, although it did seek to outlaw certain types of semiautomatic assault weapons. Yet this proposal to place limits on the production and availability of such guns was met with fierce protest from pro-gun women, as I show below.

Banning Guns That Are Good for Women

Pro-gun women activists argue that gun control efforts potentially rob women of their ability to defend themselves and their families in case of attack. Related to this line of argument, many pro-gun women take issue with efforts to limit the sale of semiautomatic assault weapons or guns that use more than ten rounds of ammunition in a single magazine, such as the firearm used in the shooting at Sandy Hook Elementary School. Sales of semiautomatic assault weapons and high-capacity magazines were banned by 1994 federal legislation known as the Public Safety and Recreational Firearms Use Protection Act, which expired in 2004. Among other reforms, the Obama administration's failed gun control plan sought to reinstate and expand the assault weapons ban and to limit the sale of magazine ammunition rounds to ten. Such a move would have limited sales of the AR-15 rifle, which is a lightweight semiautomatic weapon that is especially popular with some women gun owners.[47]

In response to such criticism, Vice President Joe Biden, who was charged with leading the task force examining gun control in wake of the Sandy Hook school shootings, urged women to use shotguns instead of semiautomatic weapons. In a Facebook Town Hall hosted by *Parenting* magazine, Biden took questions from readers about gun violence, including "Kate," who questioned how gun owners would be able to sufficiently protect themselves if the government banned certain weapons and high-capacity gun magazines. Biden told her: "Kate, if you want to protect yourself, get a double barreled shotgun. I promise you, as I told my wife, we live in an area that's wooded and somewhat secluded. I said, Jill, if there's ever a problem, just walk out on the balcony here, walk out, put [up] that double barreled shotgun and fire two blasts outside the house . . . You don't need an AR-15. Buy a shotgun! Buy a shotgun!"[48] Pro-gun advocates, including women, ridiculed Biden's advice. In the Smart Girl Politics Google Hangout, pro-gun activist Celia Bigelow said Joe Biden "has no idea what he is talking about. . . . AR-15s range in size, they are significantly lighter than shotguns and they are much more accurate than shotguns." She goes on to praise the AR-15 as a gun that is especially good for women in a *National Journal* op-ed: "The AR-15 is lightweight and practical. As light as five pounds, it produces low levels of recoil, and it's easy to shoot. It also looks intimidating, which is what you want when facing an assailant or intruder. But don't let its appearance intimidate you. Assault rifles such as the AR-15 aren't more 'dangerous,' as liberals claim. They don't fire faster than other rifles, and don't normally contain more powerful ammunition. Accuracy? Check. Ease in handling? Check. Intimidation factor? Check. An AR-15 might be a woman's best friend."[49] In her testimony before the Senate Judiciary Committee, IWF's Gayle Trotter also argued that the AR-15 was particularly well suited for women. When asked by Republican Senator

Charles Grassley whether she thought semiautomatic weapons, such as the AR-15, have a "value in self-defense," Trotter argued that women praise this gun, in particular, as their "weapon of choice": "The guns are accurate. They have good handling. They're light. They're easy for women to hold. And most importantly, their appearance. An assault weapon in the hands of a young woman defending her babies in her home becomes a defense weapon. And the peace of mind that a woman has as she's facing three, four, five violent attackers, intruders in her home with her children screaming in the background—the peace of mind that she has knowing that she has a scary-looking gun gives her more courage when she's fighting hardened violent criminals." Trotter continued to defend her position when challenged later in the hearing by Democratic Senator Sheldon Whitehouse, a fierce opponent of semi-automatic assault weapons such as the AR-15. Whitehouse pointed out that Sarah McKinley, who Trotter had referenced earlier in her testimony, had used a shotgun in self-defense, which would not have been banned under the Obama administration's proposals. As Whitehouse intimated that Trotter's position against semiautomatic assault weapons was not reasonable, she shot back, "So would it have been unreasonable for [McKinley] to use a different gun to protect her child?"[50]

Anna Rittgers of IWF also took issue with the Obama administration's plan to limit firearm and magazine sales, again framing her argument in terms of the safety of women and their families. She writes that semiautomatic guns and other weapons that allow for larger magazine capacities may be critical to women who face intruders in their home: "It often takes several shots to stop one attacker. If the maximum magazine capacity is 10 (or if all semiautomatic handguns are banned, but 6 shot revolvers remain), and a woman in danger has to stop and reload her weapon while trying to protect her children (who are likely hysterical at this point), it gives the bad guy an opportunity to react— potentially fatally. Laws limiting magazine capacity and availability of semiautomatic handguns will directly impact women, who use these weapons for self-defense inside and outside the home." Rittgers goes on to urge Obama not to pursue Executive Orders that would regulate the sale of select firearms apart from Congress, as such a move could "limit a woman's capability to fight back against attackers and protect herself and her family."[51]

Gun Rights as a Feminist Principle

Linked to the broader arguments conservative women make concerning guns rights is the stand taken by many pro-gun women that limiting access to guns is antifeminist. In essence, such conservative women argue that a woman's right to carry is not only constitutionally required, but it is an empowering, feminist act, allowing women to take care of themselves. Attempts to regulate certain types of weapons or magazines are viewed as paternalistic and belittling to women. Writing for Smart Girl Politics, Maya Grim had this to say of Joe Biden's suggestion that women use shotguns instead of semiautomatic guns: "The Vice President seems to think women won't be able to properly handle an AR-15 . . . Well, Vice President Biden, just like the school my kids goes to, the birth control I choose, or the car I drive, you really don't have a say in the matter."[52] Grim elaborated on this theme during Smart Girl's Google Hangout:

> I'm getting sick of Joe Biden . . . and all of these people telling me I can't handle a certain caliber or I can't carry a certain round or I can't have this many rounds in my magazine. It just sounds like "Honey, that's too much vehicle for you" or "Honey, that horse is too loud for you. Let me give you the sweet mare." I'm tired of it, and I think a lot of women who don't even agree with us would say where is the outcry? Where are all of the women saying, "Hey, stop talking to me like that." I can make these decisions for myself.[53]

Other Tea Party women, such as Dana Loesch, also contend that the "real war on women" is gun control. Much of this dialogue stems from current debates regarding concealed carry laws on college campuses. In Colorado, for example, although the state in 2013 passed new restrictive gun measures, it was not successful in passing a college campus gun ban (current concealed carry laws permit anyone over twenty-one with a permit to carry guns on public college campuses). One particular statement by Democratic state representative Joe Salazar raised the ire of many Republican and Tea Party women when he argued that guns should not be allowed on campus because of the possibility that women may end up shooting someone by mistake and that women have other options to defend themselves. Said Salazar, "It's why we have call boxes. It's why we have safe zones. That's why we have the whistles, because you just don't know who you're going to be shooting at. And you don't know if you feel like you're going to be raped, or if you feel like someone's been following you around or if you feel like you're in trouble when you may actually not be, that you pop out that gun and you pop . . . pop a round at somebody."[54] Republican women in the Colorado General Assembly, such as state representative Polly Lawrence, denounced Salazar's comments as insensitive and insulting: "No matter what sort of policy position you're trying to advance, questioning the rational ability of women to perceive threats around them is something Democrat leaders should condemn."[55] Dana Loesch harshly criticized Salazar's comments as patronizing, writing on her blog that women, according to him, "are hysterical things which shoot indiscriminately at any and everything," adding sarcastically, "Even if women feel like they're going to be raped, they may not, so who needs a firearm for protection?"[56]

During hearings for the Colorado bill, college rape survivor Amanda Collins testified about her experience in 2006, when she was raped while a student at the University of Nevada, Reno, in a parking garage. Despite having a concealed carry permit, she did not have her gun with her at the time of the attack because of university rules that prohibited firearms on campus. Now active in promoting campus carry laws throughout the country, Collins told committee members that measures often touted to provide safety for women on campus such as call boxes, safety zones, and carrying rape whistles "just give a false sense of security." She told lawmakers that "a call box above my head while I was straddled on the parking garage floor being brutally raped wouldn't have helped me one bit. The safe zone? I was in a safe zone and my attacker didn't care."[57] However, while Collins's points about allowing women to carry guns echo the other gendered arguments pro-gun women make about their personal safety, she goes further by arguing that concealed carry laws are important as a feminist principle. In a piece for the NRA's *America's First Freedom* blog, Collins wrote that laws banning guns from campus entail turning women into victims, essentially violating the rights of women: "All my life, I've been told there is a war being waged on women. Until recently, it was a fight I could agree with—a right to education and workplace equality. Lately, though, it seems the focus has shifted to whether we can have the ultimate control over our lives by exercising our right to self-defense—and that debate stands as a new war on women."[58] In this regard, Collins brings to mind a common refrain heard from many conservative women who denounce modern, liberal feminism more generally: the notion that intrusive government programs and regulation paint women as victims and keep women from being fully empowered. Many conservative women, then, view gun control efforts as just another attempt by progressive activists to restrict women's choices.

Moreover, pro-gun women such as Maya Grim of Smart Girl Politics, Jennifer Coffey of Second Amendment Sisters, and Tea Party radio host Dana Loesch argue that placing limits on gun ownership smacks of hypocrisy on the part of progressive women's organizations that often champion both gun control and abortion rights. Wrote Maya Grim, "How many times have you heard, from progressive feminists, that if you don't have lady parts or haven't had an abortion, you are not permitted to have an opinion on abortion, unless it's that you support abortion? How often do you hear women telling men they can't tell them what to wear, if they should fight on the front lines, or who they can love? But on being able to protect myself with the carry-firearm, or home defense firearm of my choice, what do you hear? Silence."[59] Jennifer Coffey, national director of legislative affairs for Second Amendment Sisters, a pro-gun women's advocacy group, recently told the *Christian Science Monitor*, "We always hear about a woman's right to choose, and we are women who want the right to choose how to protect our lives."[60] Returning to the issue of campus rape, Dana Loesch lashes out at the feminist blog *Jezebel*, whose writers according to Loesch "support disarming women on campus."[61] When *Jezebel* posted a blog post critical of Yale University's response to charges by the Department of Education's Office of Civil Rights that it created a "hostile sexual environment," Loesch complained, "It's like progressive women are just now discovering the brutally high college rape statistics."[62] While Loesch largely agrees with Jezebel's criticism of Yale University, deriding the school for allowing six male perpetrators of what was called "non-consensual sex" to remain enrolled, her solution to the problem resides in concealed carry laws: "If only these women were allowed the pro-choice right of choosing their self defense."[63]

As these statements demonstrate, Tea Party and other conservative women often employ gendered rhetoric to defend their right to bear arms, arguing that access to guns is particularly necessary for women, who lack the physical strength to face male attackers. They vehemently oppose attempts by lawmakers to restrict access to semiautomatic assault weapons, believing that such firearms are better suited for women when it comes to their own self-defense. Moreover, pro-gun women are often on the front lines in state legislatures promoting concealed carry laws, attempting to convince lawmakers that women should be allowed to carry concealed weapons everywhere, including on college campuses. In so doing, these pro-gun women argue that they advance feminist principles by empowering women to take control of their own lives.

The Tea Party and Attitudes about Gun Rights among American Women Nationally

Although many Tea Party women may support gun rights, it is not clear if American women nationally are likely to support these same pro-gun views. Past research shows that women are stronger supporters of gun control than are men, even while controlling for other factors linked to gun attitudes.[64] Moreover, while high-profile gun tragedies such as the school shootings at Columbine High School in 1999 and Sandy Hook Elementary School in 2012 often prompt national public opinion to support stricter gun control, such shifts are largely temporary. In fact, over the long term, Americans have moved toward being more supportive of gun rights as opposed to gun control, which is ironic given that fewer American households actually now possess firearms. The Pew Research Center found in 2012, for example, that "49 percent of Americans say it is more important to protect the rights of Americans to own guns, while 45 percent say it is more important to control gun ownership."[65] In the early 1990s, by contrast, Pew found that just about one-third of Americans felt that protecting gun ownership rights was more important than controlling gun ownership. Notably, although there is still a strong gender gap concerning attitudes toward gun control, Pew finds that women have become more supportive of gun rights over time. Its

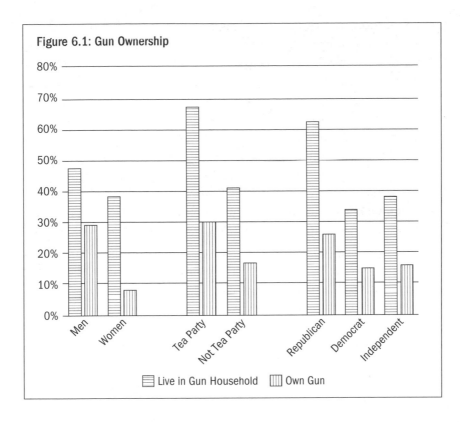

Figure 6.1: Gun Ownership

2012 study shows that 39 percent of women believe it is more important to protect the rights of gun owners, up from 26 percent in 1993.[66]

To examine the impact of sex and Tea Party status on current attitudes about gun rights, I use data collected by the Public Religion Research Institute and the Religious News Service in August 2012.[67] In addition to examining gun ownership rates among Americans, the survey asked respondents the following: (1) if they were in favor of passing stricter gun control laws or loosening current gun control laws; (2) if people should be allowed to carry concealed weapons in churches, government buildings, or a college campus; and (3) if they agreed that the constitutional right to own and carry a gun was as important as other rights.[68] Before turning to the more specific questions concerning gun control and gun rights, I examine rates of gun ownership among Americans according to the PRRI data. Figure 6.1 shows the percentage of Americans who report living in a household with a gun and the percentage of Americans who report owning a gun themselves by sex, Tea Party status, and partisanship. Respondents who identify themselves as part of the Tea Party also are significantly more likely to report living in a household with guns, as are Republicans.[69] Starker gender differences emerge when it comes to gun ownership: men are more than three times as likely as women to report owning their own gun, which corresponds to prior studies on gun ownership.[70] Rates of gun ownership also differ based on identification with the Tea Party and partisanship, in the expected ways.

Turning to women more specifically, I examine the percentage of women who live in gun households and who own their own guns by three categories: women who identify as part of the Tea Party; non–Tea Party Republican women; and "other American women" (women who identify as Democrats or Political Independents). Tea Party women are the most likely to report living in households with guns, although a solid majority of Republican women do as well (see figure 6.2). In terms of gun ownership, GOP and Tea Party women own guns at similar rates. The outlying group in both categories is women who are neither part of the Tea Party nor Republicans: they are far less likely to own their own guns or live in households that have guns.

What about attitudes on gun control and gun rights? For the first series of analyses, I consider American women's attitudes on "passing stricter gun control." As a counterpoint, I also analyze whether female respondents favor "loosening current gun control laws."[71] Combining the strongly favor and favor categories, figure 6.3 shows the percentage of Tea Party women, non–Tea Party Republican women, and "other American women" who favor either passing stricter gun control laws or loosening current gun control laws. As these data show clearly, Tea Party women are staunchly more conservative on both positions, with Republican women who do not identify with the Tea Party taking a middle position while all other American women believe that more gun control is necessary. However, when I conduct multivariate statistical analysis while controlling for similar standard political and socioeconomic controls that I employ in other models throughout the book, Tea Party status is no longer a significant predictor of gun attitudes. (See table 6.1 in appendix B for full model results.) Instead, partisanship and ideology stand out as the largest predictors explaining support for strengthen-

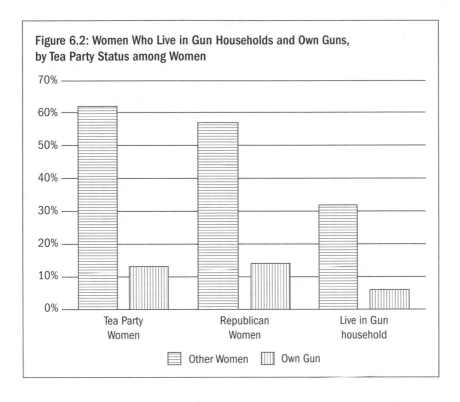

Figure 6.2: Women Who Live in Gun Households and Own Guns, by Tea Party Status among Women

ing gun control. Democratic women, in particular, are staunchly pro-gun control: compared with women who identify themselves as Political Independents, the odds ratios show that Democratic women are more than two times as likely to support gun control measures than are other women. Moreover, ideology is also a significant predictor of attitudes about gun control among American women: the more conservative American women are, the less likely they are to support strengthening gun control. When it comes to loosening gun control laws, the models report similar findings, although in this case, Republican women are two and a half times more likely than Independent women to support loosening gun control; conservative ideology remains a significant predictor of support for relaxing gun control laws, while Tea Party status fails to achieve statistical significance. These results suggest that Tea Party membership alone does not drive women's attitudes about gun

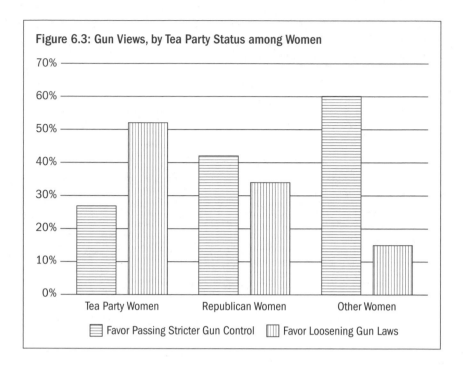

Figure 6.3: Gun Views, by Tea Party Status among Women

rights; rather, party and ideology are more important to women's orientation toward gun laws, unlike in previous chapters in which being part of the Tea Party has a conservatizing influence apart from partisanship and ideology on attitudes about many economic and feminist policies.

When it comes to concealed carry laws and where women believe people have the right to carry them, Tea Party women initially appear more likely than GOP women and especially other American women to approve of carrying concealed weapons in churches, government buildings, and college campus (see figure 6.4).[72] However, as in the last example, when Tea Party status is regressed on models that control for other factors, it is not a significant predictor in explaining support for carrying concealed weapons in any of the three places mentioned. Partisanship among women is the major driving force in explaining such attitudes, with Republican women being anywhere from 2.5 to 4 times as likely as Independent women (the comparison category) to support

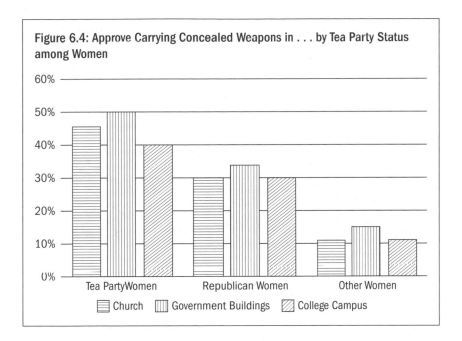

Figure 6.4: Approve Carrying Concealed Weapons in . . . by Tea Party Status among Women

carrying concealed weapons in such locales depending on the specific model. Ideology helps to explain support for carrying concealed weapons in church, but not in other locations. (See tables 6.2 and 6.3 in appendix B for full model results.)

Finally, an overwhelming majority—more than 90 percent—of Tea Party women either strongly or mostly agree that the constitutional right to carry and own a gun is just as important as other rights, which is significantly higher than either GOP women or other American women (see figure 6.5). In the final model, partisanship, region, and gun ownership lead both women and men to agree that gun rights are as important a constitutional right as freedom of speech and freedom of the press, although ideology only affects the attitudes of women about this issue: the more liberal women are, the less likely they are to agree that gun rights are as constitutionally important as other rights. (See table 6.4 in appendix B for full model results.) Women from the Midwest are more supportive of this position than are other women. However, the strongest predictor for women's attitudes on the importance of their Second Amendment rights is living in a gun household.

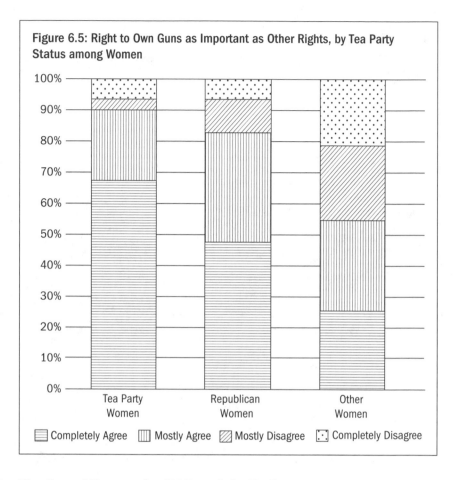

Figure 6.5: Right to Own Guns as Important as Other Rights, by Tea Party Status among Women

Legend: ▤ Completely Agree ▥ Mostly Agree ▨ Mostly Disagree ⠫ Completely Disagree

Tea Party Women, the GOP, and the Right to Bear Arms

These data and statistical models tell us several things about the attempts by conservative, pro-gun women to build more support for gun rights among American women. First, pro-gun advocates may take heart at PRRI's finding that a strong majority of American women—63 percent—agree that gun rights are an important constitutional right. While support for this position is much higher for Tea Party and Republican women, a majority (53 percent) of women who do not identify as Republicans or as part of the Tea Party also support this right. In this respect, appeals to American women to consider gun rights as an important constitutional issue may find broader support among other women than those who belong to the Tea Party or to the GOP.

At the same time, however, most American women, while generally respecting the broader rights of gun owners, also believe that some sorts of gun control are necessary and do not necessarily infringe on such constitutional rights. As is the case with many issues of public opinion, the devil is in the details. It is telling, for instance, that efforts by President Obama to impose stricter gun control laws in wake of the Newtown school shooting, which failed in the Senate in April 2013, were met with large majorities of support among the general public, but especially women. Although levels of support wavered depending on the specific reform proposed by Obama, 65 percent of American women supported a law requiring the nationwide ban on the sale of semiautomatic assault weapons.[73] The assault weapon ban or bans on any type of firearms or ammunition are adamantly opposed by gun proponents, and as the qualitative analysis shows here, it has become a gendered issue: pro-gun women argue that women should have access to automatic assault weapons such as the AR-15 because they are physically easier for women to handle. Yet most American women are not troubled by banning certain types of firearms which they believe to be more destructive than handguns or shotguns. Moreover, as the data show here, pro-gun women who lobby for *loosening* gun laws more generally, or passing legislation that allows legal gun holders to carry concealed weapons into churches, government buildings, and college campuses, are likely to face much more resistance from most American women as well.

Another lesson to be learned from the multivariate models is that Tea Party status is not necessarily linked to gun attitudes, especially among women. Partisanship and ideology appear to factor more. For pro-gun women, their appeal perhaps extends beyond the Tea Party, which likely benefits their cause. As I argued at the beginning of the chapter, there is a natural alliance between the pro-gun lobby and the Tea Party movement in that both share a passion for a conservative interpretation of the Constitution, one that calls for minimal government intrusion into the private lives of individuals, including their right to bear arms. So it is unsurprising that NRA events often feature political leaders who draw on Tea Party support. For instance, the 2014 NRA Stand and Fight Rally, where Sarah Palin implored more Mama Grizzlies to pack heat, also drew Rick Santorum, conservative talk radio hosts Glenn Beck and Mark Levin, and conservative rocker Ted Nugent, all of whom have close ties with the Tea Party. At the same time, however, the NRA and other pro-gun groups also draw support from establishment Republican leaders who have fought Tea Party efforts to shape the GOP, including Mitch McConnell, and even Democrats, particularly those who live in rural areas where hunting and gun culture are a way of life. So while many Tea Party women activists have begun championing gun rights, relatively few American women consider themselves part of the Tea Party movement; therefore, to rely on this demographic alone to advance their cause would not get such "pistol-packin" Mama Grizzlies very far. For pro-gun women to make inroads among other women when it comes to gun attitudes, they will need to build support beyond the small slice of very conservative women who identify with the Tea Party and instead reach out to moderate Republican, Independent, and Democratic women, particularly those living in areas of the country that have a cultural history with guns and hunting.

Lastly, shifting women's attitudes about gun rights is likely only to happen when, and if, American women grow more comfortable seeing women using and promoting gun rights. On this front, there has been an effort by some women politicians and activists, from both parties, to embrace gun rights more visibly. For example, Wendy Davis, the 2014 Democratic nominee for governor in Texas, came out in favor of "open carry" laws in Texas, which would allow Texans to carry firearms legally in holsters they wear openly (her Republican opponent and eventual winner, Greg Abbott, also supported this position). Joni Ernst, a Republican senator with close ties to the Tea Party who in 2014 was the first woman elected to Congress from Iowa, has also made national headlines for her promotion of gun rights. Her political ad "Give Me a Shot" features Ernst, clad in a leather jacket, riding her motorcycle to a firing range. As the narrator describes Ernst as a "mom, farm girl, and lieutenant-colonel who carries more than just lipstick in her purse," Ernst proceeds to shoot a handgun at a target, telling viewers she plans to "take aim at wasteful spending" and "ObamaCare."[74] Social media may also be key to building a stronger pro-gun culture among women. Jenny Beth Martin, who leads Tea Party Patriots, told me that she has been struck, at least anecdotally, by an increasing number of conservative women posting "photos showing them[selves] at a gun range or showing them somewhere out using their guns" on their Facebook pages or on social media in order to demonstrate their pro-gun positions.[75] Ernst, Davis, and the pro-gun women on Facebook, however, are still in the minority of American women. While anecdotes suggest that there is indeed a growing gun subculture among American women, and data suggest that rates of gun ownership among women are rising, women are still far less likely than are men to live in a household with guns or to own guns themselves. Moreover, while a majority of American women now view gun ownership as an important constitutional right, they do not necessarily believe that government efforts to regulate gun ownership interfere with such rights. Efforts by Tea Party women to promote gun rights, including the relaxation of current gun laws or the right to carry concealed weapons in a variety of public settings, by using gendered appeals among American women more broadly still face an uphill battle.

7

Conclusion

Tea Party Women and the Future of American Politics

Since the 1980s, one reliable narrative often used to explain American politics is the gender gap, in which the Democratic Party typically enjoys a wide advantage among women voters over the Republican Party. Although it has ebbed and flowed in specific elections, this gap is real, as more American women vote for Democratic candidates than men, given their higher levels of support for many of the policies promoted by the Democratic Party. Another prevailing perception among many Americans is that "pro-women" interest groups lean to the left politically. In very recent elections, both liberal women's groups such as the National Organization for Women and Democratic Party leaders have promoted the idea that the Republican Party, and by extension conservative interest groups, are waging a War on Women. Yet the emergence of women as leaders within in the Tea Party, along with the slow, but steady, ascent of a new generation of conservative Republican women in office, represents a significant development in American politics— one that challenges our perceptions of what constitutes "women's issues" and calls into question whether Democrats will continue to have a lock hold on the women's vote in future years.

This book helps shed light on why the Tea Party holds such appeal to this newer generation of right-wing, conservative women and what their emergence may mean for the future of American politics. Armed with high levels of education, work experience, and social media savvy, these conservative women have created their own opportunities within the Tea Party to speak out against a federal government that they believe threatens their liberties and usurps their personal responsibilities—particularly as an alternative to traditional Republican Party activism. Women's involvement in the Tea Party, much like their male counterparts in the movement, stems from a concern that the size and scope of the federal government has dramatically veered from what the nation's Founders intended. Frustrated with government bailouts of corporations in wake of the Great Recession of 2008, the expansion of federal social welfare programs (especially the much-hated Affordable Care Act), and taxes that they believe are too high, these Tea Party women are standing with Tea Party men to say "enough is enough!" Along the way, many Tea Party women bring to the movement a unique gendered perspective as to why the conservative policies endorsed by the movement are good for American women and their families. In so doing, they are part of an older tradition of conservative women who historically politicized motherhood to fight for conservative causes in order to protect the nation's children. But my work finds that Tea Party women differ from earlier right-wing women in other important ways. Unlike their historical counterparts, Tea Party women extend their connection between motherhood and politics to economic policy. In essence, Tea Party "Mama Grizzlies" seek to protect their children from the nation's looming debt crisis, which they believe has the potential to lower the standard of living for America's next generation. Some Mama Grizzlies also argue that protecting gun rights is an important way for mothers to protect their children. Further, some—though not all—Tea Party women argue that their conservative economic views and support for gun rights actually embody the feminist principles of self-reliance, arguing that extensive social welfare programs and gun control foster a sexist culture of dependency. Liberal feminists and women who appropriate motherhood for progressive political causes certainly take issue with these positions; however, Tea Party women's gendered rhetoric in defense of their own policy views challenges the perception often held by many that women subscribe to left-leaning politics.

What Tea Party Women Tell Us about Right-Wing Women Today

While right-wing women have found remarkable success as leaders in the Tea Party, they are not the first women to engage in conservative politics. As chapter 3 recounts, the women who engaged in far-right advocacy as part of the anticommunist cause and as part of the movement to challenge the women's rights movement in the 1970s typically employed motherhood rhetoric in defense of their conservative political stances. Conservative women played—and continue to play—a pivotal role in the antiabortion and Christian Right movements. Certainly Tea Party women's advocacy today can be viewed as an extension of this brand of conservative activism. For example, when their political goals align the Tea Party women I interviewed—most new to politics— sometimes work in conjunction with longer-standing Christian Right women's groups, including Phyllis Schlafly's Eagle Forum and Beverly LaHaye's Concerned Women for America, both of which promote biblical values and whose members are staunch social conservatives. The women leaders I interviewed from Eagle Forum and CWA likewise see the engagement of a new generation of conservative women in the Tea Party as potentially helpful to their own causes. Like the membership of these two longer-standing Christian Right organizations, the women activists of the Tea Party I spoke with are primarily white and many are socially conservative. Tea Party women in the mass public also largely fit this profile. As my analysis of national survey data shows, nine out of ten Tea Party women in the United States are white, while two-thirds identify as born-again, evangelical Christians, a group that political scientist Clyde Wilcox calls the "target constituency" of the Christian Right.[1] Additionally, strong majorities of Tea Party women in the mass public oppose both gay marriage (67 percent) and the legality of abortion in most or all cases (65 percent).

Still, there are pronounced differences between Tea Party women and religiously inspired right-wing women who are active in the Christian Right and/or the pro-life movement. While both sets of activists may share similar backgrounds and issue attitudes, women engaged in Christian Right advocacy clearly prioritize and are involved in politics because of social and religious issues. This is not to say that white, born-again Christians are not conservative on economic issues—compared with members of other faith traditions, evangelicals espouse more conservative positions on taxes and the role of government in helping the poor.[2] While there has been a deliberate attempt by some Christian Right leaders to argue that smaller government is pro-family and consistent with conservative religious values—it should be noted, as well, that one motherhood frame echoed by some Tea Party Women is that a large government usurps family responsibilities, hence threatening the sanctity of the household—it is far from clear that members of these Christian Right groups are ready to become, in a phrase coined by Christian Broadcasting Network's David Brody, "Teavangelicals."[3] My interview with Janice Shaw Crouse, senior fellow with Concerned Women for America, illustrates this point. While she notes that CWA's president, Penny Young Nance, often touts the moral dimensions of economic issues, she reports that her group has faced some criticism from its members because they believe such issues detract from the core focus of the organization, which are social concerns such as abortion and gay rights.

By contrast, Tea Party women, even those who are socially conservative, prioritize fiscal concerns. Recall my interview with one local, avowedly pro-life Tea Party activist in Maryland, who says that issues of the debt and deficits are pulling the country "in such a dramatic, opposite direction right now" that they should take precedence over the abortion issue.[4] Other Tea Party women also note that what makes their Tea Party groups "Tea Party" is their emphasis on fighting "big government." As Stacy Mott, co-founder of Smart Girl Politics, told me, their group's goal is to promote the idea of "how the economy is negatively affecting women" and to help women "see [how] these fiscal issues impact women more than the social issues are. The financial issues impact *everyone*. And you may have your beliefs on the social issues, but the bottom line, the odds are that they are not directly impacting you."[5]

Of course, this is not to say that the Tea Party's prized fiscal conservatism and its passionate defense of constitutional conservatism can't be married with the political goals of the Christian Right. Two recent areas come to mind. First, arguments about defunding Planned Parenthood, the nation's largest abortion provider, have become more common since Republicans took majority control of Congress in 2010 and a focal point for liberal activists in denouncing the GOP and the Tea Party for engaging in a War on Women during the 2012 elections. Debates about such funding reached a fever pitch in the summer of 2015, as clandestine videos surfaced that showed a Planned Parenthood staffer engaging in what appeared to be a deal to sell harvested organ tissue from aborted fetuses for research purposes.[6] However, defunding Planned Parenthood has not been viewed by the right wing as merely a pro-life cause but also as a move to rein in fiscal spending, at least according to many Republicans in Congress. For example, Republican Representative Marsha Blackburn (TN), who sponsored unsuccessful legislation in 2013 to defund the organization, told a pro-life news agency that she did so because "Americans shouldn't celebrate abortion and our taxpayers shouldn't subsidize abortion businesses like Planned Parenthood, who profit from the destruction of human life with taxpayer money. It's *fiscally irresponsible* and morally indefensible."[7] Given that all the major Republican candidates seeking the 2016 GOP presidential nomination have strongly denounced Planned Parenthood, pledging to strip it of federal funding if elected, it is likely that abortion politics will continue to be a major issue in the near future; if government funding is involved, it can unite the Christian Right and the Tea Party.

Another potential area of common ground for the Christian Right and Tea Party is religious liberty. Christian Right activists have long maintained that Christian values are under attack in American society, denouncing Supreme Court decisions as far back as the 1962 *Engel v. Vitale* case, which banned public prayer in schools, to more recent decisions that have removed religious symbols from public property as a violation of the First Amendment's Establishment Clause. Such decisions, according to conservative Christians, deny their understanding of the United States as a "Christian nation."[8] Religious liberty claims from the right wing took on more urgency with the Supreme Court's 2015 *Obergefell v. Hodges* decision, which legalized same-sex marriage nationally. Outraged by the decision, Christian Right activists argue that the court disregarded the traditional definition of marriage and in effect violated the religious beliefs of millions of Americans who oppose same-sex marriage. In some states Christian Right activists are promoting "religious liberty" bills, which would allow vendors to refuse to provide services for the weddings of same-sex couples as a matter of conscience. Many Tea Party activists, however, also support such bills as an important part of their commitment to liberty more generally—as Charlotte Hays of the secular Independent Women's Forum writes, "Religious liberty is a bedrock American value, enshrined in our Bill of Rights."[9] Thus Tea Party activists may find themselves enjoined in the fight for religious liberty along with members of the Christian Right, but they may be doing so because such activism also touches on their strong beliefs in personal liberty as defined in the Constitution (not to mention that it shores up a relationship with a potentially like-minded constituency). Like the debate about Planned Parenthood funding, religious liberty promises to remain a politically salient issue, as polls show that more Americans are accepting of gay rights and are becoming less religious, which will only serve to exacerbate tensions between Americans who value religion highly and those who do not. Yet not all right-wing women of the Tea Party are religiously conservative, and while they certainly are happy to make political alliances with social conservatives when and where their issue areas collide, their first priorities concern shrinking the size and scope of government.

Appropriation of Feminism: Conservative Issues as Women's Issues

Unlike liberal feminists and Democratic leaders, who argue that an activist government is necessary to safeguard women's equality in society and assist their families, Tea Party women maintain that such activist government is precisely the problem. The Tea Party women I interviewed believe that liberal feminist groups depict American women, in their words, as meek, needy, and dependent. Some Tea Party women go so far as to say that *they* are the authentic feminists, led by Sarah Palin, who famously declared that a conservative feminism is emerging among many women on the right—one that while acknowledging women's legal rights (save reproductive rights) primarily promotes women's self-reliance and encourages "Mama Grizzlies" to become more engaged in politics. At the same time, the pro-woman rhetoric that Tea Party women employ has largely been disassociated from the religious rhetoric used by many of the devout, right-wing women engaged in earlier battles against the ERA and abortion and which, in the words of journalist Hanna Rosin, "has helped open up space for an unfettered kind of conservative feminism"[10] among some Tea Party women.

According to this newer generation of far-right women, when government expands the social safety net to provide more programs to women and their children or enacts new regulations on businesses in the name of greater justice and equality for women, it portrays women as victims. Several examples illustrate how these conservative women make the case that progressive policies passed or proposed in the age of

Obama are bad for women and antifeminist. First, many of the right-wing women I profile cite research suggesting that ObamaCare's individual mandate, which has required Americans who do not receive insurance from their employers to buy individual policies or face stiff financial penalties, has hit women harder than men in terms of the premiums they must pay. Other women on the right, such as the Independent Women Forum's Carrie Lucas, argues that ObamaCare "lets women down" because many women are forced to buy plans for their families that often result in changes in provider networks, thus eliminating choices for women.[11] These right-wing women have also made gendered claims as to why the Affordable Care Act's birth control mandate, which requires insurance companies to provide free contraception as part of its commitment to preventative health services, promotes women's dependency on government, or, in the words of Keli Carender of Tea Party Patriots, "is the most antifeminist thing you could possibly be supportive of . . . I can take care of myself!"[12] In claiming that the birth control mandate specifically, or ObamaCare more generally, are paternalistic policies that women should avoid, Tea Party women's gendered message against such policies play into the broader narrative about self-reliance that the Tea Party promotes.

Along similar lines, Tea Party women reject calls by liberal feminists to increase regulations in the workplace aimed at preventing sex discrimination, which they argue is the primary factor driving the pay gap between men and women in the United States. Tea Party women leaders maintain that women earn less not because of rampant sex discrimination—cases of which they believe are largely overblown by liberal feminist groups—but because women choose to pursue occupations that pay less or value flexibility (and fewer hours) over higher pay. True feminists, these women argue, should support a free market that removes most workplace regulations, as that would provide women (and men) with more employment options, so they could seek jobs that pay better or provide a better work environment. As a result, these Tea Party women take issue with proposed pay equity laws, such as the Paycheck Fairness Act, that would make it easier for women to sue for pay discrimination. They believe such laws perpetuate the notion that women are, according to Krista Kafer, a senior fellow with the Independent Women's Forum, "hapless victims."[13] Tea Party women also make gendered claims against proposals to mandate that businesses provide paid work and sick leave, saying that forcing all companies to provide such benefits will ultimately make women—especially of childbearing age—more expensive and less desirable to employ. Many businesses and employers, these right-wing women argue, have increasingly found ways to accommodate talented, working parents by offering them more flexibility in terms of parental or sick leave or working from home. In other words, government should stay out of the business of regulating work/family balance and let the free market handle these issues.

Lastly, when liberal mothers call for making guns harder to obtain, often in the name of protecting their children from gun violence, pro-gun conservative women counter that such policies are downright sexist. They classify attempts by Democrats to pass comprehensive gun control that would outlaw the sale of certain semiautomatic weapons in wake of the tragic school shooting in Newtown, Connecticut, as antifeminist because it restricts women's choices. Some pro-gun women note that semiautomatic weapons are often lighter and more accurate than shotguns, and women's usage of such firearms then potentially makes it easier for women to defend themselves and their families in case of attack. Due to their lack of physical strength compared with men, such right-wing women argue that women are *more* in need of access to guns than are men to "level the playing field" in case they are assaulted. Similar to their objections to other progressive policies, right-wing women's defense of gun rights shows an alternative point of view about *which* government policies—in this case the regulation of firearms—are feminist or best for women and their families.

That these Tea Party women leaders are challenging the narrative that progressive policies are good for women and their families is not necessarily a new development in American politics. As political scientist Ronnee Schreiber's work has shown, longer-standing far-right women's organizations such as Concerned Women for America and the Independent Women's Forum have consistently challenged the ability of liberal feminist groups to, in essence, speak for all women by invoking their own, alternative conservative gender identity.[14] What makes the alternative narrative espoused by conservative women in the age of the

Tea Party different concerns both the expansion of the issue domains to which it is applied (such as gun rights, paid leave, and the Affordable Care Act) and the extent to which such policy positions are now classified as feminist.

Politically speaking, these alternative narratives matter given that such policies are likely to play a big role in the 2016 election and beyond. Hillary Clinton, for example, has made "building stronger families" a centerpiece of her campaign for the Democratic presidential nomination, which she argues will come about by helping women, especially, to better balance their work/family lives and to increase their pay. As a result, she supports increasing the minimum wage, passing the Pay Equity Act, and requiring businesses to offer paid leave and flexible scheduling to "allow parents to take care of their obligations at home without sacrificing pay at work."[15] Even if Clinton is not the Democratic nominee, these policy issues are still likely to be sold by Democratic leaders as shoring up U.S. families. Looking to the future, Republicans need a counter narrative that explains to voters—particularly women voters—why their opposition to such progressive policies and embrace of free market economics is ultimately better for women and their families. The gendered narratives that Tea Party women and other conservative women activists have developed to explain their opposition to the debt, ObamaCare, minimum-wage increases, pay equity, and gun control may be one place to start for the GOP. As my work demonstrates, however, the relationship between the Tea Party and the GOP, while certainly a necessary partnership in some aspects, is also fraught with tension, particularly for Tea Party women.

How Tea Party Women Are Shaping the Republican Party: Opportunities and Challenges

My research reveals that Tea Party women activists, particularly at the grassroots level, have often faced a cool reception from Republican Party insiders, which has propelled them into activism within the Tea Party. Ironically, though, the challenges that right-wing Tea Party women face with the Republican Party are similar to those experienced by women representing the ideologically *moderate* flank of the party. As the Republican Party has become more conservative ideologically in the past few decades, work by political scientist Danielle Thomsen shows that GOP women state legislators, who historically have been more moderate than their male counterparts, have been reluctant to seek their party's nomination for Congress, given that primary voters are far more conservative than voters in the general election.[16] Experiential studies also show that Republican voters assume that their party's female candidates are less conservative than male candidates are,[17] which again may make it more difficult for women to be elected as Republicans. Coupled with the GOP's hesitancy to "do identity politics," or recruit and train women with the express goal of promoting more of them, it is little wonder that women who are elected to office are more than three times likely to be Democrats than Republicans. The GOP's lackluster record in promoting women as candidates also spills over to its leadership ranks. In 2015 just nine out of fifty state chairs of the Republican Party were women, which was a little less than half of the women represented as party chairs within the Democratic Party.[18] By contrast, conservative women find greater opportunities to emerge as leaders within the Tea Party on their own terms given the diffuse organizational structure of the movement.

This is not to say that Tea Party women can't find success as candidates within the GOP. Several Republican women who have been identified as rising stars within the Republican Party, such as Senator Joni Ernst (IA), Senator Deb Fischer (NE), Representative Renee Ellmers (NC), and Representative Mia Love (UT), all have strong backing from the Tea Party due to their strong conservative credentials. Others, however, recognize the difficulty in challenging "establishment" Republican candidates, such as Katrina Pierson, co-founder of the Dallas Tea Party, who decisively lost the 2012 Republican primary against Representative Pete Sessions, who chairs the powerful House Rules Committee, despite her being endorsed by Sarah Palin, FreedomWorks, and Tea Party Express. The larger point here is that the GOP is not known for its welcoming embrace of Tea Party women, despite the fact that the Tea Party offers activists who hold very conservative views that may correspond better to the Republican Party's platform in ways that more moderate Republican women do not.

However, given the political realities of our nation's entrenched two-party system, many Tea Party women, as much as they grumble about the current state of the GOP, acknowledge that their policy priorities are much more likely to be adopted and promoted by the Republican Party, so they often work with Republicans to do so. My analysis of national survey data shows that on most political issues, in fact, Tea Party women and Republican women who do not identify as members of the Tea Party are far closer than they are apart in terms of their attitudes. On economic issues, Tea Party women and their Republican counterparts in the mass public overwhelmingly agree that government poverty programs create a culture of dependency and that children from all income groups have the opportunity to be successful, which belies the need for more government intervention to help the nation's poor. Nationally, GOP and Tea Party women alike are hostile to ObamaCare and tax hikes on the wealthy and are overwhelming pro-gun and pro-life.

I also find that much of the Mama Grizzly rhetoric and other gendered appeals developed by right-wing women activists is increasingly finding its way into the rhetoric of the GOP, particularly among its elected women legislators such as Cathy McMorris Rodgers, Martha Roby, and Joni Ernst, who often embrace their roles as mothers when speaking out as spokespersons for their party. That the Republican Party relies on its women leaders—however small in numbers they are compared with the Democratic Party—to promote its "brand" or defend the party against accusations that it hostile to women's interests, again, is nothing new.[19] But the emphasis on motherhood appeals, for example, when calling for Congress to cut its spending and reduce the debt, or emphasizing that a lack of jobs and lackluster economy represent a true "War on Women," takes a page out of the rhetorical playbook first used by Tea Party women. That such similar rhetoric on what is best for women and their families comes from both Tea Party women and an increasing number of Republican women elected officials should not be surprising, however, given how often these two groups of women have intermingled in recent years. For example, prominent Republican women are often featured speakers at events sponsored by Tea Party women's groups, such as the Smart Girl Politics Summit, or GOP women will often be profiled on the websites of conservative women's organizations, serving to inspire many right-wing women at the grass roots. The increasing use of gendered rhetoric by GOP women to promote conservative policy signifies that the Republican Party, pushed by the rise of women as conservative activists, is realizing that it needs a different message, and more diverse messengers, to better reach women voters across the country. In this respect, then, Tea Party women may have found a way to influence the Republican Party.

Will Tea Party Women Help Close the Gender Gap in American Politics?

At the end of the day, will the rise of women as activists and leaders within the Tea Party, and increasingly (albeit slowly) as leaders within the Republican Party, signal a shift in our politics? In other words, does the advent of Tea Party "Mama Grizzlies" signify that perhaps American women will be more likely to embrace conservative political positions and shift their voting patterns? If the endgame for Tea Party women is to get women across the country to embrace more conservative political positions, my analysis of national data shows that the Tea Party faces serious challenges. First, Tea Party women represent a small fraction of the U.S. population: PRRI data show in 2012 that just 9 percent of American women identified with the Tea Party; this level of identification fell to 7 percent in 2015.[20] Second, American women also remain reluctant to identify themselves as Republicans. In 2014 the PRRI data show that 25 percent of American women are Republican, compared with 37 percent of American women who are Democratic and 38 percent who are Independent.[21] That relatively so few women identify as part of the Tea Party or the Republican Party is not surprising; as the extensive analysis shown in this book demonstrates, the majority of American women currently hold moderate to liberal positions on economic issues, feminist concerns, and gun rights.

Moreover, on some issues, even Tea Party women in the mass public stand at odds with Tea Party and GOP leaders. My analysis of PRRI data finds that a majority of Tea Party and Republican women in the mass public believes that sex discrimination remains a problem in society, which stands in stark contrast to the position held by many conservative women leaders, such as advocates from the Independent Women's Forum, who argue that sex discrimination is largely overstated. Moreover, a solid majority of Tea Party and Republican women nationally also support the establishment of paid family and sick leave, which places them at odds with Tea Party leaders and Republicans in Congress, who believe such policies usurp the free market. While American politics are certainly nothing if not fluid, Tea Party women activists will have lots of work ahead of them if they hope to change enough women's positions on the movement's preferred, pro-market policies such that women back Republican candidates in higher numbers.

Another challenge the Tea Party faces in convincing more American women to side with its views is the increasingly negative view Americans take toward the movement. While surveys generally find that support for the Tea Party has been stable, Americans have grown more negative about the movement since its inception. In 2010, in one of the first polls conducted about the Tea Party by the *New York Times*, 46 percent of Americans said they had not heard enough about the Tea Party to form an opinion.[22] By June 2014 the *New York Times* found that 65 percent of Americans did not consider themselves supportive of the Tea Party.[23] Negative views about the movement have grown among Americans in response to the "take no prisoners" style of the Tea Party, whose Republican allies in Congress were the driving force behind an attempt to refuse to raise the debt ceiling in 2011[24] and then the government shutdown in 2013, when GOP leaders initially refused to negotiate with President Obama in a budget confrontation over the funding of Obama-Care.[25] Polls show that major damage was done to both the Republican Party and the Tea Party movement after these events. Studies show that women are less likely than men are to respond positively to attack-oriented rhetoric in politics, so the perception of the Tea Party as uncompromising may hurt its cause among American women.[26]

Other critics of the Tea Party have pointed to some Tea Party activists' commitment to polarizing issues, such as its strident opposition to immigration reform, as indicative that the Tea Party movement is less about economic reform and more about promoting a "white citizenship"[27] movement, which again may harm its attempts to broaden its appeal among American women. Some scholars argue that the Tea Party is best understood as a reactionary movement against Barack Obama, who represents for many Americans a vision of a more racially diverse world they find challenging.[28] Indeed, many Americans remember the racist signs depicting Obama as a witch doctor, or worse, that appeared at early Tea Party rallies, or the "birther" debate, driven by conservative social media and Fox News, that continuously questioned whether Obama was actually a citizen and therefore eligible to run for president, despite overwhelming evidence to the contrary. When Tea Party activists, including the Tea Party women profiled here, talk about "taking their country back," liberal critics of the movement infer that such language denotes returning to a time when racial minorities, homosexuals, and, ironically given the prominent role that women play in the movement, women had less freedom.

My own research finds mixed results here. My study, like many others, finds that identification with the Tea Party for both women and men is driven by attitudes toward Obama.[29] However, while I find that Tea Party women are certainly far more conservative on immigration reform than other women nationally, including Republicans, I find that American women—regardless of Tea Party status—hold similar attitudes on whether they believe that too much attention has been paid to the problems of blacks and other minorities. In addition, when I controlled for race in my statistical analysis of why women join the Tea Party, it was not a significant factor. While it is certainly true that the vast majority of Tea Party members are white, including most of the women I interviewed, I rarely got the sense that racial motivations or opposition to immigration reform primarily drove most of the women's activism. Of course, being "racist" is likely not something that most people would openly recognize let alone admit during an interview. While I do find empirically that opposition to Obama drives membership in the Tea Party for both women and men, my sense is that many people in the Tea Party are equally hostile to other "socialist" Democrats who they believe don't share their values. As Obama gets ready to leave the White House shortly, much Tea Party vitriol is now directed toward the likes of Chuck Schumer, Nancy Pelosi, Elizabeth Warren, and especially Hillary Clinton.

There are a few areas of potential promise for the Tea Party when it comes to reshaping the views of American women, however. The day will come in which American women, whose education levels now far exceed those of American men, will earn more money than men, in what journalist Liza Mundy calls "the big flip."[30] As studies suggest that those Americans who earn high levels of income are the most conservative on economic policy,[31] as women become larger earners, they may find free market economic positions, including reduced taxes, more appealing. On the issue of guns, studies suggest that women increasingly are likely to own guns, which is a driving factor of pro-gun attitudes. When more women own guns, they will be more likely to oppose attempts to regulate firearms in the United States, which is a Second Amendment principle shared by many Tea Party activists.

Moreover, the slow, but steady, rise of women as political leaders within the Republican Party may be a source of inspiration for more American women. Recall that many women who first got active in the Tea Party cite Sarah Palin's historic run for the vice presidency as important to first raising their interest in becoming active in politics. Studies show that women in visible political leadership positions have a positive effect on women's political participation and orientation toward politics.[32] In short, American women, who have always expressed less interest in politics than men, show more interest in politics when they see women running for office or women serving as elected officials. Up until now, the women in charge in Washington and in state legislatures have been far more likely to be Democrats than Republicans. However, a new crop of Republican women, often backed by strong encouragement from Tea Party women, threatens to challenge this partisan balance and reshape what political women in the United States look like. As Republican Representative Cathy McMorris Rodgers has said about her party's effort to diversify its pool of candidates and leaders, "messengers are important."

Whether changing the messenger—that is, having more conservative women out in front, boldly proclaiming that conservative policies are good for American women and their families—is enough to swing more American women to the side of the political right remains to be seen. At the very least, the rise of women as leaders within the Tea Party, and their steady ascent into the leadership ranks of the Republican Party, challenges our perceptions of what political women look like and even, perhaps, what feminism means today. Tea Party women's use of gendered frames, whether they touch on traditional motherhood roles or go beyond such rhetoric to directly challenge liberal feminists' contention that progressive policies and more gun control are good for *all* women, serve to demonstrate that descriptive representation—the notion that women best represent women in politics—may be difficult to achieve if women do not hold uniform political positions. Nonetheless, the advent of Tea Party women as leaders in right-wing politics shows that women can perhaps become leaders in any political circumstance and reminds us that women are far from politically monolithic.

APPENDIX A

Methodology

My book uses a combination of qualitative and quantitative methods to address the role of women in the Tea Party. First, I conducted twenty-nine semi-structured interviews with Tea Party and conservative women activists and analysts from the grassroots, state, and national level, all of which were recorded and transcribed and which lasted anywhere from one to two hours. I interviewed ten activists involved in local and/or state Tea Party organizations, most based in Maryland but one from Massachusetts and one from Texas as well; in most cases I have granted these women pseudonyms to protect their identities. I interviewed the Maryland activists in person and the others by phone. I also interviewed a Republican Maryland state legislator and have kept her identity anonymous by using a pseudonym.

In addition, I interviewed Tea Party and conservative women activists employed or engaged full-time in conservative or libertarian politics as activists, pollsters, or pundits, including Jenny Beth Martin, Diana Riemer, and Keli Carender of Tea Party Patriots (all by phone); Stacy Mott (by phone) and Tami Nantz (in person) of Smart Girl Politics; Lori Parker (by phone) of As a Mom . . . a Sisterhood of Mommy Patriots; Carrie Lukas (by phone) of the Independent Women's Forum; Janice Shaw Crouse of Concerned Women for America (in person); Colleen Holcomb, formerly of Eagle Forum (in person); Gabriella Hoffman of the Leadership Institute (in person); Amy Jo Clark and Miriam Weaver, the "Chicks on the Right" (by phone); Karin Agness of the Network of Enlightened Women (in person); Whitney Neal, formerly of Freedom-Works (in person); Patt Parker, of the National Federation of Republican Women (by phone); Yvonne Donnelly, National Chair of the 9/12 Project (by phone); Kristen Soltis Anderson, pollster and Republican consultant formerly with the Winston Group and now co-founder of Echelon Insights (in person); and Emily Ekins, director of polling for the libertarian Reason Foundation (by Skype). I also interviewed Robert Boland, former congresswoman Michele Bachmann's chief of staff (in person).

In addition to conducting these interviews, I attended several Tea Party or conservative political events, including the two-day Smart Girl Summit in July 2013 (held in Alexandria, VA); Turning the Tides in January 2013 (held in Annapolis, MD), a one-day event sponsored by MD-CAN, the Maryland Citizen Action Network; and C-PAC in March 2013 (held in National Harbor, MD). I also attended several local Tea Party meetings and national Tea Party rallies held at the National Mall in Washington DC to gain a better appreciation of the concerns of the Tea Party. During the Summit and Turning the Tides convention, I socialized and had meals with Tea Party activists, allowing me further insight into their reasons for joining the Tea Party and their thoughts as to the role women are playing in conservative political activism.

Lastly, I read and regularly followed primary documents published by these organizations, all of which were available on their websites. From 2011 to 2013 Smart Girl Politics published an e-magazine called *Smart Girl Nation*, and from 2011 to 2013 As a Mom . . . a Sisterhood of Mommy Patriots published an e-magazine called *MinuteMom*. I heavily rely on both sources. In addition, I followed many blogs, op-eds, press releases, and books issued by the conservative women's organizations that I profile in the book, although the sheer volume of material prevented me from being more systematic in analyzing the works.

In addition to the qualitative research, I also rely on survey data from the Public Religion Research (PRRI), a nonprofit, nonpartisan organization founded in 2009 which conducts national surveys about topical political issues on a regular basis. All of their surveys include a question about Tea Party status, as discussed in more detail in chapter 2. Since 2012 I have been an affiliated scholar with PRRI, so I have immediate access to their survey data, although I have not written the survey questionnaires myself. Their data are available to the public free of charge, usually after a certain embargo period. In all cases I employ the weighting scheme developed by PRRI to account for demographic characteristics. I rely on five specific surveys conducted by PRRI:

1. *2012 American Values Survey* (N = 3,003): The American Values Survey is a random, national telephone survey in English and Spanish of respondents who were eighteen or older conducted between September 13 and September 30, 2012 (1,201 respondents were interviewed on a cell phone). The margin of error for the survey is +/−2.0 percentage points at the 95 percent confidence level. For more specific details about the weighting scheme, see PRRI (2012a).

2. *2012 White Working Class Survey* (N = 2,501): The White Working Class Survey is a random, national telephone survey in English and Spanish of respondents who were eighteen or older conducted between August 2 and August 15, 2012 (1,000 respondents were interviewed on a cell phone). The margin of error for the survey is +/−2.2 percentage points at the 95 percent confidence level. For more specific details about the weighting scheme, see PRRI (2012b).

3. *2011 Millennials, Religion, and Abortion Survey.* The Millennials, Religion, and Abortion Survey is a random, national telephone survey in English and Spanish of respondents who were eighteen or older conducted between April 22, 2011, and May 8, 2011. The margin of error for the survey is +/−2.0 percentage points at the 95 percent confidence level. For more specific details about the weighting scheme, see PRRI (2011a).

4. *August 2012 Public Religion Research Institute / RNS Religion News Survey.* The PRRI/RNS Survey is a random national telephone survey in English and Spanish of respondents who were eighteen or older conducted between August 8 and August 12, 2012 (304 respondents were interviewed on a cell phone). The margin of error for the survey is +/−3.5 percentage points at the 95 percent confidence level. For more specific details about the weighting scheme, see PRRI (2012c).

5. *2014 American Values Survey* (N = 4,507). The American Values Survey is a random, national telephone survey in English and Spanish of respondents who were eighteen or older conducted between July 21, 2014, and August 15, 2014 (2,253 respondents were interviewed on a cell phone). The margin of error for the survey is +/−1.8 percentage points at the 95 percent confidence level. For more specific details about the weighting scheme see PRRI (2014).

APPENDIX B

Data Analysis

The following models are a series of logistic regression analyses that correspond with various chapters. For table 2.1 I analyze why individuals identify as part of the Tea Party and include numerous political and demographic controls.

For the remaining analyses Tea Party status is used as the major independent variable to consider whether being a member of the Tea Party significantly affects attitudes on a variety of social and political issues, all while I control for most of the same political and demographic controls first introduced in table 2.1 with several exceptions. First, I drop views on Obama in all other models save for model 2.1. Given that views on Obama are strongly correlated with whether individuals consider themselves members of the Tea Party, I opt to remove it from all other models in the study due to concerns about multicollinearity. I also drop parental status from the other models, as it does not emerge as statistically significant in any of the models and I attempted to keep the models as parsimonious as possible. Lastly, I use a series of dummy ideology variables to measure the impact of being a conservative or liberal compared to a political moderate (the reference category) in the model to explain Tea Party membership (table 2.1) but switch to an ordinal measurement of ideology in subsequent models.

Where necessary I have collapsed the dependent variables into binary measures so that I can run logistic regressions throughout the chapters. In table 2.1 the dependent variable, Tea Party membership, is coded 1 = identifies as a member of the Tea Party; 0 = does not identify as a member of the Tea Party. This coding remains the same when I employ Tea Party membership as an independent variable in the other models.

In all models I employ the following coding as control variables: sex (female = 1; male = 0); age is continuous; education (1 = high school or less; 2 = some college / trade school; 3 = college graduate; 4 = postcollege); income (1 = earns less than \$25,000; 2 = earns between \$25,000 and \$50,000; 3 = earns between \$50,001 and \$100,000; 4 = earns more than \$100,000); marital status (1 = married or partnered; 0 = not married or partnered); South (1 = lives in South; 0 = does not live in South); white (1 = white; 0 = not white); for party I use dummy variables with Republican (1 = Republican; 0 = not Republican), Democrat (1 = Democrat; 0 = not Democrat), and Independent as the reference category; I use dummy variables to measure ideology in the first model with conservative (1 = conservative; 0 = not conservative), liberal (1 = liberal; 0 = not liberal), and moderate as the reference category. In subsequent models I measure ideology as follows: 1 = very conservative; 2 = somewhat conservative; 3 = moderate; 4 = somewhat liberal; 5 = very liberal; views on Obama (1 = very favorable; 2 = mostly favorable; 3 = mostly unfavorable; 4 = very unfavorable); born-again Christian (1 = born-again Christian; 0 = not born-again Christian); and church attendance (1 = never attends church; 2 = attends church several times a year; 3 = attends church monthly; 4 = attends church weekly or more). In table 2.1 only, I control for parental status (1 = parent of children eighteen or under; 0 = not parent of children eighteen or under).

EXPLAINING IDENTIFICATION WITH THE TEA PARTY (CHAPTER 2)

TABLE 2.1 Determinants of Identification with the Tea Party (Logistic Regression)

Predictor	All Respondents (N = 3149)	Women Only (N = 1712)	Men Only (N = 1437)
Sex	−.499(.132)***	—	—
Age	−.001(.004)	.000(.006)	.002(.006)
Education	−.083(.061)	−.085(.099)	−.099(.081)
Income	.028(.044)	.123(.068)[a]	−.034(.058)
Married	.225(.147)	.386(.216)	.123(.212)
Parent	.001(.169)	−.179(.270)	.133(.212)
South	.129(.131)	.022(.203)	.188(.174)
White	.255(.244)	.429(.411)	.182(.309)
Republican	.244(.139)	.390(.231)	.136(.181)
Democrat	−.195(.271)	−.230(.377)	−.240(.387)

TABLE 2.1 (*cont.*)

Predictor	All Respondents (N = 3149)	Women Only (N = 1712)	Men Only (N = 1437)
Conservative	.924(.183)***	1.096(.293)***	.842(.231)***
Liberal	.425(.302)	.33(.436)	.690(.421)
Views on Obama	.752(.091)***	.569(.140)***	.891(.123)***
Born-Again	.520(.146)**	.782(.252)**	.358(.183)*
Church Attendance	−.095(.049)[a]	−.158(.079)*	−.050(.171)
Constant	−4.977(.593)***	−5.137(.892)***	−5.296(.810)***
Pseudo R-Squared	.19	.18	.18

Note: Data drawn from the 2012 American Values Survey and the 2012 White Working Class Survey, conducted by the Public Religion Research Institute. Cells contain binary logistic regression coefficients with robust standard errors in parentheses.
***p <. 001; **p <.01; *p <. 01; a = p <.10 (two-tailed tests).

ROLE OF GOVERNMENT ATTITUDES: REGRESSION ANALYSES (CHAPTER 4)

TABLE 4.1 Determinants of Support for Role of Government in Helping the Poor (Logistic Regressions) among American Women

Predictors	Agree That Government Poverty Programs Create Culture of Dependency (N = 1008)		Agree That Government Should Do More to Reduce Gap between Rich and Poor (N = 617)	
	B(S.E.)	Exp(B)	B(S.E.)–	Exp(B)
Tea Party Member	.622(.254)**	1.863	.941(.403)*	.390
Republican	.670(.185)***	1.953	.663(.902)	.902
Democrat	−.957(.204)***	.384	1.714(.267)***	5.553
Ideology	.285(.095)**	1.329	−.285(.119)*	.752
Education	.081(.075)	1.084	.059(.057)	1.060
Income	.113(.056)˙	1.120	−.111(.070)	.895
White	.439(.241)	1.551	−.472(.290)	.624
Age	−.003(.005)	.997	−.008(.005)	.992
Married	.348(.175)*	1.416	−.208(.204)	.812
South	.045(.164)	1.046	.049(.196)	1.050
Born-Again Christian	.023(.175)	1.023	−.027(.209)	.973
Church Attendance	.017(.061)*	1.017	−.161(.104)	.851
Constant	−2.780(.529)***	.062	2.560(.626)	12.941

(*continued*)

TABLE 4.1 (*cont.*)

Predictors	Agree That Government Poverty Programs Create Culture of Dependency (N = 1008)	Agree That Government Should Do More to Reduce Gap between Rich and Poor (N = 617)
Pseudo R-Squared	.169	.207
Percentage Classified Correctly	74.0	71.3

Note: Data for the first model are drawn from the 2012 American Values Survey. Data from the second model are drawn from 2014 American Values Survey. Cells contain binary logistic regression coefficients with standard errors in parentheses.
***p < .001; **p < .01; *p < .01 (two-tailed tests).

TABLE 4.2 Determinants of Support for Role of Government in Helping the Poor (Logistic Regressions) among American Women

Predictors	Agree That Children from All Income Groups Have Opportunity to Be Successful (N = 1259)		Agree That Most People on Welfare Take Advantage of the System (N = 946)	
	B(S.E.)	*Exp(B)*	*B(S.E.)*	*Exp(B)*
Tea Party Member	1.074(.263)***	2.927	.663(.284)*	1.940
Republican	.358(.161)*	1.431	.704(.208)***	2.022
Democrat	−.327(.150)*	.721	−.943(.175)***	.389
Ideology	.121(.071)[a]	1.128	.282(.088)***	1.326
Education	−.184(.037)***	.832	−.425(.075)***	.654
Income	.029(.044)	1.030	−.425(.075)***	1.108
White	.164(.163)	.849	.002(.004)	1.002
Age	.014(.003)***	1.014	−.002(.004)	.998
Married	.209(.131)	1.232	−.005(.165)	.995
South	.009(.124)	.939	.369(.159)*	1.446
Born-Again Christian	.344(.130)**	1.411	−.327(.169)[a]	.721
Church Attendance	−.032(.064)	.969	−.120(.058)*	.887
Constant	−.609(.371)	.544	.962(.499)*	2.317
Pseudo R-Squared	.097		.180	
Percentage Classified Correctly	61.4		69.0	

Note: Data for the first model come from the 2014 American Values Survey. Data for the second model come from the 2012 American Values Survey. Cells contain binary logistic regression coefficients with standard errors in parentheses.
***p < .001; **p < .01; *p < .01; a = p < .10 (two-tailed tests).

TABLE 4.3 Determinants of Support for ObamaCare and the Birth Control Mandate (Logistic Regressions) among American Women

Predictors	Agree That ObamaCare Should Be Repealed or Replaced (N = 638)		Support the Birth Control Mandate (N = 483)	
	B(S.E.)	Exp(B)	B(S.E.)	Exp(B)
Tea Party Member	1.383(.433)***	3.988	−.220(.350)	.803
Republican	1.545(.262)***	4.689	−.394(.264)	.674
Democrat	−1.344(.247)***	.261	.780(.285)**	2.182
Ideology	.210(.115)ᵃ	1.234	−.501(.145)***	.606
Education	−.134(.063)*	.875	−.224(.109)*	.799
Income	−.075(.073)	.928	−.072(.079)	.931
White	.930(.285)***	2.535	−.483(.328)	.617
Age	−.002(.005)	.998	−.204(.007)***	.976
Married	.201(.221)	1.222	−.100(.246)	.905
South	.402(.207)ᵃ	1.494	.415(.240)ᵃ	1.514
Born-Again Christian	.449(.211)*	1.567	.251(.260)	1.285
Church Attendance	−.075(.107)	.928	−.238(.092)**	.788
Constant	−1.062(.593)	.346	5.380(.815)***	216.942
Pseudo R-Squared	.325		.209	
Percentage Classified Correctly	76.7		75.8	

Note: Data for the first model come from the 2014 American Values Survey. Data for the second model come from the 2012 American Values Survey. Cells contain binary logistic regression coefficients with standard errors in parentheses.
***p < .001; **p < .01; *p < .01; a = p < .10 (two-tailed tests).

TABLE 4.4 Determinants of Opposition to Tax Hikes and Support for Tax and Spending Cuts to Spur Economic Growth (Logistic Regressions) among American Women

Predictors	Oppose Raising Taxes on Those Earning More Than $250,000 (N = 634)		Believe Cutting Taxes and Government Spending Will Spur Economic Growth (N = 1221)	
	B(S.E.)	Exp(B)	B(S.E.)	Exp(B)
Tea Party Member	−.779(.373)*	.459	.537(.262)*	1.711
Republican	−.439(.229)*	.632	.618(.165)***	1.856
Democrat	.863(.228)***	2.371	−.967(.158)***	.380

(continued)

TABLE 4.4 (*cont.*)

Predictors	Oppose Raising Taxes on Those Earning More Than $250,000 (N = 634)		Believe Cutting Taxes and Government Spending Will Spur Economic Growth (N = 1221)	
Ideology	−.361(.107)***	.697	.246(.074)***	1.279
Education	.065(.062)	1.067	−.072(.039)[a]	.930
Income	−.047(.064)	.954	.114(.047)*	1.120
White	.780(.242)***	.001	−.098(.171)	.907
Age	.008(.005)[a]	1.008	.012(.004)***	1.012
Married	.024(.188)	1.024	−.031(.137)	.970
South	−.164(.179)	.848	.296(.130)*	1.344
Born-Again Christian	.050(.192)	1.052	.304(.136)*	1.356
Church Attendance	−.140(.095)	.869	.073(.068)	1.076
Constant	.714(.553)	2.042	−1.797(.394)***	.166
Pseudo R-Squared	.125		.159	
Percentage Classified Correctly	64.7		67.9	

Note: Data for both models are drawn from the 2014 American Values Survey. Cells contain binary logistic regression coefficients with standard errors in parentheses.
***p < .001; **p < .01; *p < .01; a = p < .10 (two-tailed tests).

TABLE 4.5 Determinants of Opposition to Raising the Minimum Wage (Logistic Regression) among American Women

Predictors	Support Raising the Minimum Wage (N = 638)	
	B(S.E.)	*Exp(B)*
Tea Party Member	−1.131(.343)***	.323
Republican	−.850(.241)***	.427
Democrat	.604(.275)*	1.829
Ideology	−.271(.122)*	.763
Education	−.020(.062)	.980
Income	−.054(.072)	.948
White	−.440(.310)	.644
Age	−.013(.005)*	.987
Married	.240(.223)	1.271
South	.179(.207)	1.196
Born-Again Christian	−.174(.212)	.840

TABLE 4.5 (*cont.*)

Predictors	Support Raising the Minimum Wage (N = 638)	
Church Attendance	−.066(.109)	.543
Constant	3.480(.644)	32.447
Pseudo R-Squared	.150	
Percentage Classified Correctly	75.8	

Note: Data are drawn from the 2014 American Values Survey. Cells contain binary logistic regression coefficients with standard errors in parentheses.

TABLE 4.6 Determinants of Support for Paid Sick and Family Leave (Logistic Regressions) among American Women

Predictors	Support Paid Sick Leave (N = 634)		Support Paid Family Leave (N = 638)	
	B(S.E.)	*Exp(B)*	*B(S.E.)*	*Exp(B)*
Tea Party Member	−1.429(.384)***	.240	−.428(.377)	.652
Republican	−.444(.305)	.641	−.482(.281)[a]	.618
Democrat	.637(.338)[a]	1.891	.303(.295)	1.354
Ideology	−.318(.155)*	.727	−.078(.133)	.925
Education	.007(.072)	1.007	−.026(.069)	.975
Income	−.174(.083)*	.840	.096(.085)	1.101
White	.502(.349)	1.653	.155(.321)	1.122
Age	−.014(.007)*	.986	−.029(.006)***	.971
Married	.423(.264)	1.527	.198(.243)	.451
South	.737(.263)**	2.090	−.433(.224)[a]	.662
Born-Again Christian	.465(.263)[a]	1.527	−.006(.239)	.994
Church Attendance	.080(.128)	1.083	.161(.117)	1.174
Constant	2.727(.807)	15.293	2.788(.691)	16.247
Pseudo R-Squared	.097		.069	
Percentage Classified Correctly	85.7		82.7	

Note: Data for both models are drawn from the 2014 American Values Survey. Cells contain binary logistic regression coefficients with standard errors in parentheses.
***p < .001; **p < .01; *p < .01; a = p < .10 (two-tailed tests).
***p < .001; **p < .01; *p < .01; a = p < .10 (two-tailed tests).

FEMINISM ATTITUDES: REGRESSION ANALYSES (CHAPTER 5)

TABLE 5.1 Determinants of Support for Notion That Sex Discrimination Is No Longer a Problem (Logistic Regression) among American Women

Predictors	Completely or Mostly Agree That Sex Discrimination Is No Longer a Problem (N = 1055)	
	B(S.E.)	Exp(B)
Tea Party Member	.306(.213)	1.358
Republican	.161(.195)	1.175
Democrat	−.074(.202)	.929
Ideology	.145(.088)[a]	1.156
Education	−.252(.051)***	.778
Income	−.007(.032)	.993
White	.283(.222)	1.327
Age	.009(.005)	1.009
Married	.018(.166)	1.018
South	.258(.170)	1.295
Born-Again Christian	−.057(.168)	.945
Church Attendance	.122(.059)*	1.130
Constant	−1.754(.494)***	.173
Pseudo R-Squared	.069	
Percentage Classified Correctly	73.8	

Note: Data are drawn from the 2011 Millennials, Religion, and Abortion Survey. Cells contain binary logistic regression coefficients with standard errors in parentheses and odds ratios.

***$p < .001$; **$p < .01$; *$p < .01$; a = $p < .10$ (two-tailed tests).

TABLE 5.2 Determinants of Support for Notion That When Woman Has Full-Time Job, Family Life Suffers (Logistic Regression) among American Women

Predictors	Completely or Mostly Agree That When Woman Has Full-Time Job, Family Life Suffers (N = 1055)	
	B(S.E.)	Exp(B)
Tea Party Member	.389(.203)[a]	1.475
Republican	−.050(.180)	.951
Democrat	−.185(.180)	.831
Ideology	.269(.080)***	1.308

TABLE 5.2 *(cont.)*

Predictors	Completely or Mostly Agree That When Woman Has Full-Time Job, Family Life Suffers (N = 1055)	
Education	−.175(.046)***	.840
Income	.000(.030)	1.000
White	−.104(.004)	.901
Age	.015(.004)***	1.015
Married	.368(.152)*	1.444
South	−.208(.159)	.812
Born-Again Christian	.378(.153)*	1.459
Church Attendance	.037(.053)	1.038
Constant	−1.738(.449)	.176
Pseudo R-Squared	.090	
Percentage Classified Correctly	65.3	

Note: Data are drawn from the 2011 Millennials, Religion, and Abortion Survey. Cells contain binary logistic regression coefficients with standard errors in parentheses and odds ratios.
***p < .001; **p < .01; *p < .01; a = p < .10 (two-tailed tests).

TABLE 5.3 Determinants of Support for Notion That Women Are Better Suited to Raise Kids (Logistic Regression) among American Women

Predictors	Completely or Mostly Agree That Women Are Better Suited to Raise Kids Than Men (N = 1024)	
	B(S.E.)	*Exp(B)*
Tea Party Member	.451(.249)[a]	1.571
Republican	.230(.180)	1.258
Democrat	.047(.163)	1.048
Ideology	.238(.081)**	1.268
Education	−.130(.049)**	.878
Income	.084(.049)[a]	1.088
White	−.597(.192)**	.550
Age	.003(.004)	1.003
Married	.219(.150)	1.245
South	−.166(.143)	.847
Born-Again Christian	.234(.153)	1.264

(continued)

TABLE 5.3 (*cont.*)

Predictors	Completely or Mostly Agree That Women Are Better Suited to Raise Kids Than Men (N = 1024)	
Church Attendance	.035(.053)	1.035
Constant	−386(.539)	.680
Pseudo R-Squared	.056	
Percentage Classified Correctly	60.9	

Note: Data are drawn from the 2012 American Values Survey and the 2012 White Working Class Survey. Cells contain binary logistic regression coefficients with standard errors in parentheses and odds ratios.
***p < .001; **p < .01; *p < .01; a = p < .10 (two-tailed tests).

TABLE 5.4 Determinants of Opposition to Abortion (Logistic Regression) among American Women

Predictors	Oppose Abortion in Most or All Circumstances (N = 1012)	
	B(S.E.)	*Exp(B)*
Tea Party Member	.015(.264)	1.015
Republican	.719(.198)***	2.052
Democrat	−.742(.184)***	.476
Ideology	.403(.090)***	1.503
Education	−.191(.051)***	.827
Income	−.068(.055)	.934
White	.394(.208)[a]	1.483
Age	−.015(.004)***	.985
Married	−.100(.168)	.905
South	−.007(.159)	.993
Born-Again Christian	.360(.168)*	1.434
Church Attendance	.502(.064)***	1.652
Constant	−2.218(.590)***	.109
Pseudo R-Squared	.248	
Percentage Classified Correctly	71.2	

Note: Data are drawn from the 2012 American Values Survey and the 2012 White Working Class Survey. Cells contain binary logistic regression coefficients with standard errors in parentheses and odds-ratios.
***p < .001; **p < .01; *p < .01; a = p < .10 (two-tailed tests).

GUN CONTROL ATTITUDES: REGRESSION ANALYSES (CHAPTER 6)

TABLE 6.1 Determinants of Support for Strengthening Gun Control and Loosening Gun Control (Logistic Regressions) among American Women

Predictors	Support Strengthening Gun Control (N = 397)		Support Loosening Gun Control (N = 394)	
	B(S.E.)	Exp(B)	B(S.E.)	Exp(B)
Tea Party Member	−.508(.492)	.602	.804(.512)	2.234
Republican	−.570(.309)ᵃ	.565	.938(.344)**	2.555
Democrat	.768(.299)*	2.156	−.368(.367)	.692
Ideology	−.377(.120)**	.686	.290(.137)*	1.336
Education	.160(.135)	1.174	−.245(.162)	.783
Income	−.174(.083)*	.948	.001(.043)	1.001
White	−.622(.293)*	.537	.438(.358)	1.550
Age	.023(.007)***	1.023	−.008(.008)	.992
Married	−.041(.246)	.960	−.443(.287)	.642
South	.266(.255)	1.305	.920(.293)**	2.510
Church Attendance	−.122(.078)	.885	−.093(.089)	.911
Constant	2.727(.807)*	3.650	−1.727(.700)*	.178
Pseudo R-Squared	.189		.115	
Percentage Classified Correctly	69.0		78.2	

Note: Data for both models are drawn from the 2012 August PRRI/RNS Survey. Cells contain binary logistic regression coefficients with standard errors in parentheses.
***p < .001; **p < .01; *p < .01; a = p < .10 (two-tailed tests).

TABLE 6.2 Determinants of Support for Allowing Concealed Weapons in Churches and on College Campuses (Logistic Regressions) among American Women

Predictors	Support Allowing Concealed Weapons in Churches (N = 401)		Support Allowing Concealed Weapons on College Campuses (N = 406)	
	B(S.E.)	Exp(B)	B(S.E.)	Exp(B)
Tea Party Member	371(.524)	1.450	106(.528)	1.112
Republican	.920(.389)*	2.509	1.378(.379)***	3.967
Democrat	.025(.444)	1.026	.079(.419)	1.082
Ideology	.597(.178)***	1.817	.246(.154)	1.279

(*continued*)

TABLE 6.2 *(cont.)*

Predictors	Support Allowing Concealed Weapons in Churches (N = 401)		Support Allowing Concealed Weapons on College Campuses (N = 406)	
Education	.277(.177)	1.320	.234(.166)	1.264
Income	.048(.047)	1.050	−.018(.046)	.983
White	.767(.456)[a]	2.152	.516(.419)	1.676
Age	−.019(.009)*	.981	−.017(.009)*	.983
Married	−.391(.335)	.677	−.010(.316)	.990
South	.434(.335)	1.544	.587(.317)[a]	1.798
Church Attendance	.220(.108)*	1.247	.106(.099)	1.112
Constant	−5.448(.990)***	.004	−3.585(.832)***	.028
Pseudo R-Squared	.144		.107	
Percentage Classified Correctly	84.7		83.5	

Note: Data for both models are drawn from the 2012 August PRRI/RNS Survey. Cells contain binary logistic regression coefficients with standard errors in parentheses.
***p < .001; **p < .01; *p < .01; a = p < .10 (two-tailed tests).

TABLE 6.3 Determinants of Allowing Concealed Weapons in Government Buildings (Logistic Regression) among American Women

Predictors	Support Allowing Concealed Weapons in Government Buildings (N = 400)	
	B(S.E.)	*Exp(B)*
Tea Party Member	630(.524)	1.878
Republican	1.390(.388)***	4.017
Democrat	.041(.392)	1.042
Ideology	.235(.150)	1.265
Education	.208(.164)	1.231
Income	−.017(.044)	.983
White	−.190(.363)	.827
Age	−.029(.363)***	.971
Married	−.459(.301)	.632
South	−.141(.301)	.868
Church Attendance	.242(.099)*	1.174
Constant	−2.235(.742)	.107

TABLE 6.3 *(cont.)*

Predictors	Support Allowing Concealed Weapons in Government Buildings (N = 400)
Pseudo R-Squared	00.124
Percentage Classified Correctly	83.0

Note: Data are drawn from the 2014 American Values Survey. Cells contain binary logistic regression coefficients with standard errors in parentheses.
***p < .001; **p < .01; *p < .01; a = p < .10 (two-tailed tests).

TABLE 6.4 Determinants of Agreement That Right to Guns Is as Important as Other Constitutional Rights, Such as Free Speech and Religion (Logistic Regression) among American Women

Predictors	Agree That Gun Rights as Important as Other Constitutional Rights (N = 408)	
	B(S.E.)	*Exp(B)*
Tea Party Member	1.037(.699)	2.822
Republican	1.134(.346)***	3.108
Democrat	.002(.265)	1.002
Ideology	.212(.115)ᵃ	1.236
Education	−.084(.129)	.920
Income	−.035(.035)	.965
White	.542(.264)*	1.719
Age	−.004(.006)	.996
Married	.694(.237)**	2.002
South	.081(.244)	1.084
Church Attendance	.026(.075)	1.027
Constant	3.480(.644)	.429
Pseudo R-Squared	.144	
Percentage Classified Correctly	68.9	

Note: Data are drawn from the 2014 American Values Survey. Cells contain binary logistic regression coefficients with standard errors in parentheses.
***p < .001; **p < .01; *p < .01; a = p < .10 (two-tailed tests).

NOTES

CHAPTER 1. INTRODUCTION

1　Full transcript of Governor Sarah Palin's speech available at http://www.p2012 .org/photos10/palin051410spt.html.

2　Ibid.

3　See Lo (2012).

4　See Altman (2010).

5　For more on women involved in the fight against communism, see Brennan (2008); McGirr (2001); Nickerson (2012). For more on women's involvement in the antiabortion cause and as activists within the Christian Right, see Luker (1984); Diamond (1995); and Burkett (1998).

6　See Freeman (2000); Gustafson (2001); and Rymph (2006).

7　See Sommers (2013).

8　See Institute for Research and Education on Human Rights (2015). IREHR indicates that its numbers for membership are derived from a collection of online directories on the major national Tea Party faction websites: Tea Party Nation, Tea Party Patriots, 1776 Tea Party, FreedomWorks, and Patriot Action Network.

9　I took data from the Institute for Research and Education on Human Rights, which estimates Tea Party membership by state for all fifty states. I divided the membership number by state population, which I found on Wikipedia, derived from the U.S. census. For example, as a percentage of the state population, I found that .0013 percent of Maryland residents are active Tea Party members, compared with .0013 percent of California residents, .0019 percent of Texas residents, and .0022 percent of Florida residents.

10　Author interview with Emily Ekins (by Skype), June 3, 2013.

11　See Glenn (2011) and Levin (2011) for assessments on what "Constitutional Conservatism" stands for, and how its meaning has changed over time.

12　For example, Jenny Beth Martin discusses this philosophy in her co-authored book (with Mark Meckler) *Tea Party Patriots*, which has become required reading for new hires at FreedomWorks, the nonprofit grassroots libertarian organization that works to organize and facilitate Tea Party activism at the local and state levels of government.

13　See Gardner (2010).

14　Pelosi told reporter Ryan Powers of *ThinkProgress*, "This [Tea Party] initiative is funded by the high end—we call it astroturf. It's not really a grassroots movement.

It's astroturf by some of the wealthiest people in America to keep the focus on tax cuts for the rich instead of for the great middle class." See Powers (2009).

15 See Skocpol and Williamson (2012).

16 See Institute for Research and Education on Human Rights (2015).

17 See http://ffcoalition.com/about.

18 Conservative activist Jim Gilchrest started the Minuteman Project in 2005, which had "minutemen" volunteers patrol the border between Mexico and the United States to stop illegal immigrants from getting into the country. The Project disbanded in 2010 amid accusations of vigilantism and criminal charges against some of the participants of the group. The Southern Poverty Law Center labeled the organization a "nativist extremist" group, and reports surfaced indicating that some of its volunteers were also members of white supremacist groups. See Medrano (2014).

19 Author interview with Jenny Beth Martin (by phone), April 1, 2013.

20 See Favreau (2013).

21 Author interview with Kristen Soltis Anderson, Washington DC, May 20, 2013.

22 Author interview with Carrie Lukas (by phone), June 18, 2013.

23 Author interview with Stacy Mott (by phone), February 27, 2013.

24 Author interview with Tami Nantz, National Harbor, MD, March 15, 2013.

25 See Burns, Schlozman, and Verba (2001).

26 See Lawless and Fox (2010).

27 See Campbell and Wolbrecht (2006); Burns, Schlozman, and Verba (2001).

28 Author interview with Kristen Soltis Anderson, Washington DC, May 20, 2013.

29 Author interview with activist, Kent Island, MD, November 19, 2012.

30 See Tarrow (1998): 18.

31 See Palin (2010): 113.

32 See Loesch (2011).

33 The use of motherhood appeals as a rhetorical device by political organizers is not limited to conservative political causes. In the Progressive Era, for example, under the mantra of "municipal housekeeping," progressive activists compelled mothers to support political and civic reforms concerning a broad array of public causes, such as conservation, sewage, child labor, and juvenile court. See Blair (1980). Mothers' organizations were also instrumental in helping to establish government maternal health programs and protective labor legislation for women during this time. See Skocpol (1992). In more recent years, mothers have been called to support restrictive gun control laws, first through the "Million Mom March" organization in 2000 and now through the "One Million Moms for Gun Control" organization, formed in 2013 in response to the Newton school shooting tragedy (see http://momsdemandaction.org/). Established in 2006, the organization Moms Rising advocates grassroots political activism centered around liberal political causes such as the government expansion of health care, paid sick and maternity leave, and child care under the mantra "Where moms and the people who love them go to change our world" (see MomsRising.org).

34 See Fletcher (2008); Brennan (2008); and Nickerson (2012).

35 See Kim (2011) and Ritz (2013).

36 Author interview with Amy Jo Clark (by phone), June 21, 2013.

37 See Palin (2010).

38 Ibid., 139.

39 For conservative women critics of modern feminism, see Sommers (1995); Venker and Schlafly (2011); and Lukas and Schaeffer (2012).

40 See Palin (2010): 141–142.

41 See Lukas and Schaeffer (2012): 43.

42 Author interview with activist, Annapolis, MD, November 8, 2012.

43 See Schaeffer (2013) and Political Parity (2015).

44 See Sanbonmatsu (2006) and Carroll and Sanbonmatsu (2013).

45 See Pitkin (1967).

46 See Sapiro (1981) and Mansbridge (1999).

47 See Sapiro (1981): 712.

48 For a good summary of this voluminous literature, see Dolan, Deckman, and Swers (2011) and Osborn (2012).

49 See Thomas (1994) and Carroll (2006).

50 See Welch (1985) and Swers (2002).

51 See Carroll and Sanbonmatsu (2013); Swers (2002) and (2013).

52 See Cowell-Meyers and Langbein (2009); Reingold (2000); Osborn (2012); and Frederick (2010).

53 See Swers and Larson (2005).

54 Ibid.: 123.

55 See Swers (2013).

56 See Klatch (1988) and (1987).

57 See Klatch (1988): 688.

58 See Schreiber (2008).

59 Ibid.

60 Ibid.: 12.

61 Author interview with activist, Westminster, MD, April 2, 2013.

62 See Sapiro (1981); Smith (1984); Chaney, Alvarez, and Nagler (1998); Kauffman and Petrocik (1999); Kaufmann (2004); Elder and Greene (2008); and Izade (2013).

63 See Kaufmann and Petrocik (1999) and Carroll (1996).

64 See Clement (2012).

65 See Pew Forum for Religion and Public Life (2012).

66 See Brooks (2010).

CHAPTER 2. TOP CONSERVATIVES AND GRASSROOTS LEADERS

1 See Belle (2009).

2 See Zernike (2010).

3 See Smith et al. (2009).

4 Ibid.

5 See Meckler and Martin (2012): 17.

6 Kremer left to work with Tea Party Express in 2010; Meckler left after an arrest for a disorderly conduct misdemeanor in 2011 for attempting to board a plane with a gun in New York, which refused to recognize Meckler's California license for the weapon.

7 See Blumer (2009) for a full transcript of the Santelli rant.

8 See Meckler and Martin (2012): 3.

9 Author interview with Jenny Beth Martin (by phone), April 20, 2013.

10 See Meckler and Martin (2012).

11 Both women were prominently featured in the book *Boiling Mad*, published by *New York Times* reporter Kate Zernike in 2010, arguably the first national "profile" of the Tea Party movement written by a journalist.

12 Author interview with Keli Carender (by phone), April 1, 2013.

13 Author interview with Diana Reimer (by phone), April 1, 2013.

14 Keli Carender stepped down from her position as a paid employee of Tea Party Patriots after the birth of her first daughter in the spring of 2015. She plans to remain active in grassroots conservative politics, however. See Martin (2015).

15 In 2011 Sandhya Somashekhar wrote in the *Washington Post* about the enthusiasm Tea Party conservative women felt for the potential presidential candidacies of Sarah Palin and Michele Bachmann. Despite conservatives' traditional aversion to feminism or identity politics, GOP pollster Kellyanne Conway believes that women like Palin and Bachmann were appealing to conservative women voters because they could personally relate to them. See Somashekhar (2011).

16 Despite several attempts I was unable to secure an interview with Ms. Kremer.

17 See http://www.politico.com/arena/bio/amy_kremer.html.

18 See Pilkington (2010).

19 The dispute centered over Amy Kremer's affiliation with Tea Party Express while still a leader of Tea Party Patriots. Martin and Meckler were concerned that Tea Party Express was overtly partisan and tied too closely to the GOP. They also maintained that Kremer kept using her Tea Party Patriot title in activities not affiliated with the group. Both groups filed suit to maintain control of the Tea Party Patriots name in 2010, and later Kremer filed suits accusing Jenny Beth Martin and her husband, Lee, of defamation. See Mencimer (2011).

20 See Kremer (2012).

21 Ibid.

22 See Burghart (2012).

23 See Rapoport (2012).

24 See Rapoport et al. (2013).

25 See Deckman (2013b).

26 As of May 2014, women held fourteen of thirty-four national staff positions listed on the organization's website, FreedomWorks.org.

27 FreedomWorks originated from Citizens for a Sound Economy, a conservative political group funded by David H. Koch, which split into FreedomWorks and Americans for Prosperity in 2004. The Bill of Rights Institute was founded in 1999 by Charles Koch, and two members of its current board of directors work for the Koch brothers. For more on the relationship between the Tea Party and the Koch brothers, see Skocpol and Williamson (2012).

28 The Common Core is an initiative developed by the National Governor's Association in 2009 and adopted by forty-four states and the District of Columbia in an attempt to establish national standards in math and literacy. The Obama administration backs the Common Core and has encouraged states to adopt more rigorous standards by making competitive "Race to the Top" grants available to states that demonstrate innovate methods in establishing such standards. Conservative organizations have long opposed attempts by the federal government to meddle in education policy, which they believe should be the purview of state and local governments.

29 Glenn Beck, the former Fox News television host who continues to have a strong following among many activists in the Tea Party, started the 9/12 Project to bring Americans back to the unity they felt as Americans on the day after the terrorist attacks on September 11, 2001. The "9/12" in the project's title refers to both the day after the 9/11 attacks and, according to Beck, to a set of nine American principles and twelve American values, such as honesty, reverence, and hope, that the Founders established.

30 Author interview with Whitney Neal, Washington DC, July 11, 2013.

31 Author interview with Emily Ekins (by Skype), June 3, 2013.

32 Skocpol and Williamson (2012): 43.

33 I found most of the local or state women activists by researching Tea Party organizations in Maryland online or through a "snowball" sampling technique, which involves a researcher asking an interview subject to suggest other possible subjects for future interviews. Given the specialized nature of the sample population, and the fact that no systematic list of Tea Party activists exists, this snowball technique, while not random, is appropriate and frequently employed in qualitative analysis by many researchers.

34 I use pseudonyms for most of the local and state women Tea Party activists in this and subsequent chapters. However, I identify Katrina Pierson by her actual name given that she decided to run for Congress in 2014. Also, Pierson is often featured on Fox News and other conservative news outlets popular with Tea Party activists, so while she remains a local activist she has had a heightened national media presence compared with the other local activists I profile.

35 Author interview with Katrina Pierson (by phone), August 6, 2013.

36 For example, the Public Religion Research Institute's 2010 Study of the Tea Party found that just 4 percent of Tea Party members were African American, 9 percent were Hispanic, and 5 percent described themselves as "racially mixed." No Asians reported belonging to the Tea Party. See Public Religion Research Institute (2010).

The PRRI data from 2012 that I analyze in this chapter also shows that just 3 percent of women who support the Tea Party are African American and 4 percent describe themselves as "racially mixed." My earlier analysis of 2010 data from Pew show similar patterns among Tea Party women as well: 5 percent were African American, 6 percent were Latino, and 4 percent were "other." See Deckman (2012b).

37 See http://www.teapartyexpress.org/8675/tea-party-express-endorses-mia-love -for-congress-in-ut-4.

38 See Lee and Darby (2014).

39 See Swartzell (2014).

40 Ibid.

41 See TPNN (2014).

42 See Skocpol and Williamson (2012).

43 I use a pseudonym here and in subsequent profiles of local and state women activists. I italicize the pseudonyms the first time I use them.

44 Author interview with Jennifer Jacobs, Annapolis, MD, November 8, 2012.

45 This description is from the organization's website, http://www.mdcitizen.com /about/.

46 Author interview with Elizabeth Reynolds, Chevy Chase, MD, February 26, 2013.

47 Author interview with Renee Wilson, Columbia, MD, December 17, 2012.

48 See Duggan (2013).

49 See Swers (2002).

50 See Carey, Niemi, and Powell (1998) and Poggione (2004).

51 See Thomsen (2015): 302.

52 See DeSilver (2014).

53 See Thomsen (2015) and Willis (2015).

54 See Sanbonmatsu (2006) and Elder (2012).

55 See King and Matland (2003).

56 For example, Sanbonmatsu, Carroll, and Walsh (2009) found in 2009 that only eight women served as state Republican Party chairs. Women's representation in the Democratic Party as leaders was better, but only slightly: in 2009, only eleven women served as state Democratic Party chairs.

57 Lepore is highly critical of the modern Tea Party's comparison of its struggles to the patriots of Colonial Era America: "To say that we have forsaken [the Founding Fathers] and they're rolling over in their graves because of the latest, breaking political development—the election of the United States' first African American president, for instance—is to subscribe to a set of assumptions about the relationship between the past and the present stricter, even, than the strictest form of constitutional originalism, a set of assumptions that, conflating originalism, evangelicalism, and heritage tourism, amounts to a variety of fundamentalism" (2010: 16).

58 The Values and Capitalism Initiative is a program sponsored by the American Enterprise Institute, a leading pro-market think tank, that, according to its website,

"seeks to advance the case for the morality of democratic capitalism on campus, with a goal of reaching a significant number of Christian college students. The articles, books, online material, and other publications and events emphasize how the free enterprise system not only creates material wealth but also encourages the virtues of industriousness, charity, and community engagement" (http://valuesand capitalism.com/about/).

59 See Public Religion Research Institute (2013).

60 On the connection between the Tea Party and the Koch brothers, see Mayer (2010).

61 See Hays (2013).

62 Author interview with Stacy Mott (by phone), February 27, 2013.

63 Author interview with Jenny Beth Martin (by phone), April 20, 2013.

64 Quoted in Asbury (2011).

65 Ibid.

66 Ibid.

67 As a Mom published its last issue of *MinuteMom Magazine* in Fall 2013, citing reduced readership. It continues to host a chat room, run its websites, and educate its readers on a variety of political issues.

68 Among other initiatives, the 9/12 Project sponsors the Constitutional Champions Patriot Camp, in which children attend "liberty schools" to learn about colonial history, the Constitution, and the Bill of Rights.

69 Author interview with Lori Parker (by phone), July 12, 2013.

70 See Schlafly (2011).

71 Agenda 21 is a nonbinding action plan adopted by the United Nations to get member states to promote sustainable development, partly in an effort to curb climate change. While the U.S. government has signed onto Agenda 21, given that it is nonbinding, American participation is not compulsory. The Tea Party and critics of Agenda 21 believe that the program threatens American sovereignty and will potentially threaten individuals' property rights. Glenn Beck is a vocal critic of Agenda 21, and in 2012 he co-authored a dystopian novel by the same name. He routinely promotes activism among his followers, particularly at the local level of government, denouncing Agenda 21. For example, his website has developed a list of "code words" used at the local level of government that allegedly identify Agenda 21 initiatives, such as affordable housing, Common Core, conservative easement, environmental justice, high-speed rail, land use policies, smart growth, and urban revitalization. See http://www.glennbeck.com/agenda21/agenda-21 -word-list.

72 See Hall (2012): 24.

73 For a sample of Hall's writing about the "revisionist history" of the Founding Mothers, see the following: "The revisionists have been lying to us for many years. These women were not oppressed by their chauvinistic husbands to the point of servitude. They were bold and brave women of resolve." See ibid.: 27.

74 See Christianson (2012): 37.

75 See Jalonick (2012).

76 See Hulse (2012): 16–17.

77 Author interview with Lori Parker (by phone), July 12, 2013.

78 Karen Handler served for a time as vice president for public policy for the Susan G. Komen Foundation but resigned after she became embroiled in the controversy over the foundation's initial decision to stop funding Planned Parenthood, which was later reversed after public outcry among many pro-choice Komen supporters. Handler is avowedly pro-life and is largely credited with Komen's initial decision to stop funding of Planned Parenthood, which is one of the nation's largest providers of breast screening services for low-income women. Handler also served as Georgia's secretary of state. Sarah Palin, who narrated Handler's first political advertisement, also endorsed her. See Gentilvisto (2014).

79 See http://us4.campaign-archive1.com/?u=9e6bad514f8034b74b46aa1f4&id=73ee b2a496.

80 See Watkins (2012): 15.

81 Mission statement found at its website, http://www.iwf.org/about.

82 Author interview with Colleen Holcomb, Washington DC, April 30, 2013.

83 Author interview with Janice Shaw Crouse, Laurel, MD, July 26, 2013.

84 Author interview with Carrie Lukas (by phone), June 18, 2013.

85 Author interview with Emily Ekins (by Skype), June 3, 2013.

86 See Parker and Barreto (2013).

87 Ibid.: 74. Theda Skocpol and Vanessa Williamson (2012) corroborate these findings in their book *The Tea Party and the Remaking of Republican Conservatism.* They calculate the average percentage of Americans who report active participation in the Tea Party based on six national polls taken in 2010 as being around 8 percent (144).

88 The four-year average of these three polls, 26 percent, is the same as the average of 45 national polls summarized by Skocpol and Williamson (2012), although their analysis considered responses from surveys conducted in 2010 only.

89 These public opinion data on the Tea Party are found at http://www.pollingreport. com/politics.htm; however, the more recent 2015 question can be found directly on AP/GFK's website, http://ap-gfkpoll.com/main/wp-content/uploads/2015/06 /AP-GfK_Poll_April_2015-Topline_transportation.pdf.

90 See Skocpol and Williamson (2012: 143–146) for a good discussion of the effect of question wording on assessing support for the Tea Party. Their analysis of forty-five polls from the major polling and news organizations from 2010 shows that the range of support for the Tea Party varied from 18 to 31 percent depending on question wording.

91 See Public Religion Research Institute (2010) and (2014).

92 See Zernike (2010); Abramowitz (2012); and Parker and Barreto (2013).

93 See Jones and Cox (2010).

94 For example, Abramowitz's (2012) assessment of 2010 American National Election Studies data found that among self-identified supporters of the movement, 63 per-

cent were men and 37 percent were women. Parker and Barreto's (2013) multistate study finds the gender breakdown among Tea Party supporters to be 59 percent male, 41 percent female.

95 See Abramowitz (2012); Parker and Barreto (2013).

96 Combining the data sets is not problematic given that PRRI conducted the surveys using the same methodology (a random, national telephone survey conducted in English and Spanish of respondents who were eighteen or older) within six weeks of each other. The White Working Class Survey was conducted between August 2 and August 15, 2012, and the American Values Survey was conducted between September 13 and September 30, 2012. I employ the weighting scheme developed by PRRI for each survey. The margin of error for the White Working Class Survey is +/–2.2 percentage points at the 95 percent confidence level; for the American Values Survey it is +/–2.0 percentage points at the 95 percent confidence level.

97 For ease of interpretation, I only display bar charts of data in which there are statistically significant differences (p < .05 or less) at the bivariate level.

98 See Deckman (2012b).

99 Using a chi-square test, this difference between men and women in their Tea Party identification is statistically significant (chi-square = 42.721; p < .001). Data are not reported graphically.

100 In this analysis, I consider as Republicans only those women who identify themselves in the PRRI survey as Republicans; I don't "fold" Republican leaners among Independents into this category. While studies often code partisan leaners with partisans (Keith et al. 1992), including studies that analyze support for the Tea Party (Abramowitz 2012), I opt to identify the partisanship of Americans by their own self-identification here, not just for the sake of simplicity but because I am interested in isolating the most committed Republicans from Independent leaners. This distinction is important given that a majority of states have closed primaries, and the battle to control the Republican Party between Tea Party Republicans and "establishment" Republicans is most heightened at that level.

101 Data are not reported graphically.

102 Data are not reported graphically.

103 PRRI does not include Latino as a separate question from the other racial groups in figure 3.2. However, in a separate question that asks respondents if they are Latino, I find that 10 percent of Tea Party women, 6 percent of non–Tea Party Republican women, and 13 percent of other American women are Latino (chi-square = 19.470; p < .001), indicating that Tea Party and non–Tea Party Republican women are less likely to be Latino than are other American women.

104 Data are not reported graphically.

105 Trump said the following about illegal immigrants from Mexico in his announcement that he was running for president: "When Mexico sends its people, they're not sending their best—they're not sending you. They're not sending you. They're sending people that have lots of problems and they're bringing those

problems with us. They're bringing drugs. They're bringing crime. They're rapists. And some, I assume, are good people" (quoted in Burns 2015).

106 Chicks on the Right (2015).

107 See Parker and Barreto (2013); Abramowitz (2012).

108 See Parker and Barreto (2013): 270–271.

109 To ease presentation, I present bar graphs comparing Tea Party women and men only on those measures that are statistically significant at the bivariate level.

110 Data are not presented graphically.

111 See Herek (2002) and Pew Forum for Religion and Public Life (2014).

112 See Gallup (2010).

113 Data are not presented graphically.

114 I use logistic regression, in which the dependent variable is identification with the Tea Party (coded as 1 = consider oneself a part of the Tea Party; 0 = does not consider oneself a part of the Tea Party). I control for gender as the major independent variable with a host of other variables. For more details about the regression analysis and the regression results, see appendix B, table 2.1.

115 Predicted probabilities are calculated using the margins command in Stata, placing all other variables at their mean values.

116 Another difference is that income may matter for women in a way that does not for men: as income increases, women are statistically more likely to identify with the Tea Party, while income has no bearing on men's proclivity to identify with the movement. Given that income was marginally statistically significant, however ($p < .10$), and most conventional cut-offs for statistical significance are lower, typically at the $p < .05$ level or below, I have opted only to calculate predicted probabilities for variables that meet this lower threshold.

117 A chi-square test that examined the relationship between church attendance and race was 13.687 ($p < .05$).

118 See Montgomery (2012) and Brody (2012).

119 See Deckman and McTague (2015).

CHAPTER 3. A NEW CIVIC MOTHERHOOD?

1 The complete video campaign ad aired on Jamie Radtke's campaign website, http://radtkeforsenate.com/about-jamie/ (site discontinued).

2 See McAdam (1996) and Tarrow (1998).

3 For more on the frames employed by the Tea Party movement, and those frames predominately used by the media to discuss the Tea Party, see Boykoff and Laschever (2011).

4 In their analysis of what they deem the "new maternalism" promoted by conservative and progressive activists today, legal scholars Naomi Mezey and Cornelia T. L. Pillard (2012) first situate such activism historically by discussing different maternalisms across time. They describe "old maternalism" as activism by mothers' organizations fighting for Progressive Era reform and fighting against the sale of alcohol.

5 See Welter (1966).

6 Ibid.: 159.

7 See Skocpol (1992): 323.

8 Ibid.

9 See Welter (1966): 159.

10 See Parker (2002).

11 See Baker (1984) and Mezey and Pillard (2012).

12 See Blair (1980); Baker (1984); Gustafson (2001).

13 Quoted in Skocpol (1992): 331.

14 See DuBois (1998): 289.

15 See Cott (1975); Blair (1980); Kraditor (1981).

16 See Cott (1975); Blair (1980); Baker (1984).

17 See Kraditor (1981): 15.

18 See Marshall (1986) and Jablonsky (2002).

19 See Jablonsky (2002): 123.

20 Ibid.

21 See Bordin (1981) and Baker (1984).

22 See Bordin (1981).

23 See Epstein (1981): 118.

24 Ibid.

25 See Baker (1984).

26 Ibid.

27 See Skocpol (1992).

28 See Nielson (2001) and Jablonsky (2002).

29 See Nielson (2001).

30 Ibid.: 43.

31 See ibid. and Nickerson (2012).

32 See Nickerson (2012): 96.

33 Ibid.

34 Ibid.: 50.

35 See Honey (1984) and May (1988).

36 See Brennan (2008); Rymph (2006); Nickerson (2012).

37 See Brennan (2008): 91.

38 Ibid.

39 See Brennan (2008) and May (1988).

40 See May (1988).

41 See Nickerson (2012).

42 See Rymph (2006).

43 Ibid.: 112.

44 Ibid.: 118.

45 Ibid.

46 See Nickerson (2012).

47 Ibid.

48 Ibid.

49 Ibid.: 167.

50 See Mansbridge (1986).

51 See Critchlow (2005).

52 Ibid.: 48.

53 See Schlafly (1964).

54 Rymph (2006): 175.

55 See ibid.: 214.

56 See Schlafly (1977).

57 Ibid.

58 Ibid.: 70–71.

59 See Mansbridge (1986); Ryan (1992); Ferree and Hess (1994).

60 Once he was elected to the U.S. House of Representatives, Henry Hyde would become better known nationally for his pro-life advocacy as the author of the "Hyde Amendment," which forbids most federal funding for abortion. See Mansbridge (1986): 104.

61 See Mansbridge (1986).

62 Solomon (1978): 47. As Mezey and Pillard (2012) note, however, pro-ERA women activists also sought to dispel myths that they were "man-eating harpies" by plying state legislators with home-cooked meals to overcome fears that voting for the ERA would threaten traditionally domestic female values. See also Klien (2012).

63 See Klien (2012).

64 Quoted in Klatch (1988): 681.

65 See Irwin (1980) and Martin (1996).

66 Quoted in Klatch (1987): 127.

67 See Klien (2012): 10.

68 See Rymph (2006): 241.

69 Author interview with Jenny Beth Martin (by phone), April 13, 2013.

70 Author interview with Janice Shaw Crouse, Laurel, MD, July 27, 2013.

71 Author interview with Tami Nantz, National Harbor, MD, March 15, 2013.

72 Quoted in Project Vote Smart, http://votesmart.org/public-statement/528848/.

73 See Radtke (2012).

74 See Madsen 2012.

75 Author interview with activist, Kent Island, MD, November 15, 2012.

76 Author interview with activist, Baltimore, December 1, 2012.

77 Ibid.

78 Transcript from an advertisement for Sarah Palin's political action committee SarahPAC, accessed via YouTube: http://www.youtube.com/watch?v=fsUVL6ciK-c.

79 See Palin (2010): 132.

80 Author interview with activist, Easton, MD, March 29, 2013.

81 See Palin (2010): 130.

82 See Rodgers (2012).

83 Author interview with Tami Nantz, National Harbor, MD, March 15, 2013.

84 Author interview with Miriam Weaver (by phone), June 21, 2013.

85 Author interview with Colleen Holcomb, Washington DC, April 30, 2013.

86 Author interview with Jenny Beth Martin (by phone), April 16, 2013.

87 Author interview with activist, Easton, MD, March 29, 2013.

88 Author interview with activist, Westminster, MD, April 2, 2013.

89 Ibid.

90 See Loesch (2011). Article 1, Section 8 of the Constitution lists specific powers that Congress is authorized to carry out, often referred to as its "enumerated powers," including the right to collect taxes, coin money, borrow money, establish post offices, issue patents, and declare war. Strict constitutional conservatives take issue with the establishment of government programs, including politically popular programs such as Social Security and Medicare, that are not specifically listed Article 1, Section 8. However, such programs have been considered constitutional by most legal experts under Article 1, Section 8's broader "necessary and proper" clause, which states that Congress shall "make all Laws which shall be necessary and proper for carrying into Execution the foregoing Powers, and all other Powers vested by this Constitution in the Government of the United States, or in any Department or Officer thereof."

91 Ibid.

92 See Kremer (2012).

93 Author interview with Colleen Holcomb, Washington DC, April 30, 2013.

94 Author interview with activist, Columbia, MD, December 17, 2012.

95 Author interview with activist, Baltimore, December 1, 2012.

96 See Vogel (2010a).

97 See Kozub (2011): 10.

98 See Rymph (2006): 241.

99 See Diamond (1995).

100 See Gilgoff (2009).

101 From the Faith and Freedom Coalition website. See http://ffcoalition.com/about.

102 Author interview with Stacy Mott (by phone), February 27, 2013.

103 Author interview with Kristen Soltis Anderson, Washington DC, May 20, 2013.

104 Author interview with Whitney Neal, Washington DC, July 13, 2013.

105 Author interview with Keli Carender (by phone), April 1, 2013.

106 Author interview with Carrie Lukas (by phone), June 18, 2013.

107 See Klatch (1987): 152.

108 See Schreiber (2008).

109 See Meckler and Martin (2012) and Skocpol and Williamson (2012).

110 See Parker and Barreto (2013); Disch (2012); Lownes (2012).

111 See Parker and Barreto (2013): 5.

112 See Sparks (2015): 43.

113 Ibid.

114 Author interview with Kristen Soltis Anderson, Washington DC, May 20, 2013.

CHAPTER 4. THE SEXIST SAFETY NET

1 See Weiner (2012).

2 Commentators on the left were also critical of the infographic. As cultural critic Jill Lepore (2012) wrote in the *New Yorker*, it "borrows its aesthetic from *USA Today* and its narrative logic from Chutes and Ladders," and is "a bad place to start a campaign."

3 See Malkin (2012).

4 See Hawley (2012).

5 See Nantz (2012). In making this point, Tami Nantz links to a book by Deneen Borelli, an African American woman who is the author of *Blacklash: How Obama and the Left Are Driving Americans to the Government Plantation* (2012). Black conservative critics such as Borelli make the argument that government social safety net programs have been detrimental to the black community and take "old-school black leaders" to task for perpetuating "a message of victimization among their black constituents" (7). Borelli continues, "We don't need to live on the government plantation. We don't need government handouts—in fact they're bad for us. Remember one thing: there is nothing free about free money. Handouts engender dependency. They create and entrench poverty, not fix it. It doesn't matter if you are a black or white president creating entitlement programs to attract voters, it is bad policy" (7–8). In this way, their criticisms echo what many Tea Party women say about women's relationship to the federal government.

6 See Morello (2013).

7 For more on progressive organizations' views on these issues, see Human Rights Watch (2011); Center for American Progress (2014); National Organization for Women (2014); and Shriver (2014).

8 See National Women's Law Center (2013).

9 See DeSilver (2013).

10 For more on the gender gap, and how attitudes about the social safety net drive it, see Howell and Day (2000); Kaufmann (2002); Manza and Brooks (1998); Kaufmann and Petrocik (1999).

11 See Elshtain (1981); Sapiro (1983); Ruddick (1989).

12 See Carroll (2006).

13 See Howell and Day (2000).

14 See Gault and Sabini (2000); Toussaint and Webb (2005); Croson and Gneezy (2009).

15 I use dummy variables for party affiliation in the controls for the models: Republicans and Democrats with Independents (including Independents who lean Republican or Democratic as well as the relatively few respondents who identify as "other") as the reference category. Appendix A contains full details about the variables included in the analysis.

16 Author interview with Amy Jo Clark (by phone), June 21, 2013.

17 Author interview with Jennifer Jacobs, Annapolis, MD, November 8, 2012.

18 Author interview with Gabriella Hoffman, Arlington, VA, June 24, 2013.

19 Author interview with Elizabeth Reynolds, Chevy Chase, MD, February 26, 2013.

20 Here is the text of Romney's full quote: "There are 47 percent of the people who will vote for the president no matter what. All right, there are 47 percent who are with him, who are dependent upon government, who believe they are victims, who believe that government has a responsibility to care for them, who believe they are entitled to health care, to food, to housing, to you name it. That's an entitlement. And the government should give it to them. . . . These are people who pay no income tax. Forty-seven percent of Americans pay no income tax. So our message of low taxes doesn't connect. And he'll be out there talking about tax cuts for the rich. I mean that's what they sell every four years. And so my job is not to worry about those people—I'll never convince them that they should take personal responsibility and care for their lives." Quoted in Berman 2013.

21 Author interview with Janice Shaw Crouse, Laurel, MD, July 23, 2013.

22 Author interview with Colleen Holcomb, Washington DC, April 30, 2013.

23 Author interview with Carrie Lukas (by phone), June 18, 2013.

24 See Jessup (2012).

25 See Loesch (2012).

26 For a summary of its major provisions, see the Kaiser Family Foundation website, http://kff.org/health-reform/fact-sheet/summary-of-the-affordable-care-act/.

27 The Supreme Court struck down the requirement that states expand their Medicaid programs or face the penalty of losing Medicaid funding. However, it upheld the constitutionality of the individual mandate component of the Affordable Care Act, citing it as an exercise of Congress's taxing power. See *National Federation of Independent Business v. Sebelius* (2012).

28 For a summary about the specifics of the birth control mandate, see Kliff (2012).

29 I use the terms ObamaCare and Affordable Care Act interchangeably. While ObamaCare was first used a slight against the ACA by its conservative critics, including many Tea Party leaders, the White House later embraced the term. Of course, polls show that Americans' attitudes about the policy are less hostile if asked about the Affordable Care Act as opposed to ObamaCare. See Zezima (2014).

30 Author interview with Janice Shaw Crouse, Laurel, MD, July 23, 2013.

31 Quoted in Nantz (2011).

32 See Crouse (2010).

33 See House Republicans (2014b).

34 See Crouse (2010).

35 Ibid.

36 See Nance (2012).

37 See Lukas (2014b).

38 See Heath (2013).

39 Ibid.

40 See Ponnuru and Lukas (2014).

41 Ibid.

42 Author interview with Colleen Holcomb, Washington DC, April 30, 2013.

43 See Schlafly (2012a).

44 See Heath (2013).

45 See Bjorklund (2012).

46 See Zurita (2013).

47 See Schlafly (2012a).

48 Author interview with Tami Nantz, National Harbor, MD, March 14, 2013.

49 Author interview with Stacy Mott (by phone), February 23, 2013.

50 Data are not reported graphically.

51 Those respondents who strongly or mostly oppose raising taxes on those earning more than $250,000 annually are collapsed into one category (coded = 1) while those who are strongly or mostly in favor of raising taxes are coded into the other category (coded = 0).

52 See Meckler and Martin (2012).

53 Author interview with Whitney Neal, July 11, 2013.

54 Author interview with Kristen Soltis Anderson, Washington DC, June 23, 2013.

55 See Lukas and Schaeffer (2012): 67.

56 Ibid.

57 See Schlafly (2012b).

58 See Jenkins and Black (2014).

59 The Child Tax Credit Improvement Act was opposed by Democrats, who argued that the new measure failed to extend part of the child credit that was passed in 2009 to help impoverished parents who earn as low as $3,000 annually to claim some of the break on their taxes. As proposed by House Republicans, individuals earning less than $15,000 annually would not qualify for the credit. Many Democrats also argued that many military families would no longer qualify for the tax credit as written. Although the bill passed in the House in 2014, , largely along party lines, it was never introduced in the Senate (McAuliff 2014).

60 See House Republicans (2014a).

61 Those who strongly oppose or oppose raising the minimum wage are coded 1; those who strongly favor or favor raising the minimum wage are coded 0.

62 See Jones, Cox, and Navarro-Rivera (2014).

63 See Frey (2013).

64 See Vale (2014a).

65 See Borowski (2013).

66 See Lukas (2014a).

67 Ibid.

68 See IRS (2014).

69 See Currie (2014).

70 See National Organization for Women (2014).

71 See Blades and Rowe-Finkbeiner (2006).

72 From the MomsRising website, http://www.momsrising.org/issues_and_resources
   /maternity.
73 See http://www.momsrising.org/issues_and_resources/paid-sick-days-all.
74 See Gillibrand (2014).
75 See Schaffer (2014): 78.
76 Ibid.: 80.
77 See Roby (2013a).
78 See Davis (2013).
79 See Zornick (2013).
80 See Greenhouse (2007) for a summary of the decision.
81 See National Women's Law Center (2013).
82 See Mikulski (2014).
83 See White House (2014).
84 Quoted in Lieve (2014).
85 Quoted in Woodward (2012).
86 See Schaeffer (2014).
87 Quoted in Bassett (2014).
88 See Vale (2014b).
89 See Greszler (2014).
90 Ibid.
91 Quoted in Bendery (2012).
92 Quoted in Everett (2014).
93 See Fischer (2014b).
94 Ibid.
95 See Fischer (2014a).
96 See Lukas and Schaeffer (2012).
97 See Sommers (2010).
98 Ibid.
99 See Kafer (2014).
100 See AAUW (2006): 3.
101 See McCarver (2011): 22.
102 See Schaeffer (2014).
103 See Greszler (2014).
104 Author interview with Kristen Soltis Anderson, Washington DC, June 23, 2013.
105 See Schaeffer (2014).
106 See Republican National Committee (2014).
107 See Vale (2014a).
108 Ibid.
109 Author interview with Amy Jo Clark (by phone), June 21, 2013.
110 Author interview with Robert Boland, Washington DC, June 23, 2014.
111 Ibid.
112 Author interview with Carrie Lukas (by phone), June 18, 2013.

113 Author interview with Kristen Soltis Anderson, Washington DC, May 20, 2013.

114 Ibid.

115 Author interview with Keli Carender (by phone), April 1, 2013.

116 Author interview with Kristen Soltis Anderson, Washington DC, May 20, 2013.

CHAPTER 5. FREEDOM FEMINISM

1 See Deckman and McTague (2015).

2 See Krieg and Good (2012).

3 Quoted in Agiesta and Benac (2012).

4 See Walter and Scicchitano (2012).

5 See Kremer (2012).

6 Quoted in Marcus (2012).

7 Here's Hilary Rosen's full quote: "What you have is Mitt Romney running around the country, saying, 'Well, you know, my wife tells me that what women really care about are economic issues, and when I listen to my wife, that's what I'm hearing.' Guess what? His wife has actually never worked a day in her life. She's never really dealt with the kinds of economic issues that a majority of the women in this country are facing, in terms of how do we feed our kids, how do we send them to school, and why do we worry about their future." Quoted in Marlantes (2012).

8 Ibid.

9 See https://twitter.com/MichelleObama/status/190469503161860096.

10 Quoted in Kucinich and Moore (2012).

11 See Alexander (2012).

12 Quoted in Kellman (2012).

13 See Swintch (2012) for a remembrance of that quote, and its aftermath, on its twentieth anniversary.

14 See Boonstra and Nash (2014).

15 For more on how Republican women in the U.S. Senate often play the role of designated party spokespersons on women's issues, see Swers (2013).

16 See Easley (2012).

17 See Cott (1987).

18 See Friedman (2002): 4.

19 See Cott (1987): 3.

20 See Nielson (2001).

21 See http://www.nwlc.org/our-issues/employment/equal-pay-and-the-wage-gap.

22 See http://action.now.org/p/dia/action/public/?action_KEY=8961.

23 Quoted in Powers (2011).

24 See Nance (2011).

25 See Palin (2010): 129.

26 For an excellent analysis of how Palin draws on American frontier mythology to legitimate conservative feminism, and what this implies for modern feminism more generally, see Gibson and Heyse (2014).

27 See Palin (2010): 139.

28 Quoted in Kantor, Zernike, and Einhorn (2008).

29 See Palin (2010): 131.

30 Ibid.: 142.

31 Ibid.: 153. For a spirited disagreement with Palin's pro-life advocacy as being consistent with feminism, see Traistor (2010); McCarver (2011); Gibson and Heyse (2014).

32 See Dannenfelser (2010).

33 See Sommers (1995): 22.

34 Ibid.: 23.

35 See Klatch (1988): 689.

36 See Schreiber (2008).

37 Ibid.: 40.

38 Ibid.: 50.

39 Ibid.: 54.

40 Author interview with activist, Baltimore, November 19, 2012.

41 Author interview with activist, Annapolis, MD, November 8, 2012.

42 Author interview with Stacy Mott (by phone), February 27, 2013.

43 Author interview with activist (by phone), July 11, 2013.

44 Author interview with activist, Westminster, MD, February 4, 2013.

45 Author interview with activist, Chevy Chase, MD, February 27, 2013.

46 Author interview with Janice Shaw Crouse, Laurel, MD, July 26, 2013.

47 Ibid.

48 Author interview with Lori Parker (by phone), July 12, 2013.

49 Author interview with Gabriella Hoffman, Arlington, VA, June 24, 2013.

50 Author interview with Colleen Holcomb, Washington DC, April 30, 2013.

51 Author interview with activist, Annapolis, MD, January 14, 2013; emphasis added.

52 Author interview with activist, Westminster, MD, April 2, 2013.

53 Author interview with Kristen Soltis Anderson, Washington DC, May 20, 2013.

54 Conservative Republicans in the 112th session of Congress tried unsuccessfully to defund Planned Parenthood as part of its broader effort to curb government spending, but also because the organization is a leading provider of abortion services nationally. Liberal feminist organizations pointed out that federal law under the Hyde Amendment already prohibits the use of federal funds to provide abortion services and that the vast majority of work that Planned Parenthood does is to provide cancer screening, pregnancy prevention, and prenatal care to women who lack access to such services. Yet the federal ban on providing abortion funding did not prevent many conservative organizations from seeking to defund Planned Parenthood on the basis that any government grants given to the organization essentially allowed it to "free up" other funds to be spent on abortion services.

55 Author interview with Gabriella Hoffman, Arlington, VA, June 24, 2013.

56 See Deckman and McTague (2015).

57 In 2012 Sandra Fluke was a third-year law student at Georgetown University, a Jesuit institution that opposed the birth control mandate. At the request of the

minority Democrats in Congress, Fluke sought to testify before a House committee charged with oversight of the Obama administration's new rules concerning
the contraception mandate and religious exemptions. Fluke, a women's rights
advocate, supported the Obama administration's birth control mandate, and when
she was denied the right to speak to the House committee by the Republican chair
of the committee, Democrats invited her to speak to its steering committee. Her
testimony was maligned by conservative pundits, including most infamously by
Rush Limbaugh, who labeled Fluke a "slut" and a "prostitute" for her advocacy.
Limbaugh, whose remarks were strongly denounced by President Obama and
House Speaker John Boehner, apologized, but his denouncement of Fluke generated larger publicity both for the birth control issue and for Fluke herself, who
became a frequent Obama campaign speaker and who addressed the Democratic
National Convention in August 2012.

58 Author interview with Tami Nantz, National Harbor, MD, March 15, 2013.
59 Author interview with Amy Jo Clark (by phone), June 21, 2013.
60 See Loesch (2012).
61 Author interview with Jennifer Jacobs, Annapolis, MD, November 8, 2012.
62 Author interview with Keli Carender (by phone), April 1, 2013.
63 See Loesch (2012).
64 Quoted in Hays (2015a).
65 See Lukas and Schaefer (2012): 15–16.
66 See Venker and Schlafly (2011): 131.
67 Author interview with Angie Crawford, Grasonville, MD, November 12, 2012.
68 Author interview with Linda Myers, Baltimore, February 20, 2013.
69 Author interview with Carrie Lukas (by phone), June 18, 2013.
70 Author interview with Jennifer Jacobs, Annapolis, MD, November 8, 2012.
71 Author interview with Renee Wilson, Columbia, MD, December 17, 2012.
72 Author interview with Jenny Beth Martin (by phone), April 18, 2013.
73 Author interview with Amy Jo Clark (by phone), June 21, 2013
74 Author interview with activist (by phone), July 11, 2013.
75 Author interview with Whitney Neal, Washington DC, July 11, 2013.
76 Author interview with Keli Carender (by phone), April 1, 2013.
77 Cook (1989) developed a measure for feminist consciousness that combined support for the women's liberation movement and those who expressed more egalitarian views about whether women are better suited at home or at work, industry,
and government along with men.
78 See Wilcox and Cook (1989): 35.
79 The question from the 1996 General Social Survey asked respondents, "Do you think
of yourself as a feminist or not?" See Schnittker, Freese, and Powell (2003): 611.
80 See Swanson (2013).
81 Ibid.
82 The 2011 survey also asked the same question with the same options. Results were
nearly identical to the 2012 survey so I opted to use the more recent data.

83 For more on complementarianism, see Grudem (2012).

84 In recent years, however, there has been renewed debate among many evangelicals as to how patriarchal the Bible really is. For example, sociologist W. Bradford
Wilcox (2004) argues that many evangelical men are "soft patriarchs," in the sense
that they may endorse scripture that dictates men are heads of households in
fact, but in practice are far more egalitarian when it comes to their daily lives and
parenthood practices. According to *Washington Post* religion reporter Michelle
Boorstein (2014), this debate is being driven by many younger evangelicals, who
are more likely to view men and women as equal in the workplace, church, and
home.

85 See NPR News (2015) for a transcript of the State of the Union Address.

86 See Ponnuru (2015).

87 See Lukas (2015).

88 Ibid.

89 See Venker and Schlafly (2011): 174.

90 The prepper movement grew in earnest right before the year 2000, as many
individuals feared that a massive computer crash, known as Y2K, could mean
a stop to modern life and a drastic shortage of goods. As a result, many "preppers" or survivalists began to prepare for national emergencies—either natural
or man-made—that could result in shortages and electrical outages, calling on
Americans to buy generators, store fuel, and have extra food on hand. The movement has grown tremendously since. Some critics, however, believe preppers are
irrational, beholden to doomsday fantasies made popular by television shows
such as *Doomsday Preppers* on National Geographic Channel.

91 Quoted in Independent Women's Forum (2013).

92 Ibid.

93 See Swers (2013): 245.

94 See Rosin (2014).

95 See RNC Women (2014).

96 Quoted in Wong (2014).

97 See Political Parity (2015).

98 Quoted in Independent Women's Forum (2013).

CHAPTER 6. GUNS ARE THE GREAT EQUALIZER

1 See http://momsdemandaction.org/about/. The organization started with the
initial name of One Million Moms for Gun Control. See Belkin (2013).

2 See Paulson (2000). The organization later merged with several other organizations to form the Brady Campaign to Prevent Gun Violence.

3 See Palin (2014).

4 See Groeger et al. (2013).

5 My qualitative analysis is not meant to be exhaustive or systematic, particularly
given the sheer number of self-published blogs that have emerged online in recent
years, but instead is suggestive. However, I do limit my analysis to writings that

date from 2009 onward, with the start of Obama's presidency and the Tea Party movement.

6 See appendix A for more information about the survey.

7 See Tavernese and Gebeloff (2013) and Cook and Goss (2014).

8 See Cook and Goss (2014).

9 See Goode (2013).

10 See Tavernese and Gebeloff (2013).

11 See Homsher (2001) and Kelly (2004).

12 The NRA Women's Shopping portal includes the following specialized online stores marketed exclusively to women: Armed in Heels, Armed in Stilettos, Girls with Guns, Gun Goddess, Her Camo Shop, Packing in Pink, Pistols and Pumps, She Safari Outdoor Apparel, and Shoot Like a Girl.

13 See Neale (2013). Founded in 2008, Shoot Like a Girl encourages women to participate in shooting sports, as such activities are well suited to "people of all physical fitness levels," help reduce stress, and, in the case of hunting, provide "true organic food for their families" (http://www.shootlikeagirl.com/about .html). A Girl and a Gun was founded by Juliana Crowder in 2011; according to its website, the organization's mission is "to educate and encourage women about firearm usage, safety, and promote women's shooting interest and participation in the competitive shooting sports" (http://www.agirlandagun.org/about-us/).

14 See https://twawshootingchapters.org/.

15 See Cassidy (2014).

16 See Haughney (2012).

17 One Gallup poll showed that in 2011, 23 percent of women claimed to own a firearm, compared with 46 percent of men. See Saad (2011). While this poll is often cited by gun rights advocates, it appears to be an outlier compared with more recent polling, including by Gallup itself, which reported in 2013 that 15 percent of women claimed to own guns (compared with 45 percent of men). See Jones (2013). This latter poll was a compilation of Gallup polls from 2007 to 2012 with more than six thousand respondents, resulting in a margin of error of about +/−one percentage point.

18 See Goode (2013).

19 Ibid.

20 See Smith (2014).

21 See Terry (2013).

22 Of course, women who are passionate advocates for greater gun control also employ gendered appeals to defend their stands, including adopting mother-hood monikers as their organization's names. Take for instance, the Million Mom March chapters, affiliated with the Brady Campaign to Prevent Gun Violence, that promote "commonsense" gun control regulations to stop gun violence, or the more recent One Million Moms for Gun Control, started after the Newtown school shootings. An analysis of the gendered rhetoric employed by pro-gun control activists, however, is beyond the scope of this study.

23 See, for example, Homsher (2001) and Hupp (2001).

24 See Dolan (2005). Most women legislators, however, are in favor of stricter gun control, particularly in state legislatures. See Stucky, Miller, and Murphy (2008).

25 Author interview with Gabriella Hoffman, Arlington, VA, June 24, 2013.

26 See Roby (2013b).

27 See http://lummis.house.gov/issues/issue/?IssueID=9884.

28 Of course, women were not the first to describe guns as equalizers. The "great equalizer" is a nickname that was often used to describe the Colt .45 revolver, developed by Colonial Samuel Colt in the late 1800s. See http://www.pages.drexel.edu/~jj832/The_Great_Equalizer.html.

29 Author interview with Carrie Lukas (by phone), June 18, 2013.

30 See Trotter (2013).

31 See Gast (2012).

32 Whether such laws actually drive down rates of violent crime is a highly divisive topic. The work of economist John Lott Jr., author of *More Guns, Less Crime* (2010), is often cited by pro-gun supporters, as his analyses show that violent crime is reduced in states that end restrictive gun-carrying laws. However, according to Cook and Goss (2014), a panel of national experts at the National Academy of Sciences failed to replicate Lott's earlier studies, and most scholars believe Lott's empirical work is suspect.

33 See Trotter (2013).

34 See Kafer (2013).

35 See Rittgers (2013).

36 See Williams (2011).

37 See Mott (2013).

38 See Kozub (2011).

39 See Grim (2013c).

40 Grim (2013b) also advises women in another blog posting about which purses are best for carrying concealed weapons: "I just look for a bag that has a separate zippered-pocket that is easily accessible from the outside."

41 Ibid.

42 Quoted in Weingarten (2014).

43 See Loesch (2013b).

44 Ibid.

45 See Johnson (2014).

46 See Dahlberg, Ikeda, and Kresnow (2004) and Kellermann et al. (1998).

47 See, for example, Bigelow and Blankenship (2013).

48 Quoted in Bendery (2013).

49 See Bigelow and Blankenship (2013).

50 See Trotter (2013).

51 See Rittgers (2013).

52 See Grim (2013a).

53 Quoted in Mott (2013).

54 Quoted in Ferner (2013).

55 Quoted in Richardson (2013).

56 See Loesch (2013a). Even some liberal women took issue with Salazar's comments, including Katie J. M. Baker (2013) of the feminist blog *Jezebel*, who wrote of Salazar, "Democrats say dumb things about rape, too."

57 Quoted in Pavlich (2013).

58 See Collins (2015).

59 See Grim (2013a).

60 See Terry (2013).

61 See Loesch (2013c).

62 While Loesch regularly cites statistics used by progressive women's organizations and the Obama administration concerning women's rates of sexual assault on college campus to support her goal of allowing women to carry concealed weapons, other conservative women activists and organizations have called into question these statistics, including the IWF. In fact, the IWF sponsored a panel in June 2014 in Washington DC called "Straight Talk: An Honest Conversation about 'Rape Culture' and Sexual Violence," in which American Enterprise Institute scholar Christina Hoff Sommers and others questioned the validity of the statistic that one in five women on college campuses are sexually assaulted (Berenson 2014). This panel was convened in wake of U.S. Senate hearings considering proposals to combat sexual violence on campus, an issue that the Obama administration has been addressing as part of its Title IX enforcement. Sommers has long held that the one-in-five number is inflated, creating a rape culture on college campuses "where paranoia, censorship, and false accusations flourish." See Berenson (2014).

63 See Loesch (2013c).

64 On the gender difference in attitudes about gun control see Wolpert and Gimpel (1998); Pew Research Center (2012); Cook and Goss (2014); Deckman (2014).

65 See Pew Research Center (2012).

66 Ibid.

67 The survey sample size was 1,006.

68 See appendix A for exact question wording and for details about the survey methodology.

69 These differences are statistically significant according to a chi-square test (p < .000).

70 Gender differences in rates of gun ownership are statistically significant, which corresponds to earlier studies. See, for example, Jones (2013).

71 Although I don't report the data here, my earlier research on gender and gun attitudes finds that women nationally hold more liberal positions than do men on all the measures analyzed here according to the 2012 PRRI/RNS data, which is consistent with previous studies about the impact of sex on gun attitudes. See Deckman (2014).

72 In all three cases, these differences are statistically significant: favoring stronger gun control laws (chi-square = 40.251; p < .000); favoring a loosening of current

laws (chi-square = 47.636; p < .000); and believing that laws should be handled by the individual states as opposed to the federal government (chi-square = 30.773; p < .000).

73 See O'Keefe and Clement (2013). Unfortunately, the PRRI/RNS survey I use does not ask attitudes about banning assault weapons or other measures proposed by Obama in early 2013 after the Newtown shooting, given that the survey was conducted in August 2012.

74 The ad can be viewed online at https://www.youtube.com/watch?v=I3mG9f NOZp4.

75 Author interview with Jenny Beth Martin (by phone), April 16, 2013.

CHAPTER 7. CONCLUSION

1 See Wilcox and Larson (2010).

2 See Deckman, Cox, and Jones (2015).

3 See Brody (2012).

4 Author interview with activist, Westminster, MD, April 2, 2013.

5 Author interview with Stacy Mott (by phone), February 27, 2013.

6 See McCammon (2015).

7 See Ertelt (2013); emphasis added.

8 See Barton (1993) for an example of Christian Right writings that argue America was founded as a Christian nation.

9 See Hays (2015b).

10 See Rosin (2010).

11 See Ponnuru and Lucas (2014).

12 Author interview with Keli Carender (by phone), April 1, 2013.

13 See Kafer (2014).

14 See Schreiber (2008).

15 See Clinton (2015).

16 See Thomsen (2015).

17 See King and Matland (2003).

18 Data calculated by author from the Republican National Committee's website, which presents an interactive map with party leaders. See https://www.gop.com /leaders/states/. Women in 2015 make up seventeen of the Democratic state party chairs. Data calculated by author from links found on the Democratic Party's website. See http://asdc.democrats.org/state-parties/.

19 See Swers (2013).

20 Data analyzed by author. See Public Religion Research Institute (2014) for more details on survey methodology and other results.

21 Ibid.

22 See Zernike (2010).

23 See http://www.pollingreport.com/politics.htm for June 20–22, 2014.

24 See Cooper and Thee-Breenan (2011).

25 See Balz and Clement (2013).

26 See Brooks (2010).

27 See Disch (2012).

28 See Parker and Barreto (2013).

29 See ibid. and Abramowitz (2012).

30 See Mundy (2012).

31 See Gilens (2012).

32 See Campbell and Wolbrecht (2006).

REFERENCES

AAUW. 2007. "Behind the Pay Gap." *American Association of University Women Educational Foundation*. http://www.aauw.org/files/2013/02/Behind-the-Pay -Gap.pdf.

Abramowitz, Alan. 2012. "Grand Old Tea Party: Partisan Polarization and the Rise of the Tea Party Movement." In *Steep: The Precipitous Rise of the Tea Party*, edited by Lawrence Rosenthal and Christine Trout. Berkeley: University of California Press, 195–211.

Agiesta, Jennifer, and Nancy Benac. 2012. "AP Poll: Romney Erases Obama Advantage among Women." *Associated Press*. October 12. http://news.yahoo.com/ap-poll-romn ey-erases-obama-advantage-among-women-071129692—election.html.

Alexander, Rachel. 2012. "The Democrats' War on Women." *Townhall*. May 2. http://town hall.com/columnists/rachelalexander/2012/05/02/the_democrats_war_on_women /page/full.

Altman, Alex. 2010. "The 2010 Time 100: Jenny Beth Martin." *Time*. April 29. http://con tent.time.com/time/specials/packages/article/0,28804,1984685_1984864_1985462,00 .html.

Asbury, Glen. 2011. "Twitter Personality of the Week #26: 10 Questions for Teri Christoph." *Ramblings . . .* February 21. http://glenlasbury.wordpress.com/2011/02/21 /twitter-personality-of-the-week-26–10-questions-for-teri-christoph-terichristoph/.

Bachmann, Michele. 2014. "Bachmann: Celebrating Tea Party's 5th Birthday." *USA Today*. February 27. http://www.usatoday.com/story/opinion/2014/02/27/michele-b achmann-tea-party-anniversary-column/5863823/.

Baker, Katie J. M. 2013. "Colorado Rep. Thinks College Ladies Don't Know When They Are Going to Be Raped." *Jezebel*. February 19. http://jezebel.com/5985354 /colorado-rep-thinks-college-ladies-dont-know-when-theyre-going-to-be -raped.

Baker, Paula. 1984. "The Domestication of Politics: Women and American Political Society, 1780–1920." *American Historical Review* 89 (3): 620–647.

Ball, Billy. 2013. "U.S. History According to Charles Koch: The Conservative Billionaire Could Be Teaching Your Kids." *Indy Week*. February 27. http://www .indyweek.com/indyweek/us-history-according-to-charles-koch-the-con servative-billionaire-could-be-teaching-your-kids/Content?oid=3344870.

Balz, Dan, and Scott Clement. 2013. "Poll: Major Damage to GOP after Shutdown, and Broad Dissatisfaction with Government." *Washington Post*. October 22. http:// www.washingtonpost.com/politics/poll-major-damage-to-gop-after-shutdown-and

-broad-dissatisfaction-with-government/2013/10/21/dae5c062–3a84–11e3-b7ba
-503fb5822c3e_story.html.

Bamberger, Joanne. 2011. *Mothers of Intention: How Women and Social Media Are Revolutionizing Politics in America*. Houston: Bright Sky Press.

Barasko, Maryann. 2004. *Governing NOW: Grassroots Activism in the National Organization for Women*. Ithaca, NY: Cornell University Press.

Barton, David. 1993. *America's Godly Heritage*. Aledo, TX: WallBuilders.

Bassett, Laura. 2014. "Texas GOP Chief Tells Women to Become 'Better Negotiators' Instead of Suing over Pay." *Huffington Post*. March 18. http://www.huffingtonpost .com/2014/03/18/texas-gop-equal-pay_n_4985231.html.

Baumgartner, Jennifer, and Amy Richards. 2000. *Manifesta: Young Women, Feminism, and the Future*. New York: Farrar, Straus and Giroux.

Beck, Glenn. 2009. "Glenn Beck: The 9/12 Project." March 17. http://www.glennbeck .com/content/articles/article/198/22802/.

Belle, Liberty. 2009. "Conservatives Coming Out of the Closet—So to Speak." *Redistributing Knowledge*. January 25. http://redistributingknowledge.blogspo t.com/2009/01/conservatives-coming-out-of-closet-so.html.

Belkin, Lisa. 2013. "One Million Moms for Gun Control: Origins of a Movement." *Huffington Post*. January 25. http://www.huffingtonpost.com/2013/01/25/one-million -moms-for-gun-control_n_2549452.html.

Bendery, Jennifer. 2013. "Joe Biden Says No Need to Own Assault Weapons: 'Buy a Shotgun!'" *Huffington Post*. February 19. http://www.huffingtonpost.com/2013/02 /19/joe-biden-guns_n_2719330.html.

———. 2012. "Paycheck Fairness Acts Fails Senate Vote." *Huffington Post*. June 5. http:// www.huffingtonpost.com/2012/06/05/paycheck-fairness-act-senate-vote_n_1571413 .html.

Berenson, Tessa. 2014. "1 in 5: Debating the Most Controversial Sexual Assault Statistic." *Time*. June 27. http://time.com/2934500/1-in-5%E2%80%82campus-sexual-assault -statistic/.

Berman, Matt. 2013. "Mitt Romney: 47 Percent? What 47 Percent." *National Journal*. July 29. http://news.yahoo.com/mitt-romney-47-percent-47-percent-115821167 .html.

Bigelow, Celia, and Aubrey Blankenship. 2013. "Why Young Women Want AR-15s." *National Review*. January 23. http://www.nationalreview.com/articles/338418/why -young-women-want-ar-15s-celia-bigelow.

Bjorklund, Rachel. 2012. "Republican Senators Fail to Stop Obama Birth-Control Mandate." March 2. *Thoughts from a Conservative Mom*. http://www.thoughtsfroma conservativemom.com/2012/03/republican-senators-fail-to-stop-obama-birth -control-mandate/.

Blades, Joan, and Kristin Rowe-Finkbeiner. 2006. *The Motherhood Manifesto: What America's Moms Want and What to Do about It*. New York: Nation Books.

Blair, Karen. 1980. *The Clubwoman as Feminist: True Womanhood Redefined, 1868–1914*. New York: Holmes and Meier.

Blumer, Tom. 2009. "Rant for the Ages: CNBC's Rick Santelli Goes Off: Studio Hosts Invoke 'Mob Rule' to Downplay." *NewsBusters*. February 19. http://newsbusters.org/blogs/tom-blumer/2009/02/19/rant-ages-cnbcs-rick-santelli-goes-studio-hosts-invoke-mob-rule-downplay.

Boonstra, Heather D., and Elizabeth Nash. 2014. "A Surge of State Abortion Restrictions Puts Providers—and the Women They Serve—in the Crosshairs." *Guttmacher Policy Review* 17 (1). http://www.guttmacher.org/pubs/gpr/17/1/gpr170109.html.

Boorstein, Michelle. 2014. "U.S. Evangelicals Headed for Showdown over Gender Roles." *Washington Post*. September 3. http://www.washingtonpost.com/news/local/wp/2014/09/03/u-s-evangelicals-headed-for-showdown-over-gender-roles/.

Bordin, Ruth. 1981. *Woman and Temperance*. Philadelphia: Temple University Press.

Borelli, Deneen. 2012. *Blacklash: How Obama and the Left Are Driving Americans to the Government Plantation*. New York: Simon & Schuster.

Borowski, Julie. 2013. "Raising the Minimum Wage Is the Worse Idea Ever." *Smart Girl Politics Action*. December 18. http://www.sgpaction.com/raising_the_minimum_wage_is_the_worst_idea_ever (site discontinued).

Boykoff, Jules, and Eulalie Laschever. 2011. "The Tea Party Movement, Framing, and the U.S. Media." *Social Movement Studies: Journal of Social, Cultural, and Political Protest* 10 (4): 341–366.

Brafman, Ori, and Rod A. Beckstrom. 2006. *The Starfish and the Spider: The Unstoppable Power of Leaderless Organizations*. New York: Penguin.

Brennan, Mary C. 2008. *Wives, Mothers, and the Red Menace: Conservative Women and the Crusade against Communism*. Boulder: University Press of Colorado.

Brody, David. 2012. *The Teavangelicals: The Inside Story of How the Evangelicals and the Tea Party Are Taking Back America*. Grand Rapids, Mich.: Zondervan Press.

Brooks, Deborah Jordan. 2010. "A Negativity Gap? Voter Gender, Attack Politics, and Participation in American Elections." *Politics and Gender* 6 (3): 319–341.

Burghart, Devin. 2014. "Special Report: The Status of the Tea Party Movement: Part Two." Institute for Research and Education on Human Rights. http://www.irehr.org/2014/01/21/status-of-tea-party-by-the-numbers/.

———. 2012. "View from the Top: Report on Six National Tea Party Organizations." In *Steep: The Precipitous Rise of the Tea Party*, edited by Lawrence Rosenthal and Christine Trout. Berkeley: University of California Press, 67–97.

Burkett, Elinor. 1998. *The Right Women: A Journey through the Heart of Conservative America*. New York: Scribner.

Burn, Shawn Meghan, Roger Aboud, and Carey Moyles. 2000. "The Relationship between Gender Social Identity and Support for Feminism." *Sex Roles* 42 (11–12): 1081–1089.

Burns, Alexander. 2015. "Choice Words from Donald Trump, Presidential Candidate." *New York Times*. June 16. http://www.nytimes.com/politics/first-draft/2015/06/16/choice-words-from-donald-trump-presidential-candidate/.

Burns, Nancy, Kay Lehman Schlozman, and Sidney Verba. 2001. *The Private Roots of Political Action: Gender, Equality, and Political Participation*. Cambridge, MA: Harvard University Press.

Campbell, David E., and Christina Wolbrecht. 2006. "See Jane Run: Women Politicians as Role Models for Adolescents." *Journal of Politics* 68 (2): 233–247.

Carey, John M., Richard G. Niemi, and Lynda W. Powell. 1998. "Are Women State Legislators Different?" In *Women and Elective Office: Past, Present, and Future*, edited by Sue Thomas and Clyde Wilcox. New York: Oxford University Press, 87–102.

Carroll, Susan J. 2006. "Voting Choices: Meet You at the Gender Gap." In *Gender and Elections: Shaping the Future of American Politics*, edited by Susan J. Carroll and Richard L. Fox. Cambridge, U.K.: Cambridge University Press, 74–96.

Carroll, Susan J., and Kira Sanbonmatsu. 2013. *More Women Can Run: Gender and Pathways to the State Legislature*. New York: Oxford University Press.

Cassidy, W. J. 2014. "Her Right to Bear Arms: The Rise of Women's Gun Culture." *Rolling Stone*. July 14. http://www.rollingstone.com/politics/news/her-right-to-bear-arms-the-rise-of-womens-gun-culture-20140714.

CAWP. 2014. "2014 Not a Landmark Year for Women, despite Some Notable Firsts." *Center for Women and Politics*. November 5. http://cawp.rutgers.edu/2014-not-landmark-year-women-despite-some-notable-firsts.

Center for American Progress. 2014. "Why Women's Economic Security Matters for Us All." September 18. https://www.americanprogress.org/events/2014/09/10/96851/why-womens-economic-security-matters-for-all-2/.

Chaney, Carole Kennedy, R. Michael Alvarez, and Jonathan Nagler. 1998. "Explaining the Gender Gap in U.S. Presidential Elections, 1980–1992." *Political Research Quarterly* 51 (2): 311–339.

Chicks on the Right. 2015. "The Donald Trump–Univision Fight Is Getting Vicious." June 27. http://chicksontheright.com/blog/item/29596-the-donald-trump-univision-fight-is-getting-vicious.

Christensen, Carrie. 2012. "Founding Mothers: The Founders' Wives of New York." *MinuteMom Magazine* 1 (6): 36–37. http://issuu.com/minutemom/docs/feb12.

Clement, Scott. 2012. "Tea Party Opposed by Half of Americans." *Washington Post*. January 17. http://www.washingtonpost.com/blogs/behind-the-numbers/post/tea-party-opposed-by-half-of-americans/2012/01/03/gIQAsUVm5P_blog.html.

Clinton, Hillary. 2015. "Hillary Clinton: An Unequivocal Champion for Equal Pay." May. https://www.hillaryclinton.com/p/briefing/factsheets/2015/05/26/fact-sheet-equal-pay/.

Cogan, Marin. 2013. "Rise of the Female Gun Nut." *New York*. February 2. http://nymag.com/thecut/2013/02/rise-of-the-female-gun-nut.html.

Cohen, Jon, and Jennifer Agiesta. 2008. "Partisanship Appears to Sway Opinions on Palin." *Washington Post*. September 6. http://www.washingtonpost.com/wp-dyn/content/article/2008/09/05/AR2008090503932.html.

Coley, Victoria. 2013. "Statement: President Obama Seeks to Limit Women's Capability to Fight Back against Attackers: Why Women Should Fight Attempts to Ban High-Capacity Magazines." *Independent Women's Forum*. January 9. http://www.iwf.org/media/2790265/Statement:-President-Obama-Seeks-to-Limit-Women's-Capability-to-Fight-Back-Against-Attackers.

Collins, Amanda. 2015. "The Real War on Women." *NRA's America's First Freedom Blog*. June 30. http://www.americasistfreedom.org/articles/2015/7/1/the-real-war-on-women/.

Cook, Elizabeth Adell. 1989. "Measuring Feminist Consciousness." *Women and Politics* 9 (3): 71–88.

Cook, Elizabeth Adell, and Clyde Wilcox. 1991. "Feminism and the Gender Gap: A Second Look." *Journal of Politics* 53: 1111–1122.

Cook, Philip J., and Kristin A. Goss. 2014. *The Gun Debate: What Everyone Needs to Know*. New York: Oxford University Press.

Cooper, Michael, and Megan Thee-Brenan. 2011. "Disapproval Rate for Congress at Record 82% after Debt Talks." *New York Times*. August 4. http://www.nytimes.com/2011/08/05/us/politics/05poll.html?_r=0.

Costain, Anne N. 1992. *Inviting Women's Rebellion: A Political Process Interpretation of the Women's Movement*. Baltimore: Johns Hopkins University Press.

Cott, Nancy F. 1987. *The Grounding of Modern Feminism*. New Haven, CT: Yale University Press.

———. 1975. *The Bonds of Womanhood: Woman's Sphere in New England, 1790–1835*. New Haven, CT: Yale University Press.

Cowell-Meyers, Kimberly, and Laura Langbein. 2009. "Linking Women's Descriptive and Substantive Representation in the United States." *Politics and Gender* 5: 491–518.

Critchlow, Donald T. 2005. *Phyllis Schlafly and Grassroots Conservatism: A Woman's Crusade*. Princeton, NJ: Princeton University Press.

Croson, Rachel, and Uri Gneezy. 2009. "Gender Differences in Preferences." *Journal of Economic Literature* 47 (2): 448–474.

Crouse, Janice Shaw. 2010. "Obamanomics: Summary of the Analysis and Commentary Related to the Financial Impact of ObamaCare on Women and Families." Concerned Women for America. http://www.cwfa.org/images/content/Obamanomics.pdf.

Currie, Rachel DiCarlo. 2014. "Policy Focus: Why Earned Income Tax Credits Beats Minimum Wage." *Independent Women's Forum*. April 17. http://www.iwf.org/publications/2793719/Policy-Focus:-Why-Earned-Income-Tax-Credit-Beats-Minimum-Wage.

Dahlberg, Linda L., Robin M. Ikeda, and Marcie-Jo Kresnow. 2004. "Guns in the Home and Risk of a Violent Death in the Home: Findings from a National Study." *American Journal of Epidemiology* 160 (10): 929–936.

Dannenfelser, Marjorie. 2010. "2010 Elections and Pro-Life Women: A Correction for Modern Feminism." *Political Daily*. January 1. http://www.politicsdaily.com/2011/01/01/2010-elections-and-pro-life-women-a-correction-for-modern-femin/.

Davis, Susan. 2013. "GOP Presses Its Agenda on 'Mommy Blog' Sites." *USA Today*. April 30. http://www.usatoday.com/story/news/politics/2013/04/30/house-gop-mommy-blog-strategy/2121777/?AID=10709313&PID=4003003&SID=tbtmd9en3xru.

Deckman, Melissa. 2014. "Annie Get Your Gun? Women, Guns, and the Tea Party." Paper prepared for presentation at the 2014 Annual Meeting of the American Political Science Association, Washington DC, August 28–31.

———. 2013a. "A Gender Gap in the Tea Party? A Gendered Analysis of Tea Party Voters in the 2012 Presidential Elections." Paper presented at the Midwest Political Science Association's Annual Meeting, Chicago. April 11–14.

———. 2013b. "Melissa Deckman on the Limits of Libertarianism among Women." *Public Religion Research Institute.* November 22. http://publicreligion.org/2013/11 /melissa-deckman-on-the-limits-of-libertarianism-for-women/.

———. 2013c. "A New Civic Motherhood? Placing Tea Party 'Mothers' in Historical Political Context." Paper presented at the Northeastern Political Science Association's Annual Meeting, Philadelphia. November 15–17.

———. 2012a. "The GOP's Marriage Problem." *Public Religion Research Institute.* http:// publicreligion.org/2012/11/the-gops-marriage-problem/.

———. 2012b. "Mama Grizzlies and the Tea Party." In *Steep: The Precipitous Rise of the Tea Party,* edited by Christine Trout and Larry Rosenthal. Berkeley: University of California Press, 171–192.

Deckman, Melissa, Dan Cox, and Robert Jones. 2015. "Faith and the Free Market: Evangelicals' Attitudes about Economic Policies." Working Paper.

Deckman, Melissa, and John McTague. 2015. "Did the 'War on Women' Work? Women, Men, and the Birth Control Mandate in the 2012 Presidential Election." *American Politics Research* 43 (1): 3–26.

DeSilver, Drew. 2014. "The Polarized Congress of Today Has Its Roots in the 1970s." *Pew Research Center.* June 12. http://www.pewresearch.org/fact-tank/2014/06/12 /polarized-politics-in-congress-began-in-the-1970s-and-has-been-getting-worse -ever-since/.

———. 2013. "U.S. Income Inequality, on the Rise for Decades, Is Now Highest since 1928." *Pew Research Center.* December 5. http://www.pewresearch.org/fact-tank /2013/12/05/u-s-income-inequality-on-rise-for-decades-is-now-highest-since -1928/.

Diamond, Sara. 1995. *Roads to Dominion: Right-Wing Movements and Political Power in the United States.* New York: Guilford Press.

Disch, Lisa. 2012. "The Tea Party: 'A White Citizenship' Movement?" In *Steep: The Precipitous Rise of the Tea Party,* edited by Christine Trout and Larry Rosenthal. Berkeley: University of California Press, 133–151.

Dolan, Julie. 2005. "The Passage of Conceal and Carry Firearm Legislation in the Minnesota State Legislature: Political Women in Action." Paper prepared for presentation at the 2005 Annual Meeting of the Midwest Political Science Association, Chicago. April 7–10.

Dolan, Julie, Melissa Deckman, and Michele L. Swers. 2011. *Women and Politics: Paths to Power and Political Influence.* 2nd ed. New York: Longman.

DuBois, Ellen C., ed. 1998. *Woman Suffrage and Women's Rights.* New York: New York University Press.

Duggan, Maeve. 2013. "It's a Woman's (Social Media) World." *Pew Research Center.* September 12. http://www.pewresearch.org/fact-tank/2013/09/12/its-a-womans -social-media-world/.

Easley, Jonathan. 2012. "Gallup: 2012 Election Had the Largest Gender Gap in History." *The Hill.* November 9. http://thehill.com/blogs/blog-briefing-room/news/267101-gallup -2012-election-had-the-largest-gender-gap-in-history.

Ekins, Emily. 2011. "The Character and Morality of the Tea Party Movement." Working Paper.

Elder, Laurel. 2012. "The Partisan Gain among Women State Legislators." *Journal of Women, Politics, and Policy* 33 (1): 65–85.

Elder, Laurel, and Steven Greene. 2012. *The Politics of Parenthood.* Albany: State University of New York Press.

———. 2008. "Parenthood and the Gender Gap." In *Voting the Gender Gap,* edited by Lois Duke Whitaker. Champaign: University of Illinois Press, 119–140.

Elshtain, Jean Bethke. 1981. *Public Man, Private Woman: Women in Social and Political Thought.* Princeton, NJ: Princeton University Press.

Epstein, Barbara Leslie. 1981. *The Politics of Domesticity: Women, Evangelism, and Temperance in Nineteenth-Century America.* Middletown, CT: Wesleyan University Press.

Ertelt, Steven. 2013. "Bill to De-fund Planned Parenthood Re-introduced in Congress." *Life News.* January 4. http://www.lifenews.com/2013/01/04/bill-to-de-fund-planned -parenthood-re-introduced-in-congress/.

Everett, Burgess. 2014. "Senate GOP Blocks Pay Equity Bill." *Politico.* April 4. http:// www.politico.com/story/2014/04/senate-blocks-paycheck-fairness-act-105529.html.

Faludi, Susan. 1991. *Backlash: The Undeclared War on American Women.* New York: Doubleday.

Favreau, Jon. 2013. "College Republicans National Committee Report Has Grim Findings for the GOP." *Daily Beast.* June 5. http://www.thedailybeast.com/articles /2013/06/05/college-republican-national-committee-report-has-grim-findings-for -gop.html.

Ferner, Matt. 2013. "Joe Salazar Apologizes for Controversial 'Rape' Comment." *Huffington Post.* February 19. http://www.huffingtonpost.com/2013/02/19/rep-joe -salazar-apologize_n_2716653.html.

Ferree, Myra Marx, and Beth B. Hess. 1994. *Controversy and Coalition.* New York: Palgrave Macmillan.

Firestone, David. 2013. "Contraception Compromise." *New York Times.* February 1. http://takingnote.blogs.nytimes.com/2013/02/01/contraception-compromise/?_r=0.

Firestone, Shulamith. 1970. *The Dialectic of Sex: The Case for Feminist Revolution.* New York: Morrow.

Fischer, Deb. 2014a. "Press Release: Fischer, Collins, Ayotte, Murkowski Offer Amendment to Help Address Gender Pay Discrimination." April 8. http://www.fischer .senate.gov/public/index.cfm/news?ID=d6befbc8–5b71–4f9b-b054-f41665f04414.

———. 2014b. "What Women Want." *Politico.* April 9. http://www.politico.com/magazine /story/2014/04/what-women-want-105520.html#ixzz2yOaKhHzP.

Fletcher, Holly Berkley. 2008. *Gender and the American Temperance Movement of the Nineteenth Century*. New York: Routledge.

Frederick, Brian. 2010. "Gender and Roll Call Voting in the U.S. Senate." *Congress and the Presidency* 37 (2): 103–124.

———. 2009. "Are Female House Members Still More Liberal in a Polarized Era? The Conditional Era of the Relationship between Descriptive and Substantive Representation." *Congress and the Presidency* 36 (2): 181–202.

FreedomWorks. 2004. "Citizens for a Sound Economy (CSE) and Empower America Merge to Form FreedomWorks." July 25. http://web.archive.org/web/20040725031033/http://www.freedomworks.org/release.php.

Freeman, Jo. 2000. *A Room at a Time: How Women Entered Party Politics*. Lanham, MD: Rowman & Littlefield.

Frey, Brandi. 2013. "Minimum Wage Fairy Tales, Health Care Lies, and Arrogant Progressive Feel Good Politics." *Smart Girl Politics Action*. December 14. http://www.sgpaction.com/minimum_wage_fairytales_healthcare_lies_and_arrogant_progressive_feel_good_politics (site discontinued).

Friedman, Estelle B. 2002. *No Turning Back: The History of Feminism and the Future of Women*. New York: Ballantine.

Gallup. 2010. "Education Trumps Gender in Predicting Support for Abortion." April 28. http://www.gallup.com/poll/127559/education-trumps-gender-predicting-support-abortion.aspx.

Gardner, Amy. 2010. "Gauging the Scope of the Tea Party Movement in America." *Washington Post*. October 24. http://www.washingtonpost.com/wp-dyn/content/article/2010/10/23/AR2010102304000_pf.html.

Gast, Phil. 2012. "Oklahoma Mom Calls 911 Asks If Shooting an Intruder Is Allowed." *CNN*. January 4. http://www.cnn.com/2012/01/04/justice/oklahoma-intruder-shooting/.

Gault, Barbara A., and John Sabini. 2000. "The Roles of Empathy, Anger, and Gender in Predicting Attitudes toward Punitive, Reparative, and Preventative Public Policies." *Cognition and Emotion* 14: 495–520.

Gentilviso, Chris. 2014. "GOP Senate Candidate Picks Sarah Palin to Narrate Her First TV Ad." *Huffington Post*. April 11. http://www.huffingtonpost.com/2014/04/11/karen-handel-sarah-palin_n_5132762.html.

Gibson, Katie L., and Amy L. Heyse. 2014. "Depoliticizing Feminism: Frontier Mythology and Sarah Palin's 'The Rise of the Mama Grizzlies.'" *Western Journal of Communication* 78 (1): 97–117.

Gilens, Martin. 2012. *Affluence and Influence: Economic Inequality and Political Power in America*. Princeton, NJ: Princeton University Press.

Gilgoff, Dan. 2009. "Exclusive: Ralph Reed Launches New Values Group: 'Not Your Daddy's Christian Coalition.'" *U.S. News & World Report*. June 23. http://www.usnews.com/news/blogs/god-and-country/2009/06/23/exclusive-ralph-reed-launches-new-values-group-not-your-daddys-christian-coalition.

Gillibrand, Kirsten. 2014. "It's Time for Paid Family and Medical Leave to Empower Working Women and Modernize the Workplace." *Huffington Post.* February 5. http://www.huffingtonpost.com/rep-kirsten-gillibrand/its-time-for-paid-family -and-medical-leave_b_4732451.html.

Glenn, Brian. 2011. "What Is a 'Constitutional Conservative' Anyway?" *Salon.* July 4. http://www.salon.com/2011/07/04/brian_glenn_conservative/.

Goode, Erica. 2013. "Rising Voice of Gun Ownership Is Female." *New York Times.* February 13. http://www.nytimes.com/2013/02/11/us/rising-voice-of-gun-ownership-is -female.html?pagewanted=all&_r=0.

Greenhouse, Linda. 2007. "Justices' Ruling Limits Lawsuits in Pay Disparity." *New York Times.* May 30. http://query.nytimes.com/gst/fullpage.html?res=9505E4D81430F933 A05756C0A9619C8B63.

Greszler, Rachel. 2014. "How the Paycheck Fairness Act Will Hurt Women." *Heritage Foundation.* April 16. http://www.heritage.org/research/commentary/2014/4/how -the-paycheck-fairness-act-will-hurt-women.

Grim, Maya. 2013a. "Annie Get Your (Male-Approved) Gun." *Smart Girl Politics Action.* February 20. http://www.sgpaction.com/annie_get_your_male_approved_gun (site discontinued).

———. 2013b. "Packing Heat and Looking Hot." *Smart Girl Politics Action.* February 7. http://www.sgpaction.com/packing_heat_looking_hot (site discontinued).

———. 2013c. "Why I Carry." *Smart Girl Politics Action.* January 29. http://www.sgpaction .com/why_i_carry (site discontinued).

Groeger, Lena, Amanda Zamora, Kat Downs, and Dan Keating. 2013. "Where Congress Stands on Guns." *ProPublica.* http://linkis.com/JGvWk.

Grudem, Wayne. 2012. *Evangelical Feminism and Biblical Truth.* Wheaton, IL: Crossway.

Gurin, Patricia. 1985. "Women's Gender Consciousness." *Public Opinion Quarterly* 49: 143–163.

Gustafson, Melanie Susan. 2001. *Women and the Republican Party, 1854–1924.* Urbana: University of Illinois Press.

Hall, Krisanne. 2012. "Women of Principle, of Courage, and of Great Resolve." *Minute-Mom Magazine* 1 (9): 24–27. http://issuu.com/minutemom/docs/may12.

Haughney, Christine. 2012. "Garden and Gun Claws Its Way Back from the Brink." *New York Times.* September 2. http://www.nytimes.com/2012/09/03/business/media /garden-gun-magazine-survives-in-an-ailing-industry.html?pagewanted=all&_r=0.

Hawley, Kristen. 2012. "Who Is Julia?" *Smart Girl Politics.* May 31. http://www.sgpaction .com/notjulia (site discontinued).

Hays, Charlotte. 2015a. 2015b. "Portrait of a Modern Feminist: Caroline Kitchens." *Independent Women's Forum.* January 26. http://www.iwf.org/modern-feminist/2796105 /caroline-kitchens.

———. 2015b. "Why Are They Distorting Indiana's Religious Freedom Law?" *Independent Women's Forum.* April 3. http://www.iwf.org/blog/2796735/Why-Are-They -Distorting-Indiana's-Religious-Freedom-Law-.

———. 2013. "Portrait of a Modern Feminist: Stacy Mott." *Independent Women's Forum.* February 11. http://iwf.org/modern-feminist/2790520/Portrait-of-a-Modern-Feminist:-Stacy-Mott.

Heath, Hadley. 2013. "Many Young Single Women Will See Premiums Rise." *National Review.* October 24. http://www.nationalreview.com/corner/362158/many-young-single-women-will-see-premiums-rise-hadley-heath.

———. 2012. "Three Ways ObamaCare Hurts Women (and Men!)." *Independent Women's Forum.* May 15. http://www.iwf.org/blog/2787883/Three-Ways-ObamaCare-Hurts-Women-(And-Men).

Herek, Gregory M. 2002. "Gender Gaps in Public Opinion about Lesbians and Gay Men." *Public Opinion Quarterly* 66 (1): 40–66.

Homsher, Deborah. 2001. *Women and Guns: Politics and the Culture of Firearms in America.* Armonk, NY: M. E. Sharpe.

Honey, Maureen. 1984. *Creating Rosie the Riveter: Class, Gender, and Propaganda during World War II.* Amherst: University of Massachusetts Press.

hooks, bell. 2000. *Feminist Theory: From Margin to Center.* London: Pluto Press, 2000.

House Republicans. 2014a. "GOP Press Conference: Solutions to Empower." July 31. http://www.gop.gov/gop-press-conference-solutions-to-empower/.

———. 2014b. "Three Things House Republicans Are Doing to Help Women." July 9. http://www.gop.gov/3-things-house-republicans-are-doing-for-women/.

Howell, Susan E., and Christine L. Day. 2000. "Complexities of the Gender Gap." *Journal of Politics* 62 (3): 8858–8874.

Hulse, Tammy. 2012. "Are We Homemakers or Are We Homemakers?" *MinuteMom Magazine* 1 (6): 16–17. http://issuu.com/minutemom/docs/feb12.

Human Rights Watch. 2011. "U.S.: Lack of Paid Leave Harms Workers, Children." February 23. http://www.hrw.org/news/2011/02/23/us-lack-paid-leave-harms-workers-children.

Hunter, Kathleen, and Jonathan D. Salant. 2012. "Women Democratic Surge Creates Congressional Gender Gap." *Bloomberg Business Week.* November 15. http://www.bloomberg.com/news/articles/2012-11-15/women-democratic-surge-creates-congressional-gender-gap.

Hupp, Suzanna Gratia. 2001. *From Luby's to the Legislature: One Woman's Fight against Gun Control.* San Antonio: Privateer Publications.

Huston, Warner Todd. 2012. "Smart Girls on the Left's Political Manipulation of Women." April 6. *Prairie State Report.* http://www.prairiestatereport.us/2012/04/06/smart-girls-on-the-lefts-political-manipulation-of-women/.

Independent Women's Forum. 2013. "Women in the Wilderness: Charting a New Path Forward." Winter. http://iwf.org/blog/2790584/.

Institute for Research and Education on Human Rights. 2015. "The Tea Party Movement in 2015." http://www.irehr.org/2015/09/15/the-tea-party-movement-in-2015/.

IRS. 2014. "Earned Income Tax Credit: Do I Qualify?" January. http://www.irs.gov/uac/Newsroom/Earned-Income-Tax-Credit-Do-I-Qualify.

Irwin, Victoria. 1980. "Factions Seek Control of Family Conference." *Christian Science Monitor*. February 13. http://www.csmonitor.com/1980/0213/021317.html.

Izade, Elahe. 2013. "Explaining the Gender Gap on Gun Control." *National Journal*. May 30. http://news.yahoo.com/explaining-gender-gap-gun-control-072551495 —politics.html.

Jablonsky, Thomas. 2002. "Female Opposition: The Anti-suffrage Campaign." In *Votes for Women: The Struggle for Suffrage Revisited*, edited by Jean H. Baker. New York: Oxford University Press, 118–129.

Jalonick, Mary Clare. 2012. "School Lunches to Be Allowed Unlimited Meats, Grains, USDA Announces." *Huffington Post*. December 8. http://www.huffingtonpost.com /2012/12/09/school-lunches-to-be-allo_n_2267731.html.

Johnson, Kevin. 2014. "Violent Crime in U.S. Continues Decline." *USA Today*. November 10. http://www.usatoday.com/story/news/nation/2014/11/10/violence -down-fbi/18808213/.

Jenkins, Lynn, and Diane Black. 2014. "Eliminating Marriage Penalty in Family Tax Issues, Simplifying Education Credits Just Makes Good Sense." *Washington Examiner*. July 25. http://www.washingtonexaminer.com/article/2551281.

Jessup, Meredith. 2012. "'The Life of Julia'—aka, How NOT to Live." *The Blaze*. May 3. http://www.theblaze.com/blog/2012/05/03/the-life-of-julia-according-to-obama/.

Jones, Jeffrey. 2013. "Men, Married, Southerners Most Likely to Be Gun Owners." *Gallup*. February 1. http://www.gallup.com/poll/160223/men-married-southerners -likely-gun-owerners.aspx.

Jones, Robert P., and Daniel Cox. 2010. "Religion and the Tea Party in the 2010 Election: An Analysis of the Third Biannual American Values Survey." *Public Religion Research Institute*. http://publicreligion.org/site/wp-content/uploads /2010/05/Religion-and-the-Tea-Party-in-the-2010-Election-American-Values -Survey.pdf.

Jones, Robert P., Daniel Cox, and Juhem Navarro-Rivera. 2014. "Economic Insecurity, Rising Income Inequality, and Doubts about the Future: Findings from the 2014 American Values Survey." *Public Religion Research Institute*. http://publicreligion. org/site/wp-content/uploads/2014/11/PRRI-AVS-with-Transparancy-Edits.pdf.

Kafer, Krista. 2014. "Wage Gap Isn't So Simple." *Independent Women's Forum*. April 19. http://www.iwf.org/blog/2793733/Wage-gap-isn't-so-simple.

———. 2013. "We Can't Legislate Away Evil." *Independent Women's Forum*. January 18. http://www.iwf.org/blog/2790342/We-Can't-Legislate-Away-Evil.

Kantor, Jodi, and Rachel L. Swarns. 2008. "A New Twist on the Debate on Mothers." *New York Times*. September 1. http://www.nytimes.com/2008/09/02/us/politics /02mother.html?pagewanted=all.

Kantor, Jodi, Kate Zernike, and Catrin Einhorn. 2008. "Fusing Politics and Motherhood in a New Way." *New York Times*. September 7. http://www.nytimes.com/2008 /09/08/us/politics/08baby.html?pagewanted=all&_r=0.

Kaufmann, Karen. 2004. "The Partisan Paradox: Religious Commitment and the Gender Gap in Party Identification." *Public Opinion Quarterly* 68 (4): 491–511.

———. 2002. "Culture Wars, Secular Realignment, and the Gender Gap in Party Identification." *Political Behavior* 24 (3): 283–307.

Kaufmann, Karen, and John R. Petrocik. 1999. "The Changing Politics of American Men: Understanding the Sources of the Gender Gap." *American Journal of Political Science* 43 (3): 864–887.

Keith, Bruce E., David B. Magleby, Candice J. Nelson, Elizabeth Orr, Mark C. Westlye, and Raymond E. Wolfinger. 1992. *The Myth of the Independent Voter*. Berkeley: University of California Press.

Kellermann, Arthur L., Grant Somes, Frederick P. Rivara, Roberta K. Lee, and Joyce G. Banton. 1998. "Injuries and Deaths Due to Firearms in the Home." *Journal of Trauma and Acute Care Surgery* 45 (2): 263–267.

Kellman, Laurie. 2012. "Ann Romney Fires Back at Never-Worked Charge." *Associated Press*. April 12. http://news.yahoo.com/ann-romney-fires-back-never-worked-charge -150405732.html.

Kelly, Caitlin. 2004. *Blown Away: American Women and Guns*. New York: Pocket Books.

Kerber, Linda. 1976. "The Republican Mother: Women and the Enlightenment: An American Perspective." *American Quarterly* 28 (2): 187–205.

Kim, Eun Kyung. 2013. "Representative Sets Congressional Record: Most Babies in Office." *Today News*. July 19. http://www.today.com/news/rep-sets-congressional-record -most-babies-office-6C10680009.

Kim, Susanna. 2011. "Hunting and Shooting Industry Targets Women for the 'Sarah Palin Effect.'" *ABC News*. March 4. http://abcnews.go.com/Business/sarah-palin-effect -women-men-picking-hunting/story?id=13047758#.Ua8aE5V8u6E.

King, David Charles, and Richard E. Matland. 2003. "Sex and the Grand Ole Party: An Experimental Investigation on the Effect of Candidate Sex on Support for a Republican Candidate." *American Politics Research* 31 (6): 595–612.

Klatch, Rebecca. 1988. "Coalition and Conflict among Women of the New Right." *Signs* 13 (4): 671–694.

———. 1987. *Women of the New Right*. Philadelphia: Temple University Press.

Klein, Ethel. 1984. *Gender Politics: From Consciousness to Mass Politics*. Cambridge, MA: Harvard University Press.

Klien, Stephen A. 2012. "Ladies of the Tea Party: The Conservative Feminine Persona According to Palin and Bachmann." Paper presented to the 2012 Rhetoric Society of America Biennial Conference, Philadelphia. May 28.

Kliff, Sarah. 2012. "Five Facts about the Health Law's Contraception Mandate." *Washington Post*. August 1. http://www.washingtonpost.com/blogs/wonkblog/wp /2012/08/01/five-facts-about-the-health-laws-contraceptive-mandate/.

Kozub, Tara. 2011. "Why This Mom Is Riding Shotgun with Paul Revere and Mary Washington." *Smart Girl Nation*. April 10–11.

Kraditor, Aileen S. 1981. *The Ideas of the Woman Suffrage Movement, 1890–1920*. New York: Norton.

Kremer, Amy. 2012. "Tea Party Isn't Waging a War on Women—Its Women Are Waging a War." *Investor's Business Daily*. June 20. http://news.investors.com

/article/615504/201206201802/tea-party-wages-war-by-women-not-on-them
.htm?p=full.

Krieg, Gregory J., and Chris Good. 2012. "Mourdock Rape Comments Puts GOP on Defensive." *ABC News*. http://abcnews.go.com/Politics/OTUS/richard-mourdock-rape
-comment-puts-romney-defense/story?id=17552263.

Kucinich, Jackie, and Martha T. Moore. 2012. "Hilary Rosen Says Ann Romney Never Worked 'Day in Her Life.'" *USA Today*. April 12. http://usatoday30.usatoday.com
/news/politics/story/2012–04–12/ann-romney-hilary-rosen-work/54235706/1.

Lawless, Jennifer L., and Richard L. Fox. 2010. *It Still Takes a Candidate: Why Women Don't Run for Office*. New York: Cambridge University Press.

Lee, Tony, and Brandon Darby. 2014. "Sarah Palin Endorses Katrina Pierson." *Breitbart*. February 19. http://www.breitbart.com/Breitbart-Texas/2014/02/19/Sarah-Palin
-Endorses-Texas-Katrina-Pierson.

Lepore, Jill. 2012. "Oh Julia: From Birth to Death, Left to Right." *New Yorker*. May 7.
http://www.newyorker.com/news/daily-comment/oh-julia-from-birth-to-death
-left-and-right.

———. 2010. *The Whites of Their Eyes: The Tea Party's Revolution and the Battle over American History*. Princeton, NJ: University of Princeton Press.

Levin, Yuval. 2011. "What Is Constitutional Conservatism?" *National Review*. November 22. http://www.nationalreview.com/article/283326/what-constitutional-conserv
atism-yuval-levin.

Lieve, Cindi. 2014. "Career Advice from a Capitol Hill Honcho." *Glamour*. September.
http://www.glamour.com/inspired/2014/09/career-advice-from-representative-cathy
-mcmorris-rodgers.

Lo, Clarence Y. H. 2012. "Astroturf versus Grass Roots: Scenes from Early Tea Party Mobilization." In *Steep: The Precipitous Rise of the Tea Party*, edited by Lawrence Rosenthal and Christine Trost. Berkeley: University of California Press, 98–129.

Loesch, Dana. 2013a. "Colorado Democrat: Women Don't Need Guns If They Feel Like They Are Going to Be Raped." *RedState*. http://www.redstate.com/diary
/dloesch/2013/02/18/colorado-democrat-women-dont-need-guns-if-they-feel-like
-theyre-going-to-be-raped/.

———. 2013b. "Gun Control: The Real War on Women." *The Dana Show*. January 30.
http://danaloeschradio.com/gun-control-the-real-war-on-women/.

———. 2013c. "Yale's Declaration on Rape Proves Why Collegiate Females Should Be Allowed to Carry." *The Dana Show*. August 1. http://danaloeschradio.com/yales
-declaration-on-rape-proves-why-collegiate-females-should-be-allowed-t.

———. 2012. "Obama Campaign: Women Are Helpless." *RealClearPolitics*. May 4.
http://www.realclearpolitics.com/2012/05/04/obama_campaign_women_are_helpless
_279106.html.

———. 2011. "Motherhood Is Political." May 8. *ConservativeWatchNews*. http://conserva
tivewatchnews.org/?p=18923.

Lorber, Judith. 1994. *Paradoxes of Gender*. New Haven, CT: Yale University Press.

Lott, Jr. John R. 2010. *More Guns, Less Crime*. 3rd ed. Chicago: University of Chicago Press.

Lownes, Joseph. 2012. "The Past and Future of Race in the Tea Party Movement." In *Steep: The Precipitous Rise of the Tea Party*, edited by Christine Trout and Larry Rosenthal. Berkeley: University of California Press, 152–170.

Lukas, Carrie. 2015. "Parents Want Help, Not Day Care." *Independent Women's Forum*. January 23. http://www.iwf.org/news/2796090/Parents-Want-Help,-Not-Day-Care.

———. 2014a. "A Job-Destroying High Minimum Wage Won't Help Women." *Forbes*. April 30. http://www.forbes.com/sites/carrielukas/2014/04/30/a-job-destroying-high -minimum-wage-wont-help-women/.

———. 2014b. "Older Women Hit With Highest ObamaCare Costs." *Independent Women's Forum*. June 25. http://www.iwf.org/blog/2794321/Older-Women-Hit-With -Highest-ObamaCare-Costs.

———. 2013. "Policy Focus: Minimum Wage." *Independent Women's Forum*. August 14. http://www.iwf.org/publications/2791929/Policy-Focus:-Minimum-Wage.

Lukas, Carrie, and Sabrina Schaeffer. 2012. *Liberty Is No War on Women: How Big Government and Victim-Politics Undermine America's Progress*. Washington DC: Independent Women's Forum.

Luker, Kristin. 1984. *Abortion and the Politics of Motherhood*. Berkeley: University of California Press.

Madsen, Nancy. 2012. "Jamie Radtke Says 2 Percent Annual Cuts Would Balance Budget in 2016." *PolitiFact Virginia*. May 10. http://www.politifact.com/virginia /statements/2012/may/10/jamie-radtke/jamie-radtke-says-2-percent-annual-cuts -would-bala/.

Malkin, Michelle. 2012. "Mamas, Don't Let Your Babies Grown Up to Be 'Julia.'" May 4. http://michellemalkin.com/2012/05/04/mamas-dont-let-your-babies-grow-up-to -be-julia/.

———. 2009. "Signs of the Day." February 16. http://michellemalkin.com/2009/02/16 /signs-of-the-day/.

Manning, Jennifer E. 2014. "Membership of the 113th Congress: A Profile." *Congressional Research Service*. November 24. http://www.senate.gov/CRSReports/crs-publish .cfm?pid=%260BL%2BR%5CC%3F%0A.

Mansbridge, Jane. 1999. "Should Blacks Represent Blacks and Women Represent Women? A Contingent 'Yes.'" *Journal of Politics* 61 (3): 628–657.

———. 1986. *Why We Lost the ERA*. Chicago: University of Chicago Press.

Manza, Jeff, and Clem Brooks. 1998. "The Gender Gap in U.S. Presidential Elections: When? Why? Implications?" *American Journal of Sociology* 103 (5): 1235–1266.

Marcus, Ruth. 2012. "Mitt Romney Can't Leave Women Voters to His Wife." *Washington Post*. April 10. https://www.washingtonpost.com/opinions/mitt-romney-cant -leave-women-voters-to-his-wife/2012/04/10/gIQASoB88S_story.html.

Marlantes, Liz, 2012. "Hilary Rosen vs. Ann Romney: Why the Dust-Up Is Fake." *Christian Science Monitor*. April 12. http://www.csmonitor.com/USA/DC-Decoder /Decoder-Buzz/2012/0412/Hilary-Rosen-vs.-Ann-Romney-why-the-dust-up-is-fake.

Marshall, Susan. 1986. "In Defense of Separate Spheres: Class and Status Politics in the Anti-suffrage Movement." *Social Forces* 65 (2): 327–351.

Martin, Jenny Beth. 2015. "Statement on Keli Carender's Resignation." *Tea Party Patriots.* May 7. https://www.teapartypatriots.org/news/statement-on-keli-carenders-resignation/.

Martin, William. 1996. *With God on Our Side: The Rise of the Religious Right in America.* New York: Broadway Books.

May, Elaine Tyler. 1988. *Homeward Bound: American Families in the Cold War Era.* New York: Basic Books.

Mayer, Jane. 2010. "Covert Operations: The Billionaire Brothers Who Are Waging a War against Obama." *New Yorker.* August 30. http://www.newyorker.com/magazine/2010/08/30/covert-operations.

McAdam, Douglas. 1996. "The Framing Function of Movement Tactics: Strategic Dramaturgy in the Civil Rights Movement." In *Comparative Perspectives on Social Movements: Political Opportunities, Mobilizing Structures, and Cultural Framings,* edited by Doug McAdam, John D. McCarthy, and Mayer N. Zalad. New York: Cambridge University Press, 338–355.

McAuliff, Michael. 2014. "House Votes to Boost Well-Off Kids, Cut Out Poor Kids." *Huffington Post.* July 25. http://www.huffingtonpost.com/2014/07/25/child-tax-credit_n_5620014.html.

McCammon, Sarah. 2015. "Planned Parenthood Controversy Proves Complicated for Democrats." *NPR News.* July 29. http://www.npr.org/sections/itsallpolitics/2015/07/29/427419726/planned-parenthood-controversy-proves-complicated-for-democrats.

McCarver, Virginia. 2011. "The Rhetoric of Choice and 21st-Century Feminism: Online Conversations about Work, Family, and Sarah Palin." *Women's Studies in Communications* 34 (1): 20–41.

McGirr, Lisa. 2001. *Suburban Warriors: The Origins of the New American Right.* Princeton, NJ: Princeton University Press.

McGraw, Onalee. 1980. *The Family, Feminism, and the Therapeutic State.* Washington DC: Heritage Foundation.

Meckler, Mark, and Jenny Beth Martin. 2012. *Tea Party Patriots: The Second American Revolution.* New York: Henry Holt.

Medrano, Lourdes. 2014. "What Happened to the Minuteman Project? It's Still Roiling Immigration Reform." *Christian Science Monitor.* April 30. http://www.csmonitor.com/USA/2014/0430/What-happened-to-Minuteman-Project-It-s-still-roiling-immigration-reform.

Mencimer, Stephanie. 2011. "The Tea Party's Hatfield and McCoys." *Mother Jones.* October 13. http://www.motherjones.com/mojo/2011/10/tea-partys-hatfield-and-mccoys.

Mezey, Naomi, and Cornelia T. L. Pillard. 2012. "Against the New Maternalism." *Michigan Journal of Gender and Law* 18 (2012): 229–296.

Mikulski, Barbara. 2014. "Press Release: Mikulski Calls on Senate to Pass Paycheck Fairness Act and Give Women a Fair Shot at Equal Pay for Equal Work." September

12. http://www.mikulski.senate.gov/newsroom/press-releases/mikulski-calls-on -senate-to-pass-paycheck-fairness-act-and-give-women-a-fair-shot-at-equal-pay -for-equal-work.

Montgomery, Peter. 2012. "The Tea Party and the Religious Right Movements: Frenemies with Benefits." In *Steep: The Precipitous Rise of the Tea Party*, edited by Lawrence Rosenthal and Christine Trout. Berkeley: University of California Press, 242–274

Morello, Carol. 2013. "Single Motherhood in the U.S. Increases Sharply." *Washington Post*. May 1. http://www.washingtonpost.com/local/unmarried-motherhood -increases-sharply/2013/05/01/ef77c4ba-b26e-11e2–9a98–4be1688d7d84_story .html.

Mott, Stacy. 2013. "Google Hangout: Women and Guns." *Smart Girl Politics Action*. February http://www.sgpaction.com/sgpa_holds_google_hangout_on_women _guns (site discontinued).

Mundy, Liza. 2012. *The Richer Sex: How the New Majority of Female Breadwinners Is Transforming Sex, Love, and Family*. New York: Simon & Schuster.

Nance, Penny Young. 2012. "What Women Want This Year." *Fox News*. March 30. http:// www.foxnews.com/opinion/2012/03/30/what-women-want.html.

———. 2011. "Traditionalism vs. Feminism." *Concerned Women for America*. February 12. http://www.cwfa.org/traditionalism-vs-feminism/.

Nantz, Tami. 2012. "The Miserable Life of Julia." *Smart Girl Politics Action*. May 4. http:// www.sgpaction.com/the_miserable_life_of_julia (site discontinued).

———. 2011. "Game Changers: Cathy McMorris Rodgers on Women and the GOP." *Smart Girl Nation*. July 4–6.

National Organization for Women. 2014. "Women Need Paid Family Leave and Paid Sick Leave." August. http://now.org/resource/women-need-paid-family-leave-and -paid-sick-leave/.

National Partnership for Women and Families. 2013. "Fact Sheet: An Empty Promise: The Working Families Flexibility Act Would Give Workers Less Flexibility and Less Pay." April. http://go.nationalpartnership.org/site/DocServer/NPWF_Fact_Sheet _-_An_Empty_Promise_The_Working_Families_.pdf?docID=12461.

National Review. 2012. "No War on Women: Exposing the Left's Gender Politics and Pandering." October 24. http://www.nationalreview.com/article/331422/no-war -women-interview.

National Women's Law Center. 2013. "Lilly Ledbetter: Fact Sheet." January 29. http:// www.nwlc.org/resource/lilly-ledbetter-fair-pay-act-0.

Neale, Rick. 2013. "Group Caters to Rising Number of Well-Armed Women." *USA Today*. September 29. http://www.usatoday.com/story/news/nation/2013/09/29/well -armed-woman-gun-ownership/2891687/.

Nickerson, Michelle. 2012. *Mothers of Conservatism: Women and the Postwar Right*. Princeton, NJ: Princeton University Press.

Nielson, Kim E. 2001. *Un-American Womanhood: Antiradicalism, Antifeminism, and the First Red Scare*. Columbus: Ohio State University Press.

NPR News. 2015. "Transcript: President Obama's State of the Union Address." January 20. http://www.npr.org/2015/01/20/378680818/transcript-president-obamas-state-of -the-union-address.

O'Keefe, Ed, and Scott Clement. 2013. "Gun-Control Poll: Public Split on Whom to Trust—Obama or Republicans." *Washington Post*. March 12. http://www.washington post.com/politics/gun-control-poll-public-split-on-whom-to-trust—obama-or -republicans/2013/03/12/22be985e-8a82-11e2-8d72-dc76641cb8d4_story.html.

Osborn, Tracy L. 2012. *How Women Represent Women: Political Parties, Gender, and Representation in the State Legislatures*. New York: Oxford University Press.

Palin, Sarah. 2014. "Speech to NRA Stand and Fight Rally." 2014 Annual Meeting of the National Rifle Association, Indianapolis. April 26. https://www.youtube.com /watch?v=lVlQTYDFTTo.

———. 2010. *America by Heart: Reflections on Family, Faith, and the Flag*. New York: Harper.

Palmer, Barbara, and Dennis Simon. 2012. *Women and Congressional Elections: A Century of Change*. Boulder, CO: Lynne Rienner.

Parker, Alison. 2002. "The Case for Reform: Antecedents for the Women's Rights Movement." In *Votes for Women: The Struggle for Suffrage Revisited*, edited by Jean H. Baker. New York: Oxford University Press, 21–41.

Parker, Christopher S., and Matt A. Barreto. 2013. *Change They Can't Believe In: The Tea Party and Reactionary Politics in America*. Princeton, NJ: Princeton University Press.

Paulson, Amy. 2000. "'Million Mom March's Organizers Hope to Spur Congressional Action on Gun Legislation." *CNN*. May 8. https://archive.is/TtRfK.

Pavlich, Katie. 2013. "Rape Survivor: A Call Box above My Head While I Was Being Brutally Raped Wouldn't Have Helped." *Townhall*. February 20. http://townhall .com/tipsheet/katiepavlich/2013/02/20/rape-survivor-a-call-box-above-my-head -while-i-was-being-brutally-raped-wouldnt-have-helped-n1516801/.

Peters, Jeremy W. 2014. "GOP Leaders Draw Re-election Challenges from the Right." *New York Times*. February 24. http://www.nytimes.com/2014/02/25/us/politics/gop -leaders-draw-rare-re-election-challenge-from-the-ranks.html.

Pew Forum for Religion and Public Life. 2014. "Changing Attitudes on Gay Marriage." *Pew Research Center*. http://www.pewforum.org/2014/09/24/graphics-slideshow -changing-attitudes-on-gay-marriage/.

———. 2012. "'Nones' on the Rise: One-in-Five Adults Have No Religious Affiliation." *Pew Research Center*. http://www.pewforum.org/unaffiliated/nones-on-the-rise .aspx.

Pew Research Center for the People and the Press. 2012. "More Support for Gun Rights, Gay Marriage Than in 2008 or 2004." http://www.people-press.org/2012/04/25/more -support-for-gun-rights-gay-marriage-than-in-2008-or-2004/.

Pilkington, Ed. 2010. "Amy Kremer Takes Her Tea Party Express from Coast to Coast." *The Guardian*. October 18. http://www.theguardian.com/world/2010/oct/18/amy -kremer-tea-party-express.

Pitkin, Hanna Fenichel. 1967. *The Concept of Representation.* Berkeley: University of California Press.

Poggione, Sarah. 2004. "Exploring Gender Differences in State Legislators' Policy Preferences." *Political Research Quarterly* 57 (2): 305–314.

Political Parity. 2015. "Clearing the Primary Hurdles: Republican Women and the GOP Gender Gap." http://www.politicalparity.org/research/primary-hurdles/.

Ponnuru, April, and Carrie Lukas. 2014. "ObamaCare vs. Women's Choices." *Forbes.* June 12. http://www.forbes.com/sites/carrielukas/2014/06/12/obamacare-vs-womens -choices/.

Ponnuru, Ramesh. 2015. "Obama's War on Homemakers." *Bloomberg View.* January 22. http://www.bloombergview.com/articles/2015–01–22/ obama-intensifies-democrats-war-on-homemakers.

Powers, Kirsten. 2011. "Michele Bachmann: Don't Call Her a Feminist." *Daily Beast.* June 28. http://www.thedailybeast.com/articles/2011/06/28/michele-bachmann-for -president-2012-don-t-call-her-a-feminist.html.

Powers, Ryan. 2009. "Pelosi: Tea Parties Are Part of an 'Astroturf' Campaign by 'Some of the Wealthiest People in America.'" *ThinkProgress.* April 15. http://thinkprogress .org/politics/2009/04/15/37578/pelosi-astroturf/.

Public Religion Research Institute (PRRI). 2014. "Economic Insecurity, Rising Inequality, and Doubts about the Future: Findings from the 2014 American Values Survey." September 23. http://publicreligion.org/research/2014/09/survey-economic-insecurity -rising-inequality-and-doubts-about-the-future-findings-from-the-2014-american -values-survey/.

———. 2013. "The 2013 American Values Survey: In Search of Libertarians in America." October 29. http://publicreligion.org/research/2013/10/2013-american-values -survey/.

———. 2012a. "The 2012 American Values Survey." October 23. http://publicreligion. org/site/wp-content/uploads/2012/10/AVS-2012-Pre-election-Report-for-Web.pdf.

———. 2012b. "Beyond Gods and Guns: Understanding the Complexities of the White Working Class in America." September 20. http://publicreligion.org/site/wp-content /uploads/2012/09/WWC-Report-For-Web-Final.pdf.

———. 2012c. "News Release: Overwhelming Majority of Americans Agree Constitutional Right to Own a Gun Is as Important as Right to Free Speech." August 15. http:// publicreligion.org/newsroom/2012/08/news-release-overwhelming-majority-of -americans-agree-constitutional-right-to-own-a-gun-is-as-important-as-right-to -free-speech/.

———. 2011a. "Committed to Availability, Conflicted about Morality: What the Millennial Generation Tells Us about the Future of the Abortion Debate and the Culture Wars." June 6. http://publicreligion.org/site/wp-content/uploads/2011/06/Millenials -Abortion-and-Religion-Survey-Report.pdf.

———. 2011b "Fact Sheet: 'Teavangelicals': Alignments and Tensions between the Tea Party and White Evangelical Protestants." http://publicreligion.org/research/2011/11 /fact-sheet-alignment-of-evangelical-and-tea-party-values/.

———. 2010. "Religion and the Tea Party in the 2010 Election." October. http://public
religion.org/site/wp-content/uploads/2010/05/Religion-and-the-Tea-Party-in-the
-2010-Election-American-Values-Survey.pdf.

Radtke, Jamie. 2012. "My Two Cents Can Save Economy." *Richmond Times-Dispatch.*
April 5. http://www.richmond.com/news/article_c6b4ddd8–0385–5702-a97d
-6f30f7d678a1.html.

Rapoport, Ronald B. 2012. "FreedomWorks Supporters: A Report on Their Politics,
Their Political Activity, Their Media Use, and Their 2012 Nomination Preferences."
Working Paper.

Rapoport, Ronald B., Meredith Doth, Ani-Rae Lovell, and Walter J. Stone. 2013.
"Republican Factionalism and Tea Party Activists." Paper presented at the Annual
Meeting of the Midwest Political Science Association, April 11–14.

Reingold, Beth. 2000. *Representing Women: Sex, Gender, and Legislative Behavior in
Arizona and California.* Chapel Hill: University of North Carolina Press.

Republican National Committee. 2014. "Misleading Paycheck Fairness Act." April 5.
https://www.gop.com/misleading-paycheck-fairness-act/.

Richardson, Valerie. 2013. "Colorado State Rep. Joe Salazar's Comments on Rape and
Guns Draw Backlash." *Washington Times.* February 19. http://www.washingtontimes
.com/blog/inside-politics/2013/feb/19/colorado-state-rep-joe-salazars-comments
-rape-and-/.

Rittgers, Anna. 2013. "A Mother's Case for Gun Rights." *Fox News.* January 15. http://
www.foxnews.com/opinion/2013/01/15/mothers-case-for-gun-rights.html.

Ritz, Erica. 2013. "Women and Guns: Why Female Gun Ownership Is Rising and
Why Many Are Taking Notice." *The Blaze.* April 9. http://www.theblaze.com
/stories/2013/04/09/more-and-more-women-are-buying-guns-heres-why/.

RNC Women. 2014. "Press Release: RNC Launches '14 in '14' Initiative." April 14.
https://www.gop.com/rnc-launches-14-in-14-womens-initiative/.

Roby, Martha. 2013a. "Press Release: Momentum Builds for Roby's Working Families
Flexibility Act." April 25. http://roby.house.gov/press-release/momentum-builds
-roby's-working-families-flexibility-act.

———. 2013b. "Press Release: Rep. Roby Responds to President Obama's Announcement of New Gun Control Proposals." January 16. http://roby.house.gov/press
-release/rep-roby-responds-president-obama's-announcement-new-gun-control
-proposals.

Rodgers, Cathy McMorris. 2012. "House Republican Women: Working for You."
RedState. May 23. http://www.redstate.com/congresswomancathymcmorrisrodgers
/2012/05/23/house-republican-women-working-for-you/.

Rosin, Hanna. 2014. "Values Feminism." *Slate.* January 28. http://www.slate.com/articles
/double_x/doublex/2014/01/cathy_mcmorris_rodgers_values_feminism_is_the_new
_model_for_republican_women.html.

———. 2012. *The End of Men: And the Rise of Women.* New York: Riverhead Books.

———. 2011. "Good Ol' Girl." *The Atlantic.* January 4. http://www.theatlantic.com
/magazine/archive/2011/01/good-ol-girl/308348/.

———. 2010. "Is the Tea Party a Feminist Movement?" *Slate*. May 12. http://www.slate .com/id/2253645/.

Ruddick, Sara. 1989. *Maternal Thinking: Toward a Politics of Peace*. Boston: Beacon Press.

Ryan, Barbara. 1992. *Feminism and the Women's Movement: Dynamics of Change in Social Movement Ideology and Activism*. New York: Routledge.

Rymph, Catherine E. 2006. *Republican Women: Feminism and Conservatism from Suffrage through the Rise of the New Right*. Chapel Hill: University of North Carolina Press.

Saad, Lydia. 2011. "Self-Reported Gun Ownership in U.S. Is Highest since 1993." *Gallup*. October 26. http://www.gallup.com/poll/150353/self-reported-gun-owernship -highest-1993.aspx.

Sanbonmatsu, Kira. 2006. *Where Women Run: Gender and Party in the American States*. Ann Arbor: University of Michigan Press.

Sanbonmatsu, Kira, Susan J. Carroll, and Debbie Walsh. 2009. "Poised to Run: Women's Pathways to the State Legislature." Center for American Women and Politics, Eagleton Institute of Politics, Rutgers University. http://www.cawp.rutgers.edu /sites/default/files/resources/poisedtorun_0.pdf.

Sapiro, Virginia. 1983. *The Political Integration of Women: Roles, Socialization, and Politics*. Urbana: University of Illinois Press.

———. 1981. "Research Frontier Essay: When Are Interests Interesting? The Problem of Political Representation of Women." *American Political Science Review* 75 (3): 701–716.

Sarachild, Kathie. "Consciousness-Raising: A Radical Weapon." *Feminist Revolution* 144 (1978): 144–150.

Schaeffer, Sabrina. 2014. "Women at Work." In *Lean Together: An Agenda for Smarter Government Smaller Communities, and More Opportunity for Women*, edited by the Independent Women's Forum. Atlanta: IWF Press, 69–81.

———. 2013. "Out-Spent, Out-Numbered, Out-Researched: The Power of Progressive Women's Groups." *Forbes*. April 25. http://www.forbes.com/sites/sabrinaschaeffer /2013/04/25/out-spent-out-numbered-our-researched-the-power-of-progressive -womens-groups/.

Schlafly, Phyllis. 2012a. "Obama Obeys the Feminists Again." *Eagle Forum*. February 15. http://www.eagleforum.org/column/2012/feb12/12–02–15.html.

———. 2012b. "We Need Pro-Family Tax Policies." *Eagle Forum*. January 12. http:// www.eagleforum.org/column/2012/jan12/12–01–18.html.

———. 2011. "The Most Powerful Office in the World." *MinuteMom Magazine* 1 (3): 10–12. http://issuu.com/minutemom/docs/nov2011.

———. 1977. *The Power of the Positive Woman*. New York: Jove.

———. 1972. "The Fraud of the Equal Rights Amendment." *Phyllis Schlafly Report* 5 (February). https://unitedstateshistory2.files.wordpress.com/2013/01/phyllis-schlafly -the-fraud-of-the-era.pdf.

———. 1964. *A Choice Not an Echo*. Alton, IL: Pere Marquette Press.

Schnittker, Jason, Jeremy Freese, and Brian Powell. 2003. "Who Are Feminists and What Do They Believe? The Role of Generations." *American Sociological Review* 68 (4): 607–622.

Schreiber, Ronnee. 2012. "Dilemmas of Representation: Conservative and Feminist Women's Organizations React to Sarah Palin." In *Women of the Right: Comparisons and Interplay across Borders*, edited by Kathleen M. Blee and Sandra McGee Deutsch. University Park: Pennsylvania State University Press, 2012, 273–289.

———. 2008. *Righting Feminism: Conservative Women and American Politics.* New York: Oxford University Press.

Shanley, Mary Lyndon. 1988. *Women's Rights, Feminism, and Politics in the United States.* Washington DC: American Political Science Association.

Shriver, Maria, in partnership with the Center for American Progress. 2014. "A Woman's Nation Pushes Back from the Brink." *Shriver Report.* http://shriverreport .org/special-report/a-womans-nation-pushes-back-from-the-brink/.

Skocpol, Theda. 1992. *Protecting Soldiers and Mothers: The Political Origins of Social Policy in the United States.* Cambridge, MA: Belknap Press of Harvard University Press.

Skocpol, Theda, and Vanessa Williamson. 2012. *The Tea Party and the Remaking of Republican Conservatism.* Oxford, UK: Oxford University Press.

Smith, Aaron. 2014. "For the Gun Industry, Women Are the Next Big Thing." *CNN Money.* February 7. http://money.cnn.com/2014/02/07/news/companies/guns -women/.

Smith, Aaron, Kay Lehman Schlozman, Sidney Verba, and Henry Brady. 2009. "The Current State of Civic Engagement in America." *Pew Research Center.* September 1. http://www.pewinternet.org/2009/09/01/the-current-state-of-civic-engagement-in -america/.

Smith, Tom. 1984. "The Polls: Gender and Attitudes toward Violence." *Public Opinion Quarterly* 48: 384–396.

Solomon, Martha. 1978. "The Rhetoric of STOP ERA: Fatalistic Reaffirmation." *Southern Speech Communication Journal* 44 (1): 42–59.

Somashekhar, Sandhya. 2011. "Conservative Women Enthusiastic about Bachmann, Palin." *Washington Post.* June 5. http://articles.washingtonpost.com/2011–06–05 /politics/35234955_1_bachmann-and-palin-gop-women-sarah-palin.

Sommers, Christina Hoff. 2014. "Rape Culture Is a 'Panic Where Paranoia, Censorship, and False Accusations Flourish.'" *Time.* May 15. http://time.com/100091/campus -sexual-assault-christina-hoff-sommers/.

———. 2013. *Freedom Feminism: Its Surprising History and Why It Matters Today.* Washington DC: American Enterprise Institute.

———. 2010. "Fair Pay Isn't Always Equal Pay." *New York Times.* September 21. http:// www.nytimes.com/2010/09/22/opinion/22Sommers.html.

———. 1995. *Who Stole Feminism? How Women Have Betrayed Women.* New York: Simon & Schuster.

Sparks, Holloway. 2015. "Mama Grizzlies and Guardians of the Republic: The Democratic and Intersectional Politics of Anger in the Tea Party Movement." *New Political Science* 37 (1): 25–47.

Stephenson-Abetz, Jenna. 2012. "Everyday Activism as a Dialogic Practice: Narratives of Feminist Daughters." *Women's Studies in Communication* 35 (1): 96–117.

Stucky, Thomas D., Geralyn M. Miller, and Linda M. Murphy. 2008. "Gender, Guns and Legislating: An Analysis of State Legislative Preferences." *Journal of Women, Politics, and Policy* 29 (4): 477–495.

Swanson, Emily. 2013. "Poll: Few Identify as Feminists, But Most Believe in Equality of Sexes." *Huffington Post.* April 16. http://www.huffingtonpost.com/2013/04/16 /feminism-poll_n_3094917.html.

Swartzell, Nick. 2014. "Representative Pete Sessions Defeats Tea Party Challenger Katrina Pierson." *Trail Blazers Blog.* March 4. http://trailblazersblog.dallasnews .com/tag/katrina-pierson/.

Swers, Michele L. 2013. *Women in the Club: Gender and Policy Making in the Senate.* Chicago: University of Chicago Press.

———. 2002. *The Difference Women Make: The Policy Impact of Women in Congress.* Chicago: University of Chicago Press.

Swers, Michele L., and Carin Larson. 2005. "Women in Congress: Do They Act as Advocates for Women's Issues?" In *Women and Elective Office: Past, Present, and Future,* 2nd ed., edited by Sue Thomas and Clyde Wilcox. New York: Oxford University Press, 110–128.

Swers, Michele L., and Stella Rouse. 2011. "Descriptive Representation: Understanding the Impact of Identity on Substantive Representation of Group Interests." In *Oxford Handbook of Congress,* edited by Eric Schickler and Frances Lee. New York: Oxford University Press, 241–271.

Swintch, Kirsten. 2012. "Hillary Clinton, Cookies, and Rise of Working Families." *CNN.* March 12. http://www.cnn.com/2012/03/16/opinion/swinth-hillary-clinton/.

Tarrow, Sidney. 1998. *Power in Movement: Social Movements and Contentious Politics.* Cambridge, UK: Cambridge University Press.

Tavernese, Sabrina, and Robert Gebeloff. 2013. "Rate of Gun Ownership Is Down, Survey Shows." *New York Times.* March 9. http://www.nytimes.com/2013/03/10 /us/rate-of-gun-ownership-is-down-survey-shows.html?pagewanted=all&_r=0.

Terry, Allison. 2013. "Why Gun Ownership among U.S. Women Is Climbing." *Christian Science Monitor.* February 14. http://www.csmonitor.com/USA/Society/2013/0214 /Why-gun-ownership-among-US-women-is-climbing?nav=87-frontpage-entry NineItem.

Thomas, Sue. 1994. *How Women Legislate.* New York: Oxford University Press.

Thomsen, Danielle M. 2015. "Why So Few (Republican) Women? Explaining the Partisan Imbalance of Women in the U.S. Congress." *Legislative Studies Quarterly* 40 (2): 295–323.

Tilly, Charles. 1978. *From Mobilization to Revolution.* New York: McGraw-Hill.

Toussaint, Loren, and Jon R. Webb. 2005. "Gender Differences in the Relationship between Empathy and Forgiveness." *Journal of Social Psychology* 145 (6): 673–685.

TPPN. 2014. "National Tea Party Leader Joins Tea Party Leadership Fund." August 7. http://www.tpnn.com/2014/08/07/national-tea-party-leader-joins-tea-party-leadership-fund/.

Traister, Rebecca. 2010. *Big Girls Don't Cry: The Election That Changed Everything for American Women*. New York: Simon and Schuster.

Trotter, Gayle S. 2013. "What Should America Do about Gun Violence?" Testimony to the Senate Judiciary Committee on Gun Control. January 30. http://www.judiciary.senate.gov/imo/media/doc/1–30–13TrotterTestimony.pdf.

Tumulty, Karen. 2008. "Can Obama Win Back Wal-Mart Moms?" http://content.time.com/time/politics/article/0,8599,1839930,00.html.

U.S. Department of Labor. 2009. "An Analysis of the Reasons for the Disparity in Wages between Men and Women." January 12. http://www.consad.com/content/reports/Gender%20Wage%20Gap%20Final%20Report.pdf.

Vale, Elizabeth. 2014a. "500 Economics Send Letter to Washington Opposing Minimum Wage Hikes." *Smart Girl Politics Action*. March 16. http://www.sgpaction.com/500_economists_send_letter_to_washington_opposing_minimum_wage_hike (site discontinued).

———. 2014b. "President Obama and the Politics of Equal Pay." *Smart Girl Politics Action*. April 8. http://linkis.com/www.sgpaction.com/noVl4 (site discontinued).

Venker, Suzanne, and Phyllis Schlafly. 2011. *The Flipside of Feminism: What Conservative Women Know and Men Can't Say*. Washington DC: WorldNetDaily Books.

Vogel, Kenneth P. 2010a. "Face of the Tea Party Is Female." *Politico*. March 26. http://www.politico.com/news/stories/0310/35094.html.

———. 2010b. "The New Tea Party Bible." *Politico*. July 31. http://www.politico.com/news/stories/0710/40492.html.

Walter, Kathleen, and Paul Scicchitano. 2012. "McMorris Rodgers: War on Women 'Democratic Myth.'" *Newsmax*. June 28. http://www.newsmax.com/Newsfront/democratic-war-women-rodgers/2012/04/24/id/436881.

Watkins, Kami. 2012. "We Need Not Fear . . . God Is On Our Side." *MinuteMom Magazine* 1 (5): 15. http://issuu.com/minutemom/docs/jan12.

Weiner, Rachel. 2012. "'The Life of Julia' and the New Frontiers of Presidential Politics." *Washington Post*. May 3. http://www.washingtonpost.com/blogs/the-fix/post/the-life-of-julia-shows-obama-camps-web-savvy/2012/05/03/gIQAIy1YzT_blog.html.

Weingarten, Benjamin. 2014. "Dana Loesch: 'Gun Control is the Ultimate War on Women.'" *The Blaze*. June 12. http://www.theblaze.com/blog/2014/06/12/dana-loesch-gun-control-is-the-ultimate-war-on-women/.

Welch, Susan. 1985. "Are Women More Liberal Than Men in the U.S. Congress?" *Legislative Studies Quarterly* 10 (1): 125–134.

Welter, Barbara. 1966. "The Cult of True Womanhood, 1820–1860." *American Quarterly* 18 (2): 151–177.

White House. 2014. "Did You Know That Women Are Still Paid Less Than Men?" http://www.whitehouse.gov/equal-pay/myth#top.

Wilcox, Clyde, and Elizabeth Adell Cook. 1989. "Evangelical Women and Feminism." *Women and Politics* 9 (2): 27–49.

Wilcox, Clyde, and Carin Larson. 2010. *Onward Christian Soldiers: The Religious Right in America.* 4th ed. Boulder, CO: Westview Press.

Wilcox, W. Bradford. (2004). *Soft Patriarchs, New Men: How Christianity Shapes Fathers and Husbands.* Chicago: University of Chicago Press.

Williams, Erin. 2011. "New Mama Grizzly." *MinuteMom Magazine* 1 (2): 22–23. http://issuu.com/minutemom/docs.

Willis, Derek. 2015. "GOP Women in Congress: Why So Few?" *New York Times.* June 1. http://www.nytimes.com/2015/06/02/upshot/gop-women-in-congress-why-so-few.html.

Wolpert, Robin M., and James G. Gimpel. 1998. "Self-Interest, Symbolic Politics, and Public Attitudes toward Gun Control." *Political Behavior* 20 (3): 241–262.

Wong, Scott. 2014. "The GOP's Rising Female Stars." *The Hill.* October 24. http://thehill.com/homenews/house/221879-the-gops-new-stars.

Woodward, Chris. 2012. "Male-Female Gap a Myth." *OneNewsNow.* October 21. http://www.onenewsnow.com/business/2012/10/21/male-female-wage-gap-a-myth#.VKGVG7gAA.

Zernike, Kate. 2010. *Boiling Mad: Inside Tea Party America.* New York: Times Books.

Zezima, Katie. 2014. "Obama: 'In Five Years, It Will No Longer Be Called ObamaCare.'" *Washington Post.* May 20. https://www.washingtonpost.com/news/post-politics/wp/2014/05/20/obama-in-five-years-it-will-no-longer-be-called-obamacare/.

Zornick, George. 2013. "The GOP's New Outreach to Women: It's a Trap." *The Nation.* May 7. http://www.thenation.com/blog/174210/gops-new-outreach-women-its-trap#.

Zurita, Brenda. 2013. "Make Love, Not War (on Women)." *Concerned Women for America.* October 7. http://www.cwfa.org/make-love-not-war-on-women/.

INDEX

ABOUT THE AUTHOR

Melissa Deckman is Louis L. Goldstein Professor of Public Affairs at Washington College, where she also chairs the Political Science Department. An expert on gender, religion, and American politics, she is the author or co-author of four books, including *School Board Battles: The Christian Right in Local Politics*, winner of the 2007 Hubert Morken Award from the American Political Science Association Religion and Politics section for the best book on religion and politics. She chairs the board of the Public Religion Research Institute, and her political commentary has appeared in the *Washington Post*, the *Huffington Post*, and the Brookings Institution's *FixGov* blog.